Studies in Emotion and Social Interaction

Paul Ekman
University of California, San Francisco

Klaus R. Scherer
Justus-Liebig-Universität Giessen

General Editors

Emotion in the Human Face

Studies in Emotion and Social Interaction

This series is jointly published by the Cambridge University Press and the Editions de la Maison des Sciences de l'Homme, as part of the joint publishing agreement established in 1977 between the Fondation de la Maison des Sciences de l'Homme and the Syndics of the Cambridge University Press.

Cette collection est publiée en co-édition par Cambridge University Press et les Editions de la Maison des Sciences de l'Homme. Elle s'intègre dans le programme de co-édition etabli en 1977 par la Fondation de la Maison des Sciences de l'Homme et les Syndics de Cambridge University Press.

Emotion in the human face
Second edition

Edited by Paul Ekman

Department of Psychiatry,
University of California,
San Francisco

Cambridge University Press

Cambridge
London   New York   New Rochelle
Melbourne   Sydney

Editions de la Maison des Sciences de l'Homme

Paris

Published by the Press Syndicate of the University of Cambridge
The Pitt Building, Trumpington Street, Cambridge CB2 1RP
32 East 57th Street, New York, NY 10022, USA
296 Beaconsfield Parade, Middle Park, Melbourne 3206, Australia
and
Editions de la Maison des Sciences de l'Homme
54 Boulevard Raspail, 75270 Paris Cedex 06

First edition 1972 by Pergamon Press Inc.
Second edition first published by Cambridge University Press 1982

Printed in the United States of America

Library of Congress Cataloging in Publication Data
Main entry under title:
Emotion in the human face.
(Studies in emotion and social interaction)
Rev. ed. of: Emotion in the human face /
Paul Ekman. 1972.
Bibliography: p.
Includes index.
1. Emotions – Research.   2. Facial
expression – Research.   3. Psychological
research.   I. Ekman, Paul.   II. Series.
[DNLM: 1. Emotions.   2. Facial expression.
BF 591 E54]
BF531.E49   1982   152.4   81-21621
ISBN 0 521 23992 3 hard covers   AACR2
ISBN 0 521 28393 0 paperback

Portions of Chapter 8 are drawn from an article by Paul Ekman and Harriet
Oster, Facial expressions of emotion, *Annual Review of Psychology*, 1979, *30*,
527–554.

To M. A. & E.

Contents

Contributors

Paul Ekman
Department of Psychiatry
University of California
San Francisco

Phoebe Ellsworth
Department of Psychology
Stanford University

Wallace V. Friesen
Department of Psychiatry
University of California
San Francisco

Joseph C. Hager
Department of Psychiatry
University of California
San Francisco

Harriet Oster
Department of Psychology
University of Pennsylvania

Maureen O'Sullivan
Department of Psychology
University of San Francisco

William K. Redican
Behavioral Medicine
Associates
Santa Rosa, California

Silvan S. Tomkins (emeritus)
Department of Psychology
Rutgers University

Preface to the second edition

This second, revised edition of *Emotion in the human face* is more than twice as long as the first edition, which was published in 1972. Totally new chapters, some by authors not involved in the first edition, cover new work currently at the forefront of research on the face and emotion.

In Chapter 8, Ekman and Oster critically review much of the research published since 1970. Their chapter, based on one in an *Annual Review of Psychology* published in 1979, has been considerably expanded and updated.

In Chapter 9, Ekman and Friesen discuss the development, use, reliability, and validity of their new technique for measuring facial movement – the Facial Action Coding System (FACS). Many of the data reported are published here for the first time.

In Chapter 10, Redican considers research since 1965 on facial expressions in nonhuman primates from the vantage point of what has been discovered about human expression and integrates the two bodies of literature.

In Chapter 11, O'Sullivan examines one of the most popular problems of the last decade, yet one in which there has been marked inconsistency in the results reported by different investigators. Studies of individual differences in the ability to recognize facial expression are evaluated in terms of how well they meet the requirements for test construction in terms of both reliability and validity.

In Chapter 12, Hager carefully and critically assesses studies of asymmetries in facial expression. Recently this topic has generated a number of controversial and contradictory studies.

In Chapter 13, Tomkins provides a concise, up-to-date overview of his theory of affect. Tomkins' was the first theory of emotion to place great emphasis on facial expression. His two volumes, published in the early 1960s, reawakened interest in the face but are now out of print. Chapter 13 makes his ideas accessible again.

The material retained from the first edition (Chapters 1–7), annotated and cross-referenced to the new chapters, bears reading today if investigators are to avoid repeating past methodological and conceptual errors (Chapters 1 and 2) and to stop the unwitting reiteration of findings already well established.

Preface to the first edition

Our aim in this book is to integrate knowledge about the face and emotion, describing what we know, indicating what we need to know, and providing some guidelines for study of this complicated but intriguing phenomenon. We have both students and researchers in mind as the readers – those interested not only in psychology but in anthropology, ethology, sociology, and biology. Although some may be engaged with questions other than those raised here, they nevertheless may profit from knowing the answers to many of the psychological questions that have been asked about the face and emotion; and some of the methods of study might well be appropriate to their own interests in the face. This book should also be useful to those who are not primarily interested in the face and emotion but who can gain through this book a better appreciation of how a field of behavioral science progresses – the problems, the mistakes – and how experiments conducted over five decades fit together. There will be excitement as answers emerge.

The second audience for whom this book is intended consists of those planning or already conducting research on the face. This book provides current information, integrating experiments conducted over a long period of time. Some of the conceptual ambiguities that have hindered research and the methodological decisions that must be made in planning research on the face and emotion are discussed. How past investigators handled these matters is presented critically, and a set of standards is offered, which should at least provoke thought and at best provide guidelines for research.

Our hope is that the reader will be better able to profit from the past and avoid asking questions that have actually already been answered, alerted to the methodological pitfalls into which others have fallen and sensitive to some of the new, challenging questions that can be asked. Most of the research analyzed in this book has already been published, but important new findings are reported for the first time and integrated with the past results.

Acknowledgments

My own interest in the face and emotion stems from a longer and broader interest in the whole range of nonverbal behavior – body movements, gesture, and posture, as well as facial behavior. In studying nonverbal behavior, I have found it crucial to understand how the information provided by the face may differ from that which can be derived from the body. Reluctantly at first, I was led to focus on the problem of the face and emotion. My reluctance stemmed from my trust of past reviews of that literature, which suggested it was a difficult area of research with only meager findings.

I am grateful to Carol Ammons, editor of the journal *Perceptual and Motor Skills*, who was kind enough to put me in touch with Silvan S. Tomkins, after noting the overlap in our interests from articles that each of us had submitted to that journal. Tomkins has taught me much about the face. Watching him interpret facial behavior dissipated my resistance, convincing me that this would be a rich and exciting area for study. In the last fifteen years, Tomkins has been a consultant on many of my experiments and a collaborative investigator on one.

As my own research on the face proceeded, I became perplexed as to why there had been so many failures in the past when I and other current investigators were obtaining positive results. This led me to read with care some of the earlier literature. When I discovered that many of the questions I had been asking had already been answered but that either the original investigator was not aware of the implications of his data or his findings had been misreported or ignored by reviewers, the idea for this book began.

I am extremely grateful for the generous support I have received from the National Institute of Mental Health, both from the Research Fellowships Branch and the Clinical Research Branch. After finishing my master's thesis on body movement in 1955, I received a predoctoral research fellowship to continue studies of nonverbal behavior. Since that time, my research on nonverbal behavior has been supported by a postdoctoral research fellowship, a Career Scientist Development Award, a Research Scientist Award, and research grants from the Clinical Research Branch of NIMH. Some of the studies reported and the time for writing both the first and this second, revised edition were supported by NIMH grant 5 RO1 MH11976-15 and NIMH Research Scientist Award 5 KO2 MH06092.

Wally Friesen, one of the co-authors of this book, has been my close friend and collaborator for more than twenty years. We have worked together so intimately at every stage of research that it would be difficult to distinguish his ideas from mine.

The first edition of this book was dedicated to four psychologists who at different times and places each gave me encouragement and opportunity during my education. Margaret Tresselt, my teacher in an undergraduate research course, encouraged me to pursue a career in psychology. Robert Berryman was my mentor in graduate school at Adelphi University; he taught me the excitement of research. Gordon Derner, the director of the clinical psychology training program at Adelphi, supported my work in too numerous ways to describe. The late Robert E. Harris, when he was chief psychologist at Langley Porter Institute, made it possible for me to go there for postdoctoral research training; I have never left.

Paul Ekman

University of California, San Francisco
The Langley Porter Psychiatric Institute
Spring, 1982

PART I
Research foundations

PAUL EKMAN, WALLACE V. FRIESEN,
AND PHOEBE ELLSWORTH

The human face – in repose and in movement, at the moment of death as in life, in silence and in speech, when seen or sensed from within, in actuality or as represented in art or recorded by the camera – is a commanding, complicated, and at times confusing source of information. The face is *commanding* because of its very visibility and omnipresence. While sounds and speech are intermittent, the face even in repose can be informative. And, except by veils or masks, the face cannot be hidden from view. There is no facial maneuver equivalent to putting one's hands in one's pockets. Further, the face is the location for sensory inputs, life-necessary intake, and communicative output. The face is the site for the sense receptors of taste, smell, sight, and hearing; the intake organs for food, water, and air. It is the output location for speech. The face is also commanding because of its role in early development; it is prior to language in the communication between parent and child.

The complexity of the face is apparent when we consider its sending capacity, the information it may convey, and its role in social life. Although there are only a few words to describe different facial behaviors (*smile, frown, furrow, squint*, etc.) human facial muscles are sufficiently complex to allow more than a thousand different facial appearances; and the action of these muscles is so rapid that these appearances *could* all be shown in less than a few hours' time. (Current work shows that there are tens of thousands of expressions; see Chapter 11.) The face is also a complex information source. We can learn different things from looking at a person's face. The face can send messages about such transient and sometimes fleeting events as a feeling or emotion or the moment-to-moment fluctuations of a conversation. The face can show more enduring moods, perhaps even stable personality characteristics and traits, and such slow progressive changes as age or state of health and such immutables as sex. The complication occurs because the opportunity to

1

glean such a wide variety of information from this single source is combined with the possibility of drawing inferences that may not be correct.

Certainly physiognomic or environmental factors can result in misinformation from the face – for example, the prematurely wrinkled face in a young person. But the face can also misinform by intention or habit. Although smiles may be a reliable index of pleasure or happiness, a person may also smile to mask a feeling he wishes to conceal or to present a feeling when he has no emotion at all. Is the face like an involuntary system or is it subject to voluntary activation and thus capable of purposeful control and disguise? Clearly, it is both.

The very richness of the face, the number of different facial behaviors, the number of different kinds of information we may derive from observing the face, and the uncertainty about whether we are obtaining correct, incorrect, or even purposely misleading information can give rise to *confusion*. How can the movements of the face be described when there is no vocabulary to label them, when there are so many different facial appearances, and when they can change so rapidly? Which of these facial appearances are relevant to learning about a person's emotions, which to learning about his personality? Which will tell us whether he is listening or wants to interrupt us and speak himself? And how can we know when the face is purposely misleading us?

Our purpose is to clarify such confusion about the face by critically evaluating a body of research to provide answers to these questions. It will be necessary to restrict our focus to the consideration of only one type of information that can be obtained from the face (information about emotion), from only one type of organism (human adults), using only one type of evidence (empirical research). The vastness of the research literature, the variety of problems encountered in the study of the face, and the difficult conceptual issues that must be considered in order to integrate the multitude of studies require these restrictions.

We chose to focus on questions concerning how the face provides information about *emotion* because these have been the most frequently asked questions, certainly by investigators, and perhaps also in life when people see each other's faces.[1] The face of the human *adult* was selected because some of the methodological problems involved in work with children and nonhuman primates are quite different and because there has been much less work on these now rapidly developing areas. (A review of recent research on infants and children is given in Chapter 8;

---

[1]The reader is referred to Vine (1969) for a review of the face excluding emotion and to Ekman (1978) for a review of 17 types of facial signals other than those relevant to emotion.

research on facial expression in nonhuman primates is discussed in Chapter 10.) Finally, we will consider only evidence that is based on scientific research (largely in psychology) because our aim is to aid further research by providing a discussion of the obstacles that have impeded it and, most importantly, to provide answers, not speculations, about what we now know about the face and emotion.

Of the many intriguing questions that can be and have been asked about the human face and emotion, we shall discuss the evidence from seven major lines of research. (1) What words can be used to describe the emotional information that we observe in the face? How many different emotions can be seen? Can we discover not only whether someone feels good or bad but also whether he or she is interested, happy, angry, disgusted, sad, or afraid? (2) Are there types of emotional information that are fundamental to understanding the face, such as how pleasant a person feels, how active, how intense? When people are left to their own devices, how do they usually handle the information about emotion they glean from the face? The research on these questions will be discussed in Chapters 3 and 8.

(3) Is the information about emotion that can be derived from the face always an accurate measure of how a person feels? How often does the face provide *no* basis for accurate judgment of emotion? How often does the face provide incorrect information? Some people may be poker faced or may habitually mask their true feelings; does the face provide accurate information about emotion for only some people and not for others? Does one require some special tutoring in order to know how to judge emotion accurately from the face? The research on these questions will be surveyed in Chapters 4 and 8.

(4) Which of the movements and wrinkles in the face provide accurate information about a particular emotion? Is there one wrinkle that means sadness and another that means anger? Does one area of the face, such as the eyes, provide more information, or more accurate information, than other parts of the face? (5) Can we link particular facial movements and wrinkles to particular impressions about emotion? The research on these questions will be analyzed in Chapters 5 and 9.

(6) How does the face compare with other sources of information about emotion? A face is usually seen in context, that is, with words, voice, body, social setting, etc. Can we really read any information from the face alone, or is most of the information about emotion inferred from its context? If we can read information about emotion in the face and it differs from that contained in the context (i.e, a sad face shown when a

person says, "I feel great"), which is correct? Which will most people believe – face or context? Or will they combine both bits of information when forming a judgment? The research on these questions will be discussed in Chapter 6.

(7) How does the facial behavior[2] associated with emotion differ across cultures? Are there any universal associations between a facial behavior and a given emotion, or is the distinctive facial behavior for anger in one culture not relevant for anger in another culture? Do cultures differ in what makes someone angry or sad or happy? Do they differ in whether members of the culture show or conceal any clues to such feelings in their face? Do they differ in the particular facial movements that will occur when someone is angry or afraid or sad? The research on these questions will be examined in Chapters 7 and 8.

More than five decades of empirical research have addressed these questions. Reading this literature from its early beginnings, we have found that the results were not as negative, contradictory, or chaotic as past reviewers have maintained.[3] Our more optimistic picture, that there are answers to many of these questions, is based in part on a reanalysis of key experiments and an emphasis upon studies that have been ignored. In addition, by examining systematically and in detail the research design and results of certain experiments, we have been able both to correct past misinterpretations of results and to furnish the basis for discrediting some experiments that have managed to survive past criticism.

This fundamental reevaluation of the literature required that we develop a conceptual and methodological framework in terms of which each experiment could be considered, for much of the confusion, both in the experiments themselves and in past reviews, occurred because of the absence of any such framework. It is no wonder that such confusion has persisted; the conceptual issues are hazy and complex and the methodological decisions that must be made in designing research on the face and emotion are difficult and intricate.

In Chapter 1 some of the conceptual issues that need clarification will be discussed. The first difficult conceptual problem is deciding what we

[2]We have avoided the phrase *facial expressions of emotion* because it implies that some inner state is being manifested or shown externally or that the behavior is intended to transmit information. Instead we have used the phrases *face and emotion* or *facial behavior*. Note that in the later chapters we shall give up this purity of terminology and revert to the less-awkward term *expression*.

[3]Most notable, see the comments by Landis (1924, 1929) and Sherman (1927a) in their own research reports and Hunt (1941) in his review of the literature; also see Bruner and Tagiuri (1954) and Tagiuri (1969).

mean by *emotion*. The lack of a clear definition of emotion has caused much difficulty for those trying to study the face and emotion. How does emotion differ from other facets of human experience? For example, is anger an emotion? If so, how does anger relate to hostile or aggressive behavior? How can we tell when an emotion is experienced?

Another difficult conceptual problem is specifying just what we mean by the term *accurate*. How do we know whether information provided by the face is accurate? Is there some one criterion to determine what emotion has actually been experienced? We shall examine this problem by analyzing the ways past investigators have dealt with it.

A third conceptual problem is the various applications of the term *generality*. If evidence is obtained that observers can distinguish fear from anger, how are the limits of these findings determined? A number of different kinds of generality must be considered. Are the findings general to settings other than the ones studied? Can they be generalized to people other than those studied? Do they have generality in time, in the sense of showing that the face *often* permits this distinction? Do the findings have generality in the sense that most people could make the same distinction?

Another conceptual problem is to determine the extent and effect of people's ability to disguise and *control* their facial behavior. Does control entail both omitting the sign of a felt emotion and simulating the sign of an unfelt emotion? Does such control occur only in some settings or only with some people? If people can disguise and control their facial behavior, then how does the investigator determine when facial behavior is genuine and when it is simulated?

The final problem discussed in Chapter 1 is whether to conceive of the face as a single message system, which, at a given moment, can show information relevant to only one emotion, or as a multimessage system, which can simultaneously show the *blend* of two or more emotions.

In Chapter 2 each of the decisions that a researcher of face and emotion must make will be presented, along with a review of past decisions and their ramifications. The choice between two alternative research approaches and the relationship between the findings of each will be discussed. The types of circumstances that may elicit facial behavior relevant to emotion will also be evaluated. In addition, a number of questions about sampling will be considered: How many people need to be studied in order to learn about the face and emotion? How much of the facial behavior of each person should be included and how should it be selected from the total facial behavior? How many different emotions should be studied to answer questions about accuracy, cross-cultural similarities, etc? If the research utilizes observers who are to record their impressions of emotion, how many words, categories, or scales should they be given? The last methodological decision considered will be the selection of a recording technique from a number of alternatives.

In separate chapters discussions will be presented on the research that has been done and the answers that have emerged to the fundamental questions about the face and emotion, which were the focus of research from 1914 to 1970 and which continue to be studied today.

1. Conceptual ambiguities

PAUL EKMAN, WALLACE V. FRIESEN,
AND PHOEBE ELLSWORTH

1.1. Historical review

The lack of a broad methodological or conceptual framework for reviewing research on the the face and emotion and the pessimistic attitude that has characterized past reviews have had serious consequences: Errors in experimental design have been repeated, recent experimenters have been uninformed or misinformed by relevant past work, and interest has at times lagged because of the seemingly discouraging state of the field. These problems are traceable in part to the nebulous nature of the concept of emotion itself and in part to the disjointed history of research characterized by major, disjunctive shifts of interest, which we shall consider in three successive time periods. An unjustified pessimism culminated the first period (about 1914 to 1940) and was followed by a shift of interest to other issues in the second period (about 1940 to 1960). When in the third period (about 1960 to 1970) many of the issues addressed in the first period came again into vogue, the investigations did not sufficiently profit from either the mistakes or the progress made earlier.

During the first period, the face and emotion was a popular topic in the field of psychology. There were many studies, some by investigators well known today, although not primarily for their work on this topic: F. Allport, Goodenough, Guilford, Landis, Munn, Woodworth. Despite differences in both variables studied and research designs, most experiments addressed one of two issues: (1) Does the face provide accurate information about emotion? (2) Are the facial behaviors related to emotion innate or learned? For a time, there was considerable argument in the literature, but a pessimistic view became dominant. At the least, the results appeared contradictory, and certain advocates, most notably Hunt, Landis, and Sherman, argued that the face was a poor source of information about emotion; there was no accuracy, either as judged by observers or through direct measurement of the face. What little agreement about emotion could be achieved depended more on knowledge of the eliciting circumstance than on observation of the face. And no evidence for innate elements could be found. Commenting in disbelief on this period of research, Hebb (1946) wrote, "These studies have led to the conclusion that an emotion cannot be accurately identified by another observer" (p. 90).

The second period of research on the face and emotions saw less research by fewer people concerned with different aspects of the phenomenon. The field became largely defined and known by the work and interest of one man, Harold Schlosberg, the only person to publish consistently. A student of Woodworth's Schlosberg continued Woodworth's (1938) interest in the vocabulary of observers' judgments of emotion from the face, but Schlosberg did not pursue Woodworth's finding that judgments made in terms of emotion categories agreed with actors' intended poses. Instead, Schlosberg (1941, 1952, 1954) developed verbal dimensions, which he considered to underlie Woodworth's emotion categories. He later proposed a geometric model of how those dimensions interrelate, which he considered relevant not only to facial behavior but also to developments in the psychophysiology of emotion. Although a few others (Fulcher, Coleman, and Thompson) published articles during this time challenging, at least in part Landis's and Sherman's earlier negative findings, each published only once and received little attention. Accuracy and the question of innate versus learned components of facial behavior became dormant issues.

In the third period of research on the face and emotion, covering 1960 to 1970, there has been a resurgence of interest, sparked by clinical investigators looking for behavioral measures applicable to studies of psychotherapy, by the publication of two theories of emotion that emphasized the face (Plutchik's and Tomkins's), and by the development of the field of semiotics (see Sebeok, Hayes, & Bateson, 1964). Some investigators have continued the line of study initiated by Schlosberg on the dimensions of emotion relevant or useful in observers' judgments of the face. However, many of the current investigations have revived issues that had been dormant since the first period: issues of accuracy, early development, and cross-cultural similarities. Rather than avoiding the methodological pitfalls of that first period and building upon some of its promising positive findings, much current work has seemed either uninformed about the early work or, conversely, directed toward refuting the legacy of pessimism about the face and emotion. (A somewhat different historical review is contained in the beginning of Chapter 8.)

Because of the lack of an orderly progression in development of research issues, concepts, methods, and findings over these three time periods, no framework has emerged within which a survey of findings might have meaning. We shall attempt to supply such a framework. In this chapter we shall examine some of the conceptual ambiguities and oversimplifications that have hindered research and in Chapter 2 we shall then discuss the methodological problems that have impeded research in the area throughout its history.

1.2. What do we mean by "emotion"?

Most writers have disagreed in their definitions of emotion, often describing different phenomena. Izard (1969), in reviewing the literature, wrote, "The area of emotional experience and behavior is one of the most confused and ill-defined in psychology."[1] Another volume would be needed to review all the various definitions and underlying theoretical positions, but a brief outline of the different phenomena considered by those defining emotion will be relevant to issues discussed later.

Some authors have considered central to their definition of emotion a special class of *stimuli* that usually elicit emotional behavior, but there has been little agreement about what might characterize such stimuli or distinguish them from stimuli that rarely elicit emotion. No one has provided a description of either the social variables (e.g., the nature of the setting, the roles of the persons, the tasks underway) or the individual differences that might clarify why and when certain classes of stimuli evoke emotional behavior. A further problem is the inability to verify that a stimulus frequently kindles emotion except from the occurrence of consequent emotional behavior; unfortunately, it is equally difficult to verify whether the consequent behavior *is* emotional. There is some agreement, however, that there may be stimuli that elicit emotional behavior because of innate factors as well as stimuli to which the emotional response is learned, and that, in addition to internal events of the organism, such emotional reactions would also be induced by external or environmental stimuli.

The lack of agreement about what stimuli bring on emotion and the circularity in the verification of such stimuli leave the investigator with-

---

[1] For recent attempts to define emotion, see Izard (1971), Ekman & Friesen (1975), and, for a quite different view, Mandler (1975).

out guidance in choosing the particular setting or eliciting circumstance that may be likely to inspire emotional facial behavior for study. Thus, when an investigator finds no relationship between some aspect of the face and emotion, there is always the possibility that he failed to utilize stimuli that draw out "emotional" facial behavior.

Physiological responses have been viewed as relevant to some definitions of emotion, including visceral activity, other signs of autonomic activation, and hypothalamic activity. It is generally accepted that the occurrence of such physiological responses is not a sufficient indication of the presence of emotion, and there is little evidence indicating that different emotions are associated with the different patterns of autonomic activity investigated to date.[2]

Some motor responses have been considered central to the definition of emotional behavior. Involuntary motor attitudes, voluntary action tendencies, presumed basic patterns of aggression, flight, or immobility, and such phenomena as tics and restlessness have been considered. And, of course, the movements of the facial muscles have been regarded by many authors as relevant to or a primary element of emotional behavior. The nature of the relationship between facial behavior and other presumably emotion-related phenomena is the topic of this book.

Certain kinds of verbal responses have been part of some definitions of emotion. These include what Mandler (1962) called *referential verbal behaviors*, which are descriptions referring to internal somatic states, presumably reflecting awareness of physiological activation. They include, too, the vocabulary of emotion names, categories, dimensions, attributes, or qualities that could be used to describe felt or observed emotional experiences.

The interactive consequence of certain behavior has been considered by some to be the necessary criterion for defining emotional behavior. Those investigators of nonhuman primates who speak of emotion define it in terms of a sequence of events between two or more organisms in which a behavior on the part of one is immediately followed by a particular kind of response by another. Although some investigators of human nonverbal behavior have begun to study interactive sequences, the only studies of the face that utilized this approach were not concerned with emotion and isolated only the one aspect of facial behavior for study,

[2]There has been little study of the relationship between facial responses and physiological indices. The few studies compared only one physiological index, the galvanic skin response (GSP), and only a gross measure of the face (Buck, Savin, Miller, & Caul, 1969; Jones, 1950; Lanzetta & Kleck, 1970), but they found evidence of a negative correlation. (See a review of current studies in Chapter 8.)

looking or not looking at the face of the other person. (This remains so in the work from 1970 to the present.)

The lack of a clear definition of emotion presents problems for investigators, some of whom have simply sidestepped the problem of specifying why the behavior they studied may be presumed to have anything to do with emotion, and also for the editor of this volume. How should we determine just which studies are relevant, and how should we utilize this ambiguous concept? Our selection procedure was to take into account, with a few exceptions, any article that the author *said* was about emotion and where the face was studied in relation to one of the other phenomena listed above. The most common experiment has been to study the face in relation to emotion vocabulary, usually that of the observer, although there have been some studies that have analyzed facial responses under different natural or experimentally arranged environmental conditions. We found no studies of the relationship between referential verbal behavior and facial behavior, although these would have qualified for inclusion, and only a few that included physiological measures.

Studies of the face in which the investigator reported focusing on traits, attitudes, or personality, not emotion, have not been incorporated. Also excluded were experiments in which drawings of the face rather than photographs, film, videotape, or live facial behavior were employed; the rationale for this exclusion will be given in Chapter 2, Section 2.7.

When we use the word *emotion*, in many cases the discussion will apply equally to the various aspects of the term, and therefore there will be no need to specify one. In scrutinizing the results of particular experiments, we will attempt to specify what notion of emotion the investigator had in mind or at least why the investigator felt the behavior studied was relevant to emotion. In most studies, the behavior investigated was thought to be emotional because observers were able to reach some agreement in utilizing the lay vocabulary of emotion terms to describe the behavior. When interpretations of results are challenged primarily on grounds of relevance of the behavior studied to emotion, the different sources of evidence (stimuli, motor responses, verbal responses, physiological responses, interactive consequences) will be discussed.

1.3. How do we determine whether judgments of emotion are accurate?

Can the face provide accurate information about emotion? This simple question, the answer to which may seem patently obvious on an intuitive basis, has baffled investigators. Past reviewers have claimed that the findings from equally reputable investigations are contradictory and that therefore no answer can be proposed. We shall challenge this reading of the literature and, in establishing that the face can provide accurate information, shall criticize in detail and then dismiss as worthless certain experiments; we shall reanalyze and reinterpret others. We shall have to consider how investigators solved many of the methodological problems examined in Chapter 2, and shall need to take careful stock of how they established their criteria of accuracy, for this has been one of the main sources of error and confusion.

If we are to show that the face provides accurate information, we must do two things. We must use some measurement procedure to decipher the information shown in a face, and we must establish some other index of what occurred, which we will call an accuracy *criterion*, so that the information from the face can be compared with this index. If they coincide, we conclude that the face provided accurate information. The accuracy criterion is the index of what occurred; this is compared with the facial information. Part of the confusion in interpreting the past literature has arisen because investigators used different methods to derive their information from the face. Some simply asked observers of the face what emotion was shown, and others measured some aspect of the face (for example, the lowering or raising of the brows). With either kind of measurement, the investigator had the same problem – to find some independent criterion of what occurred to compare with the measurement of information from the face. If, for example, he could ask the person whose face was being measured how he felt at that time, and if he could trust the adequacy and veracity of the person's self-report as his accuracy criterion, he would employ this criterion regardless of which measurement procedure he had used for determining the information shown in the face. If he had asked observers about what the face showed, he could compare their judgment with the person's self-report; or, if he had measured some facial behavior, such as brow lowering, he could determine whether it varied when the person reported different emotions. Thus, a definition of accuracy criteria must allow for the use of either measurement procedure.

We have mentioned one source of information about emotion, the person's self-report, which could be used as an accuracy criterion. Our previous discussion of definitions of emotion showed that there were various events that have been taken to be relevant to emotion (certain stimuli, motor responses, verbal responses, physiological responses, interactive consequences). We shall consider these various sources of information as possible accuracy criteria. Further, we shall argue for the need to use multiple sources of information.

We shall use the term *accuracy* to refer to "correct" information of some nature being obtained by some means from facial behavior. The criterion for determining what actually did happen, in terms of which to check whether information derived from the face was correct, might be based on one or more of the following phenomena: (1) antecedent events (e.g., the behavior of another interactant or experimentally introduced or naturally occurring environmental events); (2) concomitant behavior (e.g., physiological measures, simultaneous verbal behavior, body movements); (3) consequent events (e.g., self-report, motor responses of the person being studied, the other interactant's behavior); or (4) consensus by a panel of experts about the individual's experience or behavior.

Few investigators have employed information from more than one such source as their accuracy criterion, yet variability across subjects, in their interpretation of similar events or instructions and in their attempts to control rather than show emotion, suggests the wisdom of obtaining multiple indexes and combining or comparing them in order to establish accuracy. Each of the possible criteria we have suggested may be incomplete; each may be subject to some sort of error; each may be more useful for one emotion than for another, for one setting than another, for one type of person than another. If these criteria have at least partial independence, in that they are subject to different kinds of error, then, as more criteria are employed, alternative explanations based on associated error become less plausible (see D. T. Campbell & Fiske, 1959).

Our definition of accuracy refers to *correct* information but does not require that the information be relevant to emotions. Establishing that the information derived from the face is correct does not guarantee that this information concerns emotion, in any of its various definitions. For example, it may be possible to show that observers are able to distinguish accurately between facial behaviors emitted during the stressful and nonstressful portions of a standardized interview. However, this correct judgment need not necessarily be based on information about emotion; if, in the stressful phase, the subjects become exhausted, facial cues associated with tiredness could provide the basis for accuracy. The investigator would need other means to show that the accurate judgment is relevant to emotional phenomena. For example, the verbal behavior of the subjects during the stress interviews could be examined, other observers who knew nothing about the interview procedure could be tested to see if they agreed about judgments, utilizing an emotion vocabulary, and whether such judgments would differentiate facial behavior emitted during the nonstressful from that during the stressful parts of the interviews. Or, the correctly judged facial behaviors could be compared with facial behaviors emitted in situations where emotional behavior is presumed to have occurred.

There is no reason to derogate findings that show accuracy. Correct information from the face is important evidence of the face's ability to provide information about personality, state of exhaustion, etc., but it may or may not be related to the construct of emotion. Maintaining the distinction between accurate information from the face and accurate information about emotion is fundamental to resolving some of the confusions in the relationship between the two general research methods for studying the face, to elucidating problems inherent in the choice of eliciting circumstances, and to interpreting substantive findings on accuracy (all discussed in Chapter 2).

Today the construct of emotion is still far from validated. Some authors even question the utility of such a construct, suggesting that its only use is as a chapter heading in survey textbooks. Multiple methods and multiple criteria for obtaining accurate information relevant to emotion are, therefore, essential to the pursuit of research in this field. Accuracy obtained with different criteria, all relevant to the different aspects of the phenomena labeled *emotional* and relevant to the distinctions among emotions (made either in terms of such categories as anger, fear, sadness, etc., or such dimensions as pleasantness, intensity, control, etc.) is crucial to increasing confidence in the utility of the emotion construct.

One further part of our definition of accuracy requiring comment is the phrase, "by some means," referring to how correct information is obtained from the face. Shortly, we shall discuss two interrelated methods of research, judgment studies and components studies (Section 2.1), one requiring observers to describe the information they derive from facial behavior and the other requiring measurement of some component of facial behavior. Accuracy can be a question in each of these methods, and an accurate finding with one can indicate the probable outcome of the other.

Let us now consider accuracy criteria that have been employed in studies of the face. The most popular accuracy criterion has been the emotion intended by an actor posing facial behavior. If observers can tell what emotion was posed or if measurement of the face can show that different facial muscles were involved in different poses, then one type of accuracy is established. The *generality* of such results may be open to question, without diminishing the finding that correct information about the actor's intended emotion can be obtained from the face. Four types of questions about the generality of findings from studies of posing can be raised: Are the findings relevant to spontaneous facial behavior (generality across settings and eliciting circumstances)? Do the results depend on the few specially gifted actors (generality across persons)? Are the findings attributable to those rare moments when someone emits a decipherable pose (generality across time)? Is exact judgment the privilege of only those who are specially trained as observers (generality across observers)? We shall weigh these questions further in the next section of this chapter when we distinguish among these types of generality.

The second basis for an accuracy criterion, employed much less often than actor's intent, is the circumstance in which the facial behavior occurred. If observers can tell what was happening or if measurements of the face show systematic variations with changing eliciting circumstances, then accuracy is established. One of the problems with this criterion is that it presupposes without substantiation (although there are empirical tests that have rarely been employed) that the same eliciting circumstance evokes the same reaction (emotion?) across persons and, further, if observers are utilized, that the observers know what reaction is likely to occur in each eliciting circumstance. For if the same eliciting circumstance evoked different reactions across persons or if the circumstance was not thought by observers to elicit a particular reaction, there would be no possibility of achieving accurate results. Even if the situation did elicit the same reaction across subjects, it is necessary to determine whether the subjects were similar in regard to attempts to control or disguise their facial behavior. These problems will be further examined when we review the control of emotion and later in the report of Landis and Coleman's experiments (Chapter 4).

Sometimes observers have been asked to judge the emotion shown in the face rather than the eliciting circumstance, typically with the investigator assuming, but not verifying, that a particular emotion was associated with a particular eliciting circumstance for stimulus persons. This problem will be further elaborated in Chapter 4 also.

Even when the accuracy criterion is based on a spontaneous eliciting circumstance, there are still questions about the generality of the findings. Although spontaneous eliciting circumstances better approximate real life than does posing, the question still remains as to how general the findings are to real-life settings. Further, one must consider whether the stimulus persons and/or the observers are representative or in some way special or unique. In addition, there is a need to establish how often, within the situation studied, facial behavior provides accurate information.

1.4. What does establishing generality entail?

There are four types of questions to be raised about the generality of the findings from any accuracy study. To establish generality across *eliciting circumstances and settings*, we must determine whether the findings in one eliciting circumstance or setting would be valid for another such circumstance or setting. This determination is relevant to studies that employ either posed or spontaneous eliciting circumstances.

This type of generality has been a major source of doubt about accuracy studies involving posed behavior, which some writers have claimed has little generality to spontaneous facial behavior. Even if observers can tell what emotion the poser intended, posing may involve the use of special facial conventions that are irrelevant to the facial behavior occurring when people are engaged in spontaneous behavior. We shall scrutinize this argument further when we weigh the choice of eliciting circumstances (Chapter 2), when we report findings on accuracy (Chapter 4), and when we examine cross-cultural studies of posing (Chapter 7). We shall argue that posed facial behavior, while special, is not unique and does have generality to spontaneous facial behavior.

Regarding the use of spontaneous behavior, if a laboratory event such as a stress interview is devised, the investigator must provide some assessment of the types of real-life events to which the laboratory eliciting circumstance is relevant. The stress interview might elicit facial behavior that is accurately judged, but that situation might be unique as to the extent of stress induced or the constraints against retaliation and have generality only to a limited set of circumstances when people are severely put-upon and cannot fight back. Even if a naturally occurring eliciting circumstance is employed, rather than a laboratory event, questions can be raised about generality across settings. For example, it might be possible to derive accurate information from the facial behavior shown during childbirth labor, but there might be few other events in life that evoke such prolonged pain and where the setting permits or encourages uncontrolled facial behavior.

Generality *across persons* refers to whether the findings are general to most people, just to specially trained persons, such as actors, or just to people with certain personality characteristics, such as extroverts. Generality is severely limited when the posers have been actors but not when untrained persons pose the emotions. Generality across persons is in doubt in studies of spontaneous behavior if some special group of persons is recruited as subjects, e.g., mental patients.

The third type of generality is *across time* within an eliciting circumstance. How frequently does the face provide true information? In posing, how often does the poser emit facial behavior that is accurately judged; does he give eight poses inaccurately judged for every one judged accurately? In studies of spontaneous facial behavior, has the investigator chosen for his sample the infrequent moment when the face showed something, or does the facial behavior shown in the situation provide precise information at many points in time? The answer to this question about generality depends upon how the investigator sampled facial behaviors from his record, whether of posing or of spontaneous behavior, and will be discussed in Chapter 2. The problem of achieving generality across time will be explored in relation to the spontaneous facial behavior studies that used photographs from magazines as their stimuli (Chapter 4).

The last question on the generality of accuracy findings applies only if observers judge the information shown in the face. Generality of *decoding* asks how readily other observers could make those judgments. Were specially trained or gifted observers used, or was enlargement or slowed motion required for their making exact judgments?

1.5. Can facial behavior be controlled or disguised?

Many writers (Hebb, 1946; Honkavaara, 1961; Klineberg, 1938; Murphy, Murphy, & Newcomb, 1937; Plutchik, 1962) have commented that a subject's control over his facial behavior and the social pressures that dictate such control can conceal the very behavior that experiment was arranged to draw out. Ekman and Friesen (1969a, 1969b, 1975) described four management techniques for the control of facial behavior: (1) intensifying, (2) deintensifying, (3) neutralizing, and (4) masking a felt emotion with the facial behavior usually associated with a different emotion. They hypothesized that these control techniques for managing facial behaviors associated with emotion are operative in most social situations and that *display rules* learned, usually early in life, for each facial behavior specify what management technique should be applied by whom in what circumstances. The display rule dictates the occasion for the applicability of a particular management technique in terms of (1) static characteristics of the persons within the situation (e.g., age, sex, physical body size), (2) static characteristics of the setting (e.g., ecological factors, social definition of the situation, such as funeral, wedding, job interview, waiting for a bus), (3) transient characteristics of the persons (e.g., role, attitude), and (4) transient regularities during the course of the social interaction (e.g., entrances, exits, transition points, periods in conversation, listening). Display rules govern facial behavior on an habitual basis such that they are more noticeable when violated than when followed. The face appears to be the most skilled nonverbal communicator and, perhaps for that reason, the best "nonverbal liar," capable not only of withholding information but of simulating the facial behavior associated with a feeling that the person in no way is experiencing.

In the choice of an eliciting circumstance for sampling nonverbal behavior (Chapter 2), the question of which display rules may be operative for which persons should be considered, otherwise the investigator may unintentionally obtain samples of deintensified or masked facial behavior. The investigator can utilize questionnaires as well as observations to determine the display rules or the social norms about the probable visible facial behavior for the particular eliciting situations employed. Individual differences in knowledge of display rules or in skill in the management techniques for controlling facial behavior, which might affect the behavior during an experiment, could be explored through self-reports by the subjects about just those questions.

It is difficult for the investigator to determine the effect of display rules, but in the past, investigators have rarely even raised the question of whether their findings might be influenced by and their negative results attributed to display rules. Conceivably, there may be circumstances where the display rule specifies that no management technique need be applied to control the facial behavior, and unmodulated facial behavior would occur. Most investigators have assumed, with little evidence for that assumption and much reason to question it, that their eliciting situations were those kinds of circumstances. How the failure to consider display rules obscured cross-cultural comparison of facial expression is described by Ekman (1973, pp. 176–179).

It is possible, of course, to make the operation of display rules itself the focus of research on the face and emotion. For example, differences in facial behavior could be compared between the subject in isolation and in interaction or aware of being observed. Some such studies are reported by Ekman (1973, pp. 214–218).

1.6. Can two or more emotions be shown simultaneously?

Several authors (Ekman & Friesen, 1967a, 1969a; Nummenmaa, 1964; Plutchik, 1962; Tomkins & McCarter, 1964) have commented on the capacity of the face to show more than one emotion at a given instant. These writers claimed that the facial muscles are sufficiently complex and independent for discrete muscle patterns in different parts of the face to combine so as to present the elements of two or more emotions, observable even in a still photograph. *Blends* may also occur through the very rapid succession in time of two different emotions. Affect blends are thought to occur when (a) the emotion-eliciting circumstance by its very nature elicits more than one feeling or (b) habits (common to a group, or idiosyncratic) link the elicited emotion to another as, for example, when a second emotion is generated in response to the initially inspired one.

Nummenmaa (1964) directly studied this phenomenon by having an actor attempt to show blends in his face. Nummenmaa confirmed that blends could be posed by finding that observers tend to select a blend judgment (e.g., happy and angry) more often than a single affect judgment for the stimuli intended to portray blends but not for the stimuli intended as single-emotion portrayals. In unpublished research, Ekman and Friesen found that some of the photographs that past investigators found to yield a bimodal distribution of judgments when observers were allowed only one judgment choice yielded agreement about the presence of both emotions when observers were allowed to indicate the presence of more than one emotion in the face.

Most investigators have failed to take into account the occurrence of blends in their stimuli. The frequent finding that observers disagree about which of two emotions is present can no longer be interpreted only as evidence of low information in the face but, alternatively, as the consequence of presenting a multiple-message stimulus and allowing the observer only a single-message judgment. In other words, low agreement may be a result of the insensitivity of the dependent-variable measure to complex forms of facial behavior.

The phenomenon of blends complicates not only the judgment procedure to be utilized but also the measures of facial behavior that need to be taken in studies where such measures are related to eliciting circumstances.

1.7. Review

We discussed five conceptual problems that need to be reviewed in planning or evaluating research on the face and emotion. Although no clear agreement about the meaning of the concept emotion has yet merged, consensus suggests that there are some stimuli that typically elicit emotion, that certain physiological, motor, and verbal responses are relevant to emotion, and that there may be specific interactive consequences of emotion. The ambiguity about the meaning of emotion causes problems for the investigator in determining what to study and how to establish that the facial behavior observed is relevant to emotion.

The term *accuracy* was defined as referring to correct information of some nature being obtained by some means from facial behavior. Four sources of information were described for determining what actually did happen. We argued that multiple sources of information should be used in establishing the criterion of accuracy. We hypothesized that the control and disguise of facial behavior are dictated by socially learned display rules, which specify how facial behavior is to be managed in particular social settings, by deintensifying, intensifying, neutralizing, or masking the facial behavior associated with an emotion. Investigators must determine whether the eliciting circumstance they chose for obtaining facial behavior is subject to display rules that might inhibit or diminish the display of the elicited emotion.

Four kinds of generality were considered, all of which are relevant to findings obtained with posed or spontaneous, artificial or natural eliciting circumstances. Is the finding general to eliciting circumstances and settings other than those studied, and if so, to which? Is the finding relevant to the facial behavior of people in general or only to some special class of persons? Is the finding general to most moments in time within the eliciting circumstance studied, or does the face provide information only occasionally? Finally, in judgment studies, is the finding general to most persons who might observe facial behavior or does it require some special skills in the observer?

We suggested that the face can probably provide information about blends of two or more emotions at a given instant. The existence of blends requires that in judgment studies observers be given the option of reporting an impression about more than one emotion. In studies where measurement is made of facial components, it is necessary to examine various areas of the face in order to determine whether a particular facial behavior is relevant to one or more than one emotion.

In Chapter 2 we shall discuss how these conceptual issues translate into specific methodological decisions to be made in planning research on the face and emotion.

2. Methodological decisions

PAUL EKMAN, WALLACE V. FRIESEN,
AND PHOEBE ELLSWORTH

In this chapter we shall take into consideration each of the decisions an investigator confronts in planning research on the face and emotion. The choices made in the past will be evaluated and a recommendation will be made regarding each methodological decision. Although the chief aim of this chapter is to provide some guidelines for those planning research on facial behavior, the discussions of problems encountered in trying to do research on the face provide the critical framework that will be applied when we review and evaluate the research findings on each of seven substantive questions.

2.1. Selecting a research design

One source of confusion in research on the face and emotion has been an oversimplification of the relationship between results obtained from two separate research approaches that address related, but not identical, questions. In *component studies*, facial behavior is treated as a response, and the question addressed is whether a certain position or movement of the subject's face is related to some measure of the subject's emotional state or circumstances. For example, do the inner corners of the eyebrows lift when the subject reports or simulates sadness? In *judgment studies*, facial behavior is treated as a stimulus, and the question addressed is whether observers who judge a subject's face can agree about the subject's emotion or can distinguish among facial behaviors emitted under different emotional states or circumstances. For example, can observers correctly distinguish facial behaviors emitted when the subject reports or simulates happiness from those reflected when sadness is reported or simulated? Whereas in the natural flow of social interaction the faces of the participants provide both stimuli and responses, in most research, one or the other aspect is studied, with quite different methods.

Throughout the history of research, judgment studies have been much more popular than component studies. This has been only partly because of the impression that they are easier to perform, in that the investigator can avoid the problem of what to measure in the face and decide only what faces to show and what judgments to require. In addition, the attraction of judgment studies has been in the possibility of answering both judgment and component questions with one study. The investigator has attempted not only to discover whether observers can judge emotion but also to infer from that result whether components of facial behavior are related to eliciting circumstances. Most investigators have failed to understand that the answer to the components question can be inferred only when the answers to the judgment study are accurate, not when they show inaccuracy or disagreement among judges.

If from a judgment study an investigator finds that the observers were accurate, then it could be inferred that a component study of the same facial behavior would find that the faces varied with the eliciting circumstance. This relationship between the outcomes of these two research approaches is logically required because observers would not have any basis for making accurate judgments if the facial behavior did not vary with the eliciting circumstance. But a judgment study may not be successful; the observers may disagree, or they may agree but be inaccurate rather than accurate. If either of these unfortunate outcomes occurs, it is not logically possible to determine what is at fault. Typically, investigators who failed to obtain accuracy in judgment studies concluded that the faces they studied did not contain information relevant to the accuracy criterion and that, if a component study were performed, no relationship would be found between facial behavior and eliciting circumstances. But this is not logically necessary. When a judgment study fails, the information *may* have been there in the face, and it *might* be unearthed by a component study, if for some reason the observers failed to utilize the available information. Observers might have missed the clues if they did not know what components of facial behavior were related to a particular eliciting circumstance, or if they had mistaken notions of how the components related to the eliciting circumstance, or if an atypical sample of facial behavior was selected for showing to the observers, or if there was an atypical sampling of observers, or if the facial behaviors were difficult to see without slowed motion viewing.

Still tentative findings (Ekman & Friesen, 1969a; Haggard & Isaacs, 1966) on micro affect displays suggest that a failure of observers to agree (or, if they agree, to be accurate) may signify not that the facial behaviors are unrelated to the eliciting circumstances but that they are too brief for the observers to perceive. Micro affect displays have been defined as facial behaviors of so short a duration that most untrained observers do not notice their occurrence, even though inspection of slow-motion film reveals behaviors associated with emotions that observers can readily judge. Such micro facial behaviors may be indicators of conflict, repression, and/or efforts to conceal the emotion experienced. (Our most recent work using the fine grained measurement technique described in Chapter 9 suggests microfacial expressions are very rare events. Nevertheless, observers often miss the information that component studies can reveal.)

Thus, if a judgment study fails to yield accuracy, the investigator must be cautious about inferring that the facial behavior is unrelated to the eliciting circumstances. Although this might be so, it is just as possible that the observers' failure was a result of one of the problems we mentioned briefly, which we shall explore at greater length in this chapter.

In this examination of the relationship between judgment studies and component studies, we avoid the term *emotion* when speaking of accuracy. It may be that observers can correctly judge a poser's *intention* to show a particular emotion, and thus we could infer that some of the components of the facial behaviors emitted when posing the different emotions were different, yet such a finding would not, in and of itself, be evidence that the observers recognized emotion. A variety of behaviors (i.e., lip bites, hesitations, sighs, refusals) might have occurred in reaction to a particular posing instruction and thus allowed accurate judgment. Similarly, if the investigator arranged eliciting circumstances such that the subject was given a severe electric shock on his leg in one circumstance and not in another, it might be that observers told of the circumstances would correctly identify the facial behavior that occurred in each and might also judge the electric shock behavior as fear and the nonshock facial behavior as happiness. Such a finding would logically require the inference that some of the components of the facial behavior were related to the eliciting circumstance. But we cannot assume that the accuracy necessarily involved emotional phenomena. Analysis of the facial components shown in that situation could reveal that during shock the subject bent down to look at his leg, completely obscuring his face, and in nonshock the subject looked straight into the camera. There certainly would be a difference in facial behavior related to eliciting circumstance and a ready explanation of the observer's accuracy, but it would be rather poor evidence for asserting that the face provided accurate information about emotion. This is admittedly an extreme example, intended to emphasize the necessity for the investigator to demonstrate that the accuracy findings, whether from a component study or a judgment study, have sufficient relevance to phenomena described as emotional to warrant the use of that term.

2.2. Choosing the eliciting circumstance

Three requirements must be met in the choice of circumstances during which facial behavior is to be sampled. (1) There must be some basis for claiming the circumstance has relevance to emotion. (2) There must be some way to determine when emotion is aroused or stimulated and, if possible, which emotion is aroused or stimulated when, so as to provide an accuracy criterion for use in either component or judgment studies. (3) A clear record must be obtained if the crucial components are to be either measurable or evident to observers. The two alternatives, posed and spontaneous situations, each satisfy only one of the first two requirements and each has potential liabilities where the other has strength. Posing provides clearer indications than do spontaneous situations of *which* (intended) emotion is shown *when*. Spontaneous situations can, however, claim to have greater relevance than posing to more usual emotional circumstances.

Posing is easy to arrange; clear records are readily obtained; and the record is composed of separate units identified in terms of specific emotions according to the poser's intent. But there are problems. Although posing may differ from other situations in terms of the relative lack of display rules to deintensify, neutralize, or mask facial behavior, posers may well differ in their ability to simulate given emotions, and the typical study has unfortunately used only one or two posers. Although the actor may intend to show only one emotion, posed behavior may contain blends of intended and unintended simulated emotions. Another difficulty is in choosing which poses to consider because most actors will not achieve a pose acceptable to them or the investigator on every attempt; this problem will be discussed later in regard to sampling of behaviors.

The most serious question about posing, raised throughout the history of research on the face and emotion, is whether posed facial behavior has relevance to spontaneously occurring emotion. Hunt (1941) has been the most forceful proponent for the view that posed facial behavior is a specialized, conventionalized language, which, although related to emotion words, is unrelated to the facial behavior occurring when emotion is spontaneously experienced. Thus, positive findings on the judgment of poses were not considered by Hunt to challenge his conclusion that spontaneous facial behavior, when emotion is aroused, is a meager source of information, if not a random phenomenon. But that view depends on argument, not direct evidence, and recent findings suggest its opposite.

Only two investigators directly compared posed and spontaneous facial behavior from the same subjects: Coleman (1949) in a judgment study and Landis (1924, 1929) in both a judgment and a component study. Unfortunately, few conclusions can be derived from their work. Coleman used only two subjects, and the relationship between posed and spontaneous behavior differed for each. Landis's studies are open to criticism on a wide variety of grounds, which will be examined later. Recent cross-cultural studies, which found that the same posed facial behavior was judged as showing the same emotion across various cultures and languages, including a preliterate culture, offer indirect evidence against Hunt's view. If posed facial behavior were an arbitrary language, it would be highly improbable that the same poses would develop in the same way and be associated with comparable verbal labels across cultures (see the end of Section 4.2 and Section 7.2 for discussion of these findings).

Nevertheless, it would be important to have both judgment and component studies directed to this question in order to examine the differences and similarities between posed and spontaneous facial behavior on the same set of subjects. Such studies would be useful because of the history of frequent use of the posing method and the need to answer Hunt's criticism more decisively. In addition, judgment studies could be used to determine whether observers can distinguish felt (spontaneous) emotion from simulated (posed) emotion, and component studies could lead to greater understanding of simulated or deceptive facial behavior as it occurs in spontaneous social interactions. Later (Chapter 4), when we review experiments on the accuracy of judgments of the poser's intentions, we shall again consider the relationship between posed and spontaneous behavior and suggest some hypotheses about their similarities and differences.

Spontaneous eliciting circumstances have been presumed to be more relevant to emotion, although it may be more difficult to record the behavior and specification of *what* emotion is shown *when* may be impossible (or possible only in gross terms). The most frequently used spontaneous circumstance (e.g., by Coleman, Dunlap, Landis, Lanzetta, and Kleck) has been the experimentally arranged, emotion-evoking event such as electric shock or tickling. The record is segmented, with a different emotion presumed to be induced in each of the evocation episodes and the episode, or the emotion, presumed to be elicited in it serves as the accuracy criterion. As discussed earlier (Sections 1.3–5), there are problems with this type of procedure. The event arranged by the experimenter may or may not evoke an emotion and the event may or may not, for most or some subjects, lead to inhibiting or disguising the facial behavior. In some experiments the self-reports of subjects showed variability as to whether they experienced emotion and, if so, which emotion, but these data were usually disregarded. Given the ambiguous status of the concept of emotion stimuli, some attempt should be made to assess, independently of the face, whether the experimentally arranged situation is normally associated with any emotion and whether it is associated with emotion for the subjects in the study.

Remarkably little use has been made of naturally occurring, spontaneous situations. The exception is the use of magazine photographs of presumably emotional events (e.g., by Hanawalt, Munn, and Vinacke). In these studies, the investigators did not specify how they decided a situation was relevant to emotion nor did they make any attempt to verify independently whether the situations they selected were normatively associated with emotions. In addition, selecting photographs from magazines deprives the investigator of any knowledge of representativeness of the behavior shown in the stimulus, leading to doubts about the generality of the results (see the discussion in Section 4.1 entitled "Accuracy in judging candid photographs").

A few investigators have looked at naturally occurring or experimentally arranged interactions where there is independent evidence that emotion occurs, but their studies suffer from their inability to make more than a gross distinction between positive and negative emotion (see the discussion in Section 4.1 entitled "Accuracy in the judgment of spontaneous behavior").

It should be noted that the distinction between posed and spontaneous behavior is not directly parallel to the distinction between artificial and natural occurrences. Though posing is by definition artificial (perhaps having only remote resemblance to the simulation of emotion naturally occurring during conversations), spontaneous behavior may or may not be natural. Spontaneous behavior is natural when some part of life itself leads to the behavior studied. Spontaneous behavior elicited in the laboratory may be representative of some naturally occurring spontaneous behavior, or conceivably it could be artificial if the eliciting circumstance is unique and not relevant to any known real life event. The investigator must be concerned with demonstrating that results gathered in the laboratory have relevance (generality) to some type of naturally occurring facial behavior. The difficulty in many studies utilizing spontaneous laboratory situations has not been a lack of relevance to real life but a failure to appreciate what aspect of life has been represented in the laboratory. For example, telling the subject a joke or shocking him may be most relevant to nonlaboratory situations where the person disguises or conceals his emotional reaction from authoritative figures, rather than being representative of how the persons shows emotions with friends. By choosing to study naturally occurring spontaneous facial behavior, the investigator avoids the problem of demonstrating relevance to actual life, but usually at the cost of greatly increasing the difficulties in recording the phenomena and specifying what emotion has occurred when.

Some standards can be listed as guides:

1. Experiments should select more than one eliciting circumstance. If only posing is used, then posing under different instructions, roleplaying, acting, etc., could be used to avoid the hazard that peculiarities in one way of eliciting the pose will bias the sample. If only spontaneous situations are used, then there should be quite a variety of such situations; for example, when an individual is alone, when the investigator is present, or when the emotion is aroused by a noxious event, a film, or the action of another person.
2. Some attempt should be made to assess whether the situation was associated with a particular emotion for subjects in general as well as for the particular subjects studied. With posing, the poser's impression as to whether the intended emotion was shown on each trial would be useful. In spontaneous situations, simultaneous or retrospective self-reports could be gathered about felt emotion, and the emotion-provoking situations could be judged by other groups of subjects in terms of whether they would expect a particular emotion in that situation and whether they would expect display rules to be operative.
3. If an artificial eliciting circumstance is used (either posing or experimentally elicited emotions), the investigator must provide some estimation of the relevance of the findings to naturally occurring emotions.

2.3. Sampling persons

Bruner and Tagiuri (1954) emphasized the need for representative sampling of persons whose facial behavior is recorded in order to avoid error due to either morphological characteristics or differing ability to show certain emotions. In our terms, such sampling of persons is crucial if the results from either component or judgment studies are not to be unduly biased by the habitual emotion blends or the idiosyncratic application of display rules by a particular person. Since Bruner and Tagiuri's review, the size of the sample of stimulus persons in judgment studies has generally increased (although some investigators have persisted in publishing on judgments made of one actor's poses), which may, in part, explain the better results recently obtained.

Although inadequate sampling of persons could bias results and limit the generality of findings, individual or group differences in facial behavior could also be a substantive issue. Tomkins and McCarter (1964) hypothesized personality variables that might account for differences in ability to emit emotions, but the one study on this topic (Levitt, 1964) did not reveal correlates of the substantial differences among posers in their ability to show facial behaviors that observers could understand. Other investigators also sought correlates of individual differences in posing ability, with little success to date, but some promise for the future (see Chapter 8, Section 8.4 for a review of recent work on individual differences in facial expressiveness).

The standard here is a simple one. Studies employing many subjects are more trustworthy than those using only a few. A more complex formulation of this standard is that the more subjects for which the eliciting circumstance succeeded in evoking the intended response, the sounder the study.

2.4. Sampling behavior from a record

Usually only a part of a permanent record of facial behavior can be either shown to observers in a judgment study or measured in a component study. Sampling is necessary, often because there is just too much material to analyze, sometimes because a record contains a number of episodes in which the eliciting circumstance obviously backfired or the subject failed. For example, not every person may be able to pose every emotion on every attempt or a presumably humorous situation may simply not be funny for everyone. There is nothing sacrosanct about eliciting circumstances that would argue against sampling only some of the facial behavior recorded, unless the circumstance itself is the primary object of study. When the eliciting circumstance is not the object of study but the means for gathering records of facial behavior, quite selective sampling is permissible.

Investigators have typically sampled the behavior they thought was "best" without stating the basis of their choices or the amount of behavior and number of subjects excluded. Without such information, it is impossible to determine the generality of their findings across persons, settings, or time within the circumstance they studied; and uncertainty about generality has created unwarranted suspicion about their substantive findings as well. If, however, the question addressed is, for example, whether observers *can* be accurate in their judgments or whether the movements of the eyebrows are *ever* related to fear-arousing stimuli, sampling that may restrict generality does not invalidate the findings. Unless the sampling procedures have been specified, the related question of *how often* the face provides accurate information (for what kinds of persons, observers, emotions, circumstances, etc.) cannot be answered.

A number of specific bases for sampling can be developed to allow determination of generality and comparison with findings from replications. Extensive pretesting could provide the basis for evaluating particular instructions, eliciting circumstances, or even types of subjects. For example, pretesting a set of instructions for posing, by having subjects use a multidimensional rating instrument to record the emotion they would try to display, might reveal that certain instructions tend to induce an affect blend rather than a single affect; such instructions could be discarded or modified. Describing an eliciting circumstance or showing it on film and having subjects describe the emotion they would expect to experience might reveal that a particular eliciting circumstance does not evoke the particular emotion the investigator expected, and it could be modified. Pretesting subjects might show that certain people are generally embarrassed in a posing situation and will not provide variable facial behavior. If the demographic, attitudinal, and/or personality characteristics of such people were determined, others who share these characteristics could be excluded as stimulus persons or the results treated separately. All of these procedures would eliminate, before records are collected, the likelihood of obtaining facial behavior not relevant to the purposes of the experiment. The investigator would avoid the procedure of subjectively picking the best stimulus persons, as has often been the case in studies of both spontaneous and posed behavior. Instead, the investigator could draw a representative sample from the records and specify the basis for excluding stimulus persons or eliciting circumstances so that the generality of the findings across persons, circumstances, and time within the situation would be known.

This same objective can also be reached by obtaining other sources of information at the time records are collected. For example, posers could be asked to describe whether or not they think they responded with a good pose for each pose attempted; or subjects in a stress interview could listen to the interview afterward and indicate the points at which they were maximally uncomfortable; or galvanic skin conductance records during a stress interview could be consulted for the points of maximal arousal. Again, the investigator would not be forced to sample subjectively but could specify the basis for the sampling, thus providing the relevant data for evaluating the generality of the findings.

It is least preferable to utilize the appearance of the facial behavior itself as the basis for sampling. If the investigator does this, the principle underlying the selection of the "good" faces should be specified, along with information about the number of rejected faces.

The standard in regard to sampling of behavior from a record is that the investigator should specify how this was done so that generality of findings can be determined.

2.5. Sampling emotions

Over- or underrepresentation of some emotions within a sample of facial behavior may seriously bias the outcome of both judgment or component studies. Almost all of the empirical research has shown that happiness is most easily recognized and distinguished from other emotions, and this result seems to occur across a number of cultures and languages (see Table 7.1). Although the evidence is not yet as firm, it would appear that some discriminations among emotions, whether made by an observer or by some measurement of facial components, are more difficult than others. Fear and surprise, for example, are probably more similar to each other in both facial components and semantic connotations than either is with disgust. Very different findings on judgment agreement, accuracy, components, or judgment of underlying dimensions of emotion may occur because experiments have sampled emotions differently. An example of this problem is a study by Abelson and Sermat (1962), in which dissimilarity ratings of observers on a sample of faces were analyzed in order to determine the dimensions underlying judgments of emotion. We checked the previously published norms on the facial stimuli they utilized and found the selection to be very skewed: six *fear* and four *happiness* pictures, only one *anger*, one *contempt*, one *disgust*, and no *surprise*.

As discussed earlier, the lack of agreement among theorists about the definition and names of emotions makes it difficult for an investigator to know what emotions should be included in the sample of facial behavior if it is to be representative. Almost all of the procedures previously discussed under "Sampling behavior from a record," can also be utilized to ascertain what emotions may be represented within a sample of facial behavior; and the results from a judgment study can also be examined for this purpose. In our discussion of findings about the categories and dimensions of emotion (see Chapter 3) we shall show that there are some consistencies across studies to help an investigator ensure that the sample includes at least those commonly found by others.

The standard regarding this problem is that the investigator should provide information about what emotions have been sampled in his study. The more emotions sampled, the greater the generality. In data analysis, results should be presented so that it is possible to determine how many of the findings can be attributed to the straightforward discrimination of *happiness* from everything else. (It is still rare to find studies that follow this suggestion.) Preferably, results should be reported in terms of each emotion, dimension, or circumstance sampled.

2.6. Sampling emotion words, categories, or dimensions in judgment studies

In a judgment study, the observer's decision about the emotion shown in a face must be recorded by utilizing either a restricted set of terms provided by the investigator or the observer's own words. Although in a few experiments the observer did not utilize emotion vocabularies (at least in ways known to the investigator) but instead, grouped photographs (e.g., Hulin & Katz, 1935), interpretation of the results has been difficult; the basis for grouping or of similarity ratings between pairs of stimuli has not usually been made explicit, and only one study (Boucher, 1973) has allowed a direct comparison between the results of this method and the more usual judgment task.

Free responses in the observer's own words have been less popular in recent years, perhaps because of Woodworth's (1938) finding that organizing such free responses into categories yielded considerably higher agreement and accuracy (see Section 3.1). Yet restricting the observer's choice to a preselected list seriously limits the import of the results, if the purpose of the study is to determine the nature of the emotion vocabulary or to check some formulations about the basic or primary emotion categories or the underlying dimension of emotion. Although such a study can reveal the differential applicability of any set of preselected terms, it cannot indicate whether more categories or dimensions might have been found if the investigator had not limited the observer's choices.

A commonly applied solution to this problem has been unsatisfactory because of inadequate sampling of stimuli. In a number of experiments, the vocabulary given observers was based on the words provided most frequently by another set of observers who were allowed to select their own words when looking at a set of facial stimuli. If, as was usually the case, the facial stimuli consisted of the behavior of just one or two persons, with no evidence that emotions were representatively sampled, then the verbal list derived from the most frequent words might be quite limited and the findings could not claim generality about the nature of the emotion vocabulary to more than the particular pictures judged.

There are, however, many experiments in which the focus of the study justifies the use of a preselected emotion vocabulary in the judgment task. When the aim of the study is not to determine comprehensive answers to questions about the nature of the emotion vocabulary or judgment procedure applicable to facial behavior, the use of preselected lists of words, categories, or dimensions may be the most economical procedure in both observer time and subsequent data analysis. If the purpose of the study is to measure differences in accuracy depending, let us say, on whether the eye area or mouth area is observed, a preselected list of emotion categories or scales is an appropriate judgment procedure. However, the investigator must be aware that different results might have been obtained if other emotion choices had been given to the observers, and the results will be more credible if he shows that the preselected emotion terminology is sufficiently comprehensive for the purposes of the study.

A last problem in connection with judgment procedure was considered earlier in regard to the phenomenon of emotion blends (see Section 1.6). We have conclusive evidence, still unpublished, that this occurs; see photographic example of blend facial expression in Ekman & Friesen, 1975. Still photographs of the face frequently contain components of more than one emotion and that observers may well be able to determine the presence of particular combinations, or blends, if the investigator allows them to do so. If the stimulus does contain an emotion blend and the investigator allows only a single choice from a preselected list that does not contain blend terms, then spuriously low levels of agreement may result, since some of the observers may choose a term for one of the blend components, some for another. There are a number of judgment procedures that could be utilized to allow observers to indicate the presence of blends as well as the particular emotions involved in a blend. The problem, of course, is less severe if observers are allowed to use their own words (and more than one), but then the investigator must, in his data analysis, be sensitive to the possibility of blend responses in perhaps differing words.

There are two standards. Attention to the question of representative sampling of emotion terms, inclusion of more, rather than fewer, terms, and, at some stages of the research, allowance for free responses would be desirable in most judgment experiments and crucial in those having as their purpose a determination about the nature of the emotion vocabulary applicable to judgments of the face. Second, some provision should be made for the possibility that the stimuli might contain emotion blends by providing a means for the observers to indicate their perception of more than one emotion if such is the case.

2.7. Choosing a method of recording

There has been some argument over the relative merit of motion (film or videotape) versus still (photographs) records of facial behavior. An influential opinion has been that of Bruner and Tagiuri (1954), who decried the use of still photographs because "judgment based on a frozen millisecond of exposure" (p. 638) is not representative of the type of judgment made in naturally occurring conditions. If, however, the purpose of a study does not require a judgment of sequential behavior, then still photographs may be useful for some research questions.

Stills may be appropriate when the information obtainable from the muscle actions at the apex of a facial movement is of interest rather than the information derived from such time variables as latency, duration, and different rates of onset and decay from different facial muscles. But still photographs may lead to judgments or measures that include information based on permanent physiognomic features rather than transient muscle movements, if only one picture of a stimulus person is shown; without a baseline, permanent facial wrinkles may not be distinguishable from wrinkles caused by a particular muscle contraction. Nevertheless, the savings in cost and ease of use may justify the use of stills in studies of posed facial behavior, where the poser holds the pose for the camera; a still will provide the same information as five seconds of film or videotape of the frozen position. Certainly, there is considerable evidence that the frozen few milliseconds of a still photograph can provide quite a bit of information.

In spontaneous eliciting circumstances, however, still photographs may mutilate the natural flow of behavior into meaningless units, particularly if the photographs are taken arbitrarily, in disregard of the natural flow of events and the timing of changes in facial behavior. Motion picture film or videotape must be used in such situations and when the aforementioned time variables are to be studied.

There are only three experiments that compared observers' judgments made on the basis of a motion picture film record with those made from selected still frames from the same record. Dusenbury and Knower (1938) found that observers who had seen the motion picture film were more accurate in identifying the posed emotion of two stimulus persons than were those who had seen a selected still frame, although even the latter achieved an accuracy level far better than chance. Frijda (1953) obtained the same result, but his eliciting circumstance included elements of posing as well as spontaneous situations, and his scoring procedure for determining the accuracy of the observer's judgment was admittedly subjective. Kozel and Gitter (1968) found that observers were more accurate in judging the intended emotions of ten professional actresses in a silent motion picture film compared with selected still frames for anger, surprise, and fear but there was no difference in accuracy between the observers who saw motion picture film and still photographs for the poses of happiness, disgust, and sadness. A significant level of accuracy was obtained by the observers who saw the still photographs for all the emotions. Thus, the evidence suggests that still photographs may not be as adequate a method for presenting posed facial behavior as motion picture film, but this stilted recording procedure does present sufficient information for accurate judgments of static events.

Some experiments have not used a permanent record, either motion or still but instead have had the actor pose live in front of the audience of observers. There are a number of problems with this procedure. Replication with the same stimuli is not possible; control over the stimulus input to the observers is difficult; and at least one investigator noted that extraneous behaviors (e.g., blushing or refusing to pose "love") contributed to accuracy. Feedback from the observers as to whether or not they seem to be getting the message can lead posers to vary their performances and to utilize behaviors other than the facial behaviors ordinarily associated with emotions.

The last technique of recording facial behavior, which was quite popular in the early years of research, is to rely on artists' drawings. Although drawings have the virtue of allowing control over demographic characteristics, lighting, and various physiognomic features, they have the enormous failing that they may include as facial behavior components that simply do not occur or cannot co-occur and possible idiosyncratic or stereotypic views of the artist. Until a systematic means of scoring facial behaviors is widely accepted and drawings as well as large numbers of actual photographs and films are scored, there is no way of knowing to what extent the drawings represent fantasy or reality. Consider, for example, a drawing of the face when the lips are drawn back. It is not possible to know how many usually occurring behaviors have been left out, how many "behaviors" that cannot occur with a particular movement have been added to an area of the face; and how many facial features that just do not occur at all have been added. We do not, for this reason, consider[1] any research in which drawings were used, such as experiments in which the Piderit faces or the Rudolf faces (drawings presumably from photographs but retouched and having the additional problem of a thick beard and moustache covering the lower part of the face) were used or the more recent studies in which simple moontype cartoon faces, which reduce facial behavior to a few curved lines, were used.[2]

2.8. Review

We began by distinguishing two research approaches to the study of the face and emotion, a component study and a judgment study. We emphasized that failure to find that the observers made accurate judgments or agreed in their judgments did not necessarily signify that the facial components were unrelated to the eliciting circumstances. Certainly, that is one explanation of a failure in a judgment study – the facial behavior was meaningless and would be shown to be so if measurements of the components were taken. But negative results in a judgment study could also arise because of defects in the judgment task, in the

---

[1]It is interesting to note that most of the studies of the face that produced negative results were studies of some artistic analog to the face rather than studies that used a record of actual behavior (see Chapter 3).

[2]The use of drawings of the face, even highly simplified ones, may provide some leads to understanding which facial components are relevant to the judgment of which emotions. This question will be discussed in Chapter 4, where one study that utilized the drawings of the face for this purpose will be analyzed.

sampling of observers, in the sampling of facial behavior, in the recording procedures employed, or in the sampling of persons. All of these considerations apply also to the design of component studies, with the exception of the sampling of words used in a judgment task.

In reviewing the literature in the next chapters, we shall see that there have been relatively few component studies, probably because judgment studies are much easier to perform and because determining how to measure facial components is a complex problem. This paucity of component studies may change now that there are three new systems for measuring facial components (see Chapters 4 and 9). Knowledge would be best advanced by research strategies that combine the use of both component and judgment approaches to the same facial behavior. Then it would be possible to determine how much information observers can interpret, what facial components relate to their inferences about emotion, and what facial behaviors systematically vary with emotion but are not recognized or consistently interpreted by observers.

We described guidelines regarding each of the methodological decisions the investigator must make in planning research, which will also be useful as standards in evaluating the past research literature. We argued that investigators should utilize more than one eliciting circumstance from which to draw the facial behavior they intend to study, and they should obtain some evidence that their eliciting circumstance was associated with a particular emotion(s) for their subjects. The standard in regard to the sampling of persons was that there should be more than a few stimulus persons, in order to rule out bias due to idiosyncrasies in facial behavior. In sampling behaviors from a record, we recommended a number of procedures to give investigators a basis other than their own intuition for selecting faces from records for study. Information about the sampling procedures followed is necessary if the generality of the findings is not to be in doubt. Investigators should also specify the emotions sampled in their studies and present data for evaluation of whether the results can be reduced to the simple distinction between positive and negative emotions or whether finer discriminations have to be made. In judgment studies, we argued that the investigator should at least include the emotion terms and scales consistently found by others and, preferably, should allow free verbal response by observers at some stage in the study. Provision should also be made for observers to indicate a judgment of affect blends. We argued that motion records (film or video) are preferable to still photographs, although stills are appropriate for such frozen events as poses. Neither live, nonpermanent records nor drawings from imagination are useful recording techniques.

No single experiment should be expected to meet fully every one of the standards we described. The importance of a particular standard depends on the particular study at issue. In the following chapters, where research findings will be considered, we shall emphasize some methodological standards more than others when examining each substantive question. We shall integrate findings from many different experiments to review and, where possible, resolve seven major questions about the face and emotion. We have not attempted to include every experiment relevant to every question discussed, only those that have been influential, those that have been misinterpreted, those that deserve more attention than they have received, and those that clarify fundamental issues or raise important new questions. In order to clarify some of the contradictory results about some of the questions, it was necessary to evaluate each group of experiments in terms of the methodological standards explored in previous chapters. Studies that did not report their methods in sufficient detail to permit such an evaluation were usually excluded if their findings did not contradict the interpretation we suggested. It was also necessary to reanalyze or to recast results from different experiments if consistencies were to be revealed. Studies in which data were not reported in a way that allowed such a reanalysis were excluded if other studies with similar findings could be used instead. As described earlier, almost all of the studies in which drawings of the face were used were also excluded.

No claim can be made that the substantive questions considered in the next five chapters are the only basic ones, but they certainly have been the most frequently raised in past studies. By focusing attention on these, in some cases bringing together evidence to indicate that the questions have been answered and in other instances indicating where further evidence is now needed, we hope to provide some sense of the state of the field.

In the next chapters, we shall utilize tables as the primary means of reporting information about experiments. We urge the reader to consider, not skip, the tables. We shall usually not summarize in the text material described in the tables. Our discussion will always presume familiarity with material shown there.

3. What emotion categories or dimensions can observers judge from facial behavior?

PAUL EKMAN, WALLACE V. FRIESEN,
AND PHOEBE ELLSWORTH

Most investigators, regardless of the particular question they have asked, have employed a judgment rather than a component study, requiring observers to use some kind of emotion vocabulary and judgment procedure to identify the emotions perceived. Two judgment procedures have been used, an emotion *category* task, in which the observer selects one category or sometimes two categories for each example of facial behavior, and a *dimension* task, in which the observer rates each face on a series of scales. These two judgment procedures represent and have been utilized to study two distinct theoretical viewpoints about the emotional information obtainable from the face.

Some theorists have postulated a set of basic emotion categories, or primary affects. Each of these categories includes a set of words denoting related emotions, which may differ in intensity, degree of control, or, in minor ways, in denotative meaning. Although the principle of inclusion is not always explained, the words within a category are held to be more similar than the words across categories. Presumably, different facial behaviors are associated with each of these emotion categories, although no theorist has ever fully explicated the exact nature of such differences in facial components. Some category theorists have further hypothesized interrelationships among all or some of their emotion categories, which allow representation of their categories within a geometric model and a delineation of certain dimensions that differentiate among the categories.

The dimension theorists, on the other hand, have been most interested in such scales or dimensions postulated to best describe and underlie (again, in a manner usually unspecified) the emotion categories. These theorists have formulated a small set of independent dimensions (smaller in almost all cases than the number of primary emotion categories proposed by the category theorists) that best describe the differ-

39

ences among facial behaviors associated with emotion and, further, are relevant to descriptions of emotional phenomena other than facial behavior.

Judgments of the face have been used by some to test, at least in part, their theory of categories or dimensions and by others to derive empirically some proposed set of categories or dimensions. First, we shall consider the evidence on categories of emotion and then turn to studies of emotion dimensions.

3.1. Emotion categories

Research on this question extends over thirty years, from Woodworth's (1938) to Frijda's studies (1968, 1969). Actually, the first experimental investigator to propose a set of emotion categories was F. Allport in 1924. The choices made in sampling stimulus persons and emotions from differing eliciting circumstances, and with observers allowed to utilize a wide variety of emotion words in making their judgment, are the most crucial for a decisive answer to this question. Table 3.1 lists these and other methodological decisions for the five investigators who focused upon the question of what emotion categories can be judged from facial behavior.

Inspection of Table 3.1 shows that each experiment had serious methodological deficiencies. (1) Only posed behavior was utilized as the eliciting circumstance. (2) Most studies used only one or two stimulus persons; although Osgood had 50 people pose, he had each emotion posed by only 5 people, thus allowing, as did the other investigators, the possibility that the idiosyncrasies of a few people could bias the results. Even Tomkins and McCarter's 11 persons do not represent a sufficient sampling of persons. (3) Most experimenters presented as stimuli only the handful of emotions they believed to be relevant to their theoretical formulation; Osgood is a noteworthy exception, presenting 40 different emotion poses. (4) None of the studies permitted free responses by the observers, although both Osgood and Frijda did the next best thing by including many words, rather than limiting the observers' choice to prescribe emotion category labels. Their evidence deserves more weight than that from the other investigations because instead of showing that observers could agree in their use of a preselected set of emotion categories, Osgood and Frijda both showed that a set of categories emerged from the judges' use of the larger list of words they were given. (5) None of the investigators used motion picture film or video-

Table 3.1 *Methodological considerations for five studies of emotion categories*

Methodological consideration	Woodworth (1938)	Plutchik (1962)	Tomkins & McCarter (1964)	Osgood (1966)	Frijda (1968)
Number of different stimulus persons	1	2	11	50 or 5[c]	2
Number of different emotions posed	10	[a]	8	40	Not reported
Number of stimuli	19	26	69	200	130
Number of emotion words or categories given observers	10	8	8	40	100
Method of deriving emotion words or categories	Most frequent when given list of 107 words	Theory	Theory	Past literature	Not reported
Eliciting circumstances	Pose	[a]	Pose	Pose	Pose
Recording technique	Still	Still	Still	Live	Still
Evidence for author's categories	Correlation poser's intent and observer's judgment	[b]	Observer agreement	Cluster analysis and factor analysis	Factor analysis

Notes: [a]Had actor attempt to move each facial muscle in all possible ways rather than pose emotions.
[b]Ratings of words separately, judgments of parts of the face, combining partial faces into total face, and then naming the emotion shown.
[c]See explanation in the text.

tape; Osgood used live behavior but, for reasons discussed in Section 2.7 live behavior raises the possibility of other sources of error.

Although these methodological problems raise doubts about the findings of each experiment if it is considered singly, some of these problems can be remedied by considering the findings across all five studies. If we credit only those results that were consistent across experiments, they derive from a sufficient sampling of stimulus persons, emotion, stimuli and emotion words. (The only limits on generality remaining would be in the use of stills and the sampling of behavior from only one eliciting circumstance, posing.)

It is a tribute to the robustness of the phenomena that, despite the span of time over which this research was done and the very different theoretical viewpoints of the investigators, the results are, by and large, consistent. Table 3.2 shows these similarities in the categories of emotion words used to describe emotions seen in the face. All investigators proposed a *happiness* category (the only variation being Osgood's two categories for happiness), all proposed a *surprise* category, and all proposed an *anger* category. There is further agreement among all other investigators, with the exception of Woodworth; they found an *interest* category and combined *disgust* and *contempt* into one category. Work by Izard (1971) and by Ekman and Friesen (1975, ch. 6) seem to show conclusively that disgust and contempt are indeed separable, as Woodworth proposed.

The only major disagreement is that Woodworth combined *fear* and *suffering* into one category, and all the other authors kept *fear* as a separate category, proposing another category for words similar to *sadness*. Ekman and Friesen (1967a) hypothesized that Woodworth's decision to combine the two categories resulted from his failure to distinguish sadness from pain (a state not considered to be an emotion but one associated with a discriminable facial appearance). Woodworth's term *suffering* may have been applied by observers to faces that showed either sadness or pain or the blend of both sadness and pain. There is a parallel ambiguity in the referent of Tomkin and McCarter's term *anguish*; it might be applicable to pain or to the blend of sadness and pain. Boucher (1969) provided support for Ekman and Friesen's view in an experiment in which stimuli judged as *fear and suffering* in Woodworth's data and stimuli judged as *distress and anguish* in Tomkins and McCarter's data were found to be judged either as *fear*, *sadness*, or *pain* or as blends of two of these terms when observers were allowed only these choices. On the basis of these data, we propose that *fear* should be considered a separate category and that there should also be a separate category for *sadness*.

Table 3.2 also shows a number of categories found or proposed by only one investigator. For the most part, these categories had no opportunity to emerge from the findings of the other investigators because they were not used as stimuli or judgment responses by most of the other authors. Until research is done with a wide sampling of words, preferably with free choice allowed the observer, and a wide sampling of stimulus persons and emotions, it will not be possible to know what to make of these other possible categories. Another unsettled question concerns the boundaries and inclusion rules for defining each category.

Table 3.2 *Emotion categories proposed by five investigators*

Woodworth (1938)	Plutchik (1962)	Tomkins & McCarter (1964)	Osgood (1966)[a]	Frijda (1968)[b]	Proposed
Love	Coyness		Complacency Quiet pleasure		
Mirth Happiness	Happiness Joy	Enjoyment Joy	Joy Glee Worried laughter	Happy	Happiness
Surprise	Surprise Amazement Astonishment	Surprise Startle	Surprise Amazement Bewilderment Awe	Surprise	Surprise
Fear	Apprehension Fear Terror	Fear Terror	Fear Horror	Fear	Fear
Suffering	Pensiveness Sorrow Grief	Distress Anguish	Despair Boredom Dreamy sadness Acute sorrow Despair	Sad	Sadness
Anger Determination	Annoyance Anger Rage	Anger Rage	Sullen anger Rage Stubbornness Determination	Anger	Anger
Disgust Contempt	Tiresomeness Disgust Loathing	Disgust Contempt	Annoyance Disgust Contempt Scorn Loathing	Disgust	Disgust/ Contempt
	Attentiveness Expectancy Anticipation	Interest Excitement	Expectancy Interest	Attention	Interest
	Acceptance Incorporation	Shame Humiliation	Pity Distrust Anxiety	Calm Bitter Pride Irony Insecure Skepticism	

[a] All categories found in at least two of Osgood's three types of data analyses were listed.
[b] All categories that emerged in the analysis of judgments of both stimulus persons were listed.

What are the related words that might be included in a category – those that are synonyms, those that show variations in intensity, or those that define the limits of a category? Plutchik (1962) made a beginning on this question, but there has been insufficient study.

All six investigators were interested in the related question of relationships among categories, and all but Tomkins and McCarter and Frijda proposed their own set of such relationships. In addition, a number of investigators examined their own data, searching for category relationships (e.g., Boucher & Ekman, 1965; Dickey & Knower, 1941; Dusenbury & Knower, 1938; Frois-Wittmann, 1930; D.F. Thompson & Meltzer, 1964). The data examined in most studies were consistent judgment errors, or what Tomkins and McCarter (1964) called "common confusions." These are instances in which a stimulus judged by a majority of observers as one emotion is judged by a minority of observers as another emotion. Only two category relationships found by more than one investigator were not directly contradicted by more than one other investigator

The categories of fear, surprise, and interest seem to be interrelated in that fear and surprise are confused with each other, and surprise is mistaken for interest (but interest is not mistaken for surprise). Recent work on facial measurement by Ekman & Friesen (1978) shows that these commonly confused emotions share many facial actions. The confusion may therefore be attributable to shared appearance clues. Anger and disgust/contempt have also been found to be commonly confused. It should be noted that the other category relationships found by Schlosberg[1] and widely cited in textbooks have repeatedly been contradicted by other investigators, in one case in a study (Boucher and Ekman, 1965) utilizing Schlosberg's own stimuli.

It is not surprising that findings on category interrelationships have been, for the most part, contradictory for the evidence used to establish common confusions is itself confusing and most investigators have been vague about their theoretical bases for expecting relationships among categories. Because of limits in the usual judgment task, common confusions might occur for two very different reasons, with quite different implications, and the term itself is probably a misnomer. One of the phenomena is not a confusion at all but signifies the probable presence of a blend, and the other phenomenon is an uncommon confusion made by only a small and, in some way, unusual group of observers.

[1]Schlosberg (1941) agreed with Woodworth that the six emotion categories placed adjacent to each other formed a scale, with the exception that the two end points of the scale, *happiness* and *contempt*, should be considered as also adjacent, thus changing the linear scale into a circle; see Table 3.2 for the adjacent Woodworth categories.

If the distribution of responses to a particular face was 60% anger and 40% disgust, the stimulus might well be a blend, containing facial components of both of these emotions (see Section 1.6). The confusion may be neither in the face nor with the observers but in the fact that the investigator gave the observers only a single-response judgment task for a multiple-message stimulus. Some observers reported one response, some the other.

Work by Kiritz & Ekman (1971), entailing a judgment task that allowed observers to indicate either a blend or a single emotion, showed that stimuli having about a 60/40 distribution of judgment responses from previous single-choice judgment studies were now judged by the majority of observers as showing both emotions (a blend). The use of such a judgment task, which allows the observer to record an impression of affect blends, should eliminate this type of confusion.

If the distribution of responses to a particular face was more skewed, however, let us say 80% anger and only 20% disgust, then a different phenomenon might have occurred. Kiritz and Ekman found that faces that in previous research had a distribution such as this were not perceived by most observers as a blend. Instead, there was a deviant minority of observers who consistently labeled most stimuli for a particular emotion differently from the majority. In this case, they judged as *disgust* most of the faces that the majority called *anger*. The phrase *uncommon shared confusions* might describe this phenomenon. Only Tomkins and McCarter (1964) have attempted any hypotheses to explain this, and they regarded their hypotheses as only a beginning attempt to disentangle the phenomenon. Work has been done (Zlatchin & Ekman, 1971) that investigates whether such uncommon shared confusions are related to semantic and/or personality differences. Unfortunately, the work of Zlatchin and Ekman failed, and the issue remains unsettled.

Summary of studies on emotion categories

What emotion catgories can observers judge from facial behavior? The question cannot yet be answered in this general form because only still photographs and posed behavior have been studied. However, it is possible to answer a related question: What emotion categories can be judged from still photographs of posed facial behavior? Seven categories of emotion have been found (see the column labeled Proposed in Table 3.2): happiness, surprise, fear, anger, sadness, disgust/contempt, and interest. This is not necessarily an exhaustive list, even for posed behavior, but it appears to be the minimal list. More categories may be found in experiments that allow observers free choice of response but show them facial behavior in motion from spontaneous situations.

Such research would be particularly valuable in determining whether commonly occurring affect blends (which should be more frequent in spontaneous than posed behavior, and in motion than still presentations) will be described by the observer by combinations of these seven categories. If the choice of two or more of these categories is sufficient to permit observers to record their impressions of a stimulus containing an affect blend, then the categories can be considered primary, and the blends secondary. For example, it may be that the term *smugness* would be used to describe specific facial behavior when observers are given a free choice to use any word in their vocabulary and that this same facial behavior would be described as both *angry* and *happy* when observers are limited to choosing among the seven categories but allowed multiple choices. If that were the result, then smugness would be considered a secondary affect blend term for the combination of anger and happiness. But if the face freely described as smug did not elicit agreement among observers in the use of two or more of the seven categories, this would suggest that another primary affect category is still missing from that list or that smugness itself should be included in the list of primary emotion categories.

It should be emphasized that the consistent emergence of the seven categories across the array of experiments is remarkable. Even though the studies shared the use of still posed photographs, they varied enormously in the theoretical bias of the investigators, the stimuli shown, and the judgment task employed. These seven categories of emotion seem likely to remain as a minimum group of possible distinctions made by observers in describing facial behavior. Later (Chapter 7) we shall see further support for the generality of these categories in the findings that observers across literate and preliterate cultures agree in their use of these categories to describe facial behavior. In subsequent chapters, when we consider questions about accuracy, components of facial behavior in relation to judgments, the influence of context in the judgment of facial behavior, and cross-cultural comparisons of facial behavior, we shall employ these seven categories as the means for recasting and reanalyzing data to facilitate comparisons across experiments.

Although these seven categories seem well established, there is little information about category boundaries and interrelationships. What is the range of words that might be included within each category as synonyms or as variants in intensity? The relationships among categories and the possible areas of overlapping meaning, either in the terminology or facial behavior itself, have not been elucidated to date.

In the next section, we shall examine a different approach to the question of measuring what observers say about facial behavior, searching for dimensions of emotion rather than categories.

3.2. Emotion dimensions

Investigations of the dimensions of emotion, like the investigations of categories of emotion, are focused on establishing the vocabulary that can be utilized by observers of facial behavior. The theoretical model of emotion assumed by the dimensions approach is, however, quite different. Rather than considering an emotion as having a separate, distinguishable status, the dimension theorists believe that an emotion can be better described and represented as a point located on a small set of continuous scales, or dimensions. That is to say, rather than ask whether a facial behavior shows anger or fear or sadness, etc., these theorists seek to determine where a facial behavior may be located along such scales as pleasant to unpleasant, passive to active, etc.

It was important for the dimension theorists to establish the smallest number of nonredundant dimensions capable of capturing the information about emotion observable in the face. There has been continuous interest in this question from the 1940s to the present time, in contrast to the disjunctive history of research activity on many of the other questions we shall consider. Schlosberg (1941) was the first investigator to attempt to derive a minimal set of scales for the judgment of emotion from facial behavior, proposing first a two- and then a three-dimensional model (1954), which he thought might underlie Woodworth's six categories of emotion. His interest in dimensions, and that of subsequent investigators, stemmed from two sources. Obtaining ordinal, or interval, data through the use of scales rather than nominal data through the use of emotion categories offered statistical techniques for obtaining better measures of agreement among observers. Second, the discovery of a set of scales that could best account for judgments of emotion from the face could prove to be relevant to a more general theory of emotion. Osgood (1966) recently reiterated this view, suggesting that scales can produce better agreement than categories, not merely because of the advantage of continuous scaled data over nominal data, but because scales that represent connotative meaning (e.g., the three factors from his semantic differential work in verbal behavior) are more relevant to the kind of information provided by the face than are any denotative emotion categories.

Two types of experiments have been conducted. In one, observers judged faces on a set of scales provided by the investigator; in the other, observers rated the amount of similarity between pairs of faces, usually without the investigator or the observer specifying the basis for judgment or type of similarity being judged. In both types of experiment, the sampling of stimulus persons, emotions, and eliciting circumstances is crucial. Almost all of the experiments can be faulted on several grounds, but there are additional methodological problems particular to each of the two types of experiments.

Table 3.3 lists the methodological decisions crucial to the studies in which the observers judged faces on a set of scales or terms. As in the studies of emotion categories discussed earlier, posing has been the sole eliciting circumstance employed. Just as serious a problem is the use of a very few stimulus persons,[2] because the dimension results could have reflected their idiosyncracies.[3] The number of stimuli shown appears adequate in most studies, as does the number of emotions represented in those stimuli. (The latter is not known for the Hastorf, Osgood, & Ono study, nor for the Frijda & Philipszoon experiment; Fridja has acknowledged Stringer's (1967) evidence that anger was underrepresented in their study.) In most of the studies, from 6 to 13 categories were represented, the stimuli having been judged also in terms of emotion categories, the results of which were reported in Table 3.2.

There is serious question about the number of scales or terms provided the judges in two of these studies and about the basis of selecting those scales. Schlosberg (1952, 1954) and Hastorf, Osgood, and Ono (1966) provided the smallest number of scales for judgment and used only the scales they thought relevant to their theory. Needless to say, both confirmed their expectation that there are only three dimensions of emotion; in the studies using more scales, however, more factors were found (see Table 3.4).

---

[2]Although Osgood's sample of 50 persons is larger than any of the other samples, the fact that only 5 persons posed each emotion allows a small number of persons to bias the results. (See the text discussion on Table 3.2.)

[3]Frijda's factor analysis of judgments of three separate stimulus persons (his two actors and the actor in Schlosberg's Lightfoot pictures) was reassuring, in that the same factors emerged for all three; the problems remain, however, that all three were actors, all were posing emotions specifically for a psychological study of emotion dimensions, and a sample of three is very small.

Table 3.3. *Methodological considerations for studies of emotion dimensions*

Methodological consideration	Schlosberg (1954)	Osgood (1966)	Hastorf, Osgood, & Ono (1966)	Frijda & Philipszoon (1963)	Frijda (1969)[b]	Frijda (1968)
Number of different stimulus persons	3	50 or 5[a]	1	1	1	2
Number of different emotions represented in stimuli	6	40 Intents, 9 categories from judgment results		Not reported	Not reported	13 Categories from judgment results
Number of stimuli	200	200	35	30	Not reported	130
Number of scales or terms given observers	3	40 labels	12	22	28	40
Method of deriving scales or terms	Inspection of photographs	Past literature	Chosen because of high factor loadings on Osgood's three dimensions	Most frequent in free naming	Not reported	Not reported
Eliciting circumstance	Pose	Pose	Pose	Pose	Pose	Pose
Recording technique	Stills	Live	Stills	Stills	Stills	Stills
Evidence for author's model	Scale scores predict category judgments	Factor analysis	Factor analysis	Factor analysis	Factor analysis	Factor analysis

[a]See text discussion on Table 3.2.   [b]This study used Schlosberg's Lightfoot photographs as stimuli.

Table 3.4. *Dimensions found by the investigators who had observers judge faces using scales or terms*

Dimension	Schlosberg (1954)	Osgood (1966)	Hastorf, Osgood, & Ono (1966)	Frijda & Philipszoon (1963)	Frijda (1969)[b]	Frijda (1968)
Pleasant-unpleasant	X	X	X	X	X	X
Attention-rejection	X					
Sleep-tension	X					
Activation		X	X			
Control (Osgood) or emotional intensity–control (Frijda)		X	X	X	X	X
Interest (Osgood) or attentional activity (Frijda)	X			X	X	X
Social evaluation or natural–artificial				X	X	X
Surprise				X		X
Simple-complicated				X		X
Strength					X	
Positive-negative social attitude					X	
Self-assertive-dependence						X

[a]Frijda's reanalysis in 1969 of these data is reported.
[b]This study used Schlosberg's Lightfoot photographs as stimuli.

Another serious problem germane to almost all of the experiments is ambiguity about what aspect of the face and emotion the investigator is attempting to study or represent in his dimensions, and the inclusion in his scale of words that refer to quite different aspects of the phenomenon. Are the judges asked to evaluate the physical appearance of the face?[4] The subjective feelings of the person?[5] The genuineness of the poses?[6] The connotations of words in general?[7] The defenses or ways of coping with emotion, or action consequences?[8] The more enduring per-

[4]For example, Schlosberg's attention–rejection scale was defined for his observers as, "the person is making every effort to see something, or the person is trying to shut out or keep out stimulation" (1952, p. 230).
[5]For example, Schlosberg's, Frijda's, and Osgood's pleasant–unpleasant scale or Frijda's happy–sad scale.
[6]For example, Frijda's artificial–natural scale.
[7]For example, Osgood's and Frijda's soft–hard or deep–shallow scales.
[8]For example, Osgood's and Frijda's controlled–uncontrolled scale and Frijda's withdrawing–approaching scale.

sonality traits or attitudes rather than transient emotions?[9] There is no argument with the attempt to determine whether observers can agree about each of these aspects of emotion; it would be interesting to compare dimensions that emerged from a factor analysis in which sets of scales for each of these aspects of emotion were systematically represented. The problem is that some investigators utilized scales that are inconsistent in the aspects of emotion to which they refer, without explicitly acknowledging that or examining their data in light of that fact. Others utilized terms for one aspect of emotion in their scales and then argued for the generality of their dimensions without acknowledging that other dimensions might well have emerged if scales relevant to other aspects of emotion had been included.

A last inadequacy of most of these studies is in the use of still photographs rather than videotape or motion picture film recordings of facial behavior.[10]

As was noted in discussing the results across a number of experiments on categories, although the findings from any single experiment are open to serious question because of major methodological defects, by summarizing the common findings across a number of experiments, at least those methodological shortcomings that limit the generality of the findings become less crucial. In considering this set of experiments on dimensions, the need for broad sampling of persons and of emotions is at least partly met by considering the results across all the experiments listed in Tables 3.3 and 3.4. However, problems remain, both in regard to determining the limits on generality because only posed still photographs were studied and, perhaps most importantly, in regard to explaining the lack of consistent findings across studies because the number, sampling, and method of deriving scales have varied widely. Table 3.4 shows that the only consistent finding across experiments is a dimension of pleasantness–unpleasantness. If we are willing to consider Osgood's interest factor as similar to Frijda's attentional activity (which is how Frijda interpreted Osgood's factor) and also to consider Schlosberg's attention–rejection as similar to Frijda's attentional activity (and Frijda reported a high factor loading of that bipolar scale with this factor), then there would be a second common finding, attentional activity, in all but one study. Again, if we consider Osgood's control factor to be comparable to Frijda's emotional intensity–control, which is how Frijda interpre-

---

[9]For example, Frijda's authoritarian–submissive scale.
[10]Although Osgood used live performers, there were problems also with that procedure (see Section 2.7).

ted his own and Osgood's result, then, with the exception of Schlosberg, we have a third common finding, an intensity–control factor. Beyond these three factors, the findings are not very consistent, even within the work of a single investigator such as Frijda when he varied the stimulus persons judged.

The investigators listed in the table disagreed about how many dimensions are necessary. Osgood and Schlosberg held that three dimensions are enough to account for the full range of emotional expression; Frijda believed there must be at least five. Applying Osgood's injunction that evidence for more dimensions from studies sampling many scales should be given greater weight than evidence for fewer dimensions from studies sampling few scales and applying a similar injunction with regard to representative sampling of stimulus persons, we suggest that Frijda's and Osgood's findings should be given more weight than Schlosberg's, or those of Hastorf, Osgood, and Ono. More than three dimensions are probably necessary; what these might be remains an unsettled question.

Let us turn now from the method of studying dimensions in which observers judge faces on some set of scales to the method in which observers rate similarity. Abelson and Sermat (1962) pointed out that the verbal labels chosen by the experimenter to define the observer's rating scales may impose on the observer a form of response not normally elicited by facial behavior. A number of investigators attempted to avoid this biasing effect by asking their observers to rate pairs of stimuli in terms of global similarity. Unfortunately, this judgment procedure has its own set of problems.

Most of these studies have used only one stimulus person, and very few samples of that person's behavior, probably because all possible pairs of the stimuli must be shown to the observer for judgment. If 20 or 30 stimuli were to be included, the number of paired judgments required would be very large. There has often been a lack of assurance that the few stimuli provided a representative sampling of different emotions (e.g., see page 53 for our analysis of how this pertains to the Abelson & Sermat experiment).

Frijda (1969) suggested that there may be a lack of comparability between findings from similarity rating experiments and dimension rating experiments because the two judgment tasks require different cognitive operations: "There is a distinct difference in task between labeling or scale rating on the one hand, and similarity estimation on the other, as Stringer (1967) himself pointed out. In the first, the subject is asked to discriminate aspects; in the second, to overlook differences, to search for similarities" (p. 32).

A major problem noted with the experiments in which judgments are made on scales relates to the various aspects of the phenomenon to which the scales might refer. A parallel in the similarity studies is the possible ambiguity about what the observer should or does attend to when judging a pair of faces. Similarities could be judged in terms of the appearance of the facial muscles, or in terms of inferred feeling states, or in terms of likely action consequences, or, if different stimulus persons are included, on the basis of physiognomic or demographic variables. If the observer is overlooking differences and searching for some basis to assess similarity, as Frijda suggested, then the observer might consider a different kind of similarity (appearance, feeling, etc.) for each pair of stimuli judged.

In analyzing similarity judgments, some investigators found evidence for two independent dimensions, others for three. Abelson and Sermat found two dimensions, pleasantness and activation, as did Shepard (1963) and Kauranne (1964). Nummenmaa and Kauranne (1958) and Nummenmaa (1964) found evidence for two dimensions, but they replaced the activation dimension with a dimension more like Schlosberg's attention–rejection. Their two dimensions were described as pleasant–anger and surprise–rejection, with each varying in intensity.

Royal and Hays (1959) and Gladstones (1962) discovered evidence for three dimensions. Both discerned a pleasantness and an activation dimension, but they differed in their third dimension. Stringer (1967, 1968, pers. comm.) also performed a similarity analysis and perceived three dimensions, and whereas one of them, happy–worry, is similar to pleasantness, the other two are different from those proposed by anyone else (thoughtful–surprise and thoughtful–disgust–pain).

Summary of studies of emotion dimensions

An answer cannot be given to the general question under consideration because only still photographic records of only posed behavior have been studied, but it is possible to provide a partial answer to a more limited question. What emotion dimensions can observers judge from still photographs of posed facial behavior? In the studies based on the facial behavior of more than one person (Osgood, 1966; Frijda, 1969) with extensive sampling of emotion words in the scales, the evidence suggested at least four or five dimensions. Certainly, one of these dimensions is something like pleasantness–unpleasantness, another activation or intensity. Beyond that, there is little consensus among investigators. Part of the problem is the limited sampling of persons, stimuli, and scales; part of the difficulty is that the investigators had very different hypotheses about what the dimensions might be (e.g., Osgood believed the dimensions should be the same as the dimensions of semantic meaning found in his studies of verbal behavior; Frijda believed the dimensions should refer to action tendencies).

Schlosberg, Osgood, and Frijda all proposed that their dimensions were related to the emotion categories. But Schlosberg and Osgood thought there were fixed relationships among emotion categories to locate them within geometric models of the emotion dimensions. Frijda, on the other hand, proposed a hierarchical model, which allowed the emotion categories to be independent of each other, though sharing on another level of consideration attributes or qualities represented by the dimensions. This question of the relationship between judgment of emotion categories and judgment of emotion dimensions is far from settled.

It seems doubtful that consistent findings about dimensions of emotion will be found until investigators utilize stimuli that have been shown by other means to represent a number of different emotion categories (at least those listed in Table 3.2), until they sample the behavior of many different persons, and until they select scales that systematically represent all or, at least, many of the aspects of emotion that might be judged from the face – appearance, feeling, action consequences, etc. It would be useful to compare findings from both scale judgment and similarity judgment experiments in which the same set of faces have been judged and the same referents represented in the scale terms and in instructions about the aspects of similarity to be judged.

Some of the dimension theorists (e.g., Frijda) believe that the judgment task they employ, rating a face on a series of scales, is much closer to the phenomenology of how people actually do perceive faces in nonexperimental settings than is the judgment task employed in the emotion category approach in which the observer is asked to choose among such categories as fear, anger, sadness, etc. Their thinking seems to be that in usual social intercourse either the face does not provide enough information for us to make the category distinction or we just do not respond to and think about faces in that way. Of course, some of the emotion category theorists (e.g., Tomkins) hold just the opposite view, which is that in actual social intercourse people respond to other people's facial behavior in terms just like those used in the category approach: the person is angry, afraid, sad, etc.

There are no data available on this question. We do not know the vocabulary utilized by observers who witness social interaction, hearing as well as seeing, knowing the social context, and observing the sequence of behavior which occurs. Nor do we know the thoughts and vocabulary of the interactants themselves at those points at which they may attend to or comment on each other's facial behavior. Though it would be important to determine which approach, categories or dimensions, is more similar to the phenomenology of social interaction, this is not the sole or even necessarily the most important criterion for choosing between these two schemes and judgment tasks.

One may also ask, which approach offers the more economical approach for measuring emotional information? That is, which employs the smallest number of independent variables to account for the information observed from the face? Probably the dimensions approach does, but the matter is not settled. Which approach allows more sophisticated statistical treatment in data analysis? Certainly the use of continuous scales is preferable to data from nominal categories. Which approach allows finer discriminations by observers? The data are not definitive on this question, although it may be that the category approach may allow more distinctions. Evidence on this matter could be derived from studies in which observers' judgments are linked to measurements of facial components (see Chapter 5). Although one study has successfully linked facial components to observers' judgments on emotion categories, the dimension approach has not received a sufficient test because the one experiment on this question where observers had judged faces utilizing dimensions did not employ an adequate measure of facial components.

It is not possible, then, from the evidence reviewed in this chapter, to say whether a categories or dimensions approach is preferable. The investigator will have to choose according to hunch, theoretical bias, or perhaps, preferred method of data analysis. If he selects a category approach, we have proposed that he include at least the seven categories of emotion that have been consistently found in past research. If he selects a dimension approach, he should include scales relevant to pleasantness/unpleasantness, attentional activity, and intensity/control. Beyond these three, the investigator should take note of the evidence suggesting that probably two or three more dimensions are necessary, but it is not clear what they are.

4. Does the face provide accurate information?

PAUL EKMAN, WALLACE V. FRIESEN,
AND PHOEBE ELLSWORTH

The question of whether the face can provide accurate information
about emotion has been the central issue since the beginning of research on the face. Although there may even well be legitimate research questions if the face provides only inaccurate information, for
example, in understanding a source of stereotyping and misinformation in person perception, the determination of accuracy has been piv-
otal in the ebb and the flow of research activity on the face. In this
chapter we shall document our claim that there is now sufficient evidence of accurate information to merit renewed and vigorous research
on the face and emotion. In so doing, we shall directly challenge the
misinterpretations, based in part on misinformation, provided by past
reviewers of this work.

The reader may wish to refer to Chapter 1, where the problems of
establishing accuracy criteria were discussed. *Accuracy* was defined as
correct information of some nature being obtained by some means from
facial behavior. As such, accuracy does not necessarily entail accurate
information about emotion; in addition to the finding of accuracy, relevance of the accuracy to some aspect of the phenomena described as
emotional must be demonstrated. Major methodological problems encountered in the main types of accuracy criteria, which will be discussed
in this section, were reviewed. In this chapter, we shall say that an
investigator obtained evidence of accuracy whenever the observers were
correct more often than would be expected by chance (p < .05).

Although either a judgment or a component approach (see Chapter 2)
could be employed in experiments on accuracy, almost all of the research has used a judgment design. We shall consider these first and
then discuss the few studies that examined accuracy by measuring facial
components.

4.1. Can judgments of emotion be accurate?

The question of whether observers could make accurate judgments of emotion was the key issue in the first period of research from 1914 to 1940, and the answer to this question was an important determinant of interest in the face and emotion, except for those who turned to the study of the vocabulary of emotion judgments. In their highly influential reviews of this literature, Bruner and Tagiuri (1954, p. 635) and Tagiuri (1968, p. 399) wrote:

> Some writers have reported that, whatever the nature of the expressive stimulus, the number of correct recognitions of emotions on the part of their subjects did not exceed the number that would be expected on a chance basis (for example, Fernberger, 1927, 1928; Guilford, 1929; Jarden & Fernberger, 1926; Landis, 1924, 1929; Sherman, 1927a – all of whom employed photographs of real emotions elicited in the laboratory). Others have shown that emotional expressions can be labeled with considerable accuracy (for example, Darwin, 1872; Feleky, 1914; Goodenough, 1931; Langfeld, 1918; Levitt, 1964; [P.K.] Levy, 1964; Munn, 1940; Ruckmick, 1921; Schulze, 1912; Stratton, 1921; [D.F.] Thompson and Meltzer, 1964; Woodworth, 1938).

It is no wonder that investigators might lose interest in this uninviting topic or, at the least, in the question of whether the face provides valid information about emotion. But Bruner and Tagiuri were factually incorrect and misleading. They enhanced the credibility of the negative findings on accuracy by saying that all of these experimenters utilized photographs of real emotions elicited in the laboratory. This is true only of Landis and Sherman. Fernberger, Guilford, and Jarden and Fernberger, whom they also credited with such laudable research methods, instead studied artists' drawings, not photographs, of posed or remembered behavior, not of real emotions elicited in the laboratory. Guilford studied the Rudolph faces, which are sketches made from photographs of an actor posing; Fernberger and Jarden and Fernberger studied the Boring and Titchener (1923) version of Piderit's drawings of the face, which presumed to show emotions in terms of separate facial features. Earlier (Section 2.7), we discussed the reasons why the use of drawings of the face have only the most dubious relevance to studies of accuracy and why we have excluded all such studies from this review. Among the studies cited by Bruner and Tagiuri as providing positive evidence on accuracy, we have excluded Langfeld because he also used the Rudolf faces, Levy and Stratton because they did not study the face, Schulze because his book was not available, and Ruckmick because he used only nine observers. The negative studies remaining in Bruner and Tagiuri's list, those of Landis and Sherman, were widely criticized and at least partially contradicted in the literature prior to their 1954 review.

No research on accuracy has completely satisfied the requirements outlined earlier in our methodological framework. Nevertheless, we shall show that reliable evidence of accurate judgment can be obtained for studies of posed behavior by taking into account findings across a number of experiments; judgments do coincide with the posers' intent. Although there is not as much evidence in regard to spontaneous behavior, what there is suggests a positive, rather than a negative, answer. Before considering these studies, however, we shall first analyze the Landis and Sherman experiments, bringing together past criticisms, our own framework, and relevant other experiments, all of which raise doubts about their findings, in an attempt to lay these two experiments finally to rest.

The Landis and Coleman experiments

In his 1924 and 1929 studies Landis took still photographs of his 25 subjects in a series of 17 situations, which included listening to music, looking at pornographic pictures, smelling ammonia, being shocked, decapitating a live rat, etc. Brief introspective reports were obtained after each situation, but these were kept short because Landis wanted a "cumulative disturbance" (an aim that provides the basis for one of the methodological criticisms to be discussed shortly). Four of the subjects were later asked to remember each situation and pose a facial behavior for each. Photographs were taken by the investigator when he noticed a change in the face. Landis selected 77 from the 844 photographs for use in his judgment study; 56 were from the initial situations, 21 from the remembered, posed situations; the sampling included the behavior of 22 of the 25 stimulus persons. Landis said he selected pictures for use in his judgment study that he thought were expressive. Forty-two observers judged the photographs, describing in their own words the emotion felt by the stimulus person, the situation that might have elicited the reaction, and their feeling of certainty about their judgment.

Landis reported that the results clearly showed that the emotions judged and the situations described by the observers were completely irrelevant to both the actual and the posed situations as well as to the introspective reports made during the actual situations. He attributed the discrepancy between the inaccuracy of his observers and the accuracy found by other investigators to the latter having used posed facial behavior, considered by Landis to be a specialized, conventional, languagelike behavior, which does not occur when people actually feel emotion.

Although there are many grounds for criticizing Landis's experiment, we shall look into only three of these, which can, at least in part, be supported by reexamination of Landis's data.

The first criticism arose from Davis's (1934) reanalysis of Landis's data on the components of facial behavior (a separate study by Landis of the records from this experiment). Davis found a tendency for the behaviors shown in the later situations to correlate with each other more than with the earlier situations. Davis interpreted this as resulting from the cumulative effect of experiencing the various situations in Landis's experiment, and as previously noted, Landis purposely kept the subjects' self-reports brief in order to enhance a cumulative disturbance. If, however, the disturbance were cumulative, that is, if there were a tendency for the emotions experienced in one situation to carry over to the next and for a disturbed or stressed reaction to build, then it would have been extremely difficult for observers, when they saw the facial behavior from each situation, either to discriminate separate, different emotions or to guess the specific eliciting circumstance. Only if the situations were not cumulative, only if each situation elicited a different reaction, would there be a chance for the occurrence of differing facial responses that could provide a systematic basis for the observer to appraise the particular emotion or situation when viewing a particular face. (Coleman, 1949, took Davis's criticism of Landis's experiment seriously, built rest periods into his experiment to diminish any cumulative effect, and attributed his positive results to his succeeding in eliminating a cumulative effect. We shall consider Coleman's study shortly.)

A second criticism of Landis's experiment, first raised by Frois-Wittmann (1930), is that Landis's situations might not have elicited the same emotion in all of his subjects; Arnold (1960) and Honkavaara (1961) later raised the same question. Furthermore, it is possible that each situation might have evoked more than one emotion, either simultaneously as a blend or consecutively. Looking at pornographic pictures, for example, or reading Krafft-Ebing case histories might elicit disgust in one subject, happiness in another, disgust–anger in a third, etc. If such variations did occur, then it would be highly unlikely that observers would be able to achieve accuracy on one of Landis's two accuracy criteria, correctly guessing the eliciting circumstance. But his other accuracy criterion, the subjects' self-reports of their experiences, could provide a more useful basis for measuring accuracy because, if subjects responded differently and reported these differences, observers might correctly judge information related to these self-reports, even if they failed to identify the eliciting circumstance. Such was not the case, however; Landis explained failure on this second accuracy criterion as error inherent in such flimsy data as introspection. After first considering the criticism under review, that Landis's situations were not emotion-specific across subjects, we shall then consider a third criticism, that Landis's experimental procedures led his subjects to mask or control their facial behavior and not to reveal their actual feelings. If that were so, then self-reports would indeed be a poor source of information for establishing accuracy.

Let us examine now two aspects of Landis's data that support the second criticism, that the eliciting situations were not emotion-specific across subjects. Landis's listing of the subjects' introspective reports showed that in only 2 of his 17 situations did even half of his stimulus persons report feeling the same emotion. Furthermore, his observers failed to judge accurately the posed facial behavior that his subjects recreated for these situations, thus contradicting Landis's belief that stereotyped posed behaviors would be accurately judged. Landis did not attempt to explain why his observers were unable to judge his subjects' poses accurately. An explanation consistent with the second criticism is that most of his 17 situations were probably not associated with any single emotion for all of his posers, who thus emitted various facial behaviors, depending on the emotion they believed to be associated with a given situation. Landis's negative results on the judgment of spontaneous behavior in his situations would be more credible if he had found that poses of behavior thought to be relevant to these situations could be accurately judged.

The third basis for criticism, first made by Murphy, Murphy, and Newcomb (1937) and repeated by both Arnold and Honkavaara, is that Landis might have unintentionally encouraged his subjects to inhibit or mask their facial responses to his situations. Landis mentioned this possibility but, unaccountably, dismissed it. A number of aspects of the experimental setting indicate the operation of display rules, either to neutralize the facial responses or to mask them with a positive affect. All of Landis's subjects knew him; most were psychologists who had had other laboratory experiences. Not only did they know they were being photographed, but, because Landis had marked their faces with burnt cork in order to measure the components of facial behavior in his other use of these records, they knew that Landis was interested in their facial behavior.[1]

Some other aspects of Landis's results are also consistent with this criticism. Landis reported that smiles were frequent in all of his situations, though he was convinced that his subjects were not feeling happy. Landis interpreted this as evidence against the meaningfulness of the smile; we interpret it as possible evidence of masking. A second source of support for the contention that Landis's experiment encouraged the operation of masking and neutralizing display rules is the introspective data. More than a third of the 17 situations elicited a report of "no feeling" from the majority of the subjects. If that is true, Landis failed with some frequency to elicit emotion. However, these self-reports, which he did not believe, do appear improbable in view of the anecdotal evidence he provided and the experience of others with such eliciting circumstances. The alternative, then, is that the reports of no feeling suggest an unwillingness to acknowledge being emotionally aroused, which could well have been duplicated in the facial behavior. In a completely different situation, Ekman and Friesen (1969a) provided some evidence that when individuals want to conceal their feelings and mask their emotions with a socially acceptable feeling, their faces typically either display deceptive masks or convey contradictory information. This may well have happened in Landis's experiment.

In summary, Landis's findings, that observers could not make accurate judgments, as compared with either the expected emotional nature of the eliciting circumstance or the subject's self-reported experience, should be credited only if (1) the same or similar reactions were elicited during at least some of the situations in most of the subjects, (2) the elicited reactions were different for at least some of the different situations, and (3) the selection of subjects and experimental arrangements did not encourage the subjects to mask or otherwise to control their facial behavior and/or to falsify their self-report.[2] The three criticisms discussed suggest that these conditions were probably not met.

[1] It is interesting to note that Hunt (1941), a supporter of Landis, belittled the importance of Munn's (1940) accuracy findings on the grounds that his subjects might have known that they were being photographed but failed to consider that this criticism was even more applicable to Landis.
[2] Our analysis does not presume that all of these problems operated in a similar fashion for all subjects. Some might have shown cumulative disturbance; others might have been more concerned with concealing their responses; it is also possible that concealment was more salient at the beginning of the experiment for most subjects, whereas toward the end, the effects of the cumulative disturbance became manifest.

The last argument against Landis's findings is based on Colman's (1949) study using comparable eliciting circumstances in which the observers did achieve accuracy. Coleman took motion pictures of the facial responses of six men and six women to eight situations, comparable to Landis's and of their subsequent attempts to pose the appropriate facial response for each situation. Because Coleman's interest was in comparing judgments of the top and bottom half of the face, which required the tedious chore of blacking out part of each motion picture frame, he utilized the films of only 2 of the 12 persons in his judgment experiment. He selected stimulus persons whose behavior he believed to be natural, not exaggerated, but showing a variety of expressions, and whose self-reports revealed that they were strongly affected by the experiment. Later we shall consider his results on the judgments of the partial faces and consider now only his results on the judgments of the full faces.

The motion pictures of the natural, or original, responses and the posed responses of two subjects were shown to 379 observers, who judged which of nine situations was the one in which the pictures were taken; (in addition to the eight actual situations, a ninth was added to decrease judgment by elimination). Judgments were accurate, in that the correct situations were identified for each stimulus person, in both the natural and posed versions, more than would be expected by chance. Posing enhanced accuracy, but for different situations for the two stimulus persons.

Why did Coleman obtain positive and Landis negative results?

First, Coleman's situations might have elicited more similar emotions across his two stimulus persons, with different reactions to at least some of the situations by both subjects. Coleman did, after all, purposefully select subjects whom he thought had been affected by the experiment, which might mean that he picked those who had shown or reported different experiences across his eight situations. Coleman explained the difference in his results from Landis's as a result of his inclusion of rest periods to diminish any cumulative disturbance, which might obscure different reactions to his eight situations. Evidence in support of the possibility that most of Coleman's situations were associated with different emotions (and by both subjects) comes from his positive results on the judgment of posed behavior. Landis's failure to obtain accuracy in judgments of posed behavior suggests, it will be recalled, that his subjects might not have shared the same emotional experience and therefore did not attempt to pose the same emotions. The fact that Coleman did obtain accuracy in judgments of posed behavior suggests, contrarily, that at least some of his situations were associated with the same emotion by his two subjects.

Second, Coleman's judgment task may have allowed for more complex or inferential judgments in that he did not ask his observers to judge emotion, as did Landis, but instead to pick the situation during which a film was taken. If an observer sees a subject smile and knows nothing of the situation, he may simply call that smile "happy."[3] But if he knows the nature of the various eliciting situations, he may well consider the possibility that the smile is a mask or an embarrassed reaction to the feelings elicited by one of the situations (e.g., Coleman's situation of crushing a snail). Coleman's judgment task of matching a situation with a film clip leaves open, however, the question of whether the accuracy obtained was dependent on information about emotion. Perhaps accurate judgments could have been based on behavior not usually described as emotional, i.e., defensive behavior. It would be helpful if Coleman had shown the same films to another group of observers and asked them to judge the emotions shown.

Third, Coleman showed motion pictures, whereas Landis obtained judgments on still photographs. Earlier, we argued that film or videotape were more appropriate than stills for recording spontaneous behavior because they do not fragment the natural flow of behavior. Still photographs are more appropriate for recording static poses. Although Landis fired his camera whenever he thought something was happening, his basic unit, a single still, would provide less information about the onset and duration of the facial response, even if his own reaction time was so rapid that he adequately captured the response at its apex, or most extreme moment. The type of complex, inferential judgment referred to previously would probably be easier to make from films, which show the sequence of reactions, duration, etc., than from still photographs.

Fourth, Coleman's subjects might have been less motivated to inhibit or mask their facial behavior than Landis's subjects. Unlike Landis, Coleman did not select subjects who knew him nor did he mark their faces; thus he may have avoided Landis's error of inadvertently encouraging the operation of those display rules that inhibit candid facial responses.

Certainly Coleman's study is far from conclusive as an accuracy study. The generality of the findings across persons cannot be determined with only two stimulus persons nor, for reasons just mentioned, can it be

---

[3]In instances where it is unavoidable, the masculine pronoun has been used in the generic sense to mean he or she.

determined that the accuracy obtained necessarily involved judgments of emotion. But Coleman's study does underline the three major methodological problems in Landis's experiment and strengthens our contention that the results of Landis's experiment should be discredited. Correcting some of the flaws in Landis's experiment, Coleman was able to achieve accuracy. It is regrettable that no further work has been done utilizing such eliciting circumstances, for the most conclusive evidence for discounting Landis' findings would be further studies similar to Coleman's with a larger number of stimulus persons.

The Sherman experiment

As previously mentioned, the only other study that obtained negative results on accuracy among those described by Bruner and Tagiuri (1954) and Tagiuri (1968) as utilizing real behavior elicited in the laboratory, and that actually did so, was Sherman's (1927a) study of observers' judgments of very young infants. His research has remained influential, despite challenges to his interpretation of his results as long ago as 1931 by Goodenough, again by Murphy, Murphy, and Newcomb (1937), and by Honkavaara (1961) and despite the results of other inquiries contradicting his findings. As with Landis, we shall critically examine his results in detail, not because of the merits of his study, but because of its continuing acceptance despite enormous flaws. We shall suggest a number of grounds for challenging the validity of his results, as well as his interpretation of them, and shall present a summary of contradictory results from a number of studies from the same era.

Sherman actually performed four separate experiments, with different conditions, only one of which is sufficiently free of confounding sources of variability to be considered. In that experiment, he recorded, on motion picture film, the behavior of two infants, one 74 hours old and the other 145 hours old, as they were subjected to four eliciting circumstances: hunger, defined as prolonging the time for the infants' scheduled feeding by 15 minutes;[4] suddenly dropping the infant; restraining the infant by holding the head and face down on a table; and applying a needle to the cheek six times. Two groups of observers (graduate and freshmen psychology students) were shown the behavior immediately after

---

[4]Sherman did not explain the basis for the presumption that, in infants of that young age, the feeding schedule would be sufficiently established for a 15-minute deviation to make a sufficient difference to elicit any reaction. It is to be hoped that Sherman had other bases for knowing that his two infants were hungry at the time of the experiment.

the elicitation and asked to judge the emotion and the eliciting circumstance in their own words.

His second experiment was said to be the only instance in which accuracy and agreement were achieved. Here the observers saw, not only the postelicitation films, but also the filmed behavior during the elicitation itself. The results are difficult to interpret for the following reasons: These observers had two, not one, sources of additional information – knowledge of the eliciting circumstance, which Sherman intended, and access to the full range of the infants' facial behavior during the elicitation procedure, which may have been redundant with or different from the postelicitation facial behavior shown in the first experiment. Another problem in comparing the results from the first and second experiments is that Sherman coached the subjects in the second, but not in the first experiment, about what behaviors to observe. A third problem is that half of the observers in the second experiment were observers in the first study. Thus any difference in performance between the first and second experiments could be, not only because of coaching, knowledge of the elicitor, or exposure to additional facial behavior during elicitation, but also because of the benefits of practice or memory for those observers who were already in the first experiment.

The third set of data was gathered from medical students and nurses who were shown the live, not the recorded, postelicitation behavior of an unspecified number of infants. (A screen blocking their view was present during elicitation and then removed.) We reject these data because the judgments are confounded by the observers' exposure not only to the facial behavior as in the first study but also, as Sherman readily acknowledged, to the vocal behavior; all infants cried during postelicitation. We should note that these two groups of observers were small and that, in most instances, the majority of their judgments were of events, not emotions, e.g., colic, just awakening, tight bandage.

The last study is one in which the eliciting circumstance film from one situation was followed by the postelicitation film from another situation as if they were sequential. This experiment suffers from most of the same flaws as that in which the observers saw the films of the actual eliciting circumstance in addition to the postelicitation films.

Based on methodological flaws in all of the other experiments, our decision to consider only the data from the first experiment, in which observers saw only the postelicitation behavior, does not ignore the results Sherman himself considered crucial. Sherman interpreted the data from that experiment as most damaging to any claim that accurate judgments could be made from infants' facial behavior.

There are three major flaws in Sherman's first experiment that serve to raise serious doubt about the validity of his conclusion. First, Sherman's data analysis is oversimplified. He did not distinguish between judgments of emotion, utilizing the usual emotion vocabulary, and judgments of events or internal states, i.e., taking medicine or being hungry. Instead, he counted both types of responses in his measures of whether observers could make accurate emotion judgments. Further, he ignored the possibility that some of the emotion terms might have been synonyms, although F. Allport had published his emotion categories a few years earlier (1924); thus, Sherman considered rage and anger, for example, as different emotion judgments and pain and hurt as different judgments.

The second and more serious criticism of Sherman's experiment is the probability that all four situations might have elicited the *same* reaction from the infants and, of course, as explained earlier in connection with Landis, if the situations do not elicit different reactions, then there is little reason to expect the observer to make different judgments. In other words, Sherman's accuracy criterion was the emotion *he* expected in each of his four situations; but he provided no empirical basis for his expectation and, if he were wrong, if the situations all elicited the same response, then the failure to find accurate judgments would be meaningless. Two aspects of Sherman's data suggest that the reactions across the four stimulus situations were similar. Anger was the most frequent judgment for all four of his situations, which Sherman saw as evidence of inaccuracy; but quite conceivably his infants *were* angry, either during all four situations or after each of the four stimulus situations. For it must be remembered that we are considering judgments made of postelicitation behavior; it is possible that each of the four elicitations immediately produced a distinctive response, was rapidly dissipated a few moments later and not seen in the postelicitation behavior, which may well have shown anger. Honkavaara (1961) might have had this in mind in criticizing Sherman for sampling infant behavior only during crying. From Sherman's other article (1927b), describing a separate study in which observers listened to the sounds made by the infants but did not see the films (again, failing to achieve accuracy in terms of Sherman's expectations), Honkavaara discovered that the infants in the study we are discussing here cried in all four postelicitation situations. Although crying does not necessarily signify that *only* anger (or only some other emotion) was present in the postelicitation behavior, one must question whether Sherman really did succeed in preserving different emotions for the four situations, without which he could have no basis for interpreting his results as showing inaccuracy.

The third criticism of Sherman's experiments, raised by Goodenough (1931), Murphy et al. (1937), and Honkavaara (1961), involves the age of the infants, both less than one week old. They argue that the failure of such young infants to show a differentiated facial response across the four eliciting situations would not be a conclusive demonstration that the face is unrelated to emotion nor that social learning provides the sole basis for any such relationship, which might exist later. Maturation may be such that the differentiated perception of the situations necessary for differential facial response, or the differentiation of the facial responses themselves, is not unfolded prior to an age of 150 hours.

The last criticism is that a sample of two infants is far too small to permit any conclusions; and, further, Sherman did not report his data separately for the judgments of the 74-hour-old and the 145-hour-old infant, so it cannot be determined whether the observers' judgments were similar for both or different because of maturational or other factors.

Although we shall not consider as a separate substantive issue the nature of the development of facial behaviors associated with emotion, we shall explore four articles reporting findings that indirectly contradict Sherman's to complete the case we have constructed for dismissing Sherman's experiment.

Goodenough (1931) showed eight photographs of a 10-month-old infant to 68 observers. The observers were given a choice among 12 possible judgments, each judgment describing both an emotion and an eliciting situation. There were four more choices provided than stimuli to decrease the chance that the observers would choose by elimination. Goodenough reported that 47% of the judgments were accurate. In our reanalysis of her data, we first discarded all of the stimuli and judgments involving the description of facial appearance rather than an inference about emotion (satisfied smile; roguish smiling; crying). We also omitted two stimuli described too generally to be relevant to accuracy regarding specific emotions (grimacing, dissatisfaction). This left three stimuli that were relevant to the question of whether accurate judgments could be made of the infant's emotions. In considering these data, we counted a judgment as correct if it accurately identified the emotion, regardless of whether or not it included a correct identification of the particular eliciting situation. For example, for the photograph taken when the infant had been astonished by the sight of a bright-colored toy, we decided that the observers were accurate if they chose that judgment or if they chose the judgments of "astonishment at the mother counting loudly," or "astonishment while listening to the ticking of a watch." The results were as follows: 94% correct judgments for the astonishment face; 79% correct judgments for the pleasure face; and 21% correct judgments for the fear face. With only one stimulus person and only three relevant stimuli, Goodenough's study was certainly enormously limited but showed accuracy on two out of three emotions tested.

In another article, Goodenough (1932/1933) reported data she felt contradicted Sherman's. She observed a 10-year old, blind–deaf child who, because of these handicaps, had little opportunity to learn facial behaviors. Goodenough dropped a doll inside the child's dress and described the facial reactions as being similar to the facial behaviors associated with different emotions in normal children. This is interesting anecdotal evidence of an innate tendency to show emotion in the face, but the nature of the data reported limits it to that.

J. Thompson (1941) and Fulcher (1942) both conducted studies of blind and sighted children, and we shall revaluate them in Section 4.2 with regard to the components of facial behavior. Thompson studied spontaneous behavior in 26 blind and 29 sighted children ranging from 7 weeks to 13 years of age; Fulcher studied the posed emotions of 50 blind and 118 sighted children ranging from 4 to 21 years old. Both noted maturational factors; both noted, in their analysis of the components of facial behavior, similarities between the blind and sighted children in at least some emotional facial behaviors – laughing, smiling, crying, and anger for Thompson and happiness, sadness, anger, and fear for Fulcher. Although differences in the extent of muscular movements were found between blind and sighted children, there was evidence of similarity in the particular muscles moved for each emotion.

Both investigators also utilized a judgment procedure with observers. Thompson had four trained psychologists observe the facial behavior of the blind and sighted children and judge emotion in 11 categories, which she then analyzed in terms of F. Allport's category scheme. There was both high agreement among observers and accuracy between observers and investigator in that the emotion judged corresponded with the investigator's impression, based on situational context as well as total behavior shown, for judgments of both blind and sighted children with no significant differences as a function of sightedness. Fulcher had five observers who knew the intended emotion judge the "adequacy" of the pose. For both blind and sighted children, happiness and sadness were judged as more adequately portrayed than anger and fear, but across all emotions the sighted portrayals were judged as more adequate than the blind ones. In discussing their results, Thompson and Fulcher cited Landis and Sherman as providing the main evidence for contradiction of their findings.

To summarize our discussion of Sherman's work and related studies, Sherman's evidence for inaccuracy rests on the presumptions that a different emotion was elicited in each situation, that it was the same emotion for each of the two infants, and that the emotion elicited during the situational manipulation was preserved long enough to appear in the postelicitation film shown to the observers. These presumptions are of dubious validity. Further, the validity of Sherman's findings can be questioned because of his failure to consider maturational processes and the small size (two) of his sample of stimulus persons. A brief review of studies by Goodenough, Thompson, and Fulcher, all studies of children's facial behavior that considered blind as well as sighted children and some of which studied different age periods, shows consistent contradiction of Sherman's conclusions.

The Landis and the Sherman experiments, with their questionable negative findings, have, in our opinion, had unmerited influence in the investigation of judgment of emotion from facial behavior. Our lengthy discussion of these studies has been an attempt to set them in perspective. We shall now turn to the positive evidence.

The first set of studies (Hanawalt, 1944; Munn, 1940; Vinacke, 1949) used as stimuli commercial magazine photographs of presumably spontaneous, naturally occurring, emotional behavior. Accuracy was measured in terms of the observers' ability to judge the emotion that presumably occurred in the situation. In the second set of studies (Ekman & Bressler, 1964; Ekman & Friesen, 1965b; Howell & Jorgenson, 1970; Lanzetta & Kleck, 1970), spontaneous reactions elicited in a standard stress interview, spontaneous behavior when anticipating electric shock, and clinical interviews with psychiatric patients were used as stimuli. Accuracy was measured in terms of the correspondence between the observers' judgments of emotion and anticipated differences between the stress and catharsis portions of standard interviews, between the pre- and posthospitalization interviews of psychiatric patients, and between observers' judgments of the eliciting circumstance, shock or nonshock. The last set of studies (Drag & Shaw, 1967; Dusenbury & Knower, 1938; Ekman & Friesen, 1965; Frijda, 1953; Kanner, 1931; Kozel & Gitter, 1968;

Levitt, 1964; Osgood, 1966; D.F. Thompson & Meltzer, 1964; Woodworth, 1938) used posed behavior as stimuli. Accuracy was measured in terms of the observers' success in judging the emotion intended by the poser.

Accuracy in judging candid photographs: Munn, Hanawalt, and Vinacke

Munn (1940) explained his decision to have observers judge the emotion shown in magazine photographs, taken during presumably emotional situations, as an attempt to resolve Woodworth's (1938) doubts about whether accuracy was possible for spontaneous as well as posed facial behavior. Munn's primary aim was to determine the influence of knowledge of the situation upon judgment of emotion from facial behavior by comparing the judgments of observers who saw the face alone with those who saw the entire photograph. Though he found that the number of observers making an accurate judgment increased when the entire picture was seen, accuracy was achieved with most of his stimuli even when only the face was seen. These comparative results will be discussed later in connection with the question of how contextual information influences the judgment of emotion from facial behavior (Chapter 6). We shall take into account here only Munn's data on the judgments of the face alone.

Hanawalt (1944) borrowed Munn's procedure of utilizing candid photographs from magazines and used a number of Munn's actual stimuli in addition to ones of his own. His purpose was not to study accuracy but to compare judgments made when either the top or bottom half of the face was seen; these results will be considered later in connection with the question of how judgments of emotion are influenced by the components of the face observed (Chapter 5). Only Hanawalt's results on the judgments of the full face will be considered here.

Vinacke (1949) also drew stimuli from magazines but chose his own different set of pictures. His purpose was not to study accuracy but to compare judgments made by different ethnic groups; those results will be scrutinized later in connection with the question of how judgments of emotion may vary across cultures (Chapter 7). Here we shall consider only Vinacke's results on the judgments by Caucasian observers.

Munn recognized that there were difficulties with his two accuracy criteria. He should have sought some means for estimating what emotional reaction was experienced independent of the facial behavior which occurred. He could have approximated that by showing the full photographs but obscuring the face so that the observer could see only the situation and determine whether there were any agreed upon expectations about the probable emotion. (This procedure might not be workable if the photograph of the situation did not adequately show what the nature of the setting was or what the elicitor was, etc.; see Chapter 1). However, he did not do that; instead, both of his accuracy criteria were contaminated by knowledge of the face as well as knowledge of the situation. One criterion was his own expectation which was an unreliable basis because he was not present when the behavior occurred and was contaminated by his inspection of the faces. The other criterion was the judgment of the observers who saw the situation and the face; it was similarly contaminated so that it is not possible to know whether their expectation about emotion was influenced primarily by the situation or by their judgment of the face. Neither Hanawalt nor Vinacke concerned himself with accuracy criteria; they analyzed their results solely in terms of observer agreement under the different conditions employed in their experiments.

The best basis for building an accuracy criterion for use with candid photographs from magazines is not available, precisely because the pictures are selected long after the event, with no access to the relevant sources of information, viz., the self-report of the individual, the reports of other people present in the situation, and the data on the antecedent and consequent events. Though less satisfactory, another basis for establishing an accuracy criterion for such stimulus materials is to determine what single emotion, if any, is usually associated with the situation in which the candid photograph appeared to have been taken. We conducted a simple experiment in which 35 college students were given the list (but no photographs) of situations as described by Munn, Hanawalt, and Vinacke and were asked to judge the most probable emotion, utilizing the list of proposed emotion categories from Table 3.2 and also the choice of "no emotion." Only situations yielding at least 50% agreement about a particular emotion were taken to be relevant for examining the accuracy of observers' judgments. The data on 5 of the 14 Munn stimuli were excluded because of lack of agreement about probable emotion as were the data on 7 of Hanawalt's 20 stimuli and 14 of Vinacke's 20 stimuli. Correspondence between the majority of original judgments of the faces in the photographs and the judgments we obtained of the verbal descriptions of the situations constituted the measure of accuracy. Table 4.1 gives the verbal description of the situation as it was noted in the articles by these authors and as it was given to our college students, the percentage agreement about the expected emotion made

Table 4.1. *Results on selected stimuli from candid photograph studies (in percentages)*

Verbal description	Judgment of verbal description	Judgment of face Munn (1940)	Hanawalt (1944)	Vinacke (1949)
Girl laughing	100 Happy	—	97 Happy	—
Jitterbug clapping hands to music	97 Happy	86 Happy	—	—
Girl running into ocean	91 Happy	97 Happy	—	—
A man smiling standing between two other men	88 Happy	—	—	59 Happy
Baseball fan vociferously cheering	82 Happy	—	—	47 Happy
Girl in sack race	66 happy	49 Sad	—	—
Man escapes Nazis	56 Happy	—	65 Fear	—
Girl escapes explosion	53 Happy	—	96 Horror	—
Man in shower as water is unexpectedly turned on	89 Surprise	—	87 Surprise	—
Girl discovers photographer as she lifts hoop skirt to go through door	85 Surprise	—	80 Surprise	—
Girl in amusement park with dress going up	74 Surprise	—	90 Happy	—
Girl discovers photographer has her covered	58 Surprise	—	62 Surprise	—
Girl photographed over transom while dressing	56 Surprise	66 Surprise	89 Surprise	—
Girl photographed over transom while in bath	38 Surprise 12 Fear	26 Surprise 28 Fear	—	—
Girl running from ghost	96 Fear	94 Fear	92 Fear	—
Boy caught in revolving door attended to by policeman	61 Fear	—	—	1 Fear
Porter leading burned man from scene of airplane crash	56 Fear	8 Fear 33 Anxiety	—	—
Man with hand stretched toward hostile crowd	54 Fear	63 Distress/ Anxiety	—	—
Frenchman shows grief as colors of lost regiment are exiled to Africa	79 Sad	—	84 Sad	—
Man wrapped in blanket after failure to swim English Channel	71 Sad	—	—	4 Sad 16 Exhaustion

Table 4.1 (*cont.*)

| | | Judgment of face | | |
| | Judgment of | Munn | Hanawalt | Vinacke |
Verbal description	verbal description	(1940)	(1944)	(1949)
Woman disheveled weeping telephoning	60 Sad	—	—	51 Sad
Girl sitting in a police station after one of her suitors was killed in a quarrel over her affections	53 Sad	—	—	32 Sad
Man who is holding strikebreaker by the coat collar	68 Anger	8 Anger	65 Anger	—
Lady awaiting news of mine disaster	94 Disgust/ Contempt	—	71 Sad	—

on the basis of reading the verbal descriptions and the judgments made by the original observers of the face alone. (These last data were reorganized in terms of the categories listed in Table 3.2 to facilitate comparisons across experiments.)

Accuracy was found with all three sets of data: for 6 of the 9 Munn stimuli listed, for 8 of the 12 Hanawalt stimuli, for 4 of the 6 Vinacke stimuli. The table also shows that this accuracy was achieved with happiness, surprise, fear, and sadness stimuli; the one anger and the one disgust/contempt stimulus yielded either inconsistent or inaccurate results.

The instances of inaccuracy are difficult to explain. Either set of observers could be wrong; or both could be correct if the stimulus person experienced more than one emotion and the camera captured the nonnormative one, or if the stimulus person had an idiosyncratic reaction, or if the verbal description of the situation failed to include relevant information. But this is the limitation of this indirect method of establishing an accuracy criterion.

To summarize, these three experiments show that observers can make accurate judgments of spontaneous behavior, in the sense that observers of a face can judge the emotion that other observers who read a description of the situation predict. There are four limitations on these results. First, the behavior studied (candid photographs taken from magazines) may not all actually have been spontaneous. The person shown in the photographs might have been aware of the photographer or, even worse, might have completely reenacted or staged the behavior for the press.

The second limitation is the accuracy criterion. Although the one we fashioned (determining what emotion would be expected in the eliciting circumstance) is preferable to the one employed by the original authors, it is still not totally satisfactory for reasons previously discussed.

A third limitation is the sampling of emotions; accuracy was shown for four of the seven emotion categories listed in Table 3.2; the sample for the other two emotion categories was very small (only one stimulus each).

The fourth and, perhaps, most serious limitation is in regard to the representativeness of the findings. Hunt (1941) appropriately noted the need to establish how often facial behavior in situations like those studied by Munn can provide the basis for accurate judgments of emotion. Are informative faces a rare event, usually lost within a sequence of noninformative facial behavior? Or is such informative facial behavior shown only by some special group of people, highly extroverted persons, for example, but not by a more representative sample? Did Munn or the photographer pick out the one rare moment, or the few rare people, who happen to provide accurate information in their spontaneous facial behavior? The answers to these questions would require information about sampling that is not available. Information would be needed both from the photographer (how the subject of the photograph was chosen and how the photographs that were published were chosen from those shot) and from Munn, Hanawalt, and Vinacke (how many published photographs they inspected in choosing the particular ones employed in their studies).

Although it can be said that accuracy did occur, it is not possible to specify how frequently facial behaviors in situations such as those studied by these authors provide the basis for accurate judgments. Thus, there is doubt about the representativeness of their findings, in terms of generality across persons and of generality across time within the situation. The next group of experiments to be considered remedies this limitation, but they are weaker than the ones just discussed in that accuracy was sought on gross discriminations rather than on specific emotions.

Accuracy in the judgment of spontaneous behavior

Let us first note how the design of experiments on spontaneous behavior, which we shall next examine, answers Hunt's criticism of the candid photograph studies by providing evidence of generality across persons and generality across time. The first question about generality is resolved if there is representative sampling of stimulus persons, that is, if the experimenter does not preselect some atypical group of people, who, because of special training, instruction, or proclivity, are likely to be more facially facile than others. Although there was no information about the sampling of persons in the candid photograph studies, in the studies of spontaneous behavior, the sampling of persons was reasonably random within the constraints of utilizing volunteers and the usual sources for subjects. The stimulus persons were either college students or mental patients, but in neither case were good expressors preselected. The number of stimulus persons in each experiment was small; but by considering the finding of accuracy across all of the experiments, this limit is remedied.

The matter of how to design experiments to resolve doubts about the generality of the findings across time is more complicated. Let us examine how answers could be furnished to a skeptic who, like Hunt, holds the view that the face rarely emits information that allows for accurate judgment. This skeptic would have no problem in dismissing the candid photograph studies discussed earlier, for there is no evidence on the sampling of behaviors in those studies to counter the skeptic's claim that both photographer and investigator probably chose that one-in-a-million slice of life in which the face happened to show something decipherable and relevant to the eliciting circumstance. If the skeptic is shown evidence of accuracy in an experiment where the investigator did not take a single slice but showed observers a continuous sample of some length on film or videotape (Howell and Jorgenson used 60-second samples, Lanzetta and Kleck used 12-second samples), then the skeptic would have to yield, but only somewhat. The skeptic could no longer claim that the rare moments when facial behavior is informative are usually lost when embedded in the total sequence of random, meaningless, facial behavior. If that were so, then observers who saw a sequence would not achieve accuracy. However, the skeptic could still argue that only in *rare* moments is the face informative, but rather than being lost, those rare moments provide the basis for accurate judgment. Perhaps one signal in 12 or 60 seconds of facial noise was the basis for accurate judgment, the skeptic would argue, and this provides no evidence that the face often conveys accurate information.

The answer to this remaining claim, that the face is an infrequent output system, requires an experiment in which many separate samples of facial behavior are randomly drawn from within an eliciting situation.

If observers are able to make accurate judgments for most of the samples, the skeptic is answered and the representativeness of findings in
terms of generality across time is established. There is one artifact in
such a research design that can decrease the probability of obtaining
accurate results. Selecting slices of behavior in a random fashion may
well fragment the natural flow of behavior. For example, a 5-second slice
might show the end of one facial behavior and the beginning of another
rather than the beginning, middle, and end of a facial behavior and
thereby increase the difficulty of judging the behavior. Nevertheless, in
the experiments by Ekman and his associates, randomly drawn multiple
samples of behavior did provide the basis for accurate judgments, establishing that the face often provides accurate information, and thus answering doubts about the generality of findings across time.

Let us now consider this set of experiments. Tables 4.2 and 4.3 show
the methodological features and results of these studies. In some of the
studies, the sample of facial behavior was obtained by recording a naturally occurring event; Ekman and Bressler (1964) and Ekman and Rose
(1965) used facial behavior shown during interviews conducted at different points in inpatient psychiatric hospitalization. Some utilized a
laboratory-contrived situation to elicit emotion; Ekman (1965) and Howell and Jorgenson (1970) used standardized interviews in which the interviewer's manner and style changed; Lanzetta and Kleck (1970) used
the anticipation of receiving either a shock or nonshock. Only the studies by Ekman and his associates were designed primarily to study accuracy, but the other studies do provide information relevant to this issue.
For all but the Lanzetta and Kleck experiment, the observers who judged
emotion knew nothing about either the situation in which the stimuli
had been recorded or the nature of the persons photographed.

In the first study listed in Table 4.2, the accuracy criterion was the
expected difference in emotions elicited by the interviewer being hostile
(stress-inducing) and then explaining the purpose of his hostility and
praising the subject for resiliency under stress (catharsis-inducing). The
observers rated stimuli from the stressful parts of the interviews as more
unpleasant than those from the cathartic parts of the interviews.[5] Whereas
the difference in pleasantness rating is small, it is significant, and it
should be remembered that these stimuli were selected at random. As
mentioned earlier, selecting still photographs at random may well frag-

[5]There were also significant differences in the ratings on the attention–rejection dimension, but these were not reported because ratings on this scale were highly intercorrelated
with ratings on pleasantness.

Table 4.2. *Methodology and results of three accuracy experiments of spontaneous behavior*

	Ekman (1965)	Howell & Jorgenson (1970)	Lanzetta & Kleck (1970)
Methodology			
Number of stimulus persons	5	4	12
Number of stimuli	60: with 12 of each person, half from each of the 2 conditions	8: with two 1-minute film clips of each stimulus person one clip from condition one film clip from relief condition	—
Type of record	Still photographs of face, randomly selected from larger record	Motion picture film of head and shoulders	12-Second videotape of stimulus person while they anticipated shock or nonshock; each observer judged 20 episodes for each of 6 persons
Number of observers	35	53	6 Observers for each stimulus person
Judgment task	Ratings on Schlosberg's three dimensions: pleasant–unpleasant, attention–rejection, sleep–tension	Pleasant–unpleasant dichotomy	Whether the videotape shows shock anticipation trial or nonshock trial
Sampling situation	Standardized interview with stressful and cathartic parts	Standardized interview with stressful and relief parts	Stimulus persons saw a red light if they were to receive a shock, a green light if no shock on that trial
Accuracy criterion	Compare judgments of stimuli from two parts of interview expected to differ in emotion experienced	Compare judgments with emotions expected in two parts of the interview	Is judge correct in identifying whether person is in shock anticipation (red) or nonshock anticipation (green)?
Results	Median stress stimuli: 4.6 unpleasant Median cartharsis stimuli: 5.7 pleasant	61% Correct identification	Accuracy significant across stimulus persons observed, although also significant differences among stimulus persons observed. Chance judgment would be 50% correct, and the range across stimulus persons was 55% to 83% correct, with a median of 62%

Table 4.3. *Methodology and results of two accuracy experiments of spontaneous behavior*

	Ekman & Bressler (1964)	Ekman & Rose (1965)
Methodology		
Number of stimulus persons	10	6[a]
Number of stimuli	40 sequences; each was five photos taken in 5 seconds; four sequences for each person; half from each of the two conditions	96 Sequences, each was five photos taken in 5 seconds; 16 sequences for each person, half from each condition
Type of record	Five rapid stills, showing face and body, randomly selected from larger record	Five rapid stills, showing face and body, randomly selected from larger record
Number of observers	34	244
Judgment task	Ratings on: pleasant–unpleasant scale, mobile–immobile scale	Ratings on: pleasant–unpleasant scale, Immobile–mobile scale
Sampling situation	Standardized psychiatric interview with in-patients, two interviews with each patient, one rated as most depressed and one rated as most improved by interviewer	Standardized psychiatric interview with in-patients, two interviews with each patient, one at time of admission to hospital and one at time of discharge from hospital.
Accuracy criterion	Compare judgments of stimuli from the two inter-views when different emotional experience would be expected	Compare judgments of stimuli from the two interviews when different emotional experience would be expect-ed
Results	Median depressed stimuli: 3.9 unpleasant, 2.3 immobile, Median Improved stimuli; 5.1 pleasant, 3.7 immobile	Median admission stimuli: 2.8 unpleasant, 2.9 immobile median discharge stimuli: 5.0 pleasant, 4.9 mobile

Notes: [a]These six patients were also stimulus persons in Ekman & Bressler's (1964) study.

ment the natural flow of behavior and, for that reason, provide a low estimate of accuracy, but this random sampling procedure was used because the study was intended to evaluate what the face might show over the course of an entire interview, not what the face might show at its most informative moments. In another study designed to assess the *maximum* accuracy possible, Ekman used as stimuli photographs that observers who saw both face and body had rated as maximally stressful or cathartic. When just the faces of these pictures were shown to another set of observers who judged the pictures on Schlosberg's three dimensions of emotion without knowledge of the interview situation, the difference in pleasantness ratings was large – a mean difference of 3.5 points on a 7-point scale.

Howell and Jorgenson (1970) performed an experiment that was very similar in both the eliciting situation and judgment task. Their major interest, however, was in comparing accuracy when the observers saw the face, read or heard the words, or received a combination of sources. We shall report here only on their results on the judgment of the facial behavior. Their interviewer's behavior changed from unfriendly and challenging to reassuring, in order to induce stress and relief from stress. The observers were shown 60 seconds of motion picture film from the stress phase and a 60-second sample from the relief phase and were asked to judge whether the person felt pleasant or unpleasant. Despite differences in accuracy achieved for particular stimulus persons and differences in level of accuracy achieved for the relief compared with the stress sample, overall accuracy was found.

Lanzetta and Kleck (1970) focused primarily on the interrelationships among three phenomena: how accurately the stimulus persons' facial behavior could be judged, the galvanic skin response (GSR) indication of psychophysiological arousal during the elicitation, and the stimulus person's performance as an observer of others. We shall discuss only the results on accuracy in judging the facial behavior.[6] Stimulus persons were recorded on videotape for 12 seconds while they watched a red light signaling that they would receive shock or a green light signaling nonshock. The observers were shown the short videotape episodes and

[6]Lanzetta and Kleck did not attempt to study accuracy but rather to determine the relationship among observers' abilities to judge facial behavior, the extent to which their own facial behavior could be judged by others, and psychophysiological measures. The results on these interrelationships are quite interesting but are not reported here because the authors considered the findings tentative owing to the small number of stimulus persons. This study is very suggestive of the fact that explorations of these variables will be fruitful (see also Buck, Savin, Miller, & Caul, 1969; Jones, 1950). These studies and later ones by these and authors are discussed in chapter 8.

were required to indicate whether they were watching persons anticipating shock or nonshock. There were 12 stimulus persons; each was judged by five other persons and a self-report was obtained. As in the preceding experiment, accuracy varied with the stimulus person observed, from a low of 55% to a high of 83% correct judgments, with the median accuracy across all stimulus persons observed better than chance, 62%. There are two problems with this experiment as an accuracy study of facial behavior. The videotapes showed more than the face; the body from the waist up was seen, and the observers may have used nonfacial sources for some, or most, of their judgments. Judgment of the eliciting circumstance may or may not have required any information about emotion; perhaps coping behavior provided the basis for accuracy.

The accuracy criterion in the next two experiments was based on the expected differences in emotions between the acute and remitted phases of a psychotic disorder, confirmed by the ratings of the treatment staff. Ekman and Bressler (1964) found that stimuli randomly selected from interviews of depressive patients during the acute phase of their illness were rated as more unpleasant and more immobile than those selected from the remitted phase. In a replication (Ekman & Rose, 1965) with a larger sampling of stimuli for each person but a smaller number of persons than in the prior experiment, stimuli from the interview closest to the patient's admission to the hospital were judged as more unpleasant and immobile than those from the interview closest to the patient's discharge from the hospital. The mobility ratings were, however, a description of actual movement, not an interference about emotions.[7]

In summary, these five studies consistently show that observers can accurately judge emotions shown in spontaneous facial behavior, in the sense that their judgments agreed with the emotion expected by virtue of the nature of the eliciting circumstance. This set of studies is particularly important because it establishes that accuracy has generality across persons judged and across time. Through the use of representative sampling of stimulus persons and behaviors, these experiments refute the argument, raised in connection with the candid photograph experiments, that perhaps accuracy is possible for only the rare stimulus person or the rare moment in time.

[7]Whereas in both of these studies on depressive patients the body and the face were shown in the photographs, there is little likelihood that the observers' judgments of pleasantness could have been based on body cues rather than facial behavior because in other experiments Ekman and Friesen (1965b, 1967a) found that observers could not agree in pleasantness judgments when they were restricted to viewing just the body in still photographs.

The major limitation in these experiments is that the emotion judged was general rather than specific. Accuracy has been shown only for the distinction between positive and negative emotional states, not for any of the distinctions within those groupings, such as happiness, interest, anger, fear, and disgust. The next set of experiments to be explored provides evidence on just this point, showing that accurate judgments are possible for specific emotions. However, we shall no longer be dealing with spontaneous behavior, but with posed behavior, and must evaluate the problem of the relevance of posed to spontaneous facial behavior.

Accuracy in the judgment of posed behavior

Why consider posed facial behavior in a discussion of accuracy? One answer is that there *is* an accuracy question: can an observer viewing a pose accurately judge the emotion intended by the poser? If, however, posing is a very special or unique eliciting circumstance, then establishing accuracy in the judgment of poses has little bearing on whether spontaneous facial behavior provides accurate information (see the discussion of posing in Sections 1.2 and 2.2). This issue will be addressed after we direct our attention to the set of experiments to be discussed next.

Whereas most investigators of the judgment of emotion from facial behavior have employed posed photographs as their stimuli, only a few presented their data in a manner that allows examination of whether the observers accurately judged the emotion intended by the poser.[8] Most of these studies have methodological problems, many of which can be resolved by considering the findings across all of the experiments.

Table 4.4 shows both the methodological features and the results of the eight experiments having as their focus, at least in part, accuracy in the judgment of posed emotions. In the early experiments, the sample both of stimulus persons and of stimuli for each emotion was small; but, as the table shows, these problems were resolved in some of the later studies. Most of the studies used still photographs; three studies used live behavior, a kind of stimulus introducing potential problems (see section 2.7). However, in two studies (Levitt and Kozell & Gitter), rec-

[8]Frijda (1953) performed an accuracy study, but it will not be reported because he utilized an admittedly subjective rating of whether the observers had successfully judged the emotions intended or experienced by the two stimulus persons. With both the still photograph and motion picture film presentations, Frijda concluded that he had demonstrated accurate judgments of emotion.

Table 4.4. Methodology and results of nine accuracy studies of posed behavior

	Kanner (1931)	Woodworth (1938) / Feleky (1914)	Dusenbury & Knower (1938)	D. F. Thompson & Meltzer (1964)	Levitt (1964)	Osgood (1966)	Drag & Shaw (1967)	Kozel & Gitter (1968)	Ekman & Fiesen (1965)
Methodology									
Number of stimulus persons	1	1	2	50	50	50 or 5[a]	48	10	6
Number of stimuli for each emotion	1–3	2	2	100	50	5	10	5	2
Method of presenting stimuli	Still	Still	Still	Live	Motion picture film	Live	Live	Motion picture film	Still
Number of observers	409	100	388	4	24	110	4	44	57
Number of judgement categories other than those listed below	[b]	1	5	2	0	6	3	1	3
Percentage of accurate judgments on:									
happy	—	93	100	76	86	55	71	86	65
surprise	76	77	86	—	43	38	68	69	—
fear	75	66	93	74	58	16	62	80	35
anger	32	31	92	60	62	39	42	79	—
sad	33	70	84	52	—	19	49	59	88
disgust/contempt	66	74	91	67	45	50	41	55	0
pleasantness factor	—	—	—	—	—	0.38[c]	—	—	—
intensity factor	—	—	—	—	—	0.32[c]	—	—	—
control factor	—	—	—	—	—	0.50[c]	—	-	—

[a]See text discussion on Table 3.2.

[b]Kanner allowed free labeling; in reanalyzing his results, many of his responses, which were not obviously in one of the categories, were not verified.

[c]These are correlations between intended emotion and observed emotion when the emotion word data were reordered in terms of factor

ords of sequential behavior (motion picture film) were used, and because their results are broadly comparable to the others, the finding of accuracy is not limited to still photographs. Though earlier studies used only professional actors and only a selected sample of the presumably best photographs of them, all but one of the studies since 1938 used untrained posers, and all but one of the studies presented all poses, not just the best attempts. (Both exceptions were in the Kozel & Gitter experiment.) Thus, the findings can be said to have generality across a large number of persons and to a broader range of behavior than might be represented by a preselected photograph of the possibly rare moment when a good pose was emitted. The number of observers is adequate, except in the Thompson and Meltzer and Drag and Shaw studies, the findings of which are substantially the same as those of the other experiments.

Before considering the results shown in Table 4.4, a few words of explanation are necessary about particular experiments. (1) Both Kanner's and Woodworth's data are based on judgments of the Feleky posed photographs; and Woodworth's findings are a reanalysis of Feleky's data. (2) Drag and Shaw found significant differences in observer accuracy depending on whether the male or female posers were judged.[9] But even the most poorly judged group (men) was judged with better than chance accuracy. In the table, we combine data for male and female stimulus persons. (3) The Ekman and Friesen (1965a) study falls somewhere between posed and spontaneous behavior. Psychiatric patients were asked to show a camera how they were feeling. The patients did not simulate a specified unfelt emotion as in all of the other studies described in the table. On the other hand, their facial behavior cannot be taken as spontaneous because it was occasioned by the investigator's request. Ekman and Friesen asked the patients to describe their feelings in their own words after they had shown their facial expression. Depressive patients were asked to engage in this task upon admission to the hospital and again at discharge as it was expected that they would have different feelings at these two points. The still photographs taken at these two times were shown to observers who did not know that the pictures were of psychiatric patients. The observers utilized the emotion

[9]There have been a few more recent studies that have attempted to isolate some of the variables associated with whether an individual is a well understood or poorly understood emotion poser. The race and sex of the poser have been found to interact with the emotion posed and the race and sex of the observer (Black, 1969; Gitter & Black, 1968; Kozel, 1969), and personality measures and skin conductance have been found related to posing (Buck et al., 1969). These issues will be considered along with other studies in Chapter 8.

category system proposed by Tomkins (see Table 3.2) to record their judgments of the emotions shown in the photographs. The accuracy criterion was conformity between observer judgment and patient self-description.

The results of each experiment reported in Table 4.4 were reanalyzed in terms of the emotion categories proposed earlier (Table 3.2) to facilitate comparison across experiments. Kanner had subjectively scored his observers' free emotion labels and judgments of the situation; these data were not used; instead his published raw data were analyzed to provide the results shown in the table. Woodworth himself recast Feleky's data, which we then further modified in terms of the seven emotion categories.

Do these studies show that observers can accurately judge the emotions intended by the posers? Generally, looking across emotions and across experiments, the answer is yes.[10] All of the percentages listed are the modal, or most frequent, response to the intended emotion. In all but a few instances the poser's intended emotion was the emotion most frequently perceived by the observers. Although the results are far from perfect for any single emotion category across experiments or for any single experiment across categories, there is certainly more correspondence between intended and judged emotion across these data than might be expected by chance.

It has been customary to dismiss accurate judgments of posed behavior as by and large irrelevant to the question of whether facial behavior is systematically related to emotion and, more specifically, to the study of spontaneous behavior. As we described earlier (Section 1.2), the argument (see Hunt, 1941; Landis, 1924) has been that posed behavior is a specialized, language like set of conventions or stereotypes, which might conceivably be understood, but that, by definition, such behavior is different from what the face actually does when emotion is spontaneously aroused. As we mentioned in our discussion of eliciting circumstances (Section 2.3), the only direct study of the differences in the components of posed and spontaneous facial behavior was the dubious experiment by Landis, who failed to find any relationship between the face and emotion for either kind of eliciting circumstance.

---

[10]For all the experiments except those of Levitt and Osgood, there were more emotion categories in the original data than those listed in Table 4.4. Therefore our estimate of accuracy is low in that the percentages were calculated by dividing the number of correct responses by the total responses to the stimulus including unlisted categories rather than by dividing by the total number of responses that fit into the six categories used by all these authors.

Indirectly, however, there is considerable evidence that posed behavior is not a specialized, languagelike set of conventions unrelated to real emotional behavior. If it were not in some way reflective of emotion, posed behavior in one culture would not be understood by people from different cultures. Later, in exploring cross-cultural studies (Chapter 7), we shall review a large body of data from a number of experiments in which the posed facial behavior of Westerners was judged as the same emotion by members of 13 literate cultures and one preliterate culture and one experiment in which the poses by members of a preliterate culture were accurately judged by members of a literate culture. For these findings to emerge, the behaviors occurring during posing must have developed in the same way across cultures. One reasonable explanation of such development would be that they are in some way based on the repertoire of spontaneous facial behaviors associated with emotion.

We believe that when an investigator asks a poser for an emotion there is an implicit request that the person show an extreme, uncontrolled version of the emotion. When the investigator asks for a pose of anger, the subject typically will imagine and try to show extreme anger and will not attempt to deintensify, mask, or neutralize facial appearances. If the investigator were to ask him to pose an emotion by specifying a low-intensity word, such as annoyance, then the subject would attempt to show facial behavior appropriate to moderate or low-intensity emotion. It would also be possible to ask the subject to show the facial behavior that would occur if a display rule were operating; e.g., anger at a superior in a situation in which the poser could not directly manifest anger. With such an instruction, posing might well yield facial behavior that is quite similar to much spontaneous conversational behavior where display rules for the management and control of facial appearance are operative.

If we are correct in our speculation about how the subject typically interprets the posing instruction (viz., as an occasion to display an uncontrolled version of the emotion), then the obtained poses are not dissimilar from all spontaneous behavior but approximate only that spontaneous facial behavior that occurs when a person is not applying display rules to deintensify, mask, or neutralize. However, poses of extreme, uncontrolled emotion may still differ from spontaneous, unmodulated, high-intensity emotion in duration and in complexity of muscle use.

Grouping the results from a number of experiments allows the conclusion that posed facial behavior can be accurately judged, in that the majority of the observers will correctly identify the intended emotion. This result is not limited to expert posers, to the best moments in the posing situation, or to still-photographic representations of posing. The results are limited, however, to the six emotion categories considered. Conceivably, further studies might achieve accurate judgments of poses of other emotions.

Summary on the accuracy of judgments

At the outset of this section, we quoted Bruner and Tagiuri's listing of studies that produced negative and positive evidence on accurate judgments of emotion. Most of the negative studies they cited were irrelevant to the question of accuracy because those studies utilized drawings rather than real behavior, thus providing only the artist's conception of emotion as the basis for determining correct judgments. The remaining two negative studies on accuracy, those of Landis and of Sherman, were thoroughly criticized, and contradictory findings from other studies were presented to support our contention that these two experiments henceforth should be disregarded.

Contrary to the impression conveyed by previous reviews of the literature that the evidence in the field is contradictory and confusing, our reanalysis showed consistent evidence of accurate judgments of emotion from facial behavior. Without question, the evidence based on posed behavior is far stronger than that based on spontaneous behavior, where a fully adequate study remains to be done. Such a study is needed in order to show accuracy in the judgment of specific emotions in addition to the judgment of positive and negative state. There is a need for further study of accurate judgments among the different negative emotions in spontaneous facial behavior, but it seems unnecessary to continue to question whether accurate judgments are possible. More useful research would determine under what conditions, for what kinds of people, in what kinds of roles and social settings, and with what types of accuracy criteria facial behavior provides correct information about emotion; and, conversely, research would also determine in what kinds of settings and roles and for what kinds of people facial behavior provides either no information or misinformation.

As we mentioned at the beginning of this chapter, there are two research approaches to the question of whether the face can provide accurate information about emotion. Thus far we have considered in this chapter only studies that use the judgment approach, determining whether observers can make accurate inferences about emotion from viewing facial behavior. The success of such studies makes the other approach, the measurement of facial components, very important because the judgment studies can only tell us that the information is there, somewhere in the face, and capable of being interpreted accurately by observers. The judgment approach cannot tell us what facial behaviors are providing this accurate information, what particular muscular movements or wrinkles in the face allow the observer to determine that an individual is in a stressful rather than a cathartic part of an interview, or how to distinguish when an individual is posing anger rather than disgust. To resolve these problems and to specify just which facial behaviors are distinctively related to which emotions, we must consider the second approach to the study of accuracy and measurement of facial components and this will be the subject of the next section.

4.2. Can measurement of facial behavior provide accurate information?

In component studies, facial behavior is the dependent variable, or response measure, rather than the independent variable, or stimulus, as it is in judgment studies. We do not attempt to determine what observers can say about faces but what the measurement of facial components can indicate about some aspect of a person's experience. In a component study, we might ask, for example, "What components of facial behavior differentiate among faces sampled when the subject was afraid and those sampled when the subject was disgusted?" In a judgment study, we might ask, "Can observers tell when looking at a face whether the subject was afraid or disgusted?" (the difference between component studies and judgment studies was reviewed earlier; see Section 2.1).

There have been remarkably few component studies. The scarcity of research is not due to the difficulty in establishing independent variables, that is, eliciting circumstances in which to sample facial behavior with some criterion of how the person feels, because these difficulties are also encountered with judgment studies, of which there have been many. It is probably due to the difficulty in deciding what to measure in the face. Today there is still no accepted notion of the units of facial behavior nor any general procedure for measuring or scoring facial components. (This may soon be changing; see Chapter 9.) Investigators have improvised their own techniques, rarely using techniques tried by others and almost invariably combining the facial component units into a few global scores. Progress is being made, and three measurement procedures have been developed, and there is some evidence to support the validity of one of them.

Tables 4.5 and 4.6 summarize the methodological features and findings from seven studies.[11] All obtained positive results, but each has shortcomings in either interpretation or generalization of the results. In the Landis and Hunt (1939) study, strong evidence of a specific facial response to a startling stimulus was detected. However, the facial responses documented for reactions to a sudden noise (a pistol shot) do not resemble the stimuli that observers customarily judged as showing surprise. The startle facial reaction was extremely brief, followed by a secondary reaction, presumably an emotion about the initial startle, which varied across subjects; Landis and Hunt did not determine whether this secondary reaction had systematic properties related to the subjects' reported feelings or to manipulations in the setting, which might have caused the sudden noise to be associated with fear, interest, or anger.

Trujillo and Warthin's (1968) finding that ulcer patients have more vertical creases in their brow when asked to frown than have other medical patients may or may not be relevant to emotion. They cite Darwin's (1872) and Bell's (1847) notion that the permanent creases in the face result from the most frequently experienced emotions and, on that basis, suggest their findings have relevance to emotion. However, they acknowledge that they did not control for chronic pain, which is not considered to be an emotion by most authors, although there is evidence (Boucher, 1969) that it does have some distinctive facial components. Their findings, even if relevant to emotion, are too general to be useful, because vertical creases in the brow can be found with anger, fear, or sadness, and they did not examine other facial components that might further distinguish among these emotions.

Leventhal and Sharp's (1965) findings are open to similar questions about whether facial components of pain or of some specific emotion during childbirth are responsible for their results. They use Tomkins's term *distress* to describe the emotion they studied. Earlier (in Section 3.1),

---

[11]Landis also conducted a component study on the same materials he showed to observers and failed to find any components related to his eliciting circumstances or the subjects' self-reports. His results will not be discussed, both for the reasons already outlined (Chapter 4), which raise serious doubts about his study, and because of two additional problems relevant to his components analysis. In computing the participation of the various muscles, he included pictures taken before and after the actual eliciting stimuli; to what extent the ubiquitous nervous smile he refers to is a function of including one "expectancy" situation (the before-elicitation pictures) with every situation cannot be gauged. Also, in analyzing his data, Landis used a technique that was both extremely conservative (Frois-Wittmann) and inappropriate for the problem (Davis).

Table 4.5. *Methodology and results of four component studies of facial behavior*

	Landis & Hunt (1939)	Trujillo & Warthin (1968)	J. Thompson (1941)	Fulcher (1942)
Methodology Eliciting circumstances	Experimental presentation of sudden, intense stimuli (primarily .22 pistol shot)	Chronic duodenal ulcer	Naturally occurring activities; a few stimuli introduced; emotion inferred from context	Instruction to pose different emotions
Emotions sampled	Startle	Not specified as emotion	Laughter, smiling, crying (also isolated inferences of fear and anger)	Anger, fear, happiness, sadness
Number and type of subjects	Normals; also infants, animals, psychotics, epileptics, deaf persons, patients with neurological disorders, subject injected with adrenalin, hypnotized subjects	126 ulcer paitents, 274 patients with other medical disorders	29 Seeing children, 7 weeks–13 years; 26 blind children 7 weeks–13 years	118 Seeing children, 4–16 years; 50 blind children, 6–21 years
Type of facial components measured	Eyeblink, widening of mouth, forward movement of head	Number of vertical folds between eyebrows	Three-point scale: some/much/no involvement of	Six-point scale: amount of movement; six-point scale: amount of distortion (eye and mouth separately); Yes–no judgement of involvement of 18 muscles; six-point "adequacy" scale.
Results	Strength of response varies directly with intensity and suddenness of stimulus. Some facial response (minimally eyeblink) *always* elicited by stimulus of sufficient strength except in epileptics. Primary stimulus of sufficient pattern shows very little variation; secondary responses vary across subjects	Three or more vertical folds in 85% of ulcer patients as compared with only 6% of control patients when asked to frown	Pattern of muscular activity same in blind and seeing for each type of emotional behavior; seeing subjects show more uniformity of pattern	More facial activity in seeing subjects; blind subjects show same general patterns but less differentiation among emotions

Table 4.6. *Methodology and results of three component studies of facial behavior*

	Leventahl & Sharp (1965)	Rubenstein (1969)	Ekman & Friesen (1972)
Methodology			
Eliciting circumstances	Prechildbirth labor, total time in labor divided into four intervals	Depressed patients asked to smile before shock treatment and 1 hour after treatment; control group of nonpatients tested twice	Each subject watched a neutral travelogue and a stress-inducing film of sinus surgery
Emotions sampled	Distress	Happiness	The self-report of the subjects showed that the emotion experienced in the neutral film was slight happiness and in stress film was interest, surprise, fear, pain, disgust, and sadness
Number and type of subjects	52 Women with prior childbirth experience; 19 women with no prior childbirth experience (55 subjects returned Welch anxiety scale and were divided into high/low anxious by median split).	17 depressive patients; 16 control subjects	25 college students
Type of facial components measured	Forehead: 4 behaviors, 2 index[a] Brow: 8 behaviors, 3 indexes Eyelids: 6 behaviors, 2 indexes Nose: 5 behaviors Eyes: 12 behaviors, 2 indexes Mouth: 36 behaviors, 3 indexes Score: frequency of behavior during 5-minute observation interval	Amount of development of facial muscles derived from obtaining a series of profile shots taken rapidly on motion picture film within a facial expression	Facial Affect Scoring Technique measured the presence of fear, anger, surprise, disgust, sadness, happiness: Brow: 8 behaviors Eyes: 17 behaviors Lower face: 45 behaviors
Results	Forehead, brow, eyelid indexes show increased discomfort (wrinkles, movement) as labor progresses; other facial indicators insignificant	More displacement of facial muscles during smile following shock treatment than before; no change from pre- to post treatment in the control subjects	More surprise, sadness, disgust, anger in stress than neutral; more happiness in neutral than stress stituation

[a] Indexes of comfort, discomfort (major, minor, or unspecified), change, created by grouping individual behavior measures

we pointed out that the term is problematic in that it can refer either to sadness–grief or to pain–hurt–suffering. Their discomfort indexes, built from scores on the eyebrows, forehead, and eyelids, may well have measured either pain or sadness or both. Their study is noteworthy, however, in that their facial behavior measures were related not only to the severity of labor but to the number of previous births and anxiety.

Both Fulcher (1942) and J. Thompson (1941) analyzed their results primarily by comparing blind and sighted children. They reported their data in a way that makes it difficult to determine what the precise differences in the facial components were for each emotion they studied within either sample of children, yet they both reported more extensive lists than most other investigators of facial components, which they hypothesized as distinctive for each emotion. Thompson's results on smiling, laughing, and crying showed similarities in the distinctive movements of the facial components for each of these reactions for her blind and sighted subjects. Less information is provided about anger and sadness, although she said they also had distinctive facial components in both blind and sighted children. Fulcher's study of the posed emotions of blind and sighted children provides information on a wider sampling of emotions and with more information about the distinctive components for each emotion, but not in sufficient detail to check his hypotheses about whether the components of facial behavior are distinctive for each emotion posed. His findings do suggest that facial components unique to each posed emotion could be isolated and measured. For new studies on this question utilizing posing procedures with sighted adults or children see Section 8.2.

Rubenstein's (1969) procedure for measuring facial components is novel but quite cumbersome. A 16-mm motion picture camera was rotated around the subject's face rapidly, acquiring a series of profile frames during a facial expression. His method of recording requires, however, that the subject freeze an expression for at least 5 seconds while the camera travels around the face and that the subject be in a rather immobilized position. This procedure is not only questionable in terms of its applicability to spontaneously occurring facial behavior, but the subjects are constantly made aware that their facial behavior is of interest. His finding, that depressive patients smile more broadly when asked to do so after shock treatment than before, does demonstrate that his measurement procedure works, but it adds little information about the facial components.

The most elaborate and complex study is the experiment by Ekman and Friesen (Ekman, 1972, 1973; Friesen, 1972) listed in Table 4.6. We shall report this experiment in some detail because of its complexity, the import of the findings, and the relevance of the methods and results to our discussion in two later sections, 5.2 and 7.2.

In conjunction with Averill, Opton, and Lazarus, Ekman and his associates collected records of the facial behavior, skin resistance, heart rate, and self-reported emotion of subjects in the United States and Japan, as they watched a neutral and a stress film. We shall discuss here only their findings on the facial behavior of the American subjects; in Chapter 7 we shall discuss the cross-cultural comparison with the Japanese subjects.

In this study a new tool for measuring facial behavior was utilized, viz., Ekman, Friesen, and Tomkins's Facial Affect Scoring Technique (FAST). The derivation of this technique and the details of its use are reported elsewhere (Ekman, Friesen, & Tomkins, 1971), but it will be necessary to provide some information about how the scoring procedure was used in order to explain the findings and convey something about the comprehensiveness of this measurement system. We shall first describe the use of FAST and then the experiment in which it was used, explaining the results listed in Table 4.6.

The Facial Affect Scoring Technique requires scoring of each observable movement in each of three areas of the face: (1) brows/forehead area; (2) eyes/lids; (3) lower face, including cheeks, nose, mouth, and chin. Rather than defining each scoring category in words, FAST employs photographic examples to define each of the movements within each area of the face that, theoretically, distinguish among six emotions: happiness, sadness, surprise, fear, anger, and disgust. For example, instead of describing a movement as "the action of the frontalis muscle which leads to raising of both brows in a somewhat curved shape, with horizontal wrinkles across the forehead," FAST utilizes a picture of just that area of the face in that particular position to define that scoring item. Figure 4.1 shows as an example the items across the facial areas considered to be relevant to surprise.

The FAST system is applied by having independent coders view each of the three areas of the face separately, with the rest of the face blocked from view. It should be emphasized that the FAST measurement procedure does not entail having the coders judge the emotion shown in the face they are coding. Rather, each movement within a facial area is distinguished, its exact duration determined with the aid of slowed motion, and the type of movement classified by comparing the movement observed with the atlas of FAST criterion photographs. If, for example, the coder is looking at the brows/forehead and sees a particular

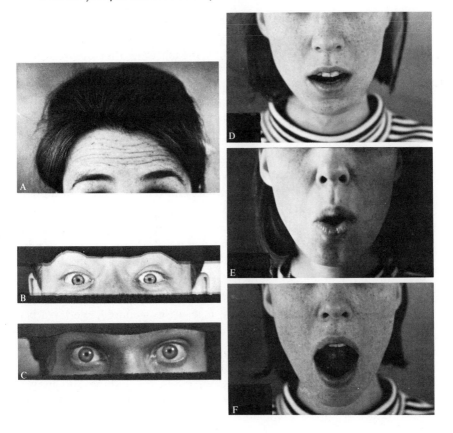

Figure 4.1 Examples of criterion items from the Facial Affect Scoring Technique (FAST) showing the brow/forehead (A), the eyes/lids (B and C), and the lower face items (D–F) for surprise.

movement in that area of the face, he compares the movement with the eight photographs of brow/forehead movements in the FAST atlas and assigns to it the FAST atlas number of the criterion picture it most closely resembles. In addition to those for the brows, there are 17 criterion photographs of eyes/lids, and 45 criterion photographs of the lower face in the FAST atlas.

Once the coders' scoring is complete, formulas are used to derive the emotion prediction for each facial movement, taking into account the scoring of more than one independent coder. For example, if the facial movement is coded by more than one coder as most closely resembling the FAST brow/forehead picture B9 (shown in Fig. 4.1), then that movement is labeled surprise. The output of the scoring system is a series of duration scores for anger, fear, surprise, sadness, disgust, and happiness for the brows/forehead, the eyes/lids, and the lower face.

Data analysis can be performed by measuring either the *frequency* of occurrence of each emotion within each facial area or the *duration* of each emotion within each facial area. The frequence or duration scores can be analyzed separately for each of the three facial areas or emotion scores for the total face can be obtained by utilizing another formula, which combines the scores for emotions shown across the face into a total face score for a single emotion or a blend of emotions. In the results reported in Table 4.6, total face scores were calculated only for a movement occurring at least two of the three facial areas and only for single emotions.

With a scoring system such as FAST, a system intended to measure facial behavior and which distinguishes among six emotions, the question must be raised as to whether or not it is valid. There are two types of validity, which we may call *personal* validity and *social* validity. In the next chapter we shall present the results of a study of FAST's social validity – whether measures of facial behavior can predict how people will judge the emotion shown in a face. In this chapter we have been discussing personal validity – whether measures of facial behavior can provide accurate information about the person, that is, about some aspect of his emotional experience or circumstance.

Let us turn now to the question asked in the Ekman and Friesen, experiment: Can the measurement of facial behavior accurately distinguish whether subjects watched a stressful or a neutral motion picture film?

In the data pool collected jointly by Ekman and his associates and by Averill, Opton, and Lazarus, each subject had been seated alone, watched first a film of autumn leaves and then a 3-minute stress-inducing film of sinus surgery. Unknown to the subjects, a videotape record was made of their facial behavior. Subsequently, the subjects answered a questionnaire about their emotional experience during the stress film. The FAST scoring system was applied to every observable movement in each of the three areas of the face for the 25 American subjects; approximately 3 minutes of their facial behavior during the neutral film and 3 minutes during the stress film were scored.

The results reveal an enormous difference in the facial behavior shown in these two eliciting circumstances. The total face scores, the scores for each of the separate facial areas, the scores based on frequency, and the scores based on duration all indicate that there was more behavior that FAST measured as surprise, sadness, disgust, and anger shown during the stress film and more behavior that FAST measured as happiness shown during the neutral film.

This study shows that measurement of facial behavior accurately discriminates between two eliciting circumstances, watching a neutral and a stress film. It is important to note that this difference between facial behavior shown in two different eliciting circumstances was obtained with a measurement system designed to measure six different emotions rather than being limited to the occurrence of one or two emotions or to the distinction between positive and negative feelings.

The experiment was not designed to provide evidence that FAST can accurately indicate each of the six emotions it was designed to measure. The only accuracy criterion available is the two film conditions, stress and neutral. Although self-reports were gathered, they are a poor accuracy criterion in this experiment because, although the stress film appears to have elicited different emotions in each subject, the self-report did not provide any information about the sequence of emotions experienced and the self-report data were gathered some time after the experience. What is required is a self-report on the felt emotion obtained immediately after a particular facial behavior occurs.

There are two other sources of information that imply that FAST does succeed in accurately differentiating particular emotions. The first, which we shall discuss in Chapter 7, is the high correlations between the specific emotions shown by American and Japanese subjects as measured by FAST. Although it cannot be said from those findings that FAST accurately measured each emotion, it can be said that FAST differentiated types of facial behavior and that these different types of facial behavior occurred with the same frequency in subjects from two different cultures who were placed in the same eliciting circumstances. For example, even though we cannot conclude that there is evidence that the FAST scores for disgust do actually measure disgust and those for surprise do actually measure surprise, it is encouraging that the FAST measurements show the same ratio of disgust to surprise behavior across members of two cultures subjected to the same eliciting circumstance.

The second piece of evidence that suggests that FAST can accurately measure specific emotions comes from a study to be outlined in the next chapter on the social validity of FAST. In that experiment, FAST scores accurately forecasted the specific emotions judged by those who simply observed the face.

One reason why we have described Ekman and Friesen's experiment at some length is because of the importance, in our view, of research that directly measures facial components. There has been too little of such research. Although judgment studies in which observers tell us their impressions about a face can be quite informative, they cannot provide knowledge about the specific facial behaviors relative to specific emotions, and many of the questions that need to be answered about the face and emotion cannot be approached solely through the use of judges. Most investigators have avoided direct measurement of facial components, and the few who did measure facial behavior, discussed earlier in this chapter, did not offer a general tool for measuring the occurrence of a number of different emotions. Ekman, Friesen, and Tomkins's FAST is intended as a general-purpose tool to measure the occurrence of six different emotions and blends of these six. Chapter 9 reports on a new technique for directly measuring facial behavior, which has been developed by Ekman and Friesen.

Two other scoring systems for measuring facial behavior have been developed by investigators following an ethological approach, Blurton-Jones (1969) and Grant (1969). Neither has yet performed any validity studies. All three systems, FAST and those developed by Blurton-Jones and Grant, have considerable overlap, although they differ in a number of regards. The FAST system is based on theory, attempting to specify only those facial behaviors that can distinguish one emotion from another, and the other two systems have attempted inductively to derive a descriptive system to cover all facial behavior observed in their samples of adults or children. The scoring items are depicted in terms of a photographic atlas in FAST, whereas the other two systems utilize a verbal description of particular muscular movements and wrinkles. The appearance of these three scoring systems is an exciting development, offering investigators a choice where there previously was none for measuring the face.

Summary on accuracy of measurements of facial behavior

The few studies on components of facial behavior are encouraging, suggesting that accurate information about some aspect of a person's experience (whether it be response to a gunshot, to childbirth, to a stress-inducing film) can be derived from measures of facial components; but much more work is needed to supply a definitive answer as to whether measurements of the face can provide accurate information about specific emotions. The evidence to date is limited to showing that accurate information about the distinction between positive and negative emotional reactions can be obtained from measurements of the face. (Accuracy is considered again in the review of studies from 1970 to 1977 in Chapter 8, Section 8.4. Unfortunately, not much progress has been made to answer the questions raised here.)

We believe this is one of the most crucial areas for further research and that the ability to measure the face directly, rather than solely relying on observers' global judgments, will be the key to a breakthrough in the next generation of questions about the face and emotion. (Chapter 9 critically reviews a number of new facial measurement procedures. See also, Chapter 8, Section 8.3.)

5. What components of facial behavior are related to observers' judgments of emotion?

PAUL EKMAN, WALLACE V. FRIESEN,
AND PHOEBE ELLSWORTH

Studies designed to determine what facial components provide the observer with information about emotion differ from those reviewed in the last half of Chapter 4. Whereas those relate facial measurements to some accuracy criterion, these relate measurements to the observer's judgment of emotion, regardless of whether the judgment is correct. That is to say, rather than relating facial components to some aspect of the experience of the person who showed the facial behavior, here we relate facial measurements to the observers' interpretations of the stimulus person's face. Although our discussion is limited to the judgment of emotion, this is more broadly a question of person perception. What connections are there between a person's particular physical aspects (various facial components) and the perceiver's impressions of that person (judgment of emotion)?

The major obstacle to all research on facial components, regardless of whether such measurements are related to accuracy or to observers' judgments, is the problem of determining just what aspect of facial behavior should be measured. What are the size and number of the component units, and how can they be quantified? In most of the studies relating components to observers' judgments, this difficult issue has been bypassed. The investigators did not directly measure facial components but, instead, limited the area of the face that the observer could see. Inferences about the importance of facial components (e.g., horizontal wrinkles) within particular areas (e.g., forehead) were made by comparing judgments made from one facial area with judgments made from another. We shall consider these studies of facial areas first and then discuss the few studies that directly measured facial components.

5.1. Judgment as a function of facial area observed

In all but one of the seven studies we shall examine in this section, the judgments of observers who saw only part of the face were compared with the judgments of observers who saw either another part of the face or the whole face. A question asked in such studies is whether a specific emotion (e.g., happiness) or even all emotions might be better judged from one facial area than from another? Even when successful, such studies do not provide information about the particular facial components relevant to the judgment of a particular emotion, but they do delimit the location of such components. The most popular division of facial areas has been the top (including the eyes) from the bottom. In a few studies, three or four divisions have been made, and Frois-Wittmann was the first to note that anatomical possibilities for independent movements of the facial muscles argue against a simple dichotomy of facial areas.

All of the experiments suffer from severe methodological handicaps. No study had a sufficient sampling of stimulus persons, of behaviors of each person, of eliciting circumstances, or of emotions to justify any conclusions; and each study utilized somewhat different judgment tasks and methods for presenting stimuli. We shall not provide any tables summarizing methods and results because our inspection and reanalysis of the data did not suggest interpretations different from the authors', and considering results across the set of seven does not resolve methodological problems or suggest any common findings. Two authors discovered evidence for the superiority of the mouth area (Ruckmick and Dunlap), two found evidence of no reliable differences between facial areas (Frois-Wittmann and Coleman), and three provided evidence that the importance of facial area depended on the particular emotion judged (Hanawalt, Nummenmaa, and Plutchik).

Ruckmick (1921) performed the first study in which observers saw either the top or bottom half of the face. Posed facial behavior of one stimulus person was employed, and the judgments of the bottom half of the face were found to be more similar to the judgments of the full face than were judgments of the top half. The data were not reported, so it is not possible to verify these results. Dunlap (1927) reported similar findings. He sampled facial behavior in laboratory situations similar to those used by Landis. Observers were given four photographs at once, two of which were composites of the top and bottom halves of the other two.

The observers' task was to select the original that most resembled each composite. Dunlap found that the bottom half of the face dominated in the sense that the composites were usually judged as most similar to the original sharing the same bottom. But, acknowledging that his eliciting circumstances were not completely successful, many of his photographs were of poor quality, and the composites were difficult to make, he restricted his conclusion to the importance of the mouth as a clue for the judgment of happiness.

Frois-Wittmann (1930) showed the top of the face to one group of observers and the mouth area, excluding the nose and cheeks, to another. Both groups were told to choose a single word from a list of 43 emotion terms. The stimuli were posed photographs of himself and drawings made from these photographs. Comparing judgments of the whole face with those of the top or mouth, he concluded that there was "no consistent dominance of either eyes or mouth in the determination of the judged expressions of the face." Coleman (1949), utilizing quite different eliciting circumstances, came to the same conclusion. The stimuli were motion picture films of two subjects' facial behavior during eight spontaneous situations similar to those employed by Landis and Dunlap and of the subsequent posed behavior of remembered reactions to the eight situations. Observers saw the top, bottom, and whole face, with the judgment task requiring that they select the correct eliciting circumstance from a list. Coleman concluded, "In general, identifications of the facial expressions of emotion were not made more reliably from either the mouth region or eye region. The identifiability of a specific facial expression of emotion was found to be dependent upon the subject, the facial region viewed, and whether or not the expression was acted or natural."

Hanawalt (1944) compared observers' judgments of emotion from top, bottom, or whole face versions of candid magazine photographs and of Ruckmick's posed faces. His evidence on judge agreement suggested that the area of the face most likely to elicit judgments similar to those for the whole face depends on the emotion. For both his candid and posed pictures, the bottom of the face was better judged than the top on happiness, and the top was better judged on surprise, anger and fear; the results on sadness were equivocal. His results, like those of Coleman and Frois-Wittmann, did show marked differences among areas of the face for particular stimuli.

Nummenmaa's (1964) findings partly contradicted Hanawalt's. Nummenmaa had an actor attempt to pose three "pure" emotions (hap-

piness, surprise, and anger) and blends of each of the pair combinations. Different groups of observers were shown the forehead, the eyes,
the nose, or the mouth and were asked to judge the presence of a single
emotion, any of the emotion pair blends, or the blend of all three.
Because there were only two stimuli for each of the intended emotions,
"pure" or blend, of only one actor, the results must be treated with
considerable caution. Inspection of the stimuli themselves suggests to us
that this actor was rather atypical in not utilizing brow/forehead movements.

High agreement (70%) for happiness was obtained with the eyes and
nose but not the mouth or brow. This contradicts Hanawalt's and Dunlap's
findings on the mouth, but because they treated the mouth as part of the
bottom of the face and Nummenmaa separated the mouth from the
nose, the difference in results is difficult to explain. High agreement
(97%) on surprise was found only for the mouth, contradicting Hanawalt's
findings for the top half of the face. Anger was judged with high agreement both on the eyes (67%) and on the mouth (73%). The presence of
blends was judged with moderate agreement (between 40 to 56% with a
choice among seven categories) from each area of the face, for at least
one of his stimuli. However, often the stimulus judged as a blend when
seen in a whole-face version was judged as either of the two separate
emotions involved in the blend when the separate areas were seen.
Nummenmaa interpreted his findings as showing that the eyes were the
only region that usually conveyed to the observers the presence of both
of the blended emotions. Considerable caution is necessary regarding
Nummenmaa's interpretation of his findings. As mentioned before, there
were only a few stimuli from the poses of only one person, who perhaps
displayed a less than usually active brow. Further, the data suggest that
for half of the intended blend stimuli, the actor failed in the sense that
less than half of the observers judged a blend when they saw the full
face. If only those stimuli are considered that did convey a blend to the
majority of the observers when the full face was seen, then there is no
difference in frequency of blend judgment as a function of the area of the
face observed. Nummenmaa's results have importance, however, in
suggesting that it may be possible to show that components of facial
behavior will differentiate not only among single emotions but also among
particular blends.

The last study to be considered can only be described generally because Plutchik (1962) provided little information about the stimuli and
only summarized the results. Two actors attempted to show all possible
movements of the face, without concern for associated emotions. Still

photographs presenting only one area of the face were shown to observers, who judged them with Plutchik's set of emotion categories. Translating his terminology into the category scheme proposed in Table 3.2, the mouth was most important for happiness, anger, and disgust; the eyes for fear and sadness; and the eyes, mouth, and forehead for surprise. In a parallel experiment, he presented the partial faces to other observers who were asked to compose a face for each emotion from the partial faces. He reports that happiness and sadness had a neutral brow/forehead; surprise, fear, and disgust had raised foreheads, and anger had a frowning forehead. In regard to the eyes, he did not report the distinctive components but noted overlaps between particular emotions: surprise and fear, disgust and anger. In regard to the mouth, sadness and anger were the most similar.

In sum, these seven studies of how observers' judgments of emotion might vary with the area of the face observed have yielded contradictory results. Every finding was contradicted by at least two other investigators. We believe this confusion is caused by an oversimplified view of how facial components might be related to emotion, based on an unwarranted assumption that different facial areas are independent and a questionable assumption that there is one movement in one facial area for each emotion.

Earlier we mentioned our impression that the area of the eyes will often reflect the action of muscles in other areas of the face: brow/forehead, nose, mouth, and cheek/nasolabial fold. This is not always the case; some eye movements do not anatomically cause changes in other areas of the face, and some movements in other areas of the face do not anatomically cause changes in the appearance of the eyes. But strictly on the basis of anatomy, completely apart from habitual linkages among movements in different muscle areas, the facial areas are not as independent as most of the studies presumed.

Perhaps more important, it seems doubtful that there is only one movement in only one area of the face for each emotion. Instead, we believe that for each emotion there may be a number of alternative movements within each facial area. Some of these alternatives may lead observers to emotion-specific judgments, some may permit them to narrow the choices to two or three emotions, with inspection of other areas further narrowing the choice.

The facial areas may differ in terms of the numbers of alternative components within each area that are relevant for each emotion. Whereas this is so for most emotions, for happiness there is just one muscle, *zygomatic major*, that produces the smile that must be involved. Interestingly, no change is registered in the brow, the forehead, or with a slight action, in the eyelid region with this muscle.

A further complication is that there are a number of facial movements within each facial area that are completely irrelevant to emotion. The face is not simply a display system for emotion. There are facial gestures (winks, sticking out the tongue, etc.) and instrumental actions (yawning) of the face that are not specific to any one or two emotions. The facial areas probably differ in terms of the ratio of possible nonaffective movements to possible affect-specific components. The brows/forehead probably have a smaller number of nonaffective movements and also of affect-specific components than the lower face. In both spontaneous and posed eliciting circumstances, there is probably considerable variability across persons and, perhaps, even within the performance of a particular person. As a consequence, alternative affect-specific components can be shown for the same emotion, and variation in the involvement of components across different facial areas can occur. For example, observers may be able to agree that a face shows anger if the brows are drawn together and lowered and the rest of the face is not active, but they may also judge a face as angry when there is activity in the lower face, such as pressing the lips firmly together, or even when an open square mouth is shown.

If our reasoning is correct, then the confusion in results can be dissipated only by a better definition of separate facial areas and by sampling a very large number of persons and stimuli. The actual specification of facial components and the correlation of these with judgments of the whole face may actually be a shorter research route than studies of judgments of different facial areas. We shall now consider those studies of facial components that support some of the hypotheses we have just made about alternative components in each facial area for each emotion.

5.2. Relationship between observers' judgments and measures of facial components

Each of the studies we shall consider in this section utilized a different procedure, asked somewhat different questions, and obtained some promising results. Frijda and Philipszoon (1963) asked whether measures of facial components would be correlated with observers' dimension judgments. Frois-Wittmann (1930) asked what facial components were unique and which were shared across emotion categories. Ekman, Friesen, and

Tomkins (1971) asked whether their coding system for scoring facial components would predict the emotion category judged by the majority of observers. All three were limited to measuring facial components in still photographs of posed behavior. Two of the three were further limited by having only one or two stimulus persons; the third, that of Ekman, Friesen, and Tomkins, had 28 stimulus persons, quite a large sample.

Frijda and Philipszoon (1963) had 30 whole-faced photographs of an actress judged by 12 observers on 27 bipolar scales. Frijda (1969) had 48 photographs of another actress (Marjorie Lightfoot) judged by an unreported number of observers on 28 bipolar scales. Factor analysis of these ratings yielded roughly the same five factors for both stimulus persons. The photographs of each stimulus person were scored on 29 facial components by three to five persons. These 29 scores were then combined into 11 global scores. Correlations were calculated between the 11 facial component scores and the 5 factor scores from the observers' judgments of each of the two stimulus persons. Each of the facial scores correlated significantly with usually just one of the five factors derived from the observers' judgments. But more than half of these correlations were found for only one of the two stimulus persons. If we consider only those that correlated significantly for both stimulus persons, the findings are as follows:

Facial component	Factor
Smiling/laughter and frowning	Pleasantness
Tension	Natural–artificial
Expressiveness, muscular activity, and mouth open/closed	Intensity
Muscular activity, eyes open/closed	Attentional activity

No facial component score was correlated for both stimulus persons with the surprise factor.

Frijda is not explicit about how he arrived at his original list of 29 facial component scores nor does he describe his criteria for combining them into his 11 composite measures. His composite measures cannot be considered an exhaustive consideration of the facial features, and he considered each of those 11 measure singly, without taking account of affect-specific combinations of facial components, as do Frois-Wittmann and Ekman et al. Therefore, his study does not permit any conclusion about how much of expressive meaning can be predicted by variations in facial components (1969).

Frois-Wittman (1930) utilized 227 stimuli, divided almost equally be-tween photographs of himself and drawings made from these photo-graphs and between whole and partial faces.[1] Unfortunately, he reported his data on the measurement of facial components in a way that does not allow determination of which results pertain to the drawings and which to the photographs, which to the whole faces and which to the partial faces. Each stimulus was judged by 15 to 120 observers, who employed a list of 43 emotion terms. (We have reorganized his judgment data into the six categories of emotion proposed in Table 3.2.) Each stimulus was also scored for the absence or presence of 22 facial components; (he did not report his basis for choosing those facial units). Table 5.1 shows the 22 facial components and indicates those components found for at least 80% of the photographs judged to represent a particular emotion cate-gory. Frois-Wittmann noted that only a few facial components were specific to only one emotion category; a number of pairs of components occurring jointly were specific to one emotion category; further, more complex permutations differentiated stimuli assigned to one emotion category from those assigned to another. He also found that the number of facial components shared by a pair of stimuli was a good indicator of the amount of judgment confusion among emotion categories. Frois-Wittmann interpreted his data as contradicting the notion that for each emotion there is but one muscular component; he concluded that "the significance of a muscular involvement is therefore not constant, but relevant to the rest of the pattern, for it is always conditioned by the influence exercised on each muscular involvement by all the muscular involvements of the face" (1930, p.141).

Drawing conclusions from Frois-Wittmann's results is difficult for the following reasons: only one stimulus person was used; the results were combined for partial and full faces, for drawings and photographs; no determination was made of whether facial components might be better related to stimuli eliciting high agreement than to those eliciting low agreement about emotion. His results have importance, however, in showing that a procedure for measuring facial components can yield relationships to observed emotion if the pattern of components across facial areas is considered. It is hard to explain why Frois-Wittmann's study has had so little influence. Though Coleman and Hanawalt each

[1]Although we have not considered results previously in which the investigator used draw-ings of the face, we have made an exception for Frois-Wittmann because the drawings were not the imaginings of an artist but direct tracing from photographs and because half of the results reported were obtained on actual photographs as well.

Table 5.1. *Frois-Wittmann's results on the muscle involvements occurring in at least 80% of the stimuli for each of six emotions*

Feature	Judged emotion[a]					
	Happy (N=22)	Surprise (N=32)	Fear (N=27)	Anger (N=32)	Sad (N=31)	Disgust (N=37)
Brow: frown or raised	—	—	Raised: 92	Frowning: 100	Frowning: 100 Raised: 83	—
Upper lid: raised or depressed	Depressed: 87	Raised: 91	Raised: 96	Raised: 100	—	—
Lower lid: wrinkled	Wrinkled: 100	—	—	Wrinkled: 93	—	Wrinkled: 86
Nostrils: pinched or dilated	Dilated: 90	—	—	Dilated: 88	—	—
Lips: open or closed	Open: 82	Open: 100	Open: 100	Open: 92	—	—
Teeth: exposed upper or lower and open or closed	—	Open: 95	Open: 96	Lower teeth exposed: 92	—	Closed: 94
Upper lip: raised, depressed, or protruding	—	—	—	—	—	Raised: 97
Lower lip: raised, depressed, or protruding	—	—	—	Depressed: 92	—	—
Corners of mouth: raised, retracted, or depressed	Raised: 82 Retracted: 94	—	—	—	Depressed: 90	—

[a]N equals the number of photographs in each emotion category.

cited his findings, they did not profit from his argument against dividing the face into top and bottom areas. Similarly, Frijda and Philipszoon apparently did not attend to Frois-Wittmann's findings suggesting the necessity to consider combinations of components rather than each component separately. Most surprising is that although his study, which found evidence that facial components were related to judgments of emotion, was done in 1930, it led to so little other research along these same lines.

Ekman, Friesen, and Tomkins's (1971) study utilized Frois-Wittmann's findings, although they pursued a somewhat different question and utilized different methods. In the last chapter, we reported their use of the Facial Affect Scoring Technique (FAST) in an accuracy study in which FAST scores successfully differentiated facial behavior shown during the watching of a stress-inducing film from facial behavior while watching a neutral film. We shall now consider their use of FAST to predict the social value of a face, i.e., what emotion observers would judge when they viewed a face. The reader is referred to the previous chapter (Section 4.2) for a description of the FAST system. Unlike Frijda's and Frois-Wittmann's use of verbal definitions Ekman and co-workers employed pictorial definitions of facial components for use in their measurement procedure.

Whole-face photographs thought likely to convey a single emotion were shown to a group of observers and were also separately scored on FAST. Eighty pictures were drawn from the photographic sets of a number of investigators and shown to 82 observers who were allowed to indicate the presence of one or two emotions from a list of six. Fifty-one of these stimuli (ten each for happiness, sadness, anger, and surprise, seven for fear, and four for disgust) met the criteria established to ensure that these stimuli conveyed only one emotion to the observers.[2] These 51 pictures included photographs of 28 different stimulus persons, at least 7 different persons for five of the six emotion categories (disgust being the exception with four), with at least one photograph from each of the sets developed by Frois-Wittmann, Frijda, Izard, Nummenmaa, Schlosberg, Tomkins, and Ekman and Friesen.

---

[2] The 80 photographs included all those that past studies had shown to elicit more than 70% observer agreement about a particular emotion category and others that had not been used in a judgment study but were anticipated, on inspection, to yield high observer agreement about a specific emotion category. The criteria for selecting single-emotion photographs were that the photograph be assigned to one emotion category by at least 70% of the observers for their first choice and that the observers recording the presence of any blend be fewer than 40%.

Each photograph was scored with the FAST procedure by masking it to reveal only one facial area and comparing it with the FAST criterion photographs for that facial area. It should be remembered that the FAST scoring system is composed of photographic examples of each facial component relevant to emotion in each of three facial areas (see Section 4.2). Three coders independently scored the 51 pictures. Each facial area received as its emotion category score the FAST criterion photograph it most closely resembled. The emotion predicted for the photograph was the emotion associated with the FAST criteria for the majority of the three facial areas; i.e., if a photograph was scored as being most similar to one of the brow/forehead FAST criterion photographs presenting components for sadness, and as being most similar to one of the eye area FAST criterion photographs representing fear, and as most similar to one of the FAST criterion mouth/nose/chin/nose photographs representing sadness, then the prediction would be that the photograph would be judged as showing sadness by the majority of the observers who saw the photograph.

Table 5.2 shows that the FAST scores predicted the observers' judgments on 44 of the 51 photographs. Perfect prediction was obtained with the surprise and anger stimuli, and there was only one error each on the sadness and happiness photographs. One incorrect prediction was made on the disgust pictures, and four on the fear pictures. Some of the errors on fear do not appear very serious; two of the incorrect predictions were that the pictures would be judged as fear–surprise blends. More complex decision rules, in place of the simple majority decision rule specifying combinations of particular components in different facial areas, were also developed for over 4,000 of the possible 11,000 combinations of FAST facial components. The use of these a priori decision rules attempted to take account of physiognomic differences, potential errors in the application of the FAST scores, and idiosyncrasies in affect display. When these more complex decision rules were applied to the FAST scores, four more photographs were correctly predicted, so that the final result was that 48 of the 51 photographs were correctly predicted.[3]

Predictions were also made from the facial components in the three facial areas separately, and these results were consistent with Frois-Wittmann's. In most instances, the predictions based on the components across the entire face were more correct than those made from

---

[3]Boucher and Ekman (1975) used the method in Section 5.1 to test the findings from this study. Showing observers just the brow, eye, or lower face region, they replicated the results shown in Table 5.2.

Table 5.2. *Ekman, Friesen, and Tomkins' FAST prediction of emotion judged by the majority of observers*

Emotion judged by majority of observers	FAST Prediction in terms of majority score across three facial areas										
	Happiness	Surprise	Anger	Sadness	Disgust	Fear	Happiness–surprise	Fear–sadness	Fear–surprise	Sadness–surprise	No prediction
Happiness	9	—	—	—	—	—	1	—	—	—	—
Surprise	—	10	—	—	—	—	—	—	—	—	—
Anger	—	—	10	—	—	—	—	—	—	—	—
Sadness	—	—	—	9	—	1	—	—	—	—	—
Disgust	—	—	—	—	3	—	—	—	—	—	—
Fear	—	1	—	1	—	3	—	—	2	1	—

components within a single facial area. No facial area yielded better predictions than another across all emotion categories.

This study was replicated in a recent unpublished study by Ekman and Friesen using the new facial measurement procedure, the *Facial Action Coding System*. Importantly, this new facial measurement procedure does predict blend stumuli and variations in intensity. That measurement procedure is described in Chapter 9.

5.3. Summary

There have been two approaches to the study of how components of facial behavior might be related to observers' judgments of emotion. The first and most popular type of study has been the attempt to infer the location of facial components by determining whether judgments of emotion can be made from a view of one or another portion of the face. There have been no consistent results with this approach, perhaps because of methodological mistakes, which are remedial (e.g., too few stimulus persons, oversimplified division of the face into just two areas), or because of flaws central to the design itself. If stimuli judged as the same emotion sometimes show components in one facial area, sometimes in another, and sometimes across all facial areas, then this approach would yield confusing results.

The few studies that have followed the other approach, of measuring facial components and relating these to observers' judgments of emotion made from a view of the full face, have made more progress. A system for scoring facial components has succeeded in predicting how observers will judge emotion for six emotion categories, regardless of possible psychological or physiognomic differences across a sample of 28 stimulus persons.

6. What are the relative contributions of facial behavior and contextual information to the judgment of emotion?

PAUL EKMAN, WALLACE V. FRIESEN,
AND PHOEBE ELLSWORTH

People rarely see a face alone without any context; when they do they usually make no inference about emotion. Usually the context includes the preceding and consequent facial behavior, the movements and position of the body, perhaps concomitant words and voice tone, the nature of the setting, what has been happening, who else is present, etc. All of these are sources of information about emotion, perhaps information that agrees with that derivable from the face alone, perhaps information discrepant from that shown in the face. The question to be addressed in this chapter is what are the relative contributions of context and face as sources of information? Can the face alone provide information about emotion, even though it is rare in life to see only the face? If the contextual information agrees with the facial information, is there some additive effect so that the observer is more certain about the judgment of emotion? If the two sources disagree, as, for example, if a person's face looks happy but we know that the person has just been told some bad news, does one source dominate or is some new, more complex inference drawn that could not be made from either source alone?

Here, as in our discussion of accuracy (Chapter 4), we shall present an interpretation of the literature that conflicts with those of previous reviewers (e.g., Hunt, 1941; Bruner & Tagiuri, 1954; Tagiuri, 1968). The parallel is not accidental, since their interpretation of the accuracy literature, which we disputed, was one basis for their contention that the context contributes more than, or at least always improves upon, judgments made from the face. Our disagreement with previous reviewers about the relative influences of facial and contextual information is not, however, based solely on our different interpretation of accuracy studies nor on their acceptance of studies we rejected (see Section 2.7 for our rationale for dismissing studies using artists' sketches). More importantly, the difference occurs because we drew a few simple conceptual distinctions, which led to a reevaluation of previous experimental designs and a reinterpretation of past data. Fortunately, Frijda (1969) also made some of these distinctions independently in a series of experiments and provided evidence that agrees with our reinterpretation of past experiments (including one of his own).

6.1. Conceptual issues

Misinterpretations of the literature and the frequent use of simplistic research designs may both have been due, in part, to an underlying assumption about the face. If the face were considered to provide little, if any, information about emotion, then it would be reasonable to expect that such an impoverished source would be easily overwhelmed by any other source of information. Further, that view would not suggest the necessity to consider the clarity of information provided by either source, face or context. Fernberger (1928) was one of the earliest writers to reflect this view, concluding from his study of drawings of the face that, "If a stimulus situation is indicated, the emotional state will be judged in accordance with that situation rather than in accordance with the facial expression." But, if the contextual information were itself ambiguous, in that observers did not know what emotion to expect (for example, "She looks at an animal in the corner of the room," a context story used in Frijda's 1958 study), and the face showed a very clear emotion, as determined independently by observer agreement, certainly the judgment of the combination would not conform to Fernberger's conclusion.

It would be possible to obtain results showing that the face was more important than the context or vice versa, depending on whether the investigator had combined an informative face with an ambiguous context or an ambiguous face with an informative context. All of the experiments we shall interpret failed to recognize the necessity of considering the clarity of each source, with the sole exception of Frijda's most recent experiments in which clarity was more of an afterthought than an integral part of the research design. We shall see, in considering data we have distinguished in terms of the clarity of each source, that Fernberger's conclusion is not always supported even when the clarity of the two sources is the same.

Bruner and Tagiuri (1954, p. 636) in their review of the literature (and later Tagiuri, 1968, p. 402) said, "Virtually all the evidence available points to the fact that the more information about the situation in which the emotion is expressed, the more accurate and reliable are judgments of emotion." Facts are rare commodities in psychology; but the data contradict this one, and their assertion ignores another necessary conceptual distinction. Not only is the clarity of the sources omitted from consideration, but Bruner and Tagiuri fail to distinguish between *concordant* and *discordant* combinations. Their conclusion is predicated on a simple additive relationship between sources, such that the combination will always be better than either source alone. Although this might be true for concordant combinations, in that each source alone would lead to similar judgments, it is clearly not true for discordant combinations, in that each source alone would lead to different judgments; an additive process would simply not resolve the discrepancies. (Fernberger apparently had such discordant combinations in mind, although he failed to say so explicitly.) Even for concordant combinations, the additive hypothesis ignores the possibility that the relative weight of each source may vary with particular emotions; data we shall review show that this qualification is necessary. A last problem with the additive hypothesis, less serious than the others, is that it fails to consider the constraints from *ceiling effects* where observers have reached near maximum agreement from one source and the addition of another could be of no measurable benefit – and just such instances occurred in experiments reviewed by Bruner and Tagiuri.

Bruner and Tagiuri (1954, p. 638) and Tagiuri again (1968, p. 608), made a more general criticism of research on the face and context. They wrote, "All in all, one wonders about the significance of studies of the recognition of 'facial expressions of emotions,' in isolation from context." Their wonder is doubt not curiosity and obfuscates the issues. It is legitimate, we believe, to find out what kinds of information can be provided by a single source, regardless of whether or not that source is typically combined with others in natural situations, and our discussions in Chapters 3, 4, and 5 have yielded some evidence and credible suggestion that the face, apart from knowledge of the context, can provide substantial information. The fact that the face is usually seen within a possibly informative context does not invalidate the utility of such research on the face alone; on the contrary, unless we know the contribution of each source separately, it may be impossible to untangle the complexities of the judgment process as it naturally occurs.

Contrary to Bruner and Tagiuri, we hold that understanding judgments of combined sources requires research on the information from each source alone as well as from the combination of sources and that experiments on this problem must therefore provide three values: judgments from face alone, from context alone, and from face within context, viz., the combination. This is all the more necessary because information from either source could be ambiguous or clear, matched or unequal, and could suggest the presence of the same emotion or different ones, thus allowing for concordant and discordant combinations. Those variables that are likely determinants of the judgment of the combinations cannot be specified without information about the face alone and about the context alone.

We shall briefly consider what might be implied by the term *context* and then discuss different aspects of the clarity of a source, before outlining some of the methodological problems common to the experiments we shall review. Information about the context in which facial behavior occurred could encompass quite a number of different phenomena: stable characteristics of the social setting, such as the task, the physical locale, etc.; stable characteristics of the participants, such as demographic variations and roles; and transient events preceding or following the facial behavior, such as events involving inanimate objects, the behavior of other participants, and the facial or other behavior of the stimulus person.

Three different procedures have been utilized to provide contextual information, none of them comparable in the amount or type of information they convey or in their credibility to the observer. One technique has been to show an entire still photograph, often including more than just the behavior of the stimulus person, sometimes indicating preceding and consequent events, sometimes conveying information about stable settings and personal characteristics. Another technique has been to present a verbal description or story about the context in which the facial behavior occurred; but even here, where it is most feasible to control systematically for the type and amount of information given, this has not always been done. The third technique involves preceding the facial behavior with motion picture film sequences of other contextual events.

Regardless of the technique employed, investigators should either systematically vary some of the types of contextual information in order to study them or, at least, maintain some constancy in the type and amount of contextual information provided across their experimental conditions, so that it is possible to reach some determination from their data, no matter how limited their sampling of types of contextual information. Unfortunately, neither has been done; type and amount of contextual information furnished over trials within almost all experiments have varied unsystematically.

The phrase *source clarity* refers to differences in the amount or type of information about emotion available to observers when they are exposed to a single source, either face or context. There are at least three aspects of source clarity: ambiguity, message complexity, and strength. The *ambiguity* of a source could be measured by the extent of agreement among observers about the presence or likelihood of a single emotion in terms of category judgments or the variance in their judgments if an emotion dimension task is used. Some faces, for example, will yield agreement among almost all observers; other faces will yield agreement among perhaps half of the observers, with the rest either opting for a second emotion (shortly we shall consider such bimodal distributions, which imply blends) or randomly distributing their choices; and some stimuli will be essentially ambiguous, eliciting no agreement among observers. In a parallel fashion, some stimuli will elicit a very small variance on an emotion scale such as pleasant–unpleasant, others a moderate variance, and still others a sufficiently large variance to suggest that the stimulus is ambiguous.[1]

The *message complexity* of a source could be measured by whether a single emotion or a blend of emotions is observed, the former being considered less complex than the latter. Determination of a blend is better made from a judgment task that allows observers to record their impression about the presence of two or more emotions (e.g., see the discussion of Nummenmaa's work in Section 5.1) than inferred from a bimodal distribution when only one judgment is allowed.[2] We have called a blend less clear than a single emotion stimulus because the presence of a blend might allow for a greater variety of interpretations with more potential for shifting away from the judgment of a single source when the combined sources are observed, but this is, of course, an empirical question, which has not been studied.

---

[1]The problem with bipolar scale judgments is in determining what the midpoint of the scale represents. A barely pleasant (or barely unpleasant) stimulus might appropriately be rated at the midpoint, either because the judges could not attribute any emotion to it or because a random distribution of judgments would produce a midpoint mean. But the variance may be no different for stimuli having a midpoint mean, even if that midpoint provides information for one stimulus (barely pleasant) and indicates inappropriateness for another (agreement in the use of the midpoint because the scale is not relevant to the stimulus).

[2]The problem with inferring a blend from a bimodal distribution of judgments on a task that allowed only a single choice is that this distribution may not always indicate that most observers really saw both emotions and simply chose one or the other; alternately, it can also indicate divergent, nonoverlapping judgments by the two groups of observers (see Chapter 1).

The *strength* of a source could be measured by the intensity of the emotion observed, disregarding or holding constant the judgment about the nature of the emotion. Two contexts might both be associated with anger or yield the same mean on a pleasant–unpleasant scale, but one context might yield low-intensity judgments and the other might yield high-intensity judgments.

All three aspects of source clarity need to be considered, for they are interrelated. Intensity of a source is relevant to each message if the source involves a blend; agreement may vary about intensity judgments, and thus there may be more or less ambiguity about the intensity of a source. It would be preferable in planning experiments on the face and context to utilize all three measures of source clarity, but no experiment has determined the relative clarity of its sources on more than one index. Even more problematic no experiment has systemtically manipulated clarity (even if measured only one way) by pairing high, moderate, and low clarity stimuli from each source. Unwittingly, however, some of these combinations have occurred, and the investigator has drawn unwarranted conclusions not considering that the results were limited to the particular clarity combinations used. Even when clarity of sources is not to be an independent variable systematically explored, information about the clarity of each source must be provided in order to determine whether the sources were evenly or unevenly matched. In addition, information about the clarity of each source will also reveal whether concordant or discordant combinations were studied. Some of the studies we shall examine did not specify which type of combination they investigated.

These experiments we shall discuss share some previously described methodological flaws with the experiments discussed in Chapters 3, 4, and 5. Here, too, it is important to sample a number of different emotions for each source. Only one investigator did that (Frijda, 1969), and he considered only two emotion dimensions; but because he found some differences in the relative influence of the face and context as a function of the emotion sampled, we must regard with considerable caution generalizations drawn from experiments that do not specify the relevant emotions. Again, it is important to have a reasonable sampling of stimulus persons whose facial behavior makes up one of the sources and, in addition, to have a representative sampling of contexts. Most studies have used the facial behavior of only one person, usually an actor posing.

The reader might well wonder at this point why with all these defects we bother to discuss any of the experiments. There are three reasons.

The first is to convince the reader that the conclusions of past reviewers are not only unwarranted, in that they fail to specify the relevant parameter of the phenomena, but unfounded, in that what data there are suggest just the reverse of what has been concluded. The second is to illustrate the methodological requirements for research on this topic by applying them to the interpretation of past data. And the third is to report the few findings that hint at what future research may show.

6.2. Review of experiments

Goldberg (1951) performed the only experiment in which the context was defined by preceding motion picture film sequences. Observers watched two different versions of a motion picture film containing four scenes. In both films, the fourth scene – a woman screaming – was the same, and the observers judged the emotion shown in that scene by choosing an emotion word from a list. In both film versions, the first scene was also the same – a child riding a tricycle – but in one version the two intervening scenes suggested an automobile accident, and in the other they suggested amiable play between the child and a man. Goldberg showed both versions to two groups of observers, varying the film seen first.

We believe that the most relevant data to measuring the influence of the different context (previous film episodes, accident, or play) on the judgment of the scream are only the observations from each group for the first film they reviewed. After seeing either version, the second film might well be rated quite differently simply because the subjects figured out the experimenter's hypothesis. Goldberg reported that there was a significant order effect for the judgments of the accident film; it was judged as more fearful when seen first. In analyzing Goldberg's published data, we found that there was also an order effect for the play film; it was judged as less fearful and more joyful when seen second. The presence of this order effect does suggest that the most conservative test of Goldberg's hypothesis about context would be from the first judgments of each group of observers where there is no question of their being contaminated by previous film watching.

In comparing the judgments of the accident versus the play context on the judgments of the scream scene, Goldberg had calculated chi-squares over all conditions and also within each group of observers and found significant differences. Even when our precaution is employed and only the first observations in each group are compared, a significant chi-square shows that the context had an influence, but the influence is not nearly as dramatic.

Goldberg concluded from his findings that "the concept formed by the perception of a motion picture film is not dependent upon the reaction to the individual scenes that have been cut and spliced together, but rather on the sequence as a whole" (1951, p. 71). We question this interpretation for a number of reasons. Its generality is in doubt because only one stimulus person and only one facial stimulus were studied and, further, there is no information provided about the interpretation of the separate scenes to which Goldberg's conclusion refers. Perhaps more importantly, although there was a significant shift in the judgment of some observers (24% more observers judged the scream in the play version as anger or joy than in the accident version and 21% fewer observers judged the scream in the play version as fear than in the accident version), Goldberg overlooked what his data showed in terms of the stability of judgment of the scream regardless of the preceding context. Seventy-seven percent of the observers still called the scream in the play version fear as compared with 98% in the accident version. Although no conclusion is possible from this study because of the limited sampling of emotions and stimulus persons and the lack of data on each source, the results can be used to support either the Fernberger hypothesis about contextual dominance or just the reverse, depending on which aspect of the data is emphasized. The preceding context influenced the judgment of the face for about a fourth of the sample of observers, but better than 70% of the observers judged the face as showing the same emotion regardless of differences in preceding context.

Munn's study (1940) is probably the best-known work on the influence of the context on judgments of the face and is the one most frequently cited in support of the view that contextual information is the sine qua non for judgments of emotion from the face or, at the least, will always improve judgments of the face alone. Munn utilized candid camera photographs of presumably emotional situations as his stimuli; provide contextual information he showed the full photograph including everything captured by the original photographer. Judgments made from that source were compared with judgments made from the same photographs cropped to show the face alone.

There are a number of problems in Munn's experiment. First, there are no judgments from the contextual source independent of the facial information; thus there is no way of assessing what information came from just the context and what information from just the face. We tried to remedy this defect by substituting judgment data we collected by giving Munn's verbal descriptions of each context to a group of observers and asking them to choose a single emotion from a list of six categories, with an option of *no emotion* (see Section 4.1 for a description of this study and the use of these data to establish an accuracy criterion). It would have been preferable if Munn had obscured the face from the whole photographs and shown those stimuli to observers to determine the information available from his context; but because we did not have his stimuli, we were unable to attempt that.

A second problem relates to the use of Munn's procedure for representing contextual information. Granting that contexts defined by photographers may be more believable to the observer than a verbal story of a supposed context, nevertheless, it is difficult to obtain comparable contexts that are similar in the type and amount of information they furnish; that is, one such photograph may show the emotional reactions of other participants, another may show the event that elicited the reaction, etc. If such a procedure is to be used, then there should be some systematic sampling of different photographs balanced in terms of the type and amount of information they provide. A third problem is that Munn did not consider whether he was studying discordant or concordant source combinations, and although most of his data are relevant only to the latter, there are two discordant combinations as well. A fourth problem is his failure to consider source clarity for either face or context; examination of his data and the auxiliary data we collected showed that for all but one item there was similar clarity for each source and for some stimuli the clarity was moderate, so there was room for improvement in judgment.

One virtue of Munn's procedure is that it does furnish an opportunity to assess the relative value of each source. Because he used actual photographs of actual events rather than the contrived contexts used by Goldberg and most of the other investigators considered, a comparison of the clarity of each source – face and context – provides some impression as to which source yields more information. This comparison is limited, however, by the small number of stimuli and stimulus persons, the unknown nature of the principle of selection of stimuli by first the photographer and then Munn, and by our reliance on observers' judgments of verbal descriptions of the context to measure that source, which may under- or overestimate what observers might have said if they saw the actual photograph of the situation without the face.

In reanalyzing Munn's data, we disregarded the results from 5 of his 14 stimuli, all of which were athletic events and were judged by our observers as typically not associated with any one emotion. For the remaining stimuli, we reorganized judgments into the emotion categories suggested earlier in Table 3.2.

Seven of the nine stimuli listed in Table 6.1 involved concordant combinations, where each source judged separately yielded similar results. These have been further divided on the basis of high and moderate clarity of both sources. The data permit two tests of Bruner and Tagiuri's additive hypothesis. First, the column labeled "Combination judgment minus highest single source" shows that there was no consistent pattern to suggest that the combination of face and context is always better than the source that is superior when observed alone. Second, if we compare the combination judgment with the judgment of face alone, again there is no strong trend; for three items there was no difference, for one item the face alone yielded higher agreement than the combination of face and context, and for three items the combination was better than the face alone. So the additive hypothesis, that the combination of sources will always be better than either source alone, is not supported, nor is the more limited hypothesis that the combination of face and context is better than the face alone.

Table 6.1 also allows a test of the question of which source – face or context – usually provides more information. There seems to be no general trend but a variation with the item. The face judgments were higher than the context judgments for three of the items, the context higher than the face for four items, and no difference was found on the remaining two items. Fernberger's hypothesis, that the context always dominates the face, involves essentially the same question, but can be evaluated only for discordant combinations, of which there were only two. In the one of these discordant combinations where there was similar clarity for both sources (#8) the combination judgment agreed more with the facial judgment than with the contextual. The last item does not provide a relevant case because the face was judged to be ambiguous and the context informative, and the combination was judged as the same as the nonambiguous source.

To summarize briefly our evaluation of Munn's experiment, his design can be criticized on a number of grounds. The limited sampling of faces, emotions, and contexts prevents any conclusions, but what data there were support neither Fernberger's context dominance hypothesis nor Bruner and Tagiuri's additive hypothesis.

Vinacke (1949) performed an experiment similar to Munn's, also using candid photographs and showing one group of observers only the face

Table 6.1. *Reanalysis of Munn's data on the face and context*

Type of combination	Verbal description of situation given to observers (N = 35)	Judgment of Verbal description (%)	Judgment of face alone (%)	Combination: judgment of face plus picture (%)	Combination judgment minus highest single source
Concordant: high clarity for each source	1. Girl running into ocean	91 Happy	97 Happy	97 Happy	0
	2. Jitterbug clapping hands to music	97 Happy	86 Happy	92 Happy	−5
	3. Girl running from ghost	94 Fear	94 Fear	88 Fear	−6
Concordant: moderate clarity for each source	4. Girl photographed over transom while dressing	56 Surprise	66 Surprise	72 Surprise	+6
	5. Man holding hand of drowned person	63 Sad	74 Sad	74 Sad	0
	6. Porter leading burned man from scene of airplane crash	56 Fear	41 Fear[a]	45 Fear	−11
	7. Man with hand stretched towards hostile crowd	65 Fear	63 Fear	74 Fear	+9
		65 Sad	63 Sad	74 Sad	
Discordant: low clarity for each source	8. Girl photgraphed over transom while in bath	44 Anger	26 Surprise	75 Surprise	Interpretation influenced more by face than context
		38 Surprise	28 Fear		
Discordant: moderate clarity for one source ambiguous for the other	9. Man who is holding strikebreaker by the coat collar	68 Anger	8 Anger	78 Anger	Interpretation influenced by context

[a]We credited anxiety as well as fear as a fear category response.

and the other group the entire photograph including the face. His verbal descriptions of the contexts shown in his 20 photographs were also judged by our group of observers; only six were judged by the majority as probably being associated with a single emotion. We shall not report the results on these six photographs because they are comparable to those we gave for Munn and are open to the same criticisms.

Goodenough and Tinker (1931) performed the first context experiment employing story descriptions of the context. Their study is notable because it is the only one before 1969 to include data on the clarity of each source in addition to judgments of the combinations. It is hard to understand why their findings have received so little attention and, further, why later researchers, some of whom do cite that study, did not profit from their research design. Although their substantive results are limited because of the use of just a few stimuli of just one stimulus person, that is so for every study we can report, even Frijda's more recent experiments. Goodenough and Tinker did not consider differentiating among stimuli in terms of the amount of clarity in each source, but neither has anyone else, and they deserve praise for at least measuring the clarity of each source separately.

Goodenough and Tinker selected four of Feleky's (1914) posed photographs intended to represent four emotions – fear, anger, disgust, and sympathy. Those observers who were shown only the faces rated two stimuli as having high clarity (96% agreement for the fear and disgust pictures) and two as having moderate clarity (sympathy judged as such by 75% of the observers and the intended anger picture judged as fear by 78% of the observers; we shall treat that picture as showing fear, not anger, because that is how it was judged). The four stories intended to connote these same four emotions were all rated as having high clarity, 100% of the observers having judged each story to represent the emotion intended by the authors.

Table 6.2 shows the two types of source combinations furnished by this experiment. The top part of the table shows the results for the judgments of discordant combinations in which the clarity of the two sources is comparable. These data do not support Fernberger's conclusion. There is no combination that fits the context-dominance expectation. Instead, in two of the combinations, the face dominates the context: disgust face dominates anger context, fear face dominates anger context. No conclusion can be drawn, however, about facial dominance, without replication with other stories for the anger context and other stimuli for the fear and disgust faces. The second part of the table shows combina-

Table 6.2. *Reanalysis of Goodenough and Tinker's data on face and context: emotion judgments of observers who received both face and context*

A. Discordant: high clarity for face & story

Face	Story			
	Disgust	Fear	Sympathy	Anger
Disgust	—	43 Disgust 41 Fear	47 Disgust 46 Sympathy	69 Disgust
Fear	49 Disgust 42 Fear	—	50 Fear 47 Sympathy	78 Fear

B. Discordant and concordant: story of higher clarity than face

Face	Story			
	Disgust	Fear	Sympathy	Anger
Fear	72 Disgust	96 Fear	43 Sympathy	No data
Sympathy	69 Disgust	87 Fear	—	74 Anger

tion judgments of stimuli in which the context had greater clarity (higher agreement among observers) than the face. In each instance, the combination is dominated by the context. Again conclusions are difficult because of the limited sampling of either source, but it seems reasonable to expect that with discordant combinations in which source clarity differs the clearer source will dominate. If the face had been clearer than the context, then for these same emotions the face might well have dominated the combination judgments.

In sum, Goodenough and Tinker's experiment does not provide the basis for any conclusions because of limitations in the sampling of both faces and contexts, but it is exemplary in terms of providing data on each source alone. Their findings do, however, raise serious doubt about the validity of the general assertion that one of these sources (the context) will always have more influence than the other (face) when the two sources are of comparable clarity and the combination of the two is discordant. Frijda's more recent experiments, to be interpreted next, essentially replicate Goodenough and Tinker's findings.

Frijda (1969), in a series of experiments, followed much the same design as Goodenough and Tinker.[3] The major limitation of these exper-

[3] We have not discussed the Frijda and Philipszoon (1963) study here because it did not provide information about each source, its methodology was previously criticized (Rump, 1960), and its quite ambiguous findings have been far improved on by Frijda's more recent experiments, which solved some of the earlier methodological problems.

iments, as with the Goodenough and Tinker study, is the limited sampling of stimulus persons (only one), of faces of that person (four in one study and three pictures in each of the other two studies), and of context stories (six, nine, and nine, respectively).

In all three experiments, the following procedure was used: first, photographs were rated by the observers on ten 7-point bipolar scales; next, situation descriptions were rated by these same observers on the same bipolar scales; a week later, the combinations of photographs and contexts were judged by these same observers on these same scales. In the first experiment, no systematic sampling procedures were followed in the selection of the four photographs. When the ratings on the discordant combinations were analyzed by comparing the judgments across all ten scales for each source separately, Frijda found that the face dominated, in that the shift away from the context-only rating was twice as great as the shift away from the face-only rating. The second and third experiments were planned to explore this matter by systematically selecting stimuli for both sources in terms of an emotion dimension.

In the second study, three faces were employed – one judged as pleasant, one judged as unpleasant, and one expected to be judged in the middle of the scale, or neutral, but actually judged as slightly unpleasant. There were nine situation descriptions – four unpleasant and five pleasant. Frijda did not report his data in a way that allows examination of whether there was differing clarity for the stimuli in each source (as indicated by the variance) and if this affected the results. For all discordant combinations, however, he noted that again the face dominated the context; the correlation between face-only and combination ratings was .67, and that between context-only and combination ratings was −.49. "To judge from these data," Frijda wrote, "if someone behaves [face] happily, or sadly when circumstances [context] make us expect otherwise, we rather believe his behavior than our expectations" (1969, p. 197). In the concordant combinations, there was a nonsignificant trend for the context to dominate, but Frijda attributes this to the greater polarity (perhaps indicating higher clarity) for contexts as compared with faces.

The third experiment was similar to the second except that the selection principle was in terms of his dimension of active versus passive attending. Three pictures representing each pole and a midpoint and nine stories about context varying on this dimension were used. For all discordant combinations, the face again dominated the context; the correlation between face-only and combination ratings was .87 and the correlation between context-only and combination ratings was −.36. Again, there was no significant tendency for the context to dominate in the concordant combinations or for the agreement, as measured by the variances, to be less for combinations than for the separate sources.

Frijda attempted to determine whether the clarity of the face (variance) might be related to the extent to which judgments of the combination shifted from the face to the context judgment. He found such a relationship in the second experiment but not in the first. Frijda also examined whether the shifts in judgment differed in relation to the particular emotions involved in each source. He found a greater shift from the face (context had more influence) for the happy face when it was paired with a sad story than for a sad picture when it was paired with a happy story; there was more shift from the face for the passive picture paired with an active context than for an active face paired with a passive context.

In attempting to explain these findings, Frijda examined the observers' descriptions of how they resolved discrepant information and suggested the operation of four different cognitive mechanisms, but these are the weakest data in his experiment. One of Frijda's four cognitive mechanisms implies what we earlier discussed in terms of display rules and masking of emotion (Chapter 1). The concept of display rules and our earlier interpretation of why subjects smiled so often in Landis' experiment (Section 4.2) would suggest that the difference between the sad and happy face might be attributed to the observers interpreting smiles that are discrepant from context to be a mask, but there should be no similar expectation about sad faces acting as a mask of happy feelings. The difference between the passive and active faces might arise from the former having less distinctive facial components than the latter and, thus, in that sense being more ambiguous or it might be that a passive face is more frequently a mask than is an active face. These interpretations cannot be actually tested from Frijda's data, although some of his evidence supports them.

Frijda's experiments disconfirm both the additive hypothesis and the context dominance hypothesis. They further suggest the necessity to consider particular emotions in each source and the value of including measures of the cognitive operations employed by the observers to resolve discrepant information in discordant combinations. Conclusions are not possible, primarily because of the limited sampling of emotions and stimulus persons, but Frijda's study certainly points to the fruitfulness of research on this problem.

There is another potential problem in the design employed by Frijda and by Goodenough and Tinker. Conceivably, when the context information is provided through a verbal story and that information is discordant with the information from a facial photograph, the facial source will dominate because the observers view the photograph as a more direct representation and, thus, as more believable than a verbal story. This is not to suggest that actions must always speak louder than words but that within an experiment the two sources may differ in credibility by virtue of the medium of their presentation. If that is so, such findings could misrepresent what might actually occur in natural settings, where the contextual information would be just as credible as the facial information. The use of one medium, e.g., photographs or films, to provide both the contextual information and the facial information might circumvent this potential problem.

6.3. Summary

No conclusions can be drawn about the relative influence of information from facial behavior and information about the context in judgments of emotion when both are known by the observer. The only exception is that the context dominance hypothesis of Fernberger and the additive hypothesis of Bruner and Tagiuri were shown to be unsupported by the data available. There seems to be no question that either source, face or context, can, on given occasions, be more salient or more useful or more of a determinant of the combined judgment than the other. But this statement is surely insufficient and only points to the necessity for research on three questions.

First, what are the parameters of both sources that determine their relative influence on the judgment of the combinations? We have argued that the parameters must include the clarity of each source, preferably measured in regards to ambiguity, message complexity and strength; the distinct emotions associated with each source; and the pairing of sources to yield discordant and concordant combinations. Thus moderate clarity, happy faces could be paired with moderate clarity, happy contexts; with high clarity, happy contexts; with moderate clarity, fearful contexts; with extreme clarity, fearful contexts; etc. Further, there must be representative sampling of stimulus persons and facial behaviors for each of these possibilities and different context definitions in terms of the type and amount of contextual information because high-clarity contextual sources may still differ in the type of information provided and this difference might be relevant to whether the context dominates the face or not or to the type of cognitive mechanism employed to resolve the discrepancy.

The second research problem is the specification of the particular cognitive mechanisms employed to resolve discrepant information between the face and the context. Frijda made a start toward solving this problem, and we suggested only some of the parameters of the sources to be considered in research on the cognitive mechanisms for resolving discordant combinations.

A third research problem is to investigate the nature of these occasions when the face provides more information than the context, when the context provides more information than the face, and when each provides influential information and the resolution of the discrepancy involves a reinterpretation of both sources. The answer may lie in part with individual or cultural differences; some people or peoples may generally provide trustworthy facial behavior, others may be notorious for deceptive facial behavior. The answer may lie in part also in the nature of the social setting in which the facial behavior occurs. Ekman and Friesen (1969a) specified some of the parameters of social interactions where the face is a less reliable source of information than the context, although they did not consider the converse, the nature of the social interactions where facial behavior is trustworthy, perhaps more so than social context. Goffman (1963) offered some notions about the nature of conversational behavior that might provide leads for specifying the particular points within a conversation when either face or context might be more useful.

7. What are the similarities and differences in facial behavior across cultures?

PAUL EKMAN, WALLACE V. FRIESEN,
AND PHOEBE ELLSWORTH

There has been a long and heated controversy over the question of universals in the face and emotion. Those who argue that there are universal facial expressions of emotion hypothesize that the relationship between specific facial behaviors and particular emotions is innate or is the result of certain learning experiences common to all persons, regardless of culture. Those who argue that there are no universals claim that the relationship between particular facial behaviors and particular emotions is learned in a fashion that varies within each culture or subculture. The dispute has been based largely on anecdote and unsystematized observation. The culture-specific view has been predominant, marshaling wide acceptance within psychology and anthropology. Very recently, however, it has been challenged, particularly by the ethologists, but again without much data. In the last few years, a consistent body of evidence has accumulated that conclusively demonstrates that there is a pancultural element in the association of facial behavior with emotion.

7.1. Historical review

Darwin (1872) proposed that there are universal facial behaviors for each emotion and, in support of this claim, was the first to utilize a judgment procedure in the study of facial behavior; but no quantitative research was done on this topic until 1941. Later, LaBarre's (1947, 1962) and Birdwhistell's (1963) writings on cultural differences in emotion received wide attention and were generally interpreted as evidence that the facial behaviors associated with emotions were socially learned and culturally variable. However, they had not systematically gathered quantitative data but had relied on anecdotal impressions, the descriptions of novelists, or anthropological reports.

Klineberg has recently said that the axiom, "what shows on the face is written there by culture," is an unfair view of his work (Izard, 1969, p. 18). In his original writing he anticipated some of our discussion of display rules (Chapter 1) in proposing that there are three ways in which social determinants can influence emotional behavior: by determining which situations evoke which emotions, by conditioning the amount of overt emotional behavior that is culturally acceptable in a situation, and by directing the manner in which the emotions manifest themselves. In regard to the last, he wrote, "There are undoubtedly certain types of expressive behavior which are common to all human societies," (1940, p. 176) probably the manifestations of happiness, fear, and sadness.

LaBarre took the opposite view: "There is no 'natural' language of emotional gesture" (1947, p. 55); but the statement itself emphasizes his failure to distinguish gesture from facial behavior associated with an emotion. Birdwhistell shared LaBarre's view, although he distinguished gestures from facial behaviors associated with emotion: "When I first became interested in studying body motion...I anticipated a research strategy which could first isolate universal signs of feeling that were species specific....As research proceeded, and even before the development of kinesics, it became clear that this search for universals was culture bound....There are probably no universal symbols of emotional state" (1963, p. 126).

Arguing just the opposite view, but admittedly without direct evidence to support their claim, F. Allport (1924), Asch (1952), and Tomkins (1962, 1963) provided different theoretical bases for hypothesizing invariants in facial behavior related to emotion, regardless of culture. These researchers also recognized that there would be cultural differences in facial behavior as well, and each made a partial attempt to explain these cultural variations in facial behavior.

Thus there has been considerable controversy over the question of whether there are any pancultural aspects to facial behavior associated with emotion, i.e., any invariants in the relationship between facial behavior and specific emotions, but neither side in the argument has systematically gathered quantitative data to support their view.

7.2. Literature review

Whether or not there are pancultural aspects to facial behavior is one question on which the data are now quite clear. Eight experiments were conducted on facial behavior in different cultures and all provided evidence of universals. Six studies, utilizing a judgment procedure, showed that the same facial behaviors are associated with the same emotions by observers from different cultures. One study showed that emotions posed by members of a preliterate culture are accurately judged by members of a literate culture. The eighth experiment used a components, rather than a judgment approach, directly measuring facial behavior in the same eliciting circumstance in two cultures. The data from the first two studies are somewhat confused, largely because of limitations in the sampling of facial stimuli. The other six studies, however, unfold a very consistent picture.

Triandis and Lambert (1958) compared urban Greek, rural Greek, and urban U.S. observers in their judgments of the facial behavior of Schlosberg's set of posed photographs (Engen, Levy, & Schlosberg, 1957). They found evidence of similarities and differences. For the most part, the stimuli received the same ratings on Schlosberg's three dimensions of emotion across the three groups of observers. There were significant intercorrelations between the judgments of U.S. and Greek urban, U.S. and Greek rural, and Greek urban and Greek rural on the pleasantness dimension (0.91, 0.82, and 0.86, respectively), on the attention–rejection dimension (.82, .88, .83, respectively), and on the sleep–tension dimension (.76, .67, .66, respectively).

There was a cultural difference in the relationships among the judgments on the three dimensions. The Greeks rated pictures they judged as unpleasant more toward attention and tension, and the Americans did the same for pictures they judged as pleasant. The authors mentioned that interpretation of this difference was difficult but suggested that the U.S. observers were more activist and instrumentally oriented about emotion than the Greek observers.

Another difference in dimension judgments among observer groups was between the two urban groups (U.S. and Greek) and the rural sample. On all three dimensions, the mean rating on the pictures was more similar between the urban groups than between either and the rural sample. Triandis and Lambert thought this might be because of stereotyping of judgments on the basis of having seen commercial motion pictures, but it could just as well have been because of the different types of judgment tasks used with the rural sample.

Another cultural difference was found in the judgments based on Woodworth's six emotion categories. There were more random judgments among the Greek observers on this task than on the dimension judgments. This finding led Osgood (1966) to conclude that the affective meanings (dimension judgments) of facial expression are more stable across languages and cultures than the referential or denotative meanings (category judgments). But subsequent research by others found consistent category judgments across a great number of cultures and language groups. This particular finding of Triandis and Lambert may be, as Izard (1969) said, because of peculiarities of the Lightfoot series of photographs, which Schlosberg posed specifically to represent differences on his dimensions.

In sum, Triandis and Lambert found evidence for both similarities and differences between the groups of observers they compared, but for two reasons it is difficult to untangle what accounted for either the similarities or the differences. The data are limited to judgments of only one stimulus person, and there was no control for the amount of visual contact among the groups of observers.

Vinacke expected to find differences among his groups of Caucasian, Japanese, and Chinese observers (all from Hawaii) in their judgments of Caucasian (1949) and of Oriental faces (Vinacke & Fong, 1955). The 21 Caucasian and 28 Oriental were photographs from magazines, selected by Munn's technique as showing presumably emotional behavior. The three groups of observers differed significantly only in the extent of their agreement about a particular emotion; but there was a slight tendency for the observers to reach higher agreement in judging their own than the other group's behavior. Vinacke concluded that this could be "linked with nation–racial ancestry" but admitted his evidence was weak. He did not, however, have the same set of observers judge both Caucasian and Oriental stimuli, and the slight differences he did obtain may well be because of the sampling of observers in his two experiments.

Vinacke recognized the necessity to achieve visual isolation among his groups of observers and explained his failure to show significant cultural differences as possibly because of his use of groups from Hawaii, all of whom had extensive mutual contact. Another problem with Vinacke's experiments is the questionable relevance of his stimuli to emotion; we have only investigated his information about the contexts in which the Caucasian faces occurred but that did show that only 6 out of his 20 situations were judged by observers as having relevance to emotion (see Chapter 4). Agreement among all of his groups of observers was usually low, but, in any case, despite his attempt to find evidence of cultural differences, he obtained just the opposite.

Dickey and Knower (1941) conducted the first experiment comparing groups of observers from different cultures in their judgments of the same set of facial behaviors. Junior and senior high school boys and girls in the United States and Mexico City judged 22 photographs of posed emotions, choosing among emotion categories. In both cultures, the same facial behaviors were judged as showing the same emotion, although agreement was consistently higher among the Mexican than among the U.S. observers. Dickey and Knower interpreted this difference in extent of agreement as owing to the greater sensitivity of Mexicans to the communicative symbols of action. It is difficult to know what their difference in agreement means; it was not replicated, and Izard's and Ekman's work has not revealed any similar superiority of other cultural groups over U.S. observers.

In any case, they did find that the faces were judged as showing the same emotion in the two cultures; however, the evidence for cross-cultural similarity is limited by their observers' lack of visual isolation and by the smallness of their sample of stimulus persons (only two). Their results (all age groups and sexes combined) are reported in Table 7.1, with the data reorganized for the six categories of emotion we have been considering. The table is organized so that one may examine any row, or set of photographs assumed to represent a particular emotion, and compare the percentage of each group identifing those stimuli as showing the expected emotion. The particular stimuli used to represent each emotion, of course, will differ for the three investigators listed in the table.

Izard (1969) developed his own set of 32 photographs, selected on the basis of agreement among pilot groups of observers. These were presented to observers in eight different language-culture groups, who made judgments using emotion category labels translated into their own language. The results, shown in Table 7.1, were consistent across cultures (we have not included the results on shame and interest).

Izard's weakest results (although still greater than chance in terms of cross-cultural agreement) were from his African and Japanese observers. The Africans were persons from different parts of Africa living in France, and Izard believed there may have been translation problems. The Japanese results may well have been lowered by translation difficulties; Ekman and Friesen obtained better agreement with their Japanese sample, and their translators were critical of the particular emotion translations used by Izard.

The only major limitation on Izard's findings of cross-cultural similarity in the judgment of emotion from facial behavior is the lack of visual

Table 7.1. *Percentages that same emotion is identified by members of literate culture with same stimulus within each group*

Emotion	Dickey & Knower (1941)		Izard (1969)									Ekman & Friesen (1969)				
	Mexican	U.S.	U.S.	English	German	Swedish	French	Swiss	Greek	African	Japanese	Japanese	Brazilian	Chilean	Argentinian	U.S.
Happy	97	95	97	96	98	96	94	97	93	68	94	87	97	90	94	97
Fear	71	55	76	67	84	89	83	67	68	48	58	71	77	78	68	88
Surprise	54	43	90	80	85	80	84	85	80	49	79	87	82	88	93	91
Anger	86	69	69	81	83	82	91	92	80	51	57	63	82	76	72	69
Disgust/ contempt	61	47	82	84	73	88	78	78	87	55	56	82	86	85	79	82
Sad	61	51	73	74	67	71	70	70	54	32	67	74	82	90	85	73
Number of observers	616	1244	89	62	158	41	67	36	50	29	60	29	40	119	168	99
Number of categories other than these listed here	5	5	2	2	2	2	2	2	2	2	2	0	0	0	0	0

isolation among any of the groups of observers compared, a point we shall look into shortly.

Ekman and Friesen, in collaboration with Tomkins, selected stimuli that appeared free of the influence of any display rules to control or mask emotion and showed the facial components they hypothesized to be specific to each emotion. These researchers were developing at that time their procedure for systematically scoring from photographs or films the facial components associated with emotion (see Facial Affect Scoring Technique (FAST), Chapter 4). When pictures had to be selected for the cross-cultural study, FAST was not completed and they could not select stimuli on the basis of FAST scores. Instead, they applied FAST's specifications informally as they examined and selected pictures. Thirty photographs of 14 different stimulus persons met their criteria, including pictures from Ekman and Friesen's (1968) study of mental patients and from the studies of Frois-Wittmann (1930), Schlosberg (Engen, Levy, & Schlosberg, 1957), and Tomkins and McCarter (1964). These photographs were shown to observers in five literate cultures who chose an emotion category from a list of six translated into their own language. These results, shown in Table 7.1, again reveal that in literate cultures the same facial stimuli are judged as indicating the same emotions, regardless of the culture of the observer.

But these results, like the results of Dickey and Knower, Izard, Triandis and Lambert, and Vinacke, could be regarded as not necessarily persuasive for the view that there are pancultural elements in facial behavior. Instead, these data could be interpreted as evidence that culturally variable learning is the sole basis for the association of facial behaviors with emotions. On the grounds that there was some shared visual input among the cultures compared, it could be argued that everyone had learned to recognize the same set of conventions or at least had become familiar with each other's different facial behavior through this shared visual source. This argument could be met by showing that members of a visually isolated culture recognize the same emotions for the same stimuli as do members of literate cultures.

Ekman, Sorenson, and Friesen (1969) conducted studies on the recognition of emotion in two preliterate cultures, Borneo and New Guinea. They used the same stimuli for which positive results were obtained in five literate cultures. They encountered difficulty in utilizing the usual judgment task in which the observer is shown a photograph and asked to choose an emotion label from a list of emotions. They have published only their data on those observers in these two preliterate cultures who

B   C

Figure 7.1 Examples of the photograph sets utilized in the study of emotion recognition among preliterate observers in New Guinea. (A) This photograph, one of Tomkin's stimuli, has been judged as sadness across literate cultures. (B) One of Frois-Wittmann's stimuli, this has been judged as anger within literate cultures. (C) Again one of Tomkin's stimuli, this photograph has been judged as surprise within literate cultures.

In the experiment conducted in New Guinea with observers from a preliterate culture, all three photographs were shown at once, and a translator asked the observer to pick the face that would occur if "his child died and he felt sad." 79% of the 189 observers in New Guinea selected (A) as fitting that story. This confirms that the same facial behavior is selected for the same emotion concept in this more visually isolated preliterate culture.

had the most contact with Westerners. Although their results were similar to the results from literate cultures, the data were weaker, and the pancultural theory was still open to argument, inasmuch as those observers were not visually isolated.

In a second study, Ekman and Friesen (1971) had better success, utilizing a judgment task first described by Dashiell (1927) for working with young children. Observer were given three photographs at once, each showing a face, and were told a story that involved only one emotion; the observers then pointed to the face they deemed appropriate to the story. Figure 7.1 shows a set of three photographs and one of the stories used in this study. The observers were from the Fore language group in New Guinea. The following criteria were established to minimize visual contact with Western cultures: they had seen no movies or magazines; they neither spoke nor understood English or Pidgin; they had not lived in any of the Western settlements or government towns; and they had

Table 7.2. *Percentage choice by visually isolated preliterate observers of the emotion expected in terms of agreement with the judgments of Western literate culture observers*

Emotion category described in the story	Adults	Children
Happiness	92	92
Sadness	79	81
Anger	84	90
Disgust	81	85
Surprise	68	98
Fear: from anger/disgust or sadness	80	93
from surprise	43	—
Number of observers	189	130

Source: Ekman and Friesen, 1971.

never worked for a Caucasian. Forty photographs were used of 24 different stimulus persons.

Table 7.2 shows the results for these visually isolated peoples, for both adults and children. The data were organized in terms of the emotions expected on the basis of the Ekman, Friesen, and Tomkins FAST theory, which was confirmed by the judgments of their literate culture subjects. The first row, for example, shows that when a face judged as happy in literate cultures was presented with two photographs usually judged in literate cultures as showing another emotion and a happy story was read to the observer, 92% of the observers chose the happy photograph. These data prove that the same facial behaviors are associated with the same emotions by these visually isolated members of a preliterate culture as by members of literate cultures. The only exception was in regard to fear, which, as the table shows, was discriminated from sad, angry, disgusted, and happy faces but not from surprised faces.

Ekman and Friesen (Ekman, 1972) also conducted a study on the posing of emotion, asking other visually isolated members of this New Guinea culture to show how their face would appear if they were the person described in one of the emotion stories used in the judgment task. Unedited videotapes of nine New Guineans were shown to 34 college students in the United States. Table 7.3 shows that, except for the poses of fear and surprise (which the New Guineans had difficulty in discriminating), the students, who had never seen any New Guineans, accurately judged the emotion intended by the poses. This study further confirms the results from the recognition study reported in Table 7.2.

Table 7.3. *Percentage of correct judgments by U.S.
observers of New Guineans' intended emotions*

Emotion	Percentage
Happiness	73
Anger	51
Disgust/contempt	46
Sadness	68
Surprise	27
Fear	18

These findings on both the recognition and posing of emotion by members of a preliterate culture strongly support the hypothesis that there is a pancultural element in the facial behavior associated with emotion. The only way to dismiss such evidence is to claim that even these New Guineans, who had not seen movies, who did not speak or understand English or Pidgin, who had never worked for a Caucasian, still had some contact with Westerners, sufficient contact for them to learn to recognize and simulate the culture-specific, uniquely Western, facial behaviors employed with each emotion. Though it is true these subjects had some contact with Westerners, the argument seems implausible. The criteria for selecting these subjects should decrease the probability that they could have learned such a hypothesized "foreign" set of facial behaviors well enough not only to recognize them but also to display a "foreign" set of behaviors as well as those to whom the behaviors were native. Further, Ekman and Friesen reported that the women in the New Guinean culture, who are considered to have even less contact with Westerners than the men, did just as well as the men in recognizing emotions.[1]

The best rebuttal of the culture-specific view underlying such skepticism comes from new evidence gathered with spontaneous, not posed, behavior and based on measures of the repertoire of facial behavior rather than on observers' judgments. In the study, conducted by Ekman and his associates jointly with Lazarus and his associates (Ekman, 1972), Japanese and American subjects were compared. The purpose of the study was to determine whether the same facial behaviors occurred in the same emotion-eliciting circumstances in subjects within both cultures. Japan was selected for comparison with the United States because

[1]In a study of another preliterate culture in New Guinea (the Dani), which is considerably more isolated than the Fore, essentially the same results were found (Ekman, 1972, 1973).

of the common belief that Japanese facial behavior is sufficiently differ-ent from that seen in the United States to mitigate against finding uni-versals. Ekman and Friesen hypothesized that when subjects were alone and not vulnerable to the display rules governing facial appearance in public or social situations they would show the same basic repertoire of facial expression of emotion as their American counterparts. Another reason for selecting Japan was that it made feasible the use of an eliciting circumstance that would evoke essentially the same emotions in the two cultures. Averill, Opton, and Lazarus (1969) previously conducted re-search in Japan to establish that the eliciting procedure of having sub-jects watch stress-inducing motion picture films led to self-reports of comparable emotion in Japan and the United States.

The design of this experiment and the results on the U.S. subjects were described in Chapter 4 in connection with the measurement of components of facial behavior. We shall briefly summarize the design and measurement procedure. Twenty-five subjects in the United States and 25 subjects in Japan each individually watched a neutral and a stress-inducing film while seated alone in a room. Skin conductance and heart rate measures were taken with the subject's knowledge and a videotape of their facial behavior without their knowledge.

Ekman, Friesen, and Tomkins's Facial Affect Scoring Technique (FAST) was employed to measure each movement of the face within each of three facial areas (brows/forehead, eyes/lids, lower face). This measure-ment procedure yields both frequency and duration scores for each of six emotions – happiness, anger, sadness, surprise, fear, and disgust – for each of the three areas of the face. Total face scores were also derived for any occurrences of facial activity in two or more areas at the same mo-ment in time.

We already reported (Chapter 4) that the facial behavior shown by the Americans was very different in stress from that shown during the neutral film; the same finding was obtained for the Japanese. The crucial question to test the universality hypothesis, however, is whether the facial behavior shown in these two very different cultures was similar or not, for it would be quite possible for the facial behavior shown during stress and nonstress to differ in both cultures and yet for those differ-ences to be dissimilar between cultures.

Table 7.4 shows that the repertoire of facial behavior shown during the stress film was very similar for these two cultures. In the table, the frequency measure of each type of emotional facial behavior across the 25 subjects in each culture is listed; for example, when the whole face

Table 7.4. *Frequency of emotional facial behavior shown by American (N = 25) and Japanese (N = 25) subjects while watching a stress-inducing film*

Emotion	Total Face		Brows/Forehead		Eyes/Lids		Lower Face	
	U.S.	Japan	U.S.	Japan	U.S.	Japan	U.S.	Japan
Surprise	76	50	53	24	14	12	64	65
Disgust	61	48	16	13	17	12	31	38
Sadness	59	126	29	39	57	64	2	3
Anger	29	28	18	28	14	8	19	20
Happiness	8	14	0	0	8	8	8	22
Fear	2	1	0	0	7	0	0	0
Facial behavior that was not emotion-specific	29	24	0	0	9	15	1	3
Rank-order correlation	.88 $p < .01$		.86 $p < .05$		.95 $p < .05$		.96 $p < .01$	

Source: Ekman (1972)

scores were totaled, 76 surprise faces within the U.S. sample, 61 disgust faces, etc. were found. Rank-order correlations were used for comparison of the two cultures, to see whether the relative frequency of the different emotions was similar, and these were quite high. The same calculations, made with the duration scores for each emotion rather than the frequency scores shown in Table 7.4, yielded almost identical results.

It must be acknowledged that Ekman and Friesen did not have the definitive evidence to prove that they were actually measuring the facial behavior associated with disgust, anger, fear, surprise, etc. In our discussion in Chapter 4 of whether the Facial Affect Scoring Technique actually does measure specific emotions, we concluded that more evidence was needed, although the results were encouraging. However, that determination is not crucial to the matter now under consideration. The Facial Affect Scoring Technique was successfully used to demonstrate the occurrence of different types of facial behavior in these two cultures. Even if the facial behavior were mislabeled by FAST (for example, if the behavior FAST labels disgust should be labeled anger, and vice versa), the evidence relevant to the universality question is whether the repertoire of these different types of facial behavior, whatever the label, is similar when subjects from these two cultures are in the same eliciting circumstance.

The extent of correspondence in the repertoire of facial behavior between these two cultures is remarkable. After all, these subjects live in cultures that are notoriously different in their public facial behavior. One of the elements that the investigators believe was crucial to obtaining this evidence of similarity, however, was that the subjects were not in a public situation. They did not know that their facial behavior was being observed, and thus no culture-specific display rules for managing their facial behavior should have been applicable.[2] After the subjects saw the stress film, a member of their own culture entered the room and conducted an interview about the experience. Friesen (1972) measured the facial behavior in the interview and found that the Japanese subjects showed very different facial behavior from the American subjects. During the interview, when display rules should apply, the Japanese en-

---

[2]The success of this experiment may also be based on two other factors. First, the measurement system did not describe just one type of facial behavior but was intended to measure facial behavior associated with six different emotions, so that even if the stress film elicited different emotions across the subjects, as long as these were different from the emotions elicited by the neutral film, accurate results could be obtained. Second, there was independent evidence (from the psychophysiological data and the self-reports) to indicate that the eliciting circumstance did call forth emotional reactions in the subjects.

gaged in masking, by showing happy faces when their Japanese interviewer asked them about their experience, and the Americans typically did not cover signs of negative affect when they talked with their American interviewer. This experiment further confirms the evidence for universals that was found in the studies utilizing a judgments approach to show that observers associate the same emotion with the same facial behavior across cultures (Tables 7.1–7.3).

The evidence of a pancultural element does not imply the absence of any cultural differences in the face and emotion. It implies that we must look, not at the particular facial behaviors associated with emotion, but elsewhere for those differences. Ekman (1972) and Ekman and Friesen (1967b, 1969b) suggested that cultural differences will be manifest in the circumstances that evoke an emotion, in the action consequences of an emotion, and in the display rules governing the management of facial behavior in particular settings. Izard (1969, 1971) hypothesized that cultural differences reside in attitudes about emotion and found different responses between Japanese and Western subjects to the questions, "What emotion do you least understand?" and "What emotion do you most dread?"

7.3. Summary

The same emotions were judged for the same facial behaviors by observers from different cultures in experiments that had many different stimuli of many different stimulus persons and many different groups of observers from 14 cultures or nations. Similar results were obtained with visually isolated, preliterate, New Guinea observers. A comparable repertoire of facial behavior was found in a study that measured the facial behavior shown by Japanese and American subjects while they watched a stress-inducing film. Together these findings provide conclusive evidence of a pancultural element in facial behavior and emotion. This element must be the particular association between movements of specific facial muscles and emotion concepts because the results obtained require that in every culture some of the same facial behaviors be recognized and interpreted as the same emotion. There may well be such a pancultural element for more than the six emotions reported; and in terms of the New Guinea group where visual isolation was obtained, the results were similar for only five emotions. It should be noted that these emotions for which there is pancultural evidence are not simply a random choice of possible emotion categories but include most of the emotion categories most consistently emerging in one culture from the work of investigators who focused on establishing the categories of emotion that can be judged from facial behavior (see Table 3.2).

Similarities in the association of facial behaviors with emotion concepts can be explained, from a number of nonexclusive viewpoints, based on evolution, innate neural "programs," or learning experiences common to human development (i.e., F. Allport, 1924; Asch, 1952; Huber, 1931; Izard, 1969, 1971; Izard & Tomkins, 1966; Peiper, 1963; Tomkins, 1962, 1963). The findings are consistent with studies of the facial behavior of blind compared with sighted children discussed earlier (Chapter 4) and with recent illustrative films gathered in a number of cultures by Eibl-Eibesfeldt (1970). The choice among the different viewpoints as to the basis for facial muscles being related to emotion will require further research, particularly on early development and possibly also in studies utilizing brain stimulation in relation to facial activity.

The finding of cross-cultural similarities can help clarify the relationship discussed earlier of posed behavior to spontaneous behavior (see Chapters 2 and 4). If, as Landis and later Hunt argued, posed behavior is a conventional language – socially learned and unrelated to real emotion – then it would be logical to expect, as they did, that poses would be judged differently across cultures. The fact that posed facial behavior was similarly judged across cultures and that not only were Western poses understood by New Guineans but New Guinea poses were understood by Westerners requires either that these conventionalized facial behaviors were, inexplicably, learned the same way in all 14 cultures or that Landis and Hunt were wrong and posed facial behavior resembles and grows out of spontaneous facial behavior. Our view is that posed facial behavior is similar to, if perhaps an exaggeration of, those spontaneous facial behaviors shown when the display rules to deintensify or mask emotion are not applied (see the end of Section 4.1). Posed behavior is thus an approximation of the facial behavior that spontaneously occurs when people are making little attempt to manage the facial appearance associated with intense emotion.

The findings of cross-cultural similarities in the face and emotion contradict the views of LaBarre and Birdwhistell and support the claims of F. Allport, Asch, Darwin, Tomkins, and, partly, Klineberg. There seems little basis for disputing the evidence that for at least five emotion categories there are facial behaviors specific to each emotion and that these relationships are invariant across cultures. Two major empirical questions remain. What might account for these invariants in facial behavior:

neurophysiology, constants in early learning for all humans, evolution, etc.? In what ways does facial behavior associated with emotion differ across cultures; by what means and to what extent do social–cultural determinants influence what evokes an emotion, the rules governing the visible display of emotion in the face, and the interpersonal consequences of such facial behavior?[3]

[3]Additional evidence relevant to universality in facial expression is contained in *Darwin and Facial Expression: A Century of Research in Review*, Paul Ekman, Editor, Academic Press, 1973; see especially chapters on facial expression in infants and children by William Charlesworth and Maryann Kreutzer, facial expressions in non-human primates by Suzanne Chevalier-Skolnikoff, and cross-cultural studies by Paul Ekman. Also see further discussion of this issue in Chapter 8, Section 8.1.

PART II
Review and prospect

PAUL EKMAN AND HARRIET OSTER

A number of influences have been responsible for renewed interest in facial expression of emotion since the publication of the first edition of *Emotion in the Human Face* in 1972.

Tomkins (1962, 1963) provided a theoretical rationale for studying the face as a means of learning about personality and emotion (see Chapter 13 for a newly revised and concise presentation of this theory). He and McCarter (1964) also showed that observers can obtain very high agreement in judging emotion if the facial expressions are carefully selected to show what they believe are the innate facial affects. Tomkins greatly influenced both Ekman and Izard, helping each of them to plan their initial cross-cultural studies of facial expression. The resulting evidence (see Chapter 7), that there is universality in facial expression, stimulated new work on this problem in both psychology and anthropology.

This evidence of universals in facial expression not only fits with Tomkins's theory but also with the newly emerging interest in applying ethological methods and concepts to human behavior. Interest in the biological bases of behavior, ethologists welcomed evidence of commonalities in social behavior across cultures. Human ethologists provided the first detailed "catalogs" describing naturally occurring facial behavior (Blurton-Jones, 1972; Branningan & Humphries, 1972; Grant, 1969; McGrew, 1972). In recent years developmental psychologists investigating attachment, mother–infant interaction, and the development of emotion have also begun to study facial expression (see Chapter 8).

Interest in facial expression also reflects the current popularity of "nonverbal communication." Although most of the research done under this rubric has focused on hand and body movement, gaze direction, or

Some of this material is drawn from the first edition of *Emotion in the Human Face*, some from a chapter in the *Annual Review of Psychology* by Ekman and Oster (1979).

posture, some studies have included a few facial measures or have used a judgment approach to assess the face.

A number of reviews on facial expression that appeared in the 1970s may have sparked renewed interest in this topic. The first edition of *Emotion in the Human Face* may have drawn some attention back to the face. In particular, the refutation of the negative findings of Hunt, Landis, Munn, and Sherman and the challenge to the gloomy review of the accuracy issue by Bruner and Taguiri (1954) described in Chapter 4 may have had some effect on research directions. Other influential reviews treated facial expression: in infants and children (Charlesworth & Kreutzer, 1973); in nonhuman primates (Chevalier-Skolnikoff, 1973; Redican, 1975); across cultures (Ekman, 1973); and in relation to theories of emotion (Izard, 1971).

Unfortunately, many of the new investigators of facial expression have not profited from either the successes or the failures of earlier work. Some of the questions answered in previous experiments were asked again, as if for the first time. Also, investigators have persisted at times in utilizing research designs that earlier investigators found defective.

Yet there have been advances since the 1960s. Substantive findings on certain issues are now conclusive. New methods developed for measuring facial behavior now allow study of many issues previously ignored. The availability of inexpensive videotape equipment for recording facial behavior makes possible research previously prohibitive in cost. And, once again after a 30-year hiatus, emotion has become a topic of more than marginal interest in psychology and psychiatry.

Chapter 8 reviews much of the work of the past decade, integrating what has been found and indicating what questions have not been answered or not been asked.

8. Review of research, 1970–1980

PAUL EKMAN AND HARRIET OSTER

Four topics of major importance, either because of their long-standing theoretical significance (cross-cultural, developmental, and accuracy studies) or because of recent methodological advances (facial measurement), will be discussed in this chapter. Research on the influence of facial feedback and on the neural correlates of facial expression will then be considered more briefly, as there has been much less work on these topics. This chapter was not intended to provide exhaustive coverage, but exemplary studies were selected to illustrate major findings, gaps in knowledge, or questions needing study.

8.1. Cross-cultural studies and the issue of universality

What has been found

1. *Observers label certain facial expressions of emotion in the same way regardless of culture.* Although a number of studies reviewed by Ekman (1973), attempted to show differences across cultures in the way observers judge isolated facial expressions, in fact their findings were either ambiguous or showed smiliarity across cultures. More consistent results obtained by investigators who used explicit descriptive criteria (based on theory or empirical results) to select photographs of expressions representative of each emotion. These photographs were shown to observers who selected from a list of emotion terms the one that best described each expression. The majority of observers in each culture interpreted the facial expressions as conveying the same emotions [five literate cultures (Ekman, 1972; Ekman, Sorenson & Friesen, 1969); nine literate cultures

Much of this chapter is taken from Ekman & Oster (1979). Also included are sections from Chapter 20 of the first edition of *Emotion in the Human Face*. Other material is new.

(Izard, 1971)]. Similar experiments have obtained comparable results in Malaysia (Boucher, 1973) and in two states of the Soviet Union (unpublished report by T. Niit and J. Valsiner).

Two studies investigated judgments of the intensity of emotional expression. Both found high agreement among members of literate cultures (Ekman, 1972; Saha, 1973).

In spite of this evidence, it can still be argued that facial expressions of emotion are culturally variable social signs and that the commonality of judgments is attributable solely to common learning experience. By this interpretation, exposure to the same mass media representations of emotional expression might have taught people in each culture how to label facial expressions. This explanation was disproved by studies of isolated, preliterate cultures not exposed to the mass media: the South Fore in Papua/New Guinea (Ekman & Friesen, 1971) and the Dani in West Iran (Heider & Heider reported by Ekman, 1973). These observers chose the same facial expressions to describe particular emotions as members of literate cultures.

A limitation of these cross-cultural experiments is that the facial expressions presented were not genuine but posed by subjects instructed to show a particular emotion or to move particular facial muscles. One interpreter of this literature (Mead, 1975) suggested that universality in judgments of facial expression might be limited to just such stereotyped, posed expressions. Two experiments argue against this interpretation. Winkelmayer Exline, Gottheil, and Paredes (1978) chose motion picture samples from interviews with normal and schizophrenic people to see if emotion judgments by members of different cultures would differ when spontaneous, rather than posed, expressions were shown. There was no overall difference among American, British, and Mexican observers. However, the Mexican observers were less accurate than the others in judging the facial expressions of normal but not schizophrenic subjects. This difference had not been predicted, may have been due to language and/or culture, and has not been replicated. More clear-cut results were obtained in a study by Ekman (1972) in which Japanese and American observers judged whether the facial expression of Japanese and American subjects were elicited by watching a stressful or neutral film. Observers of both cultures were equally accurate whether they judged members of their own or the other culture. Moreover, persons of either culture who were judged correctly by Americans were also judged correctly by Japanese (correlations above .75). This experiment was replicated with different subjects and observers. (See Chapter 7, pages 137–41.)

2. *Members of different cultures show the same facial expressions when experiencing the same emotion unless culture-specific display rules interfere.* Whereas many studies have compared judgments of facial expression by observers from different cultures, few studies have compared the facial expressions actually produced by members of different cultures in comparable situations. Without studies measuring actual facial activity, it is not possible to determine which specific aspects of facial expressions are universal, in what social contexts these configurations are shown, how cultural norms for managing emotional expression (display rules) operate. Such questions apply both to intended (posed) and spontaneous facial expressions. There has been but one study of each.

Ekman & Friesen (1971) found that members of a preliterate New Guinea group showed the same facial movements when posing particular emotions as did members of literate cultures. Ekman (1972) and Friesen (1972) also found that when Japanese and American subjects sat alone watching either a stress-inducing or neutral film, they showed the same facial actions. (This part of the study is reported in detail in Chapter 4, pages 91–6.) However, as predicted by knowledge of display rules in the two cultures, when a person in authority was present, the Japanese subjects smiled more and showed more control of facial expression than did the Americans.

Unanswered or unasked questions

1. *How many emotions have a universal facial expression?* Researchers in literate cultures have found distinctive facial expressions for anger, disgust, happiness, sadness (or distress), fear, and surprise (Boucher, 1973; Ekman, 1972; Ekman, 1973; Ekman, Sorenson, & Friesen, 1969; Izard, 1971; Saha, 1973). Izard (1971) also reported evidence for interest and shame, but inspection of his photographs suggests that head position, not facial expression, may have provided the clues for recognizing these emotions. There have been no other cross-cultural studies of these two emotions. In the preliterate cultures studied, fear and surprise expressions were differentiated from anger, sadness, happiness, and disgust but were confused with each other both in labeling and posing expressions (Ekman, 1973). In sum, there is unambiguous evidence of universality only for the expressions of happiness, anger, disgust, sadness, and combined fear/surprise. Further study may reveal universal facial expressions for other emotions.

Although there have been many cross-cultural studies, they were not conducted in a way that would answer other fundamental questions raised, but not settled, in earlier research about the judgment of emotion from facial expression. Earlier, in Chapter 3, we reported consistent evidence that people can obtain information about happiness, surprise, fear, anger, disgust, contempt, interest, and sadness from viewing facial expression. And, they can also describe facial expressions using dimensions such as pleasant–unpleasant, active–passive, intense–controlled. Work has yet to be done within a single culture to determine how many more emotions (categories or dimensions) have a distinctive facial expression. Other related questions from the pre-1970 literature largely ignored in the last decade are: When people view the face, do they tend to think about the information they obtain more in terms of categories or dimensions? What is the relationship between the categories and dimensions; can one be derived from the other, and do they refer to different facial behavior? Which provides more differentiated information? What cluster of words may be contained within a category, as, for example, the category *fear*; which are synonyms; which define its boundaries with another category such as *surprise*; and which, although similar in general meaning, vary in intensity?

Whereas it is evident that the face can provide information about the presence of two emotion categories at the same instant in time or in rapid sequence, there has been little study of *blends* within or across cultures. Are there specific words in the vocabulary of each culture, or just certain cultures, that describe each blend, or do people refer to them as happy–angers or sad–disgusts? Would blends be more likely to be interpreted differently across cultures than expressions that show but a single emotion? Or would the difference among cultures be manifest in whether or not there is a term for a particular blend? And if there were such differences in the naming of blends, might this reflect a difference among cultures in the frequency that particular blends of emotion are likely to occur?

2. *How many universal expressions are distinguishable for any emotion?* Tomkins (1962, 1963) hypothesized that each emotion would have both universal and culture-specific expressions, but he did not describe the appearance of the latter in any detail. The cross-cultural studies used only a few examples of each emotional expression and did not analyze observers' judgments to see whether different versions of each expression were judged differently.

Even within a single culture, it is not known how many expressions there are for any single emotion. Perhaps another way cultures might differ is in the number of facial expressions associated with a particular emotion. There might be four or five expressions for anger in one culture and eight or nine in still another culture.

3. *How great are the cultural differences in facial expression?* Most accounts of extreme cultural variability in the expression of emotion come from qualitative observations made by single observers who did not control for observer or sampling bias or take display rules into account [Birdwhistell, LaBarre, Leach, Mead, and Montague reviewed by Ekman (1973, 1977)]. One quantitative study of cultural differences is the previously cited finding by Ekman (1972) and Friesen (1972) that facial expressions in Japanese and American subjects differed in a social situation but not when the same subjects were alone. This fit the authors' hypothesis that socially learned display rules for managing facial expression in various contexts are a major source of cultural variation in facial expression. In another study of display rules, Heider (1974) confirmed his prediction that one West Irian culture but not another would substitute disgust expressions for anger when asked to portray angry themes. There has been no further cross-cultural study of display rules. A study of year-book photographs and conversations (Seaford, 1976) found evidence for a facial expression "dialect" in patterns of smiling among Southeastern Americans. The origin and interpretation of this dialect remain uncertain.

Many questions could be asked about display rules within a single culture as well in cross-cultural comparisons. What are these rules? How are they acquired – with what level of specificity in terms of the characteristics of the social situation and persons to which they apply? When facial behavior is managed in two cultures is the resultant facial behavior similar? For example, if in culture X the display rule for adult males is to deintensify sadness at funerals and in culture Y the display rule for adult females is to deintensify sadness when hearing about the husband's prolonged departure, is the facial appearance of the deintensified sadness the same in both cultures? Or does one culture deintensify sadness by restricting the expression to just the brow (producing a *partial* expression) and the other culture deintensify by reducing the time period (producing a *micro* expression)? Ekman (1972) postulated that learned triggers for each emotion were another major source of cultural variation, but he hypothesized that these elicitors may have some shared underlying characteristics. Boucher (1973) and Cunningham (1977) found evidence for similarities, but not for the hypothesized differences, in the specific elicitors of certain emotions in quite divergent cultures. In sum, there probably are important cultural differences in facial expression, attributable to learning, but precisely what these are and how they come to be are unknown.

4. *How often do people in natural situations actually show the distinctive, universal patterns of facial expression?* Are these expressions common or relatively rare? Does their occurrence vary with culture, sex, age, or the particular social context? Such questions call for detailed measurement of the facial expressions occurring in specified circumstances in different cultures as well as knowledge of each culture's display rules. These facts are not available for even one culture.

5. *What are the evolutionary and/or ontogenetic origins of facial expressions?* Why are particular facial muscles activated in particular emotional expressions? For example, why are the lip corners raised in happiness and drawn down in sadness rather than vice versa? The finding of universal facial expressions has been taken as evidence that these expressions are *innate*, prewired, specialized signals (Darwin, 1872; Eibl-Eibesfeldt, 1971; Redican, 1975; Tomkins, 1962). Other writers (F. Allport, 1924; Peiper, 1963) have proposed instead that adult facial expressions derived onto-genetically from species-constant learning and from the biologically adaptive responses of the newborn: movements related to sensory reactions, defensive and orienting responses, crying, sucking, etc.

The crucial data for understanding the origin of facial expressions of emotion – longitudinal studies involving detailed measurement of facial movements in infants in a variety of situations and in several unrelated cultures – exist only in piecemeal fashion. Detailed comparison of blind and sighted infants could reveal the importance of visual imitation and the adaptive use of facial movements involved in vision for the development of facial expressions. Studies of congenitally blind infants (reviewed by Charlesworth & Kreutzer, 1973) have provided the best evidence that direct imitation is unnecessary for the development of smiling, laughter, and crying. However, descriptions of the actual facial movements corresponding to these and other emotions (e.g. surprise, anger) in blind children have been vague and imprecise. Reports that blind infants and children are less facially expressive than sighted children (Charlesworth & Kreutzer, 1973; Fraiberg, 1974) have also lacked detailed description.

8.2. Developmental studies

Most research on facial expression in infants was concerned with the timetable of emotional development. At what age and in what order do particular emotions emerge? Unfortunately, the behavioral criteria by which various emotional responses were "recognized" and labeled were often subjective and imprecise, with little attention paid to detailed description of the facial movements themselves. Most early studies also lacked independent, convergent measures for assessing the infant's presumed emotional state. Several more recent studies attempted to deal with these methodological problems (Campos, Emde, Gaensbauer, & Henderson, 1975; Hiatt, Campos, & Emde, 1977; Lewis, Brooks & Haviland, 1978; Waters, Matas, & Sroufe, 1975; Young & Décarie, 1977). Nevertheless, it is still not known when the distinctive, universal facial expressions corresponding to certain emotions first appear, nor how they develop. Part of the problem is that the questions left unanswered by research on infants have been pursued in studies of toddlers and young children.

What has been found

1. *The facial musculature is fully formed and functional at birth.* Many observers have been struck by the newborn's considerable facial mobility (Gesell, 1945; Haviland, 1975). Using a fine-grained measurement system (described later), Oster & Ekman (1978) confirmed that all but one of the discrete facial muscle actions visible in the adult can be identified and finely discriminated in full-term and premature newborns. Evidence for organization and temporal patterning in expressive movements such as smiling, brow knitting, and pouting in young infants has also been found by fine-grained analysis (Josse, Leonard, Lezine, Robinot, & Rouchouse, 1973; Oster, 1978; Oster & Ekman, 1978).

2. *Distinctive facial expressions resembling certain adult expressions are present in early infancy.* Crying, the universal expression of *distress*, is of course present at birth, but there has been little careful description since Darwin of the facial signs of distress and no study of developmental changes, if any, in cry faces. It is not known whether different facial movements correspond to acoustically different cry types or different sources of distress. Newborn infants show expressions resembling adult *disgust* in response to unpleasant tastes (Peiper, 1963; Steiner, 1973). These facial responses were found in anencephalic and hydrocephalic

infants, suggesting a brain stem origin (Steiner, 1973). The processes by which these facial reactions become associated with a wide range of psychological elicitors are not known. The *startle* reaction can be triggered in the newborn by sudden, intense stimulation and often occurs as a spontaneous discharge in non-REM (rapid eye movement) sleep. There is disagreement about whether startle should be considered an emotional response related to surprise or a physiological reflex (Tomkins, 1962; Vaughn & Sroufe, 1976; P. H. Wolff, 1966). The facial response is quite different from surprise and is said not to change throughout life.

Contrary to previous belief, neonatal smiles are neither random nor produced by gas. They occur primarily during REM sleep and seem to reflect periodic, endogenous fluctuations in CNS activity (Emde, Gaensbauer, & Harmon, 1976; Sroufe & Waters, 1976; P. H. Wolff, 1963). Social smiling, i.e., smiling in an alert, bright-eyed infant who is fixating the caregiver, first occurs around 3 to 4 weeks of age (P. H. Wolff, 1963). The reliable, full-blown social smile emerges in the third month (Emde et al., 1976; P. H. Wolff, 1963). Smiling in 2- to 3-month olds was observed in a variety of experimental situations suggesting that it reflects active cognitive engagement, "mastery," and a sense of efficacy (Papousek & Papousek, 1977; Shultz & Zigler, 1970; Sroufe, 1978; Sroufe & Waters, 1976; Watson, 1978). Beginning around the fourth month, smiling becomes increasingly reserved for the infant's primary caregivers (Ainsworth, 1973; Bowlby, 1969). With the exception of P. H. Wolff's classic study, little is known about developmental changes in the morphology of the smile or about differences, if any, in the appearance of social, playful, or cognitive mastery smiles (Blurton Jones, 1974; van Hooff, 1972). Laughter first appears around 4 months and most studies focused on changes in the determinants of laughter (Sroufe, 1978; Sroufe & Waters, 1976). Insights into the mechanisms underlying smiling and laughter came from the study of Down's Syndrome infants (Cicchetti & Sroufe, 1978).

3. *Three- to 4-month olds show differential responses to facial expressions.* Early studies (Charlesworth & Kreutzer, 1973) indicated that infants do not begin to discriminate among facial expressions until 5 to 6 months. Several more recent studies found differential visual fixation to slides of happy versus neutral or angry faces (LaBarbera, Izard, Vietze, & Parisi, 1976) and surprise versus happy faces (Young-Browne, Rosenfeld, & Horowitz, 1977) in 3- to 4-month-olds. It is not certain which aspect of the faces the infants were responding to nor whether they perceived the stimuli (other than the smile, perhaps) as meaningful emotional expres-

sions. Measurement of infants' emotional responses and scan patterns to different facial expressions might help to resolve this question. Three-month-olds typically become "sober" or distressed when the caregiver presents an impassive face, suggesting a sensitivity to the animation and responsiveness of naturally occurring facial behavior (Brazelton, Tronick, Adamson, Als, & Wise, 1975; Techler & Carpenter, 1967; Trevarthen, 1977). Detailed study of infants' responses to the dynamic, temporally patterned, often exaggerated facial expressions used by caregivers (see Stern, Beebe, Jaffe, & Bennett (1977) might reveal a greater sensitivity to differences in the expressive movements themselves.

4. *Imitation of some facial movements is possible at an early age.* Recent studies suggest that 2- to 3-week old infants can differentially imitate actions such as mouth opening and tongue or lip protrusion (Meltzoff & Moore, 1977), but there is disagreement about the possible mechanism underlying this feat (Jacobson & Kagan, 1978; Meltzoff & Moore, 1977). It is not known whether neonates can imitate the principal actions used in emotional expression nor what role imitation plays in the normal development or "fine-tuning" of facial expression. Such a role is suggested by Kaye and Marcus's recent finding (1978) that 6-month-olds gradually accommodate their performance over a series of trials to match the movements modeled (bursts of mouth opening and closing). Many of the specific facial actions found in emotional expression can be imitated by 5 year-olds (Ekman, Roper, & Hager, 1980).

5. *Preschool children know what the most common facial expressions look like, what they mean, and what kinds of situations typically elicit them.* The general finding from recognition, discrimination, affective role-taking, and empathy studies is that performance improves from age 3 to 10 (Charlesworth & Kreutzer, 1973; Greenspan, Barenboim, & Chandler, 1976; Hoffman, 1977). The abilities to imitate and voluntarily produce facial expressions to the satisfaction of adult judges likewise increases with age (Charlesworth & Kreutzer, 1973; Hamilton, 1973). On both recognition and production tasks, the expression of happiness is easiest and fear among the most difficult. Most studies with children involved cognitive tasks tapping knowledge of emotional expressions rather than measures of spontaneous emotional expression. However, a few empathy studies have shown that preschool children's spontaneous facial expressions reflect the emotions shown by others (Hamilton, 1973; review by Hoffman, 1977). The spontaneous nonverbal expressions of preschool children watching emotion-

eliciting slides can be "decoded" by other preschool children, at least in terms of the pleasantness or unpleasantness of the "sender's" reaction (Buck, 1975). But no direct measures of the subject's facial expressions have been made in encoding/decoding studies. The only direct studies of facial behavior in children were from an ethological perspective, as discussed next.

6. *Facial expression can play a role in the development of social communication.* The young infant is increasingly being viewed as an active individual, equipped with basic signaling capacities that serve to ensure certain kinds of attachment-promoting exchanges between infant and caregivers (Ainsworth, 1973; Bowlby, 1969; Brazelton, et al., 1975; Lewis & Rosenblum, 1974; Trevarthen, 1977). Facial expression is recognized as a major component of this signaling system.

Ethological studies of natural social interaction in day care or nursery school settings typically focused on the repertoire of facial and gestural actions associated with agonistic encounters, rough-and-tumble play, and social interaction with adults and peers (Blurton Jones, 1972). Ethologists discuss these actions in terms of their presumed motivation and signal function. However, there was little quantitative documentation that particular expressive movements actually serve the presumed signaling function. Nor have ethologists systematically related the facial movements shown in such actions to emotional expressions. An exception on both scores is a recent ethologically oriented experimental study (Camras, 1977), showing that certain "aggressive" facial configurations used by children defending a desired object predicted both the child's own and his partner's subsequent behavior. The growing social control over emotional expression is suggested by observations that the presence of others can have a facilitative effect on emotional expressions such as crying (Blurton Jones, 1972b) and humor (Chapman & Wright, 1976).

Unanswered or unasked questions

1. *At what age can emotion be inferred from facial expressions seen in early infancy?* Most psychologists believe that young infants lack the cognitive prerequisites for the experience of emotion. This belief cuts across the nativist/empiricist spectrum e.g., F. Allport, 1924; Gesell, 1945; Peiper, 1963, though there have been widely differing views on the presumed cognitive prerequisites for experiencing "true emotion," on the age when

these prerequisites are attained, and on the ontogenetic mechanisms presumed to be involved. Recent articles (Emde, et al., 1976; Lewis & Brooks, 1978; Saarni, 1978; Sroufe, 1978) have interpreted expressive movements such as crying and smiling in early infancy as purely passive, reflexlike precursors of later expressions of emotion. There is said to be no "genuine" emotion until the emergence of the first signs of active cognitive processing, or "consciousness," around the third month (Emde, et al., 1976; Sroufe, 1978), or until the emergence of "self-conscious awareness" around 18 months (Lewis & Brooks, 1978). Although not denying the importance of these cognitive achievements, several researchers maintain that emotion is present at birth (Izard, 1978; Tomkins, 1962, 1963) or suggest a more gradual transition from physiological to psychological causation of emotional expressions (Oster, 1978; Stechler & Carpenter, 1967; P. H. Wolff, 1966). This issue cannot be resolved on the basis of available empirical data.

2. *When do adultlike, differentiated facial expressions for the emotions of interest, surprise, sadness, fear, and anger first appear?* "Brightening" of the eyes and face was noted in alert newborns attending to visual or auditory stimuli. But more detailed study will be needed before we can conclude that the expression of interest, as distinct from orienting and attentional responses, is present in early infancy. The typical adult surprise face is infrequently observed in infants less than 1 year old (Charlesworth & Kreutzer, 1973; Vaughn & Sroufe, 1976), even though infants in the second half-year may respond to presumably surprising experimental situations in ways suggesting that they were surprised (Decarie, 1978; Hiatt et al., 1977; Vaughn & Sroufe, 1976).

We cannot yet specify when discrete negative affect expressions (as distinct from crying) begin to appear on a regular basis nor in what natural circumstances they are likely to occur. Sadness and distress faces differ in adults, but this distinction was not made in studies of infants and children. "Wariness" and fear emerge in the second half-year of life, as inferred from the onset of hesitant, avoidant, or overtly negative reactions to situations that were not previously distressing, such as heights or the approach of a stranger. (Campos, Hiatt, Ramsay, Henderson & Svejda, 1978; Decarie, 1978; Emde et al., 1976; Sroufe, 1977, 1978). Anger was inferred from "tantrum" behaviors and from instrumental acts such as hitting, throwing, and biting (Charlesworth & Kreutzer, 1973; Sroufe, 1978). But the facial expressions accompanying these emotional responses were not described in detail. Investigators who coded infants' responses to emotion-arousing situations in terms of specific facial actions (Campos et al., 1975; Hiatt, Campos & Emde, 1977; Lewis et al., 1978; Waters et al., 1975; Young & Decarie, 1977), did not find differentiated expressions of fear, sadness, or anger, but rather affectively neutral attention and components of pre-cry or distress faces of various intensities. In one of the few studies that tried to elicit several different negative affects (Young & Decarie, 1977), the infants' reactions could not be distinguished on the basis of facial expression alone. A finer-grain coding system might reveal precursors of adult expressions of anger, sadness, or fear in the cry or pre-cry faces elicited by different events or associated with other behaviors indicative of these affects.

As just noted, 5-year-olds can satisfactorily pose expressions of anger, fear, and sadness, but there has been no systematic study of the actual occurrence of discrete negative affect expressions in natural or laboratory settings. Crying apparently remains the prepotent expression of virtually all strong negative affect throughout early childhood. However, no studies investigated Tomkins' proposal (1963) that different cry vocalizations and cry faces accompany different negative affects. Nor is it clear whether young children cry because they do not yet "use" more discrete facial expressions (which they can, however, produce voluntarily) or because all negative affect is blended with or produces distress at this age.

3. *When and how do facial expressions of emotion come under voluntary control?* The development of voluntary control and of culturally defined "display rules" for managing emotional expression remains a virtual *terra incognita*, with only impressionistic observations suggesting a gradual transition from the automatic, uncontrolled expression of emotion in early infancy to the more modulated, subtle, and voluntary expression of emotion seen in older children and adults. The first step is probably the (not fully conscious) instrumental use of crying and smiling, somewhere in the first 2 to 3 months of life, as suggested by subjective impressions of "fake" crying (P. H. Wolff, 1969), by evidence that both crying and smiling can be brought under the control of social reinforcement (Gewirtz & Boyd, 1976) and by reports suggesting that during the first half-year of life infants begin to acquire a sense of the efficacy of their own signaling behaviors (Bell & Ainsworth, 1972). By the end of the first year, one sees what seem to be smiles used as social greetings, deliberate "tantrum" behaviors, and visible efforts to hold back, or suppress, tears. The specific facial actions used in such behaviors were not closely examined, however.

As noted, one form of voluntary control – deliberately imitating or posing facial expressions when the corresponding emotion is (presumably) not felt – is present to some extent in preschool children. One recent study investigating children's verbal knowledge of social display rules (Saarni, 1978) found increasing awareness of rules for managing emotional expression from 6 to 10 years. We know of no studies that directly studied children's efforts to control emotional expression or their use of display rules. Despite the general assumption that feedback from others (e.g., "big boys don't cry") plays a crucial role in shaping children's tendencies to manage emotional expression, we know of no objective data on the amount and kind of social feedback that children actually receive in response to their facial expressions nor the extent to which parents, other adults, and peers serve as direct models.

8.3. Facial measurement

As indicated in Sections 8.1 and 8.2, many of the central questions in cross-cultural and developmental research require measurement of facial activity itself and cannot be answered solely by reliance upon observers' judgments of emotion. Methods were recently developed to allow measurement of two different, but related, aspects of facial activity: muscle tonus changes and visible actions.

Muscle tonus measurement

Schwartz and his co-workers (Schwartz, Fair, Salt, Mandel, & Klerman, 1976) showed that surface electromyographic (EMG) measurements are sensitive to differences among recalled emotions and moods and can distinguish depressive from normal subjects. The EMG leads were placed over facial areas that, according to theory (Ekman & Friesen, 1975; Tomkins, 1962, 1963), were expected to be differentially active for the emotions studied. Although a given placement of leads apparently can differentiate among two or three emotions, it is not certain whether surface EMG procedures could distinguish as many as five or six emotions. A study by Ekman, Schwartz, and Friesen (reported in Ekman, 1982) on the relationship between EMG and visible facial activity suggests that the EMG can record muscle tonus changes that are barely visible or totally invisible.

The EMG measurement of facial activity may be most applicable when the investigator can specify in advance the emotions of interest, when unobtrusiveness is not crucial, and when the subjects will not be likely to move their faces. (The leads, paste, and tape tend to inhibit movement and may be torn by strong muscle actions.) In addition, EMG should be useful when emotion is aroused by fantasy, recall, listening, viewing a film, etc. and is also the only method for studying Birdwhistell's (1970) proposal that there are stable individual differences in the pattern of muscular tension maintained when the face is at rest (see Smith, 1973).

Visible action measurement

The early attempts to measure visible facial action (reviewed in Section 4.2) have been largely ignored by those who followed. These early methods for measuring facial action did not explain the rationale for their choice of facial measurement units, yet as Altmann commented, "What stage in our research could be more crucial than this initial choosing of behavioral units. Upon it rests all of our subsequent records of communication interactions and any conclusions we may draw from them" (Altmann, 1968a, p. 501). Selection of behavioral units has been based on theory, inductive observation, or facial anatomy.

Inductively based selection. Several overlapping listings of facial actions were derived by observing spontaneous behavior in infants (Nystrom, 1974; Young & Decarie, 1977), children (Blurton Jones, 1971; Brannigan & Humphries, 1972; Grant, 1969; McGrew, 1972), and normal adults and psychiatric adult patients (Grant, 1969). These systems were useful in generating "ethograms," or catalogs of the salient behaviors in the communicative repertoire. Blurton Jones's system was adopted, with some variations, by a number of developmental psychologists. Yet all these studies suffer from major methodological flaws if considered as general-purpose facial measurement systems.

All are incomplete, with no explanation of what has been left out or why. All include, without mention, both simple muscle actions and complex movements involving several independent actions. Behavioral units are sometimes given inference-laden names (e.g., "angry frown"), making objective study of the action's meaning difficult. Many units are only vaguely described, so that investigators cannot know if they are coding the same actions. Descriptions of some actions are anatomically incorrect. Finally, individual, racial, or age-related differences in physiognomy may make it difficult to identify certain actions described in terms of static configurations (e.g., "oblong mouth").

Theory-based selection. Ekman, Friesen, and Tomkins's (Ekman, Friesen, & Tomkins, 1971) Facial Affect Scoring Technique (FAST) specified what they believed, on the basis of previous research, to be the distinctive components of six universal affect expressions. FAST proved useful in studies relating subjects' facial expressions to autonomic responses, experimental conditions, and observers' judgments. (See Sections 4.2, 5.2, and 7.2.) It is not a general-purpose tool, however and cannot be used to determine whether actions other than those specified are relevant to emotion nor to study developmental changes or individual differences in the expression of emotion. The first two criticisms of the Inductively Derived systems also apply to FAST. Izard's (1979) newly developed Maximally Discriminative Facial Movement Coding (MAX), which follows the same general approach as FAST, also suffers from the same limitations. Some investigators (e.g. Hiatt, et al., 1977; Izard, 1979) used theory-based systems (e.g., materials developed by Ekman and Friesen, 1975) for training clinicians, or Izard's MAX as the basis for scoring emotional expressions or components of those expressions in infants or young children. This approach suffers from the problems outlined for FAST also. There are additional methodological problems inherent in using a theory-based facial measurement system derived from data on adults for research on infants. More serious, such an approach cannot reveal how full-face, adultlike expressions develop and ignores possible early precursors of these expressions.

Anatomically based selection. Becau. ` every facial movement is the result of muscular action, a system for describing facial expression can be comprehensive if the measurement units are based on knowledge of how each muscle acts to change appearance. Any complex facial movement can then be scored analytically in terms of the minimal muscle actions that collectively produce the movement. Three investigators have followed this logic.

Seaford (1976) described a regional variation in facial expression that showed the utility of an anatomical approach. In addition, he provided an excellent, detailed critique of the hazards in theoretically or inductively derived systems. Ermiane and Gergerian (1978) developed a general-purpose, anatomically based facial measurement system, but they do not report reliability data nor mention whether the system can be learned without personal instruction.

Ekman and Friesen's (1976a, 1978) Facial Action Coding System (FACS), also a general-purpose system, was designed to measure all visible facial behavior in any context, not just actions related to emotion. The list of minimal units overlaps considerably with that of Ermiane and Gergerian. However, FACS specifies minimal units not only in terms of anatomically possible actions but also in terms of which actions can be reliably distinguished. Persons who learn the system without personal instruction from the developers have achieved high reliability.

FACS is slow to learn and use, requiring repeated, slow-motion viewing of facial actions. It is thus unsuitable for real-time coding. By its nature, FACS includes more distinctions than may be needed for any particular study, which increases the expense and tedium of measurement. However, once meaningful units of behavior are defined empirically, it is possible in a given study to collapse some of the elementary measurement units or to disregard subtle distinctions. Empirical evidence to substantiate which facial actions and combinations, as scored by FACS, correspond to particular emotions is reported in Chapter 9. Most of the material discussed in this section will also be described in more detail in Chapter 9.

Other facial measurement

Perhaps the most popular measure of facial activity was the direction of gaze, yet surprisingly this was rarely studied in relation to emotion or facial expressions (recent exceptions are Graham & Argyle, 1975; Lalljee, 1978; Stechler & Carpenter, 1967; Stern et al., 1977; Waters et al., 1975). Although pupil dilation was studied in relation to emotion, no study of associated changes in facial expression was done. Blood flow, skin temperature, and coloration changes in the face are other measures that so far remain unexplored.

8.4. Accuracy

How are we to determine if the information provided by a person's facial expression is accurate? We must have some criterion, independent of the face itself, for establishing which emotion, if any, was experienced at the moment of facial expression. The problem of independent validation has been the greatest obstacle to research on accuracy. A common approach has been to ask subjects to report their feelings (usually retrospectively) and to see whether their facial expressions differ when reporting emotion A as compared to emotion B. Such self-reports are error-prone because subjects may fail to remember or to distinguish among the emotions experienced, particularly if several minutes elapse before the report is made. A subject who successively felt anger, disgust, and contempt while watching a film might not recall all three reactions, their exact sequence, or their time of occurrence. This problem can be avoided by limiting self-report to the grosser distinction between pleasant versus unpleasant feelings; but we then cannot determine whether facial expressions convey accurate information about particular unpleasant or pleasant feelings.

A second common approach has been to find out if subjects' facial expressions vary according to the eliciting conditions, e.g., affectively positive versus negative films or slides; anticipation of an electric shock versus a no-shock trial; or hostile versus friendly remarks made by another person. Because it is unlikely that all subjects experience the same discrete emotion during a particular condition, this approach can usually show only that different facial expressions are used in presumably pleasant and unpleasant situations.

Attempts to pre- or postdict other information about subjects (e.g., whether they have many friends) have also been used to assess accuracy; but this approach implies that facial expressions can provide information about enduring traits in addition to transient states. If particular changes in voice pitch or quality, body movement, or speech were infallible indicators of particular emotions, these could serve as accuracy criteria. Unfortunately, there is no evidence that these channels provide any more accurate information than facial expressions. Similarly, change in autonomic or central nervous system activity could provide a useful criterion if there were evidence that different patterns of neural activity reliably accompany different emotions. The few studies that have explored the neural correlates of facial expression will be reviewed in Section 8.6. Because there is no single, infallible way to determine a person's "true" emotional state, it is unfortunate that so few investigators have followed the approach of using multiple convergent measures to gain a more reliable indication of the emotion experienced.

Regardless of the accuracy criterion used, the information provided by facial expression can be studied either indirectly, by observers' judgments (of the emotion experienced, the eliciting conditions, etc.), or by direct measurement of facial activity (using any of the techniques described in the previous section). Facial measurement and observer judgments need not yield the same results even when applied to the same facial expressions. Direct measurement can reveal expressive movements that observers missed in real-time or that they failed to interpret correctly. Conversely, observers can pick up cues that were not among the units measured. Observer judgment studies have far exceeded facial measurement studies, probably because the latter are more expensive and time-consuming than the former.

What has been found

1. *Facial expressions of emotion can provide accurate information about the occurrence of pleasant as compared to unpleasant emotional states.* Reanalysis of studies from 1914 to 1970 in Chapter 4 leads to the conclusion that both facial measurements and observers' judgment methods accurately distinguished pleasant from unpleasant states. Since then a number of experiments (cited below) have replicated these findings but have not extended them to possible distinctions among particular positive or negative emotions. There is little information pinpointing the specific facial actions that differentiate between pleasant and unpleasant states. Most investigators have used observers' judgments of facial expression without trying to determine to which configurations observers were responding to. Those who directly measured facial expression failed to report the frequency of specific actions or full-face configurations used in the expressions that provide accurate information.

2. *Facial expressions can be disguised to mislead an observer about the emotions experienced.* Among the dozens of recent experiments on interpersonal deceit, only five (Ekman & Friesen, 1974a; Harper, Wiens & Fujita, 1977; Lanzetta, Cartwright-Smith, & Kleck, 1976; Mehrabian, 1971; Zuckerman, DeFrank, Hall, Larrance & Rosenthal, 1979) explicitly instructed subjects to conceal their emotions and also obtained evidence independent of the face that they actually experienced emotion. The results were contradictory, most likely because of variations in the strength or number of emotions aroused, the subjects' motivation to deceive, and their prior practice in perpetrating such deception. However, the experiments also differed in other ways; e.g., whether subjects knew they were being videotaped, whether observers knew that deception might be involved, whether they were trained, whether they heard the deceiver's speech in addition to seeing their faces. Despite the lack of consistency, this seems an important area for further study.

3. *Individuals differ in facial "expressiveness" (encoding ability) and in their ability to judge facial expressions (decoding ability).* In encoding/decoding

studies, encoders are videotaped in emotion-arousing situations (while watching slides or undergoing shock); decoders (often the same subjects) then try to infer, from each encoder's facial expressions, the eliciting condition (category of slides or level of shock) or the encoder's rating of his or her own emotional experience. There are marked individual differences in how accurately an individual's facial expressions are judged and in how accurately an individual judges the faces of others (Buck, 1977; Cunningham, 1977; Harper et al., 1977; Lanzetta & Kleck, 1970; Zuckerman, Larrance, Hall, De Frank, & Rosenthal, 1979). This finding is consistent with observations from other experiments that were not specifically looking for individual differences. Attempts to study the relationship between encoding and decoding abilities produced negative, positive, and insignificant correlations (see Fujita, 1977, for a careful discussion). Inconsistent findings have also been obtained in the search for personality correlates of individual differences in encoding and decoding abilities. An exception is the small but consistent superiority of women in both encoding and decoding (J. Hall, 1977, 1978).

These encode/decode studies are fraught with methodological problems, which may explain some of the inconsistencies. In some studies the subjects must periodically rate their own emotional experience, a task that might affect their facial expressions or the experience itself. Many experiments do not verify which, if any, emotion was experienced by encoders. Exceptions are studies that obtained independent ratings of the emotions aroused by their elicitor (Cunningham, 1977; Harper et al., 1977) or that used psychophysiological measures to indicate arousal, though not which emotion was aroused (Lanzetta et al., 1976). Most often, the only measure of emotional arousal is the observers' success in inferring the relative pleasantness of the eliciting condition or the subjects' subsequent rating of their own feelings (Buck, Miller, & Caul, 1974; Buck, Savin, Miller & Caul, 1972; Zuckerman, Hall, DeFrank, & Rosenthal, 1976). Such judgments could be made on the basis of cues having nothing to do with facial expression, e.g., posture, gross body movements, or facial signs of cognitive activity.

Although the search for personality correlates of individual differences in encoding and decoding abilities implies that these differences are stable, there has been no study of test-retest reliability in individual encoding ability or in encoding and decoding abilities in the same subjects. Another problem is that in many decoding tasks observers must judge facial expressions that occurred during speech but with the speech omitted. Only the deaf might have sufficient experience with this condition to develop stable individual differences in decoding such stimuli. Quite a different approach to individual differences is illustrated by Schiffenbauer's (1974) finding that the emotional states of the observer influenced the emotion they attributed to a facial expression. See Chapter 11 for a critical review of studies of individual differences in decoding ability.

Unanswered or unasked questions

1. *Can facial expressions provide accurate information about the distinctions among negative and positive emotions?* The most completed answer comes from studies of posed facial expressions (see Chapter 4). However, for a variety of reasons discussed earlier (see Section 2.2 and Chapter 4), generalizations from posed to spontaneous behavior cannot be made. Accurate information might be provided about distinctions among positive and among negative emotions for posed expressions but not for spontaneous expressions. The evidence for accurate information about the distinctions among emotions from spontaneous expressions is much more limited. Ekman, Friesen, and Ancoli (1980) found that specific facial actions differentiated among variations in the intensity of positive affect, between which of two positive experiences was most enjoyed, and among variations in the intensity of negative affect. They also isolated the particular facial actions positively correlated to the experience of disgust and negatively correlated to the experience of other emotions such as anger or sadness. More evidence will be needed to specify the particular actions that might differentiate among anger, sadness, and fear; among blends of negative emotions; and among surprise, interest, pleasure, humor, contentment, etc. It still remains unknown whether the face can provide accurate information about the occurrence of these emotions when they spontaneously occur.

2. *When can we expect facial expression to provide accurate information about emotion?* Studies showing that the facial expressions of some people are difficult to judge did not detemine whether detailed measurement of their facial activity would reveal reliable cues missed by observers nor whether those individuals might be more expressive in other social circumstances. Studies showing that people can successfully disguise their facial expressions of emotion did not explore whether this ability is a stable characteristic of the persons nor whether measurement of their facial activity would reveal reliable signs (i.e., "leakage") of their actual feelings.

Quite apart from the issues of individual differences and deception, which might limit the accuracy of information provided by facial expression, there is little information about the number and kinds of situations in which facial movement expresses emotion. It has been suggested (Ekman, 1977, 1979) that most facial activity in social interaction has little to do with emotion, but no empirical studies have compared different types of facial activity in different settings.

3. *How do facial expressions of emotion differ from nonemotional facial actions, such as gestures, mock expressions, or simulated (posed) expressions?* Facial actions occur for a variety of reasons quite apart from the experience of emotion: to illustrate and punctuate speech (Ekman, 1979); to comment on an emotion being experienced; to show politely expressions that are socially required; to provide a symbolic gesture such as the wink; to make mock expressions, etc. How do these differ from spontaneous emotional expressions? Ekman, Hager, and Friesen (1981) differentiated between actions made upon request and spontaneous emotional expressions by the amount of asymmetry in the facial movements and in the proportion of asymmetrical expressions that were stronger on the left side of the face (see Chapter 12 for a discussion of this study and a review of other studies of facial asymmetries). This study is only a beginning, however, in the identification of possible differences between emotional and nonemotional facial behavior. Only one type of non-emotional facial movement (requested actions) was compared with emotional expressions and only one aspect of the expressions, asymmetries, were measured. Ekman (1977) hypothesized that symbolic facial actions, facial illustrators, and facial actions to comment on emotion differ from emotional expressions in timing and in the particular muscles recruited into the expression. Recent evidence on felt and unfelt smiles is reported in Ekman & Friesen (1982).

4. *How much information does the face, as compared with voice, speech, and body movement, provide about emotion?* A number of studies compared observers' judgments about an event perceived via different "channels": audiovisual, audio alone, or visual alone. Most experimenters found that the face is more accurately judged, produces higher agreement, or correlates better with judgments based on full audiovisual input than on voice or speech input (Argyle, Alkema, & Gilmour, 1971; Burns & Beier, 1973; DePaulo, Rosenthal, Eisenstat, Finkelstein, & Rogers, 1978; Mehrabian & Ferris, 1967; Zaidel & Mehrabian, 1969). A few experimenters found

that the face was less important than another channel (Berman, Shulman & Marwit, 1976; Shapiro, 1972) or that channel cues varied with the observer (Berman, Shulman & Marwit, 1976; Shapiro, 1972). The findings of most "channel" experiments are suspect because the behavior judged was quite contrived. The results of the most extensive series of studies (Van de Creek & Watkins, 1972) on naturally occurring behavior was that what was said mattered more than the visual input and that knowledge of demographic information produced as much accurate behavioral postdiction as exposure to an audiovisual film.

Another problem in this research is that observers judging the "face" channel are usually shown – without sound – facial expressions that occurred embedded in speech. This could cause misinterpretations of speech-related facial expressions. Moreover, observers who are limited to just the face may get more information than they would ordinarily get from the face when it is viewed in context.

Ekman, Friesen, O'Sullivan, and Scherer (1980) found that the relative weight given to facial expression, speech, and body cues depended both on the judgment task (e.g., rating the stimulus subject's dominance, sociability, or relaxation) and the conditions in which the behavior occurred (e.g., subjects frankly describing positive reactions to a pleasant film or trying to conceal negative feelings aroused by a stressful film). The correlation between judgments made by observers who saw the face without speech and judgments made by observers who saw the face with speech was quite low on some scales (e.g., calm–agitated) and quite high on other scales (outgoing–withdrawn).

Studies by Bugental and co-workers suggest that the influence of facial expression as compared with other sources depends on the expressor, the perceiver, the message contained in each channel, and previous experience. They found that children were less influenced than were adults by a smile shown by an adult female when it was accompanied by negative words and voice tone (Bugental, Kaswan, Love, & Fox, 1970). Some experiential grounds for distrusting mothers' smiles was found in a study showing that smiling in mothers (but not fathers) was not related to the positive versus negative content of the simultaneous speech (Bugental, Love, & Gianetto, 1971). Also, mothers (but not fathers) of disturbed children produced more discrepant messages (among face, voice, and words) than did parents of nondisturbed children (Bugental, Love, Kaswan & April, 1971).

Although Scherer, Scherer, Hall & Rosenthal (1977) studied judgments of personality rather than emotion, their findings also contradict the simple notion that one channel is better than another. Personality inferences were usually channel-specific, with some best made from one source, some from another. No one combination of channels (face plus speech, face plus voice, etc.) yielded the most accurate judgments. It varied with the trait judged.

The whole question of how much information is conveyed by "separate" channels may inevitably be misleading. There is no evidence that individuals in actual social interaction selectively attend to another person's face, body, voice, or speech or that the information conveyed by these channels is simply additive. The central mechanisms directing behavior cut across channels, so that, for example, certain aspects of face, body, voice, and speech are more spontaneous others are more closely monitored and controlled. It might well be that observers selectively attend not to a particular channel but to a particular type of information (e.g., cues to emotion, deception, or cognitive activity), which might be available within several channels. No investigator has explored this possibility or the possibility that different individuals may typically attend to different types of information.

8.5. Facial feedback

The next group of studies addresses the long-debated issue of how we know what we feel. Since the demise of the James–Lange theory of emotion, which postulated visceral and other somatic feedback as the source of our subjective experience of emotion, cognitive theories have prevailed. These theorists (e.g., Schacter) view emotional arousal as undifferentiated; our experience of a particular emotion, they argue, comes from interpretations of situational cues. By contrast, Tomkins (1962, 1963) holds that we experience discrete, differentiated emotions via feedback from innately patterned facial expressions.

A variant of the facial feedback hypothesis, set within the framework of self-attribution theory, postulates that we can use information from our own facial (and other) behavior to *infer* how we feel. Laird's (1974) study provided a model for later feedback experiments: subjects were instructed to contract particular facial muscles, producing, presumably without their awareness, a "happy" or a "frowning" expression which they held while viewing slides or cartoons. The face manipulation had a significant, though small, effect (compared with the effect of the slides) on their reported feelings. A subsequent series of experiments found that individual differences on the face manipulation task were related to other indexes of an individual's tendency to use "self"- versus "situation" -produced cues (e.g., Duncan & Laird, 1977).

A recent experiment (Tourangeau & Ellsworth, 1979) failed to confirm the strong version of the facial feedback hypothesis, i.e., that overt facial expression is both necessary and sufficient for the experience of emotion. Facial manipulations had no significant effect on self-reported emotion and only ambiguous effects on physiological responses. The complexity of the issues involved in studying facial feedback can be seen in the criticisms of the Tourangeau–Ellsworth study by Hager and Ekman (1981), Izard (1981), and Tomkins (1981) and in the defense by Ellsworth & Tourangeau (1981).

These contradictory findings are difficult to evaluate because of the methodological problems inherent in the expression-manipulation paradigm: the demand characteristics of the task; the implausibility of the cover stories; and the artificiality of the situation and facial "expressions," which must be held unnaturally long. As Laird (1974) cautioned, feedback that is too unnatural could be discounted by the subject (or the CNS), thus working against the hypothesis.

The strongest evidence for a positive link between voluntary facial expression and emotional experience comes from a series of experiments by Lanzetta, Kleck, and colleagues (Colby, Lanzetta, & Kleck, 1977; Kleck, Vaughan, Cartwright-Smith, Vaughan, Colby & Lanzetta, 1976; Lanzetta et al.,1976) investigating the effect of overt facial expression on the intensity of emotional arousal produced by shock. Attempts to conceal the facial signs of pain consistently led to decreases in both skin conductance and subjective ratings of pain, whereas posing the expression of intense shock significantly increased both measures of arousal. When subjects were told that they were being observed by another person, they showed less intense facial expressions and correspondingly decreased autonomic responses and subjective ratings of pain, even though they received no instructions to inhibit their responses (Kleck et al., 1976). These findings can be interpreted in various ways (see Lanzetta, et al., 1976). Before concluding that facial feedback was directly and causally related to the observed changes in arousal, it would be necessary to rule out the possibility that some other strategy used by subjects might have affected both their facial expressions and emotional experience. It is also not clear that the effect is specific to facial versus bodily signs of emotion. Nevertheless, these findings suggest that overt facial expression can affect the intensity of emotional arousal. Evidence that facial feedback can determine *which* emotion we experience is far more ambiguous. It is worth noting that little is known about the nature and quality of feedback from the muscles of facial expression.

8.6. Neural control and ANS correlates of facial expression

Psychophysiological correlates

Two different approaches were used to examine the relationship between facial expression and autonomic nervous system (ANS) responses. In one type of study gross changes in autonomic measures (usually GSR) averaged over some period of time are compared with changes in facial expression (as inferred by observers' judgments of emotion). The other approach looks for patterning in the moment-to-moment changes in autonomic and facial measures. This approach has produced more consistent results.

Correlational studies of individual differences in ANS responsivity and facial expressiveness (in encoding/decoding studies previously discussed) typically result in negative relationships; i.e., subjects whose faces can be accurately judged as anticipating shock (Lanzetta & Kleck, 1970) or as viewing slides arousing positive versus negative affect show lower GSR responses and vice versa (reviewed by Buck, 1977). In experimental, within-subject studies, however (e.g. facial feedback and deception studies discussed above), increases in facial expressiveness have been shown to be accompanied by increases in ANS responsivity (Lanzetta, et al. 1976; see other recent studies cited previously).

Malmstrom, Ekman, and Friesen (1972) in a pilot study, found that different patterns of heart rate acceleration and deceleration coincided with facial activity showing elements of disgust versus surprise when subjects viewed a stressful film. Ancoli (1978) found that facial expressions of disgust in subjects viewing a stressful film were related to respiration changes (thoracic as compared with abdominal).

In developmental studies of infants' reactions to an approaching stranger, several investigators (e.g., Campos, et al. 1975; Waters, et al. 1975), reviewed by Sroufe, 1977) found greater heart rate acceleration in 6- to 10-month-old infants who showed facial signs of "wariness" or distress than in infants who showed neutral or positive expressions. An "open" or affectively neutral, attentive face was typically accompanied by heart rate deceleration. Lewis, Brooks & Haviland (1978), although finding a relationship between heart rate deceleration and attentive faces, did not find a significant relationship between heart rate acceleration and negative affect expressions.

Face and brain

Most knowledge about the neural control of facial expression has come from clinical studies of neurological disorders. The dual control of facial movement is shown by the finding that individuals suffering from complete paralysis of voluntary facial movements (as in pseudobulbar palsy, which affects the corticolbulbar tracts) may show spontaneous facial expressions, often grossly exaggerated, when emotion is aroused (Ford, 1966). Conversely, spontaneous emotional expressions but not voluntary movement may be affected by subcortical lesions, postencephalitic Parkinsonism, or "congenital weakness of the facial muscles" (Ford, 1966). The limbic system is known to be important in emotional expression (reviewed by Lamendella, 1977), and successive states in the ontogenetic development of spontaneous and volitional facial and vocal expression are probably related to the maturation of specific brain structures and subsystems, though the evidence at present is indirect and often sketchy.

Several converging lines of evidence (brain lesion studies, research on commisurotomized patients, recognition and reaction time experiments with normal subjects) point to a right-hemisphere advantage in recognizing faces. This advantage is especially pronounced when the task requires processing in terms of the higher-order configurational properties of faces rather than isolated features (R. Campbell, 1978; Diamond & Carey, 1977). It is also greater (Suberi & McKeever, 1977) when the faces to be recognized by subjects show emotional expressions than when they are affectively neutral. The ability to use configurational information for recognizing unfamiliar faces does not develop until around 10 years of age. Younger children, like patients with right-hemisphere lesions, use piecemeal processing and can be fooled easily by salient paraphernalia such as items of clothing (Diamond & Carey, 1977). Facial expression was not found to be a source of confusion in children of any age, suggesting that, unlike clothing, it is not normally seen as an isolated cue to identify but rather as linked to the higher-order configurational properties of faces. This view was confirmed by R. Campbell's finding (unpublished report) that adults are often misled by facial expression when facial stimuli are projected to the right but not to the left hemisphere (see also Crouch, 1976).

R. Campbell (1978 and unpublished report) used chimeric face stimuli (composites of two half-faces showing different individuals or facial expressions or mirror-reversed expressions) to study lateralization effects in the production and perception of facial expression. Her findings reveal that in right-handed adults the *perception* of facial expression is dominated by the left visual field (i.e., by the viewer's right hemisphere), corresponding to the right side of the face stimuli. There is much less agreement among investigators about whether the *expression* of emotion is stronger on one side of the face. This literature will be critically reviewed in Chapter 12.

PART III
New research directions

PAUL EKMAN

As noted in Chapter 8, one major new research direction is the actual measurement of facial action itself. New techniques have been developed to make it possible to measure what the face does, no longer relying just upon observers' inferences about the possible meaning of facial movement. In Chapter 8 a number of newly developed alternative techniques for measuring facial movement were discussed. In Chapter 9 one of these methods, Ekman and Friesen's Facial Action Coding System, will be described in detail. Although part of Chapter 9 was previously published (Ekman & Friesen, 1976a, 1978) much of it reports new findings on the reliability of this measurement technique. The use of this and other techniques for directly measuring facial movement should have a marked impact on what is learned about facial expression. More than 75 investigators are now using one of these new measurement techniques to study facial movement. (For a critical review of 14 techniques for measuring facial movement, comparing Ekman and Friesen's, Izard's, and Gergerian's techniques with each other and with previous approaches to facial measurement, see "Methods for measuring facial action," by Ekman (1982).

In Chapter 10 Redican provides a new and different review of research on facial expression in nonhuman primates. Unlike previous reviews (by Redican, 1975, and by Chevalier-Skolnikoff, 1973), the focus of this chapter is on how methodological and conceptual issues from the studies of human facial expression can help to reintegrate the studies and theories about expressions in other primates. Information from this chapter about nonhuman primate facial expressions should influence the questions asked in coming years about human expressions.

There has been a great deal of recent interest in the individual differences in the expression of emotion and in the interpretation of emotional expressions. A number of investigators have developed tests that presume to measure either expression (or what has been called *encoding ability*) or interpretation (or *decoding ability*). Chapter 8 briefly mentioned some of the limitations on this body of research. O'Sullivan, in Chapter 11, provides a critical and detailed evaluation of the individual difference tests on the ability to recognize facial expression. As a developer of one of these tests, with a background in psychometrics through her work with Guilford, O'Sullivan integrates concepts from tests and measurement with distinctions made in Chapters 1 and 2. Many of the points in this chapter would apply equally well to studies of individual differences in the production of facial expression. In this chapter a set of guidelines for the development of individual difference tests in the area of facial expression is also provided.

Currently, asymmetry in facial expression is a very popular area of research. It has, however, been characterized by profound contradictions in the empirical findings reported. Much of this work has been done by investigators more knowledgeable about neuropsychology than about facial expression. Hager, an investigator new to this field, combines sophistication about both. In Chapter 12 he provides conceptual distinctions about the face itself and about the information it may convey, distinctions that have been missing in most of the research on facial asymmetries. Using these distinctions and the methodological guidelines described in Chapter 2, he integrates many recent findings, resolving a number of apparent contradictions in the literature.

It may seem peculiar to include a chapter on affect theory under new research directions. There were two reasons for doing so. Tomkins's theory played a very influential role in the renascence of interest in facial expression in the last 15 years. He was the first modern theorist to emphasize the centrality of the face. (Darwin, of course, also gave center stage to the face in his book on emotional expression.) Tomkins also advised both of the investigators who produced the cross-cultural evidence on the universality of facial expression in the late 1960s – working both with Ekman and Friesen and with Izard (see Chapter 7 and Chapter 8, Section 8.1). Tomkins also worked with Ekman and Friesen in the development of their first attempt at facial measurement, their Facial Affect Scoring Technique, which preceded their Facial Action Coding System (see Chapter 9). No presentation of new research on facial expression would be complete without acknowledgement of this very influential theory. Yet Tomkins's theory has become inaccessible. The major presentations of this theory (Tomkins, 1962, 1963) are out of print. In Chapter 13 Tomkins provides a concise statement of his theory, including revisions made in the last few years, many of which have not been previously published. No where else is an integrated statement of this theory available. It is published here so that it may influence the new directions in research as it has influenced research over the past 15 years.

9. Measuring facial movement with the Facial Action Coding System

PAUL EKMAN AND WALLACE V. FRIESEN

Most researchers on facial behavior have not measured the face itself but instead have measured the information that observers were able to infer from the face. Examples of the questions asked are: Can observers make accurate inferences about emotion? Can observers detect clinical change or diagnosis? Do observers from different cultures interpret facial expression differently? Are observers influenced by contextual knowledge in their judgments of the face? Do observers attend more to the face than to the voice?

Few studies have involved measurement of the face itself. Examples of the type of questions that could be asked are: Which movements signal emotion? Do facial actions change with clinical improvement or differentiate among types of psychopathology? Do the same facial movements occur in the same social contexts in different cultures? Are certain facial actions inhibited in certain social settings? Which facial movements punctuate conversation? The differences between these two approaches to the study of facial behavior (i.e., observers' inferences versus facial measurement) were discussed in Chapter 1.

Research focused on the face has been impeded by the problems of devising an adequate technique for measuring the face. Over the years, various procedures for facial measurement have been invented. Early work (e.g., Frois-Wittmann, 1930; Fulcher, 1942; Landis, 1924; J. Thompson, 1941) is rarely cited by current investigators. Rather, current approaches to facial measurement have varied in methodology, ranging from analogic notations of specific changes within a part of the face (Birdwhistell, 1970) to photographic depictions of movements within each of three facial areas (Ekman, Friesen, & Tomkins, 1971) to verbal descriptions of facial gestalten (Young & Decarie, 1977).

No consensus has emerged about how to measure facial behavior. No tool has been developed as a standard to be used by all investigators.

178

Investigators have almost been in the position of inventing their own tools from scratch. The only exception has been that the category lists of facial behavior described by some human ethologists (Blurton Jones, 1971; Grant, 1969; McGrew, 1972) have influenced other human ethologists studying children.

Although differing in almost all other respects, most facial measurement techniques have shared a focus on what is visible, that is, on what raters can differentiate when they see a facial movement. An exception (Schwartz, Fair, Salt, Mandel, & Klerman, 1976) used electromyographic (EMG) measurement to study changes in muscle tone not involving a noticeable movement. EMG could also be used to measure visible changes in muscle tone not involving a noticeable movement. EMG could also be used to measure visible changes in muscle tone that do not involve a noticeable movement, but such work has not been done. Although EMG could also be employed to study visible movement, we think it is unlikely that surface electrodes could distinguish the variety of visible movements delineated by most other methods. Later in this chapter we shall describe a study comparing EMG and visible movement measurement.

Vascular changes in the face are another aspect of facial behavior that can occur without visible movement and, like muscle tonus, could be measured directly with sensors. No such work has been published in coloration or skin temperature, although Schwartz, in unpublished studies, has found thermal measures useful in measuring affective responses. Some of the measurement procedures that utilize observers to rate visible movement, have included a reference to a "reddened" face.

Elsewhere (Ekman, 1982) a comparison was made between 13 other methods for measuring facial movement and the FACS method, contrasting the assumptions that underlie each method, explaining how units of measurement were derived, and providing point by point comparisons of the measurement units. Here we shall only selectively contrast other methods with FACS to explain the technique.

9.1. Background to the development of the Facial Action Coding System

Our primary goal in developing the Facial Action Coding System was to develop a *comprehensive* system that could distinguish all possible visually distinguishable facial movements. Most other investigators developed their method just to describe the particular sample of behavior they were studying. Our earlier approach, the Facial Affect Scoring Technique (FAST) (Ekman, Friesen, & Tomkins, 1971) discussed in Chapters

4 and 5, also had this narrower objective. It was designed primarily to measure facial movement relevant to emotion. Although we remained interested in describing emotion signals, to do so we needed a measurement scheme that could distinguish among *all* visible facial behavior. We were also interested in a tool that would allow study of facial movement in research unrelated to emotion; e.g., facial punctuators in conversation or facial deficits indicative of brain lesions. With comprehensiveness as our goal, we wanted to build the system free of any theoretical bias about the possible meaning of facial behaviors.

The interest in comprehensiveness also led us to reject an inductive approach to developing FACS. Most other investigators devised their descriptive system on the basis of careful inspection of some sample of the behavior they intended to measure. Thus, although their system might contain gaps, as long as its purpose was simply to measure a prescribed sample of events, it was perfectly practicable. With comprehensiveness as a goal, an inductive method would require inspecting a very large and diversified sample of behavior.

We chose to derive FACS from an analysis of the anatomical basis of facial movement. Because every facial movement is the result of muscular action, we concluded that a comprehensive system could be obtained by discovering how each muscle of the face acts to change visible appearance. With that knowledge, it would be possible to analyze any facial movement into anatomically based minimal action units.

No other investigator has so exclusively focused on the anatomy of facial movement as the basis for the descriptive measurement system. Blurton Jones (1971) considered anatomy in developing his descriptive categories, but it was not the main basis of his measurement system. He did not attempt to provide a description of the full range of minimal actions.

Our interest in comprehensiveness was motivated not only by the diverse applications we had in mind but by an awareness of the growing need for a common nomenclature for this field of research. Comparisons of the measurement units employed by other investigators would be facilitated if the particular units used in each study could be keyed to a single comprehensible list of facial actions. Also, a complete list of facial actions would reveal to potential investigators the array of possibilities, so they could better select among them. And, of course, there might be some investigators who, like us, would want to measure, not just some facial behavior, but all possible movement that they could observe.

A constraint on the development of FACS was that it deals with what is clearly *visible* in the face, ignoring invisible changes (e.g., certain changes in muscle tonus) and discarding visible changes too subtle for reliable distinction. In part, this constraint of measuring the visible was willingly adopted, based on our interest in behavior that could have social consequences. In part, the constraint of dealing only with the visible was based on our interest in a method that could be applied to any record of behavior – photographic, film, or video – taken by anyone. If our descriptive system included the nonvisible, we would be limited only to situations where we ourselves could attach the apparatus (e.g., the leads for EMG). The visibility constraint was also dictated by our belief that if subjects know their face is being scrutinized, their behavior may differ radically. The odd results obtained by Landis (1924) may have been in part because of this (see Chapter 4 for discussion of the Landis studies). A method based on visible behavior would use video or motion picture film records, which could be gathered without the subject's knowledge.

Another limitation placed on the system was that FACS would deal with *movement*, not with other visible facial phenomena. These other facial signs are important to a full understanding of the psychology of facial behavior, but their study requires a different methodology. Elsewhere (Ekman, 1977) a variety of static and slow facial signs have been distinguished, contrasting the types of information they may contain with rapid facial movement. With FACS, visible changes in muscle tonus that do not entail movement are excluded. These changes can be measured through EMG or by having observers make global inferences about brightness, alertness, soberness, etc. Changes in skin coloration are not usually visible on black and white records. Facial sweating, tears, rashes, pimples, and permanent facial characteristics were also excluded from FACS. As the name states, the Facial Action Coding System was developed to measure only movement of the face.

Ideally, the Facial Action Coding System would differentiate every change in muscular action. Instead, it is limited to what humans can reliably distinguish because it is used by human operators viewing facial behavior, not a machine-based classification. The system includes most, but not all, of the subtle differences in appearance that result from muscle action. The fineness of the scoring categories in FACS depends on what can be reliably distinguished when a facial movement is inspected repeatedly in stopped and slowed motion.

A system for measuring visible facial movements can follow one of two approaches. Either the minimal units of behavior can be specified, which can, in combination, account for any total behavior, or a list of possible facial gestalten can be given. There are several reasons for selecting the minimal units approach. First, the sheer variety of possible actions the facial musculature allows argues for the minimal units solution rather than gestalten if comprehensiveness is the goal. Also, there are too many different possible total facial actions to list all of the gestalten. Third, if the method specifies facial gestalten (e.g., Young and Decarie's, 1977, the list of 42 facial gestalten), it cannot score facial actions that show only part of the gestalt or actions that combine some of the elements of several gestalten.

Although most investigators listed minimal units, they were not explicit as to how they derived their list. How did they determine whether an action was minimal or, instead, a composite of two actions that might appear separately? Usually the decision was based on a hunch, speculation about signal value, or simply what was observed in a limited sample of facial behavior. Because we decided that an answer would come from knowledge of the mechanics of facial action, we set about determining the number of muscles that can fire independently, and whether each independent muscular action results in a distinguishable facial appearance. Such an anatomically-based list of facial appearances should allow description and differentiation of the total repertoire of visibly different facial actions.

Some might argue that there is no need to make such fine distinctions among facial actions. Indeed, there might not be a need; many differently appearing facial actions may serve the same function, or convey the same message. There may be facial synonyms, but that should be established empirically, not on *a priori* grounds. Only a measurement scheme that separately scores visibly different facial actions will permit the research that can determine which facial actions should be considered equivalent in a particular situation.

Another consideration that guided our development of the Facial Action Coding System was the need to separate inference from description. We are interested in determining which facial behavior is playful, or puzzled, or sad, but such inferences about underlying state, antecedent, or consequent actions should rest on evidence. The measurement must be made in noninferential terms that describe the facial behavior, so that the inferences can be tested by evidence. Almost all of the previous descriptive systems have combined inference-free descriptions with descriptions confounded with inference; e.g., "aggressive frown" (Grant, 1969); "lower-lip pout" (Blurton Jones, 1971); "smile tight-loose" (Birdwhistell, 1970). Each of these actions could be described without inferential terms. Because humans do the measurement the possibility of inferences cannot be eliminated, but they need not be encouraged or required. If a face is scored, for example, in terms of the lip corners moving up in an oblique direction that raises the infraorbital triangle, the person scoring the face still may make the inference that what he is describing is a smile. Our experience has been that when people use a solely descriptive measurement system, as time passes they increasingly focus on the behavioral discriminations and are rarely aware of the "meaning" of the behavior.

Another problem that plagued previous attempts to measure facial movement was how to describe most precisely each measurement unit. Blurton Jones (1971) noted that facial activity could be described in three ways: the location of shadows and lines; the muscles responsible; or the main positions of landmarks such as mouth corners or brow location. He opted for the last, although he said the other two were used also. He decided not to base his descriptions on muscular activity because it would be "...more convenient if description could be given which did not require that anyone who uses them should learn the facial muscula-ture first, although knowledge of the musculature obviously improves the acuity of one's observations" (p. 369).

We have taken almost the opposite position. The user of FACS must learn the mechanics – the muscular basis – of facial movement, not just the consequences of movement or a description of a static landmark. It is by emphasizing patterns of movement, the changing nature of fa-cial appearance, that distinctive actions are described – the movements of the skin, the temporary changes in shape and location of the fea-tures, and the gathering, pouching, bulging, and wrinkling of the skin.

It is FACS's emphasis on movement and the muscular basis of ap-pearance change that helps overcome the problems caused by physiog-nomic differences. Individuals differ in the size, shape, and location of their features and in the wrinkles, bulges, or pouches that become per-manent in midlife. The particular shape of a landmark may vary from one person to another; e.g., when the lip corner goes up, the angle, shape, or wrinkle pattern may not be the same for all people. If only the end result of movement is described, scoring may be confused by physi-ognomic variations. Knowledge of the muscular basis of action and em-phasis on recognizing movements helps to deal with variations caused by physiognomic differences.

9.2. Development of the Facial Action Coding System

Our first step in developing FACS was to study various anatomical texts to discover the minimal units. We expected to find a listing of the muscles that can fire separately and how each muscle changes facial appearance. We were disappointed to find that most anatomists were seldom concerned with facial appearance. The anatomy texts for the most part described the location of the muscles. Capacity for separate action or visible change in appearance was not the basis for the anatomists' designation of facial muscles. Instead, they distinguished muscles because of different locations, or if there was a similar location they separately named what appeared as separate bundles of muscle fibers.[1]

Duchenne (1862) was one of the first anatomists concerned with the question of how muscles change the appearance of the face. He electrically stimulated the facial muscles of a man without pain sensation and photographed the appearance changes. By this means he was able to learn the function of some of the muscles. His method was problematic for exploring the action of all of the facial muscles. Many of the muscles of the face lie one over the other, and surface stimulation will fire a number of muscles. Inserting a needle or fine wire through the skin to reach a particular muscle might fire others as well.

The work of Hjortsjö (1970) proved to be the most help. An anatomist interested in describing the visible appearance changes for each muscle, Hjortsjö learned to fire his own facial muscles voluntarily. He photographed his own face and described in drawings and words the appearance changes for each muscle. His aim was not to provide a measurement system, and so he did not consider many of the combinations of facial muscles, nor did he provide a set of rules necessary for distinguishing among appearance changes that are in any way similar.

Following Hjortsjö's lead, we spent the better part of a year with a mirror, anatomy texts, and cameras. We learned to fire separately the muscles in our own faces. When we were confident that we were firing the intended muscles, we photographed our faces. Usually there was little doubt that we were firing the intended muscle. The problem instead was to learn how to do it at all. By feeling the surface of our faces, we could usually determine whether the intended muscle was contracting. By checking Hjortsjö's account, we could see whether the appear-

---

[1]We are grateful to Washburn (1975, Pers. comm.) for explaining why the standard anatomy texts were of so little help and for encouraging our attempt to explicate the muscular basis of facial action.

ance on our faces was what he described and showed in his drawings. There were a few areas of ambiguity for which we returned to a variation on Duchenne's method for resolution. A neuroanatomist placed a needle in one of our faces, inserting the needle into the muscle about which we were uncertain. With the needle in place, the muscle was voluntarily fired, and electrical activity from that needle placement verified that indeed it was the intended muscle. As this method was uncomfortable, we used it rarely and only when we were in doubt.

One limitation of this method of deriving facial units must be noted. If there are muscles that cannot be fired voluntarily, we cannot study them. This seems to be the case only with the *tarsalis* muscle, and as best we can determine, its action and effect on appearance are not different from those of one of the voluntarily controlled muscles, *levator palpebrae*.

Our next step was to examine the photographs taken of each of our faces, scrambling the pictures so that we would not know what muscle had been fired. Our purpose was to determine if all the separate muscle actions could be distinguished accurately from appearance alone. Often it was easy to determine, although it usually required comparing the appearance change with the resting, or baseline, facial countenance.

There were instances, however, in which we found it difficult to distinguish among the many muscles in a set to account for a photograph of a facial appearance. Sometimes we could tell one muscular action from another, but the differentiation seemed so difficult that we prejudged it as not likely to be reliable. Sometimes the appearance changes resulting from two muscles seemed to differ mostly in intensity of the action, not in type of appearance. In either instance, we designated and described the result as one *action unit*, which could be produced by two or three different muscles.

Note that we call the measurements *action* not muscle units. As just explained, this is because a few times we have combined more than one muscle in our unitization of appearance changes. The other reason for using the term *Action Unit* is because we have separated more than one action from what most anatomists described as one muscle. For example, following Hjortsjö's lead, the *frontalis* muscle, which raises the brow, was separated into two Action Units, depending on whether the inner or outer portion of this muscle lifts the inner or outer portions of the eyebrow.

Table 9.1 lists the numbers, names, and anatomical bases of 33 Action Units, most of which involve a single muscle. The numbers are arbitrary and do not have any significance except that 1 through 7 refer to brows,

Table 9.1. *Single Action Units (AU)*

AU number	FACS name	Muscular basis
1	Inner brow raiser	*Frontalis, pars medialis*
2	Outer brow raiser	*Frontalis, pars lateralis*
4	Brow lowerer	*Depressor glabellae; depressor supercilii;* corrugator
5	Upper lid raiser	*Levator palpebrae superioris*
6	Cheek raiser	*Orbicularis oculi, pars orbitalis*
7	Lid tightener	*Orbicularis oculi, pars palpebralis*
8	Lips toward each other	*Orbicularis oris*
9	Nose wrinkler	*Levator labii superioris, alaeque nasi*
10	Upper lip raiser	*Levator labii superioris, caput infraorbitalis*
11	Nasolabial furrow deepener	*Zygomatic minor*
12	Lip corner puller	*Zygomatic major*
13	Cheek puffer	*Caninus*
14	Dimpler	*Buccinator*
15	Lip corner depressor	*Triangularis*
16	Lower lip depressor	*Depressor labii inferioris*
17	Chin raiser	*Mentalis*
18	Lip puckerer	*Incisivii labii superioris; incisivus labii inferioris*
20	Lip stretcher	*Risorious*
22	Lip funneler	*Orbicularis oris*
23	Lip tightener	*Orbicularis oris*
24	Lip pressor	*Orbicularis oris*
25	Lips part	*Depressor labii,* or relaxation of *mentalis* or *orbicularis oris*
26	Jaw drops	*Masseter;* temporal and internal *pterygoid* relaxed
27	Mouth stretches	*pterygoids;* digastric
28	Lips suck	*Orbicularis oris*
38	Nostril dilator	*Nasalis, pars alaris*
39	Nostril compressor	*Nasalis, pars transversa and depressor septi alae nasi*
41	Lids droop	Relaxation of *levator palpebrae superioris*
42	Eyes slit	*Orbicularis oculi*
43	Eyes close	Relaxation of *Levator palpebrae superioris*
44	Squint	*Orbicularis oculi, pars palpebralis*
45	Blink	Relaxation of *levator palpebrae* and contraction of *orbicularis oculi,* pars palpebralis
46	Wink	*orbicularis oculi*

Table 9.2. *An example of information given in FACS for each Action Unit*

Action Unit 15 – Lip corner depressor
The muscle underlying AU 15 emerges from the side of the chin and runs upward attaching to a point near the corner of the lip. In AU 15 the corners of the lips are pulled down. Study the anatomical drawings that show the location of the muscle underlying this AU.
(1) Pulls the corners of the lips down.
(2) Changes the shape of the lips so they are angled down at the corner, and usually somewhat stretched horizontally.
(3) Produces some pouching, bagging, or wrinkling of skin below the lips corners, which may not be apparent unless the action is strong.
(4) May flatten or cause bulges to appear on the chin boss, may produce depression medially under the lower lip.
(5) If the *nasolabial furrow*[a] is permanently etched, it will deepen and may appear pulled down or lengthened.
The photographs in FACS show both slight and strong versions of this Action Unit. Note that appearance change (3) is most apparent in the stronger versions. The photograph of 6 + 15 shows how the appearance changes due to 6 can add to those of 15. Study the film of AU 15.

How to do 15
Pull your lip corners downward. Be careful not to raise your lower lip at the same time – do not use AU 17. If you are unable to do this, place your fingers above the lip corners and push downward, noting the changes in appearance. Now, try to hold this appearance when you take your fingers away.

Minimum requirements to score 15
Elongating the mouth is irrelevant, as it may be due to AU 20, AU 15, or AU 15 + 20.
(1) If the lip line is straight or slightly up in neutral face, then the lip corners must be pulled down at least slightly to score 15, or
(2) If lip line is slightly or barely down in neutral face, then the lip corners must be pulled down slightly more than neutral and not the result of AU 17 or AU 20.

---

[a]A wrinkle extending from beyond the nostril wings down to beyond the lip corners.

forehead, or eyelids. The table indicates where we have collapsed more than one muscle into a single Action Unit and where we have distinguished more than one Action Unit from a single muscle. The FACS names given in the table are shortened for convenience of recall and are not meant to describe the appearance change.

Table 9.2 lists an example of how an Action Unit (AU) is described in the FACS manual (Ekman & Friesen, 1978). The description includes four types of information:

1. The muscular basis of each AU is given in words and diagrams.
2. Detailed descriptions of the appearance changes are keyed to illustrative still photograph and film examples.
3. Instructions are given as to how to make the movement on one's own face. This aids in learning the appearance changes, particularly if FACS is learned by a group of people who can observe the variations in appearance on each others' faces. Learning how to do each AU also provides the user with a technique for later analyzing movements to be scored into their component parts. The user imitates the movement to be scored, noting which muscles had to be moved to produce the movement to be scored. By this means the scoring of any novel, complex facial action can be determined.
4. A rule is given specifying the minimal changes that must be observed in order to score a slight version of each AU.

The determination of the single AUs (Table 9.1) and their description (an example of which is shown in Table 9.2) were the first steps in developing FACS. The procedure of moving muscles, photographing the movement, and inspecting the pictures was reiterated for all possible combinations of two AUs. There was no need to describe AU combinations that could not interact. For example, pulling the lip corners down is done by a muscle that cannot affect the muscles controlling the position of the eyebrows. Two-way combinations were performed separately for the AUs controlling the brows, forehead, and upper and lower eyelids and for those AUs controlling the lower eyelids, cheeks, and lower regions of the face. There were several hundred combinations to perform and examine, for only in a very few instances did we discover that two AUs could not occur simultaneously.

Study of the photographs of the AU combinations showed that most of the appearance changes were additive. The characteristic appearance of each of the two-AU combinations was clearly recognizable and virtually unchanged. There were, however, a few AU combinations that were not additive. Their appearance changes may have incorporated some of the evidence of the single AUs, but new appearance changes from their joint action were also evident. All of these distinctive combinations were added to FACS, each described in the same detail as were the single AUs.

Inspection of the photographs of the AU combinations revealed that the appearance changes might be neither additive nor distinctive and that there might be a relationship of dominance, substitution, or alternation between AUs. In *dominance*, the strong AU overshadows the weak one. It may completely conceal the appearance of the subordinant AU or it may make the evidence of the subordinant AU very difficult to detect. In order to enhance agreement in scoring, rules were established to prohibit the scoring of subordinant AUs when there is clear evidence of a dominant AU. In *substitution*, the appearance of two different AU combinations is so similar that, in order to avoid disagreements, we designated only one of the combinations as the score to be used for either of the combinations. In *alternation*, two AUs cannot both be scored because both cannot be performed simultaneously; it is hard to distinguish one from the other; or the logic of other FACS rules does not allow both to be scored. The coder determines which of the two alternatives best describes a particular action.

After analyzing the pictures of all the two-AU combinations, the processes of performing, photographing, and then inspecting were reiterated, but this time with 3-AU combinations. Instead of hundreds there were thousands to so examine. Those that produced a distinctive, rather than an additive, combination of AUs were allotted their own entry in FACS with full descriptions as shown in Table 9.2. When we were ready to explore the 4-AU combinations, the number to be considered was so great that we decided to study them only selectively. On the basis of what we learned from the 2-AU and 3-AU combinations, we extrapolated those further combinations likely to result in distinctive facial movements. In total, between 4,000 and 5,000 facial combinations were performed and examined. This included *all* the possible combinations of AUs in the upper regions of the face and *all* the two- and three-way combinations in the lower face, plus *some* of the four-, five-, six-, seven-, and eight-AU combinations in the lower region of the face.

The manual for the *Facial Action Coding System* (Ekman & Friesen, 1978) was written in a self-instructional format, to serve as an initial tutor and subsequently as a reference in scoring facial behavior. It contains the following information:

1. textual material describing each AU listed in Table 9.1 in terms of its muscular basis, appearance changes, instructions for making the movement, and requirements to be met for scoring slight verisons (see the example in Table 9.2);
2. comparable information for each of more than 44 combinations of AUs;
3. a simple, less precise account of the 11 additional single AUs listed in Table 9.3, many of which do not involve the facial muscles (We have not described them in as much detail as was done in Table 9.2.);
4. descriptors that can be used to measure head and eye position;
5. tables comparing and contrasting over 400 AUs (or AU combinations) with only subtle differences;
6. scoring rules based on the dominance, alternation, and substitution relationships among AUs;

Table 9.3. *Simply defined AUs in FACS*

AU number	FACS name	AU number	FACS name
19	Tongue out	33	Cheek blow
21	Neck tightener	34	Cheek puff
29	Jaw thrust	35	Cheek suck
30	Jaw sideways	36	Tongue bulge
31	Jaw clench	37	Lip wipe
32	Lips bite		

7. a scoring sheet and a step-by-step procedure containing a number of internal checks designed to increase inter-rater reliability.

There are also still photographic and motion picture film examples of all the single AUs in Tables 9.1 and 9.3, of the 44 AU combinations, and the head and eye position descriptors. Additional still photographs and motion picture film examples of facial behavior are provided for practice in scoring facial movement. Correct scores are given, with commentary about the source of possible errors in scoring.

9.3. An example of scoring faces

It is not feasible in this chapter, without film or video, to illustrate the actual use of FACS in scoring a facial movement. The logic underlying FACS can be illustrated, however, with still photographs. For example, consider the seven facial behaviors shown in Figure 9.1. They all involve some common elements in appearance, in particular the down curve to the line of the mouth; they also differ. Analysis of these faces in terms of the single AUs involved will allow precise differentiation among them.

These seven faces include three single AUs and four combinations among these AUs. Figure 9.1 *A* is the appearance change resulting from AU 15, described earlier in Table 9.2. Figure 9.1*B* shows AU 17, described in Table 9.4; Figure 9.1*C* shows AU 10, also described in Table 9.4. If you read the verbal descriptions from Table 9.4 and match them to the photographs, you should then be able to "dissect" the other four faces in Figure 9.1 into their component AUs. Figure 9.1*D* combines AUs 10 and 15; Figure 9.1*E* combines AUs 10 and 17; Figure 9.1*F* combines AUs 15 and 17; Figure 9.1*G* combines AUs 10, 15, and 17.

Any complex facial behavior can be similarly analyzed into its component elements, if the single AUs have been learned and if rules regarding combinations have been studied. The scoring procedure leads the

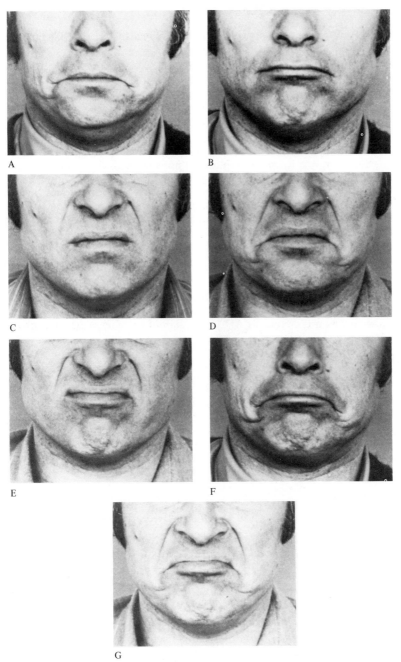

A

B

C

D

E

F

G

Figure 9.1 Action units that produce a down curve to the line of the mouth. (From "Measuring facial movement" by P. Ekman and W. V. Friesen, *Journal of Environmental Psychology and Nonverbal Behavior*, 1976, 1, 56–75. Copyright 1976 by P. Ekman. Reproduced by permission)

Table 9.4. *Appearance changes due to AU 10 and to AU 17.* (Copyright ©
Ekman & Friesen, 1976.)

Action Unit 10

The muscle underlying AU 10 emerges from the center of the infraorbital triangle[a]
and attaches in the area of the nasolabial fold.[b] In AU 10 the skin above the
upper lip is pulled upwards and towards the cheek, pulling the upper lip up.
(1) Raises the upper lip. Center of upper lip is drawn straight up, the outer
    portions of upper lip are drawn up but not as high as the center.
(2) Causes an angular bend in the shape of the upper lip.
(3) Raises the infraorbital triangle; and may cause the infraorbital furrow to
    appear, or if it is evident in neutral, to deepen.
(4) Deepens the nasolabial furrows and raises the upper part of this furrow
    producing a shape as ⟋⟍ .
(5) Widens and raises the nostril wings.
(6) When the action is strong the lips will part.

Action Unit 17

The muscle underlying AU 17 emerges from an area below the lower lip and
attaches far down the chin. In AU 17 the skin of the chin is pushed upwards,
pushing up the lower lip.
(1) Pushes chin boss upward.
(2) Pushes lower lip upward.
(3) May cause wrinkles to appear on chin boss as skin is stretched, and may
    produce a depression medially under the lower lip.
(4) Causes shape of mouth to appear ⌒⟍.
(5) If the action is strong the lower lip may protrude.

[a]Roughly the cheek area.
[b]A wrinkle extending from beyond the nostril wings down to beyond the lip
corners.

user to break down any action into a set of single AU scores. When in
doubt, the user is encouraged to consult the verbal descriptions, photographic and film examples, and tables of contrasting subtle differences.
The person is also encouraged to imitate the action seen, observing the
mirror reflection, and noting what AUs must be used in order to reproduce the action observed.

It is important not to be mislead by the example of Figure 9.1 into
thinking that FACS was designed for scoring still photographs. The
emphasis of FACS is on movement and its chief use is for scoring facial
actions seen on motion records, although it can be used with stills if
there is also a picture of a "neutral" face.

Figure 9.1 was used to demonstrate how FACS scoring differentiates
among the seven facial behaviors shown. Although these seven behav-

iors are not visibly the same, are they the same functionally, psychologically, or communicatively? Is one a sadness expression, another a pout, another a disbelief gesture, etc.? It is only if the facial measurement distinguishes among these behaviors that we can determine empirically how many of the distinctions are useful. Once we can measure their separate occurrences, we can examine the contexts in which the behaviors occur or we can study preceding or consequent actions of other persons, isolate concomitant behavior in the person showing the behavior, study observers' inferences from viewing each behavior, etc.

The Facial Action Coding System far exceeded our initial anticipation of what would be required to provide a comprehensive, descriptive system for measuring facial action. Certainly, FACS is a very elaborate system, considerably more comprehensive than any previous system. There is no facial action described by other systems that cannot be described by FACS, and there are many behaviors described by FACS not previously distinguished by others. In addition, FACS allows for measuring facial asymmetries, where different AUs appear on each side of the face. It does not, however, include a measure of the intensity of actions for every AU, although it does so for four of the AUs listed in Table 9.1. It would be possible for others to follow the procedure used for these AUs in order to provide intensity of action scoring for the other AUs.

We are reasonably confident that FACS is complete for scoring the visible, reliably distinguishable actions of the brows, forehead, and eyelids. Unfortunately, FACS probably does not include all of the visible, reliably distinguishable actions in the lower part of the face. The hinged jaw and rubbery lips allow a nearly infinite number of actions. We included everything we could see, everything anyone else included and what are probably the most common elements and combinations of actions in the lower part of the face among children and adults. As we and others use FACS, we expect that some other AUs may need to be added, although we hope not many. Also, others may be interested in more finely discriminating separate AUs from the list of broadly defined AUs in Table 9.3.

Some will ask the question whether FACS is too elaborate, too comprehensive, and too detailed? We believe it has been useful to attempt an approximation of the total repertoire of facial action, to isolate minimal Action Units that can combine to account for any facial movement. At the least, FACS provides a means to cross-reference the different scoring categories used by others with a common nomenclature. It may also serve to advise the investigators of their options, so that they may make explicit decisions about what to include in and what to omit from their measurements. No one knows at the outset how many of the variations in facial behavior can be ignored in any research study without losing important information. In preliminary observations, or pilot studies, investigators may wish to use FACS to make comprehensive measurements and, then, based on these results, to score selectively only certain AUs or AU combinations in their main study.

Apart from these more selective uses of FACS, there will be some who simply need a comprehensive measurement system. If we wish to learn all the facial actions that signal emotion (and those that do not) or whether facial emphasis markers are the same regardless of the content of speech so emphasized (to mention just two current interests), then a method such as FACS is needed.

9.4. Reliability of the Facial Action Coding System

Reliability issues

The fundamental reliability issue is whether independent persons would agree in their scoring of facial behavior; more specifically, whether persons who learn FACS without instruction from the developers would agree among themselves and/or with the developers.

To score facial behavior, two different operations, description and location, and thus two different reliability issues are required. By *description*, we mean what happened: What are the Action Units responsible for an observed change in facial behavior? By *location*, we mean when did it happen: At precisely what moment did whatever happened start and stop. Suppose the brows moved. To describe the movement, we would ask which type of movement it was: did the brows raise, lower, raise and draw together? did just the inner part raise or the entire brow, etc.? To locate the movement, we would ask at what videoframe (1/60 second) the movement, whatever it is, started and at what videoframe it ended? The two questions are independent to some extent. Reliability could be high for description but low for location, or vice versa.

For either description or location, reliability can be evaluated on either of two bases: (1) agreement among independent persons, or (2) agreement between a learner and an expert. We were interested in not only whether there was intercoder agreement but whether those who learned FACS without instruction from us would score facial behavior the way we did. Data were reported for both types of agreement. The results were about the same.

The description of facial movement with FACS involves four operations and the reliability of each was studied:

1. *Determining which AUs are responsible for the observed movement.* The coder learns how to recognize the appearance changes due to each of 44 AUs, singly and in combination. The logic of the system is that any movement can be scored in terms of which AUs produced it. Theoretically, it is possible for about 20 AUs to combine to produce a single facial movement or as few as one. (All 44 cannot combine because some involve antagonistic actions and the occurrence of some actions conceals the possible presence of others.)
2. *Scoring the intensity of action for five of the 44 AUs.* While intensity scoring could have been provided for each and every one of the 44 AUs, we used intensity scoring only where we thought the magnitude of action could influence the recognition of a particular action unit or a related action. Intensity was scored in terms of three levels: low, medium, and high.
3. *Scoring whether an action is asymmetrical or unilateral.* FACS distinguishes unilateral actions, where there is no evidence of the action on one side of the face, from asymmetrical actions, where the movement is evident on both sides of the face but stronger on one side. There were very few instances of unilateral actions in the records we scored, too few to estimate the reliability of distinguishing unilateral from bilateral or asymmetrical actions. Later the reliability of asymmetry scoring will be reported.
4. *Scoring the position of the head and the position of the eyes during a facial movement.* This descriptive system is less rigorous than that provided for the AUs. Fourteen descriptors are provided, of which up to six can be scored for any event. Because head/eye scoring is a simpler system, agreement on it could have inflated agreement measures on the total scoring of a face. Results will, therefore, be reported separately, including and excluding head/eye position scores. In fact, however, it made little difference.

A final issue to be considered is whether agreement is substantially improved by having the independent coders arbitrate their disagreements. The agreement achieved by six independent coders (intercoder agreement and agreement with experts) will be contrasted with agreement achieved by three pairs of arbitrated scores. Arbitration improved agreement, but not by much.

The behavioral sample for initial reliability studies

For our initial reliability study, we selected behavior samples from 10 of the honest–deceptive interviews we have been studying over the past eight years (Ekman & Friesen, 1974a; Ekman, Friesen & Scherer, 1976). We selected the first two actions shown by a subject who was conversing about her reactions to a film while she was watching it and the first two actions shown when the interview continued after the film ended.

In order to increase the variety of behaviors subject to scoring, if the first two actions repeated an AU or AU combination already selected more than once, then the next nonredundant action was taken. By these means, a total of 40 items was obtained. Six were dropped because the videopicture was not acceptable, leaving 34 items.

Coders were given the videotape with the instruction to score whatever occurred within each of the 34 events. Note that by defining each event ahead of time, giving the coders the start and stop frame within which they should score, we eliminated decisions about location and studied just description reliability.

The coders

Seven persons previously unfamiliar with FACS learned the system as a group during a 5-week period, working on a half-time basis. We had minimum contact with them during this time so that their performance can be considered a fair test of whether FACS produces reliable scoring when learned without instruction from the developers. The results reported are based on six persons because one coder did not continue.

The six coders consisted of five women and one man. Two were research assistants who have bachelor's level education. Two were doctoral candidates, one in psychology, another in linguistics. Another was a postdoctoral fellow trained in developmental psychology. The last was a visiting associate professor of clinical psychology whose native language is German.

Procedure

The six coders independently scored the 34 events without any communication among them. After their scoring was completed, the six were grouped into three pairs and given their scorings on any event about which they disagreed. They were required to arrive jointly at an arbitrated final scoring.

We (the authors) jointly scored each of the 34 events. We then examined the scoring of the six learners and considered whether we would want to change our scoring in light of their performance. We did so only a few times, and those decisions did not increase the agreement between them and us.

Table 9.5. *Example of raw scores on one behavioral event*

Coder	AU numbers				
Experts	1 + 4 +			7	
Blossom	1 + 4 +			7	
Kathy	1 + 4 +		6		
Charlotte	4 +		5X +	7 +	10X[a]
Linda	1 + 4 +			7	
Sonia	4 +			7	
Rainer	4 +			7	
Arbitrated					
Bl–Ka	1 + 4 +			7	
Ch–Li	1 + 4 +			7 +	10X[a]
So–Ra[b]	4 +			7	

[a]In FACS, X denotes a rating of low intensity.
[b]Note that arbitration was not necessary here as subjects were in agreement on original scoring.

Raw data matrix

Thirty-four events were scored by six independent persons producing 6 x 34 = 204 sets of action unit scores. Additionally, there are the three arbitrated pair scorings for each event. Table 9.5 shows the scores for one of the 34 items. The first row is our scoring. The next six rows show the scoring of this event by each of the six persons. The final three rows show the arbitrated scoring of the three pairings. (Note that Sonia and Rainer agreed on this event so they did not arbitrate.) The entries are the numbers for the AUs, which is the system used to record scores. The experts scored three AUs, 1, 4, and 7, which describe raising the inner corners of the brow (1), pulling the brows together (4), and tightening of the eyelids (7). There was agreement among all coders that AU 4 was present. Some did not score AU 1. One coder scored an outer eyelid action (6) rather than the inner eyelid action of AU 7. One coder also scored an upper eyelid raise (5X, the X meaning that she scored it as being low in intensity); and a low upper lip raise (10X).

An index of agreement

It was not obvious what type of measure of agreement should be employed. Reliability measures often are applied to situations where scoring involves a binary decision (e.g., present or absent) or assignment into one of a series of exclusive categories. In FACS there is a range of possible scores, from 1 to about 26 (about 20 AUs and 6 head/eye descriptors) that could be scored for any one event. There are many more opportunities for disagreement than is usually the case in psychological measurement.

We could have assessed reliability for each AU separately, determining how many times the six persons agreed about its presence or absence over the 34 items. This method, often used in reliability studies, would give as much credit to an agreement that an AU was not scored for an event as an agreement that it was scored. Such a method would have produced reliability scores much higher than the procedure we selected.

The index of agreement that we employed (Wexler, 1972) was a ratio calculated separately for each of the 34 events for each pair of coders and for each coder compared to the expert scoring. The arbitrated scoring was also evaluated with the same index. The formula was:

$$\frac{(\text{number of AUs on which coder 1 and coder 2 agreed}) \times 2}{\text{total number of AUs scored by the two coders}}$$

For example, if the scoring by one coder was $1 + 5 + 7 + 22$ and the scoring by a second coder was $1 + 7 + 16$, the ratio would be:

$$\frac{4 \ (2 \ \text{AUs agreed upon} \times 2)}{7 \ (\text{total number of AUs scored by two coders})} = .57$$

Table 9.6 shows the matrix of ratios generated with this formula for the raw data shown in Table 9.5. The first six rows of Table 9.6 give the ratios calculated for the scoring of each individual person. The last three rows of the table give the ratios when the scoring reached through arbitration by a pair of persons was evaluated. We will use the first six rows to illustrate how the ratio represents agreement. The first column of numbers shows the ratio when each coder's scoring was entered into the formula with the scoring of the experts. Perfect agreement (in the case of Blossom and Linda) generated 1.00 ratios. Disagreements generated lower ratios. The other columns in the table show the ratios between each pair of coders. One can see that Sonia and Rainer agreed exactly, as did Linda and Blossom. The maximum disagreement was between Kathy and Charlotte.

The mathematics of the formula used are such that if only one or two AUs are scored for an event, a disagreement will lower the ratio more

Table 9.6. Matrix of agreement ratios for the scoring of one behavioral event

Coder	Experts	Blossom	Kathy	Charlotte	Linda	Sonia
Single-person scoring						
Blossom	1.000					
Kathy	.667	.667				
Charlotte	.571	.571	.286			
Linda	1.000	1.000	.667	.571		
Sonia	.800	.800	.400	.667	.800	
Rainer	.800	.800	.400	.667	.800	1.000

	Experts	Bl–Ka	Ch–Li
Arbitrated pairs scoring			
Bl–Ka	1.000		
Ch–Li	.857	.857	
So–Ra	.800	.800	.667

than if six of seven are scored. If two coders disagreed about only one AU and agreed about one AU, they would earn a ratio of .50. If they disagreed about one AU and agreed about four AUs, the ratio would be .80. Even though the disagreement is in both instances about only one score, it seems reasonable that the formula rewards agreement on a high proportion of actions that are present.

We checked on how many AUs were scored for each of the 34 events by the experts. The mode was three scores for an event, with about one-third of the 34 events having one or two scores and one-third having four to seven scores. Thus, if the absolute number of scores distorted the ratio of agreement, the 34 events produced a balanced distribution in this regard.

Two matrixes were generated. One matrix was composed of the ratios derived by comparing each person's scoring of each event with the experts' scoring, generating 204 data points (6 persons x 34 events). The second matrix disregarded the experts' scoring and calculated the ratio by comparing each person's scoring with each other person. With six persons, five such ratios were generated for each person (comparing that person with every other person) for each of the 34 events scored. The mean of those five ratios was taken as the measure of a particular person's average agreement with others for a particular event. This yielded a second matrix that again had 204 points, with each point representing the mean ratio of agreement with the other person's for each event scored (34 events x 6 persons).

Overall agreement

The mean ratio across all coders (6) and all events scored (34) was .822 when scoring was compared with experts' and .756 when intercoder agreement was evaluated. Figure 9.2 shows that the distributions of ratios were skewed toward high agreement. For example, 141 out of 204 ratios of agreement with the experts were .80 or above, and only 28 out of the 204 ratios were below .60. The figure also shows that the distribution of ratios representing intercoder agreement was similarly skewed toward agreement, with just as few low-value ratios but not as many ratios above .80 as when agreement with experts was calculated.

Since FACS was first published, more than thirty investigators have learned FACS using the training materials provided without any direct contact with us. Part of the training package makes available the videotape of the same behavior sample coded by the initial group of six

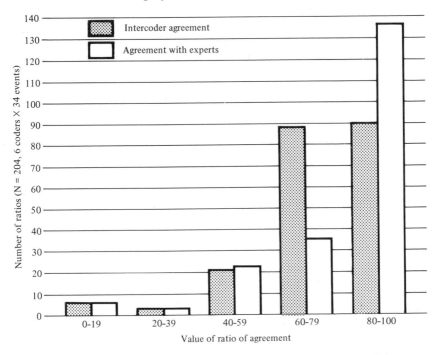

Figure 9.2 Distribution of agreement ratios among coders and between coders and experts. (From *The facial action coding system* by P. Ekman and W. V. Friesen. Palo Alto, Ca.: Consulting Psychologists Press, 1978. Copyright 1978 by P. Ekman. Reproduced by permission)

learners. All of these new investigators achieved comparable reliability to the data reported in Figure 9.2.

Did scoring head/eye position inflate reliability?

The answer is no. Recall that the measurement of head/eye position was a grosser descriptive scheme than that of the Action Units. Agreement on what might be an easier set of decisions might have inflated the agreement ratios, concealing disagreements about the scoring of AUs. When head/eye position scores were disregarded, however, and the ratios recalculated, the mean ratio across all coders and all events was .816 (as compared with .822 including head/eye) when scoring was compared against experts and .745 (as compared with .756 including head/eye) for intercoder agreement. The distributions were examined and were found to be not noticeably different from those shown in Figure 9.2. Results reported hereafter will include the head/eye position scores.

Table 9.7. *Mean ratios of agreement with experts, showing the benefits of having coders arbitrate their disagreements in pairs*

	Individual scoring	Arbitrated pairs
Blossom	.782	
Kathy	.827	.869
Charlotte	.859	
Linda	.858	.886
Sonia	.873	
Rainer	.732	.883

Does arbitrating differences enhance agreement?

The answer is slightly, but it depends on how much they disagreed and how low their individual agreement was prior to arbitration. Presenting the coders with their disagreements and asking them to arbitrate their differences could have produced lower, rather than higher, agreement. Each pair after arbitrating might diverge more from the other pairs or from the experts. Instead there was a slight increase in both agreement measures.

The mean ratio across all coders and all events went up from .822 to .863 in terms of agreement with experts and from .756 to .809 in terms of intercoder agreement. Table 9.7 shows that in terms of agreement with experts the benefit was negligible for the pair who had high agreement individually (Charlotte and Linda), moderate for a pair somewhat lower individually (Blossom and Kathy), and considerable for the pair where one member (Rainer) had the lowest coefficient of agreement. His gain through arbitration, however, was at the cost of a loss of the person with whom he arbitrated (Sonia). When the same comparisons were made utilizing the measures of intercoder agreement (rather than agreement with experts as shown in Table 9.7), the values were two to three hundredths lower but the pattern was the same. For example, the mean ratio of intercoder agreement for Sonia and Rainer's arbitrated scoring was .802 as compared with .833 for agreement with experts.

Two other methods for reconciling disagreements were explored. In one, a simple flip of the coin was used to determine who was "correct" on each disagreement. Using the coin flip as the basis for saying what the final score should be for items where a pair disagreed yielded ratios of agreement with the experts that were just as high as arbitration for the coder pairs who did not initially disagree strongly (Blossom and Kathy; Charlotte and Linda). For the pair with the one coder who showed the lowest agreement with the experts (Rainer), a coin flip did not yield as much increased agreement as did arbitration. The second method for resolving disagreements consisted of applying a set of logical rules to determine who was "correct" for any events where a pair disagreed. These rules benefited the pair who most disagreed (Sonia and Rainer) as much as did arbitration.

Agreement about intensity

The data analysis thus far has ignored any disagreements about intensity. Such disagreement could have occurred on the scoring of only 5 of the 44 AUs because FACS provides for intensity scoring on just those few. There were 19 instances in which the experts scored the AUs with an intensity rating, providing 114 opportunities for agreement with the experts (6 coders x 19 instances).

Exact agreement about intensity was reached on 55% of these scorings. Recall that intensity involves a three-point scale. There were no two-point disparities; instead about half the disagreements were one-point disparities, the other half were when one person entirely missed scoring an intensity-AU that was scored by the experts at the low-intensity level.

The scorings of the pairs of persons who disagreed on intensity were subject to arbitration, which enhanced the agreement with experts. Exact agreement about intensity rose to 74%.

Recall that the data reported previously disregarded disparities in intensity scores. The agreement ratios for each of the six coders compared with the experts' scoring were recalculated with a disagreement about intensity considered as a total disagreement. The mean ratio across all six persons and all 34 events was .778 when a difference of intensity was considered an error, as compared to .822 when intensity disagreement was ignored. Of course the reason why the ratio of agreement did not decrease further was that there were not that many instances where intensity could be scored. In another behavioral sample, in which there was a preponderance of behavior involving AUs for which intensity could be scored, the ratios of agreement might be lower.

Representativeness of the behavioral sample

The scores were tabulated for each AU across all coders and all events to provide a picture of the extent to which the behavioral sample offered opportunity for testing the reliability of all the AUs. For this tabulation we considered not only whether an AU was scored but also whether an AU was considered, even if not scored, during the coders' step-by-step scoring procedure. (Such information is readily retrieved from the scoring sheets on which the coders recorded every AU considered.)

Twenty-five of the 44 AUs were scored or considered many times; only 19 of the AUs were scored or considered less than 10 times. These 19 AUs are probably rare occurrences in most conversations between adults; for example, sticking out the tongue, tightening the *platysma* muscle, sucking the lips in to cover the teeth, puffing out the cheeks, etc. Although we cannot generalize from this study to the reliability that might be obtained if the behavior scored included such actions, there is no reason to suspect that reliability would be lower. Quite the contrary, the classification of many of these infrequent AUs probably involves an easier set of discriminations than is required for the AUs that were considered and scored in this study.

Reliability in the location of facial action

In the beginning we distinguished between two aspects of measuring facial action, description (what happened) and location (when something happened). Thus far we have considered only description. Let us now consider the reliability of scoring location.

Information is available from a dissertation by Ancoli (1979). Subjects sat alone in a room and watched two films. One film showed scenes that other subjects had rated as causing pleasant feelings. The other film had been rated as producing feelings of disgust and fear. The subjects were monitored on EEG, heart rate, EMG on skeletal muscles, and respiration. In addition, a videotape was made of their faces. Ancoli scored all of the facial behavior shown by 35 subjects, a total of 3 minutes during a pleasant film and 2 minutes during the unpleasant film for each subject.

Reliability was evaluated at two points in the study. After she scored the first 10 subjects, Ancoli randomly selected the facial behavior during one of the two films for each subject. This sample was then scored by a second person (Linda Camras, another of the people who had recently learned FACS). Later, a second sample was drawn, consisting of a 30-second period from the video records of each of the 25 remaining subjects. Again, Camras scored the randomly selected sample.

Location, unlike FACS description, can be regarded as a binary decision – something is happening or not at each frame in time. The decision should be easy with a large facial movement or when the face is completely still; it should be difficult when there is a very small movement. A set of minimum requirements is provided by FACS for the amount of change that must occur before a movement can be scored. The most difficult decision, and the main opportunity for disagreement, is when there is a small movement and the person must evaluate whether it is sufficient to meet FACS requirements for scoring. If it does not, the coders treat it as a no-movement.

When occur versus no-occur decisions are made point by point in time, a common way to assess reliability is to determine for each point in time whether two independent persons agree. Agreement is then represented as a percentage of total time considered. Each .10 second was so examined. In sample 1, the two coders agreed (as to whether or not something was occurring) 89% of the time. In sample 2, the two coders agreed 95% of the time. This calculation gave equal credit to agreement that nothing happened as to agreement that something happened. If the sample contained long periods of time in which the face was inactive, this measure of locational agreement would be inflated. In sample 1, the face was totally inactive or not scorable (action occurred but did not meet the minimum requirements demanded by FACS) 69% of the time; in sample 2, the face was inactive or not scorable 66% of the time.

There is, of course, quite a difference between agreement that nothing has occurred and agreement that something unscorable has occurred (i.e., that it does not meet the minimum requirements specified by FACS). Agreement about an unscorable action should represent the most difficult locational decision. Since Ancoli's study we have added a new action descriptor to FACS for unscorable actions. If this had been available in Ancoli's study, it would have been possible to calculate the percentage of time two coders agreed that a scorable action occurred, that an unscorable action occurred, and that no action occurred. Now that unscorable actions have been included in the scoring procedure, in future studies using FACS, we recommend that locational agreement be so examined. It will then be possible to isolate disagreements where one person said the action was scorable and another called it unscorable, and instances where one person said the action was unscorable and the other recorded no action. In either case, additional instruction can be given to increase locational reliability if a consistent pattern is found, consistent, that is, for a particular coder or a particular AU.

Another way to examine agreement about location, which avoids the problem of inflating the estimate by agreements on the absence of ac-

Table 9.8. *Percentage of agreement on total events located*

	Agree on beginning		Agree on end		Agree on beginning and end	
	within .10 sec	within .5 sec	within .10 sec	within .5 sec	within 1 sec	within 2 sec
Sample 1	25.0	59.1	13.6	38.6	47.7	68.2
Sample 2	64.5	74.5	61.3	67.7	74.2	74.2

Table 9.9. *Mean description reliability ratios on agreement*

	Including events scored by only one	Including only events scored by both	Including only events scored by both and excluding events agreed to be not scorable
Sample 1	.722	.878	.815
Sample 2	.791	.909	.824

tion, is to consider the occurrence of complete disagreements. The worst error in location is when one person scores an event that the other fails to score (either because they missed the event entirely or judged it as not reaching the minimum requirements dictated by FACS). In sample 1, such complete disagreement occurred with 18.4% of the behavior scored; in sample 2, such complete disagreement occurred with 12.9% of the behavior scored.

Location reliability can be studied in more detail by examining exactly how closely coders designated when an event began and when it ended. Table 9.8 shows that information for the two samples of Ancoli. The calculation of percentage of agreement used the total events scored by both (including events seen by only one) as the denominator. Agreement was higher for judgments of when an action began than for judgments of when it ended. Agreement was higher in sample 2 than in sample 1, perhaps because of experience. The last two columns in Table 9.8 show the percentage of events where both persons agreed within 1 second and within 2 seconds on both the start and stop of an action. A high percentage of agreement was found in sample 2.

Another look at description reliability

Ancoli's dissertation presents another opportunity to study the reliability of the FACS description. Table 9.9 reports the ratios of agreement (calculated as explained previously) for the two behavioral samples. The first numerical column shows the mean ratio when the events scored by only one coder were included in calculating the mean across all events. For those events scored by only one coder, the ratio was zero, thus allowing disagreement about location to lower the measure of agreement on description. The next column gives the percentage that include in the calculation of the agreement ratios only events scored by both persons. These ratios include agreements that in certain instances there was no scorable facial action. That is, of course, an important type of agreement, but it is not the same as agreement about how to describe what is present. In the last column are shown the ratios calculated excluding items in which both coders agreed that the event was a no-score, or neutral, action. The figures in this column are directly comparable to the ratios reported earlier for intercoder agreement among six persons because in that reliability test no neutral events were included in the behavior sample and the ratios are not deflated by disagreements about location. Agreement remains about as it was for the learners described previously.

Now that FACS provides an unscorable action descriptor, it is possible to analyze description reliability with one further refinement not shown in Table 9.9. Agreement ratios would be calculated for all events considered scorable or unscorable by one or the other of the coders, excluding from the ratio only agreements that no action had occurred. These ratios would give credit for any agreements that unscorable activity occurred.

9.5. Validity

The Facial Action Coding System was designed to measure any facial movement, not just movements that might be relevant to emotion. Although FACS contains hypotheses about the particular actions that signal each emotion, these hypotheses are quite separate from FACS and even if they were shown to be incorrect, FACS would still be valid as a measurement technique if it were found to measure the behavior it claims to measure. Conversely, the hypotheses about emotion signals could be correct and yet FACS might not be valid. There is a difference then between the validity of a measurement technique and the truth or falsity of any set of hypotheses about what the measurements might mean.

Figure 9.3

Descriptive validity

The validity of FACS requires evidence that it actually measures the behavior it claims to measure. Because FACS identifies the elemental muscular actions that singly or in combination produce any visible movement observed, the question is whether the muscular actions identified by FACS are the particular ones that actually produce a particular movement. Of course there may be more than one action that can produce a momentary change in facial appearance. Consider an expression entailing a down-curved lower lip, as shown in the drawing in Figure 9.3. If FACS scored this appearance as Action Unit 15 it is saying that the down curve to the lower lip was produced by a muscle which pulls the corners of the lips down (see Figure 9.1). Perhaps the down curve to the lower lip was produced by Action Unit 17 which pushes the chin and lower lip up in the center, or by Action 15 and Action 17 (see Figure 9.1).

In addition, FACS measures the intensity of some facial actions, such as whether the pulling down of the lower lip was slight, moderate, or extreme. The validity question is whether such measurements correspond to known differences in the intensity of such an action. The problem is how to know what facial action actually occurred; that is, what criterion to utilize independent of FACS? Two approaches have been taken: performed action and electromyography.

In the first approach, Ekman and Friesen trained a number of people to perform voluntarily various actions on request. Videotape records of such performances were scored without knowledge of the performances that had been requested. FACS accurately distinguished the actions the performers had been instructed to make.

In the other approach, in joint study with Schwartz, Ekman and Friesen placed EMG leads on the faces of subjects who were asked to produce actions on request. Utilizing the EMG measure of electrical activity in one or another muscle region as the criterion, FACS was found to differentiate accurately the *type* of action. This study also showed that FACS measurement of the *intensity* of facial action was valid; FACS scoring of intensity was highly correlated with EMG readings (Pearson $R = .85$).

Validity of emotion-signal hypotheses

The Facial Action Coding System contains more than a thousand hypotheses about the particular combinations of facial actions that signal the *type* of emotion (anger, fear, surprise, etc.), the variations in the *intensity* of each emotion, the *blends* of emotions, and the signs of attempts to control emotion. The problem in validating these hypotheses is to have some criterion independent of FACS to determine just which emotion, at what intensity, is being experienced at any given moment by a particular person. The traditional approach has been to use a poser's intent as the criterion. Such studies using FACS to measure the poser's facial actions have verified many of the hypotheses about emotion signals contained in FACS, but for the many reasons discussed in Chapter 4, one cannot generalize from posed to spontaneous emotions. Additionally, posing is probably one of the easiest types of facial behavior to measure. The onset is usually coordinated and abrupt, the apex frozen, and the scope very intense and exaggerated. Success with poses is no guarantee of success when emotional expressions occur spontaneously. Let us consider, then, a number of studies using spontaneous emotional behavior.

In one study autonomic nervous system changes were used as the criterion to test hypotheses about facial signs of emotion. The question asked was whether there was a difference in ANS activity when the face showed what FACS considered emotion or nonemotional activity? Ancoli (Ancoli, 1979; Ancoli, Kamiya, & Ekman, 1980) had female subjects watch pleasant and unpleasant films seated alone in a room, while heart rate, GSR, respiration and EEG were measured. The subjects did not know that their facial activity was being videotaped. When the subjects' ANS responses to the two films were compared, differences in the pattern of changes were found only when the face showed what FACS identified as positive or negative emotions. One limit of this study, however, was that it could only validate the predictions about the gross distinction between positive versus negative emotions, not finer distinctions within positive or negative emotional experience.

In another study of the subjects in this experiment, the subjective reports of emotional experience were utilized as the criterion to validate FACS predictions about finer distinctions among emotions. Ekman, Friesen, and Ancoli (1980) found that FACS hypotheses about a number of aspects of emotional experience predicted the subjects' report on multidimensional scales immediately after viewing the pleasant and unpleasant films. That is, FACS was able to discriminate (1) the intensity of happy feelings, (2) which of two happy experiences was the happiest, (3) the intensity of negative feelings, and (4) the occurrence of disgust as compared with fear, anger, or sadness.

In another study an environmental event was used as the criterion of what emotion was experienced. Ekman, Friesen, and Simons (1982) studied facial reactions in response to a blank pistol shot to test hypotheses about the facial startle response. They were able to discriminate the uniform pattern of facial actions that always occurs in response to such an unanticipated very loud noise from idiosyncratic responses. The pattern included the type of action that occurred and also the timing of the action, i.e., how quickly it began after the gun shot.

In yet another study, the emotion being experienced was identified in terms of the characteristics of the person showing the expression. Krause (1981) reasoned from the clinical literature that people who stutter should show many signs of anger during a conversation. Support for FACS predictions about the particular actions that signify anger was obtained because stutterers showed more of these particular actions than nonstutterers.

A variation in the experimental conditions during which an expression occurs was employed as the criterion in another study addressing a fundamental question about facial expressions of emotion. Is it possible to discriminate a purposeful facial action from a naturally occurring emotional expression? Ekman, Hager, and Friesen (1981) compared facial movements performed on request with naturally occurring movements in response to a joke or while watching pleasant or unpleasant films. They found that the requested actions were asymmetrical more often than the spontaneous emotional expressions and that the actions usually were more intense on the left side of the face for the requested, but not for the spontaneous, facial actions.

Many more studies are needed, of course, to validate all of the hypotheses contained in FACS and to replicate the studies just reported.

Utility

Because FACS was designed to measure any type of facial behavior, not just actions relevant to emotion, it is reasonable to ask whether there is evidence that FACS has general-purpose utility? Evidence of utility would require demonstration that FACS can measure people of different ages and can measure facial behavior that is providing signals other than emotional ones.

Oster (Oster, 1978; Oster and Ekman, 1978) provided information about some of the expression differences between the neonate and the young infant. For example, when the brows are raised, the horizontal furrows apparent in the child or adult will not appear in the neonate because of the fatty pad in the forehead. When FACS is used with Oster's modifications, all of the facial actions can be measured. Oster's studies provided evidence that certain complex, spontaneous facial actions observed in young infants are not random but represent organized patterns and sequences of facial muscle activity that are reliably related to other aspects of the infant's behavior.

The Facial Action Coding System has been found useful in studying conversational facial signals in which the facial action serves to illustrate or punctuate speech. Camras (in prep.) found differences in the syntactic form of questions that do and do not contain facial actions functioning as "question-markers." Ekman, Camras, and Friesen (reported by Ekman, 1980) found that the semantic context predicts which of two facial actions is used to provide speech emphasis. Baker (1982) used FACS to identify the facial actions shown by deaf persons when they sign. She was able to isolate particular combinations of facial actions that appear to serve syntactic functions.

9.6. Conclusion

Since it was first published, more than forty people have learned FACS and are beginning to use it to study quite diverse phenomena. Others have been learning Izard's (1979) technique for measuring facial movement. The next decade should see a great growth in knowledge about the face, now that the tools are available to measure facial action itself.

10. An evolutionary perspective on human facial displays

WILLIAM K. REDICAN

With almost Proustian clarity I recall an occasion when, as a fifteen-year-old high-school freshman, I was summoned by the principal to come to him. To accommodate this directive, I was obliged to walk down a long and otherwise unoccupied corridor: he, in his ominous collar and black robes, at one end, and I, slowly closing the distance, at the other. As I approached, vaguely aware of having broken one or more of the many rules of high-school life, I tried to present a composed and innocent countenance. However, a singularly unwelcome thing took place: the corners of my mouth began to be drawn inexorably down and back, exposing a thin row of teeth. I remember wondering why humans are such perverse creatures that a quite unbidden and seemingly irrepressible expression like that could appear on the face. Trying to control the corners of my mouth only produced a curious wavering expression, which I was convinced was being interpreted by the principal as a sure sign of guilt.

I decided to try to wrench my attention to a suitably sobering topic – as I recall, Dostoyevsky's Innocent Suffering Child – in a desperate but successful effort to obliterate the expression from my face, and I arrived in front of the principal with a countenance undoubtedly startling to behold.

I am pleased to report that I now have a reasonably satisfying answer to my question of several years past. Most monkeys in a comparable circumstance, though unable to resort to Dostoyevsky, would have displayed a very similar facial configuration: corners of the mouth retracted, frontal teeth exposed, and gaze averted or vascillating. Monkeys might also have emitted an occasional high-frequency scream and flattened their ears against their head as well. My point is that *Homo sapiens* and other members of the primate order often display remarkably similar facial expressions, in terms of the structural features, emotional substrates, and social contexts in which they are displayed.

In this chapter I will provide a selective overview of the major facial displays of affect that characterize nonhuman primates, draw attention to comparable human displays where possible, and indicate the sorts of issues that concern primatologists when they approach this topic. I will discuss ways in which this subject has been investigated in the past, and propose some ways it might be investigated in the future. I have assumed that most readers will not be familiar with research on nonhuman primates and have therefore made an effort to: (1) eschew or at least define primatological jargon, (2) explain underlying biological concepts or issues, and (3) introduce various taxonomic groups of animals that make up the primate order. I have compromised bibliographic thoroughness on occasion in order to present major findings in the field in a general fashion. For further detail, the interested reader is referred to my earlier review (Redican, 1975) as well as to works by Andrew (1963, 1964, 1965), Chevalier-Skolnikoff (1973, 1974b), Gautier and Gautier (1977), and van Hooff (1969, 1972, 1976). In particular, these other sources will provide information on interspecies differences, a topic largely bypassed in the present undertaking.

10.1. Introduction to primate taxonomy and nomenclature

Primate taxonomy and nomenclature can be introduced by defining taxonomy, simply, as the classification, ordering, or systemization of organisms into groups, or, more precisely, taxa (taxon, singular). *Taxa* will often be used in this chapter, not to impart a contrived sense of expertise, but rather because common expressions involving comparisons of "species" are quite often wrong. One might be comparing a species with another species, or genus, or family, etc., and usage can thus easily become chaotic. Some idea of commonly accepted taxonomic categories can be conveyed by reviewing the formal taxonomy for human beings, *Homo sapiens sapiens* (Table 10.1). The taxonomy for human beings is considerably simpler than that of some other organisms, for which categories such as superorder, infraorder, subgenus, or superspecies apply. When one considers that there are approximately 1,100,000 species of animals alone (Mayr, 1969), one is inclined to be more tolerant of such formalism.

In the case of primates – from the Latin *prīmātis*, "one of the first, principal, or chief," thus bestowing a decidedly ethnocentric name on our order – the most general division is into the prosimian and anthropoid suborders. The former is a group of small, often nocturnal, rodentlike

214   W. K. Redican

Table 10.1. *Formal taxonomy for human beings (Homo sapiens sapiens)*

Kingdom	Animalia: animals
Phylum (pl., phyla)	Chordata: chordates
Subphylum (pl., subphyla)	Vertebrata: vertebrates
Superclass	Tetrapoda: vertebrates with four limbs
Class	Mammalia: mammals
Subclass	Theria: live-bearing (i.e., not egg-laying) mammals
Infraclass	Eutheria: placental mammals
Cohort	Unguiculata: placental mammals with nails, claws, or both
Order	Primates: primates
Suborder	Anthropoidea: monkeys, apes, and humans
Superfamily	Hominoidea: apes and humans
Family	Hominidae ⎤
Subfamily	Homininae ⎟
Genus (pl., genera)	*Homo* ⎬ humans
Species	*sapiens* ⎟
Subspecies	*sapiens* ⎦

After *International code of zoological nomenclature* (Fifteenth International Congress of Zoology, 1964); Blackwelder (1967); Dewsbury (1978)

creatures that will not concern us much in this chapter. The anthropoid suborder includes monkeys, apes, and humans. Monkeys in turn are made up of Old World forms (i.e., from Asia and Africa) and New World forms (i.e., from South and Central America), and the apes are divided into *great* apes (gorillas, chimpanzees, and orang utans) and *lesser* apes (gibbons and siamangs). There is but one living species and subspecies of human being, one or more human species, such as *Homo erectus*, and one subspecies, *Homo sapiens neanderthalensis*, having become extinct.

Occasionally it will be necessary to refer to an organism's formal taxonomic name, in which case a full or partial binomial citation will usually be employed: the first name refers to the genus, the second to the species (e.g., *Macaca mulatta* refers to the rhesus macaque). Both are italicized, and the genus is also capitalized – the latter unlike the convention for musculature (e.g., *pectoralis major*). For a more thorough guide to primate taxonomy and a description of generalized primate traits, the reader is referred to the indispensable *Handbook of living primates*, by Napier and Napier (1967). In addition, Terry (1977) has authored a refreshing introductory chapter on the designation of names for a variety of nonhuman-primate taxa. In this chapter, for the sake of readability, the term *primate* will sometimes be used to refer to all taxa in the order except *Homo sapiens*.

10.2. Homology and analogy

Basic to an understanding of work in the field of animal behavior are the concepts of homology and analogy (see, e.g., Atz, 1970; Klopfer, 1976; and chapters by Cain, Masters, Senn, Wickler, and von Cranach in von Cranach, 1976). A *homology* is a similarity in structure or behavior that is attributable to the two or more organisms having a common ancestry. The homologous features may or may not have a similar function. Thus, for example, the feet of a human and a chimpanzee are homologous, but so also are the hooves of horses. Suckling behavior by a human, monkey, and seal infant would also be homologous. An *analogy* between structures or behaviors is a similarity based on function, not a common ancestry, this similarity having arisen from evolutionary selection over time. Thus, for example, a bat's echolocation and a lion's eyesight both function to locate prey. Likewise, a gorilla's chest-beating and a human's horn-honking might both be said to function as analogous means of intimidating other members of the social group.

One of the foremost questions that arises in comparisons of facial expressions of primates of different taxonomic groups is whether an apparently similar expression in different taxa represents a common ancestry or simply a common function. For our present purposes, we are much more interested in homologous expressions, as we are on a much firmer footing when attempting to generalize and extrapolate about such things as the muscles, movements, nervous pathways, endocrine responses, and eliciting circumstances involved in the expressions of human and nonhuman primates. In practice, it is often very difficult to discern homologous and analogous aspects of such complex social behaviors as, for example, territoriality. Human spatial behavior has much in common with that of birds and mammals, yet the divergencies are impressive. In general, however, the primary expressions of monkeys, apes, and humans will be found to be homologous, in view of the wide dispersal of very similar motor patterns and eliciting circumstances in both closely and relatively distantly related taxa of primates and, indeed, other mammals. One sees a continuity and progressive elaboration of facial expressions in taxa that are believed to represent ancestral groups from which *Homo sapiens* has diverged during the progression of evolution. As van Hooff (1976, p. 184) concluded: "Facial expressions may offer the best, if not the sole example of behavioural comparisons between man and his relatives, where the concept of homology can be justifiably applied and where its application is more than a mere triviality."

10.3. Displays

Although the term *expression* finds a wide usage among animal behaviorists, a more precise term used in the ethological literature to describe facial and other communicative activity is *display*. One limitation of *expression*, perhaps, is that it comes uncomfortably close to implying intentionality, although dictionary definitions of the term seem not to invoke the idea. The use of *display*, however, does offer a more operationally definable term and one that incorporates important principles of evolution.

As generally understood, a display is a signal or pattern of motor activity whose exaggerated or stereotyped characteristics suggest that it has become specialized – in form, frequency, or both – during evolution to effect or to facilitate the process of communication (e.g., Andrew, 1964, 1972; Brown, 1975; Moynihan, 1970). The term is usually reserved for visual signals, as opposed to those of other modalities (Brown, 1975; but see Moynihan, 1955). Clarity, precision, and strength of transmission are primary adaptive features of a signal, and they are achieved if the form and pattern of displays are exaggerated, emphatic, stereotyped, and distinctly different from other behavior patterns (Moynihan, 1970).

Ethologists conceive of displays as having been derived or *emancipated* from behaviors not specifically functioning as communicative signals. Thus, as Tinbergen (1952) used the concept, the behavior is said to have been freed from the causal factors that were involved in the appearance of the phylogenetic precursor (see also Hinde and Tinbergen, 1958). The process by which behaviors are emancipated into displays is called *ritualization* – one of the most important concepts in classical ethology (the biological study of behavior emphasizing observation in the natural habitat and the incorporation of principles of evolution, led in recent years by Lorenz and Tinbergen). Sir Julian Huxley first applied the term in 1914. More recently, in a valuable paper, he defined it as:

> the adaptive formalization or canalization of emotionally motivated behaviour, under the teleonomic pressure of natural selection so as: (a) to promote better and more unambiguous *signal* function, both intra- and inter-specifically; (b) to serve as more *efficient stimulators* or releasers of more efficient patterns of action in other individuals; (c) to reduce intra-specific *damage*; and (d) to serve as sexual or social *bonding* mechanisms. [Huxley, 1966, p. 250; emphasis added]

Huxley's definition is particularly helpful insofar as many authors stress simply the reduction of intraspecific tissue damage as the prime function of ritualized displays.

The traditional way that ethologists trace the general features of the evolutionary development of a display is through the *comparative method*, through which homologous behaviors in a number of closely related taxa are compared (on the basis of criteria such as those elaborated by Baerends, 1950, and Wickler, 1968). A classic example of this method is the ritualization of male courtship displays from ancestral feeding behavior in the pheasant taxon (Schenkel, 1956: reviewed by J.M. Cullen, 1972; Brown, 1975; and Eibl-Eibesfeldt, 1970). A form believed to be ancestral is shown by taxa such as the bobwhite quail in which males give a food vocalization and offer food directly to females as a prelude to copulation. In other taxa, such as ring-necked pheasants and domestic chickens, males typically peck at the ground and give food calls whether or not food is actually present; they may also pick up pebbles rather than food, and females are attracted to their proximity. The courting male impeyan phesant bows low before a female and pecks vigorously at the ground; if the female approaches, the male spreads wing- and tail-feathers while standing with his head low and tail-feathers bobbing. Male peacock pheasants give a similar display, and if food is given to males during the display they will in turn offer it to the females being courted. The point is that if one were not familiar with these intermediate ritualized forms, one might not be able to identify the origins of the highly elaborate courtship display of the male peacock: The courting male of this species spreads and shakes his prominent tail-feathers, then bends these feathers forward and simply points his beak at the ground. Although no food need be involved at all, females run in front of him and peck at the ground in the area that is the focal point of the male's arched tail feathers.

10.4. Natural selection

Although many of the facial displays of the nonhuman primates we will be considering are not as highly stereotyped or rigid as those of other mammals, birds, or reptiles, an acquaintance with the preceding ethological concepts of ritualization is helpful in understanding the very early origins of displays and their progressive development over evolutionary time. The factors that affect the direction of this development center on the concept of natural selection, where a distinction is usually made between natural selection (that seen in nature) and artificial selection (that deliberately engineered by human beings). Because the process of selection is "overwhelmingly the most important force in evolution" (E.O. Wilson, 1975, p. 67), one might expect a widespread consensus on its meaning. In fact, there is still a certain amount of controversy on the subject: "Even such an ostensibly simple concept as selection is neither consistently defined nor adequately understood by most biologists" (Darlington, 1972, p. 1239). For our purposes, *natural selection* will be held to mean a change in relative frequency of genotypes resulting from the differential survival and reproduction – and/or the differential elimination – of the associated phenotypes (Darlington, 1972; E.O. Wilson, 1975). A recent and lucid definition was offered by Trivers (in Dawkins, 1976, p. v): "Within each species some individuals leave more surviving offspring than others, so that the inheritable traits (genes) of the reproductively successful become more numerous in the next generation. This is natural selection: the non-random differential reproduction of genes." A trait is said to be *adaptive* if it renders the organism more fit to survive and reproduce – or less likely to be eliminated – relative to other members of the population (e.g., Ehrlich, Holm, and Parnell, 1974; Ruse, 1971).

Natural selection and adaptation are introduced here because of the transcendent concern shown in them by ethologists and animal behaviorists when considering a topic such as facial displays. In brief, *the employment of displays by an individual is viewed in light of the selective advantages conferred by its use to that individual and to others sharing its genes.* Thus, when investigators note that a primate typically flattens its ears during a particular display, they go on to ask what the associated costs and benefits are, and the sort of functional answer proposed is likely to sound something like "ear-flattening confers an adaptive benefit by reducing the likelihood of damage to the ears during an interaction with an opponent."

Andrew (1972) distinguished a number of factors that are important in considering the adaptiveness of display features and their evolutionary specialization as visual signals. Among the more important for a consideration of facial displays are the following, which Andrew regards as a description of the "immediate causation of...important groupings of display components" (p. 185).

Responses elicited by novel and significant stimuli

Novel stimuli are considered to be simply those that differ from preceding patterns of stimulation. Although Andrew does not define *significant*, he offers the example of conditioned stimuli associated with the acquisition of food. Three major subheadings of these responses are as follows:

Figure 10.1. A frowning adult female pigtail macaque (*Macaca nemestrina*). Note the forward position of the ears in this alert animal. Although the brows are lowered and appear to be converged, there is little evident constriction of *orbicularis oculi*. (Photograph copyright 1982 by The Zoological Society of London)

Alerting responses. The alerting responses are those elicited when major sense organs are collecting information. These can occur when the organism is either concentrating on a particular stimulus or scanning the environment. In the former case, when information is being gathered visually, a frown is often formed (i.e., the eyebrows are brought lower and closer together and the muscles around the eye may be constricted; see Figure 10.1). As we shall see, this observation is important for a consideration of several displays.

Several explanations have been offered to account for the functional significance of frowning brow movements, but a satisfying integrative account remains to be formulated (see Ekman, 1978b, for a critique of many proposals). Van Hooff (1969, p. 73), for example, suggested that frowning involves constriction of *orbicularis oculi* ("with which the muscle responsible for frowning [the *corrugator*] is connected"), which in turn steadies the eye during fixation. No data were cited to support this hypothesis, and it has never been satisfactorily explained why eye fixation is a beneficial outcome. It is well known that drifting of the eye and high-frequency, low-amplitude tremors of the eye take place during visual fixation. In fact, in humans these movements do not enhance visual acuity. They do prevent the fading or disappearance of an image that occurs when it is stabilized on the retina. This is referred to as the Troxler phenomenon because Troxler first noted the degradation of peripheral images during stabilized fixation. These images reappear immediately when the eyes are moved. Thus, the eyes must move if the perception of contours is to remain functional and if there is not to be intermittent fading and reappearance of images (Davson, 1972, p. 251; Newman, 1975; Pritchard, 1961).

A second proposal was offered by Andrew (1972, p. 188), who suggested that pupil constriction during frowning may increase the depth of sharp focus. Indeed, depth of focus does increase as pupil size diminishes: constriction of the human pupil from 4 to 2 mm accomplishes an increase of almost 50% in depth of focus (when the fixated object is at a distance of 1 m) (Davson, 1972, p. 406). Contrary to Andrew's suggestion, however, the pupil responds with dilation, not constriction, during frowning – at least when there is overhead light, as is usually the case. The interested reader can confirm this in front of an appropriately lighted mirror. Although Darwin (1872, pp. 220–226) did not mention pupil aperture, he did note that frowning when the head is held upright diminishes the amount of light striking the eye, and he cited Herbert Spencer's *Principles of Physiology* (2nd ed., 1872, p. 546) as support.

I propose that these early suggestions can be extended by arguing that, during frowning, the reduction of light striking the pupil has the effect of enhancing visual acuity ("the sharpness with which objects are perceived," Monnier, Polc, and Böhmer, 1975, p. 793) by reducing what is called simultaneous contrast (e.g., Mueller, 1965). That is, if an area focused on is adjacent to an area of greater illumination, that focal area will be perceived as dimmer than an identically illuminated area without such a brighter adjacent area. The brighter the retinal illumination (within limits), the greater will be visual acuity (Mueller, 1965).

In other words, I propose that a frown may enhance perceived focal illumination by diminishing background light (i.e., from the overhead sun), and the resultant increase in visual acuity enhances such capacities as the discrimination and resolution of stimuli. For example, I recently demonstrated to myself what I believe to be this phenomenon by focusing near a distant lamppost on a rainy night, during which time the raindrops in the area of the lamp were not visible. When I shielded the light from above with my hand (as an analog to the frown of the brow), a large area of raindrops instantly became perceptible around the lamp.

As for the particular significance of pupil dilation during frowning, it is probably most simply described as a component of the well-known direct light reflex by which pupil diameter is generally inversely related to the amount of light striking the retina (e.g., Moses, 1975). Beyond that basic declaration, the subject of pupil size becomes remarkably intricate. For example, the dilation accompanying emotional arousal (especially fear) can even largely override the direct light reflex (Moses, 1975, p. 331).

Human visual acuity is enhanced by increasing pupil diameter (e.g., Leibowitz, 1952). The upward limits to this benefit are spherical aberration, chromatic aberration, and astigmatism caused by the oblique path of light entering the eye through a wide pupil. The lower limits are determined by diffraction, which, when the pupil is at small aperture, superimposes unfocused light on the retinal image and thereby diminishes acuity (Davson, 1972; Moses, 1975). Thus, the benefits of increased depth of focus at small pupil diameters is offset by the potentially substantial detriments of diffraction. The optimal balance between diffraction on one hand and aberration/astigmatism on the other is a human pupil diameter of 2.4 to 3 mm (F.W. Campbell and Gubisch, 1966; Davson, 1972), with the diameter of the normal human pupil varying between 1.5 and 8 mm (Moses, 1975).

Thus there are at least two possible interpretations of pupil dilation during frowning. The first is that it is simply a reflexive response to the withdrawal of light induced by shading of the eye, the primary function of which is to reduce simultaneous contrast. The second is that it serves to enhance visual acuity by raising the level of retinal illumination and by reducing diffraction, short of the limits imposed by aberration and astigmatism. What are needed to resolve the question are data both on the actual magnitudes of pupil change during frowning and on the range in which such change takes place.

While one scans the environment, in contrast, the eyebrows are often raised and the eyelids are spread apart, which result in a relatively wide field of vision (particularly upward). As Andrew (1972) notes, it is difficult to look upward without raising the brows. Andrew describes pupil dilation as an accompaniment to scanning eye movements, but if more light strikes the retina the pupils should constrict, not dilate. At such times when peripheral vision is so important, it makes sense that the aberration caused by oblique light should be diminished by constriction, and, at the same time, depth of focus should be enhanced, which is also crucial in scanning. I am indulging in post-hoc speculation, which is the bane of evolutionists, but there is, unfortunately, a paucity of data on the subject. Blurton Jones and Konner (1971), however, demonstrated quite well that a situation evoking scanning (i.e., moving the eyes and turning the head) elicited more brow-raising than one evoking direct gazing. They also cite the common finding that brow-raising is used as a conversational cue, especially during questioning (Ekman, 1978b).

Protective responses. As a major category of responses involving facial displays, protective responses are said to safeguard sensory organs and other vulnerable tissue from potential damage. They are elicited by startling, painful, or potentially dangerous stimuli. Andrew (1972) distinguished several gradations of facial protective responses, each occurring at higher intensities of arousal:

1. Eye closure (perhaps intermittent), contraction of the *orbicularis oculi* muscles, brow-lowering, and ear-flattening
2. Arrested respiration (narrowing or closure of the glottis) and retraction of the corners of the mouth
3. Repeated tongue protrusion and lateral shaking of the head and body

As we shall see, most of these components are involved in facial displays associated with fear and in situations when animals "greet" each other, i.e., when individuals come into a (typically sudden) perceived proximity after some period of separation.

Responses associated with exertion. Andrew conceives of a continuum from exertion to immobility, and one can readily agree that many visual displays are associated with imminent gross body movements (e.g., the well-known fight/flight gradation). Indeed, the ethological concept of intention movements might well be invoked here. *Intention movements* are incomplete or preparatory locomotor movements; they were so named because they often afford a clue about what the animal "intends" to do next (Daanje, 1950; Heinroth, 1911). For example, several components of bird displays consist of intention movements of flight (e.g., tipping up the wings or lifting the head). Very basically, it is believed that selection pressures have led to a simplification of the more complete motor pattern into a ritualized display – either a component or its totality. In the case of facial displays of nonhuman primates, several intention movements can be recognized that are associated with preliminary or attenuated biting movements (both play biting and aggressive biting).

Two sorts of responses involved in exertion that seem to have contributed to the evolution of facial displays are respiration and thermoregulation. Changes in intensity and frequency of respiration are, of course, typical of the affective states that characterize displays. Dilation of the external nares is usually sustained during vigorous inhalation and exhalation, and it has been incorporated as a component of several facial displays. Among the thermoregulatory responses believed to be important in facial displays are piloerection (Brown, 1975) and perhaps blushing – a vascular cooling response appearing in circumstances in which imminent exertion is likely.

Responses associated with vocalizations

Some of the motor patterns originally involved with vocalizations have evolved as components of visual displays. As might be expected, these involved primarily the area around the mouth and neck. Many populations of nonhuman primates – particularly terrestrial, diurnal, group-living ones – are believed to be under strong selection pressure toward relatively silent communication, as frequent vocalizations can add greatly to an individual's conspicuousness in an environment and may therefore alert potential predators to its general location. Vocal signals are also relatively inefficient within a large social group. Thus, the vocal component of a number of signals is believed to have dropped out as the displays became increasingly ritualized in such taxa, so that eventually a silent display remains (or one in which vocalizations are emitted only at arousal levels of relatively great intensity).

Selection pressures exerted by the habitat

The habitat in which a species evolves is characterized by features that constitute significant constraints and selective pressures on the course of behavioral and morphological change. The habitat is, in many ways, similar to the economics of human societies. Animal behaviorists trained from a psychological perspective are often content to render a broad overview of the field with scarcely a mention of ecological variables, preferring instead to focus on proximate factors (e.g., the role of early experience, the contingencies of learning systems, or the effects of hormones). For such traditional psychologists, spending time considering the variables that ecologists are wont to do is almost tantamount to studying the occult. On the other hand, animal behaviorists trained from a biological perspective are thoroughly acquainted with literature that highlights the effects of the habitat on the evolution of social systems, particularly in taxa as large and as well studied as birds. They are not reluctant to consider factors such as predator and antipredator strategies, the availability and seasonality of food, the nutritional quality of diets, and, in general, the competition for limited resources (see, e.g., Crook, 1970; Clutton–Brock, 1974; Crook and Goss-Custard, 1972; Eisenberg, Muckenhirn, and Rudran, 1972; Gaulin and Konner, 1977; Tuttle, 1975). Within the field of animal behavior, psychologists have been known to be irritated with biologists for concentrating on what appear to be such remote variables and for appearing to reduce all of behavior to such things as niche adaptations; biologists have been likewise known to be vexed with their psychologist colleagues for devoting so much attention to animals in "unnatural" environments in lieu of studying some of the primary factors shaping the evolution and dynamics of social behavior. Thankfully, the emergence in recent years of a generation of animal behaviorists that is more truly cross-disciplinary has done much to ameliorate such internecine sentiment and to establish a respect for the different sorts of questions generated by different traditions.

A helpful illustration of ecological variables pertinent to the evolution of displays is afforded by a comparison of Old and New World monkeys, the former being mostly terrestrial and the latter primarily arboreal. It can be readily appreciated that visual signals in a habitat of dense foliage are often highly inefficient: the signaler is simply blocked from the percipient by foliage. Moreover, Chalmers (1968) pointed out that monkeys in an arboreal habitat are often silhouetted against a background of relatively bright sky, which makes it difficult to discriminate movements of the facial musculature and changes in coloration. (This aspect of forest illumination would not necessarily preclude the development of displays consisting primarily of gross body movements, such as head-bobbing or lunging, but this point lacks empirical assessment.)

In accord with the restrictions on visual displays that are occasioned by a forest environment, one sees a much-reduced repertoire of facial expressions in New World relative to the Old World monkeys (Andrew, 1964; Moynihan, 1969). Indeed, in considering a species of New World monkey that is both arboreal and nocturnal – the night monkey – Moynihan (1964) was led to comment that monkeys of that species simply "do not have any facial expressions" (p. 80). I would not be surprised if that statement proves to be overzealous, but the point remains that a nocturnal adaptation reduces even further the utility of visual displays.

If selection by factors involving the habitat were to play a significant role in the evolution of displays, one would expect that arboreal Old World taxa would have a relatively reduced repertoire of facial displays compared with terrestrial Old World monkeys. (That is, we would be trying to eliminate other evolutionary factors that impinged on New World monkeys after their divergence from ancestral Old World monkeys.) Of course, this is the case. Thus, for example, a particular arboreal Old World monkey – the Nilgiri langur – lacks several expressions and components thereof that are typical of terrestrial Old World species (Poirier, 1970), and the communicative repertoire of the arboreal black mangabey is considerably more vocal than visual (Chalmers, 1968; Chalmers and Rowell, 1971). As Gautier and Gautier (1977, p. 939) expressed it, the regulation of intragroup social relations in terrestrial Old World primates of an open habitat is "ceaseless and subtle, linked with frequent looks that yield continuous information on the activity of neighbors." In Old World primates living in a woodland habitat, by contrast, "the lack of facial expressiveness and the passivity of exchanges causes reactions to be less predictable and subtle, and less susceptible to modulation."

Closely associated with the openness of the habitat is the size and complexity of social groups, with the larger and more complex being typically found in a terrestrial or open habitat. A large number of individuals in a group can be supported in a habitat such as a savannah much more easily than in a forest, and the larger population of interacting individuals necessarily involves more frequent and complex communicative displays (Gautier and Gautier, 1977; Marler, 1970). In particular, the Gautiers associate the degree of gradation in the visual repertoire with the frequency of social contact. Primates involved in the close-range, intense, and complex social interactions that typify large groups have been seen to evolve comparably significant repertoires of displays such as facial expressions. By comparison, in primates whose communicative activity consists largely in long-distance and intergroup signals, the predominant mode of communication is vocal. The hazards of long-distance vocal signals in terms of conspicuousness to potential predators is believed to be offset by the difficulty of locating an auditory signal in space (Marler, 1965). Geldard's (1960) distinctions between auditory and visual coding of messages fit well with these generalizations. For example, visual coding allows for fine and rapid discrimination (e.g., during close agonistic altercations), whereas auditory coding is favored when the recipient is preoccupied, oriented away from the signaler, or at reduced alertness, and the signal must "break in" to the recipient's perceptual domain (e.g., when a feeding animal is alerted to the presence of a nearby individual).

10.5. Facial displays and their social contexts

The objective of this section is to provide an overview of the facial displays that characterize nonhuman primates. It will, of course, be a highly selective one, and for additional information, the interest reader is referred to the general references previously cited. In particular, in this section we shall limit our concern primarily to Old World monkeys and apes and to the more generalized types of facial displays. In a later section an attempt will be made to integrate these categories of facial displays with current classifications of human affect (e.g., Ekman and Friesen, 1975).

The threat display

What is widely referred to as a threat display is of interest for several important reasons: (1) structurally, it involves the activation of a number of components, many capable of separate display; (2) it is believed to be emitted when the individual is in a relatively complex motivational state (i.e., a compound of aggression and fear); and (3) it is a category of display not often discussed in the literature on human facial communication. In its complete form, as often seen in most taxa of Old World monkeys and apes, the display is characterized by a slightly to fully open mouth with upper lip tensed over the teeth and corners of the mouth brought forward, and the upper and often the lower teeth are not usually visible, especially in profile; the ears are usually flattened against the head; the gaze is fixed upon the percipient; the eyebrow may be raised; and the nostrils may be flared (see Figure 10.2). The facial display

Figure 10.2 An adult female rhesus macaque (*Macaca mulatta*) displaying a facial threat. Notice that the teeth are not prominently exposed. Ears are flattened against the head, the brow is raised, the gaze is fixed and staring, nostrils are flared, and the upper lip is rounded over the teeth. (Photograph copyright 1982 by William K. Redican)

may be accompanied by one or more body postures or movements, such as slapping, lunging, or jerking. Let us now go on to consider most of these components separately, as it appears that, with an increasing level of arousal, successive components of a threat display are exhibited in an additive manner. This statement is a qualitative and inductive one; no vigorous data exist on this point.

Direct stare. One of the first surprises awaiting the student of human communication who investigates similar processes in nonhuman primates is that monkeys and apes appear to spend remarkably little time in direct eye-to-eye contact. Indeed, a fixed direct gaze or stare by itself is typically described as a low-intensity threat (see Argyle and Cook, 1976, pp. 1–9; Redican, 1975, pp. 115–119; Shafton, 1976, chap. 8). To be sure, the gazes of primates often meet in the course of nonagonistic social interaction, but at some point a transition from an information-gathering activity to an agonistic display takes place (see Figure 10.3). The domain of this transition is nebulous, but there exist some criteria. That is, an agonistic stare is said to be more prolonged than other gazing, being

Figure 10.3 An agonistic stare by an adult female rhesus macaque (on the right in each photo) paired with an adult male. This sequence took place in a refractory period between bouts of copulation. The female looked quickly at the male and then turned and stared at the human observer, often jerking her upper body in a vertical plane. The sequence was repeated many times and culminated in the onset of a series of copulations. This form of behavioral interaction is referred to as *incitement*. (Photographs copyright 1982 by William K. Redican)

maintained for 3 to 5 seconds or longer in one species (Struhsaker, 1967c). Moreover, it may be accompanied by agonistic postures, movements, vocalizations, and perhaps piloerection. The rhesus monkey, for example, may quickly jerk its head up and then back to the resting posture while staring.

There is another feature of a stare that is observable in nonhuman primates, although it is rather elusive – i.e., the animal is not *behaving enough*. In a sense, "not behaving enough" is itself a behavior, although operationally defining such (non)activity is vexing. When an animal appears to be in a moderate state of arousal, it is characterized by a relatively great number of behaviors: it will respond to environmental changes and contingencies in a relatively direct and immediate fashion by shifting its gaze, posture, direction of outer ears, etc., in a frequent and typically smooth progression. When staring, this sequence of minor shifts appears to cease, and the individual is far more restricted in the range of observable behavioral units. Once again, there is a lack of data on this point. As the Gautiers (1977, p. 929) said, "No one seems to have tried to analyze the elements of the look (form, surface, and brilliance of the eye, or dilation of the pupil)."

The behavioral consequences of a display (used here in a loose sense) that is as subtle as a stare are often dramatic. The percipient of a stare may physically withdraw, crouch, exhibit a submissive display, scream, redirect the attention by staring at another individual, cease or avoid an activity, threaten back (although that seems to be reported rarely), and so forth (e.g., Bertrand, 1969; Kaufman and Rosenblum, 1966; Kummer, 1967). Clearly, the likelihood of these responses is contingent not only on the social status of sender and receiver but on the context in which the stare is displayed. Thus, a stare by the alpha male can precipitate flight in the percipient, whereas a stare by a low-ranking individual can pass with no observable effect on other group members. Likewise, a stare displayed by an animal running toward the percipient is far more efficacious than one displayed by a sitting animal (Struhsaker, 1967b).

Eyelids and eyebrows. The facial features of a direct stare are, for the most part, static. As a facial threat becomes more elaborate, features begin to be involved that are at least temporarily mobile. The eyelids and eyebrow are of major importance. In most Old World monkeys, a threat involves vertical movement of the eyebrow, which in many taxa exposes the bright skin of the upper eyelid and the area immediately above it (the eye coverfold); in some cases, the effect of revealing these areas can be enhanced by rapid eyelid-blinking (e.g., K.R.L. Hall, 1962; Redican, 1975; Struhsaker, 1967a, 1967c; van Hooff, 1969). It may be worth noting that this component of the threat display, along with several others to be discussed for this and other displays, involves the exposure of a previously concealed feature of the face, not simply the movement or rearrangement of visible features (in, for example, a frown or a closed-mouth human smile). A complication, in the case of nonhuman primates, is that some taxa have areas of coverfold and eyelid coloration that remain visible even when the brow is at rest, whereas other taxa reveal such areas only when the brow is raised or eyelids lowered. The taxonomic variability in this trait remains largely unsystematized as yet, although it seems reasonable to state that the sudden exposure of bright or colored areas around the eyes is a much more conspicuous event than simply the raising of brows against a homogeneous background. In the case of humans, except where the eyelids are cosmetically adorned, a morphological relationship exists that is converse to that of other primates. That is, we have retained patches of eyelid fur, from what was presumably a much furrier ancestral face, on a background of naked skin. The conspicuousness of human brow movements thus appears to consist primarily in movement of the brows against the contrasting background and, perhaps, secondarily in the onset of associated furrows, rather than in exposure of concealed bright areas of skin or fur. However, one might still look for a similar functional significance of vertical brow movement during threats in both human and nonhuman primates in spite of contrasting morphology.

Ears. Closely associated with movements of the eyebrow are those of the ears. Indeed, Andrew (1963) regards brow-raising as a byproduct of scalp withdrawal because the ears are flattened against the sides of the head. It is not yet clear, however, under what circumstances prominent ear movements can be made without accompanying brow movements. We do know that ear-flattening takes place in several types of facial display in addition to the threat, as will be seen later. It also occurs in a wide range of mammals when startled, when something is thrust close to the face, or when the individual is advancing toward an object or individual (Andrew, 1965). According to Guthrie and Petocz (1970), in most mammalian taxa the ears are erect and oriented toward the antagonist in the first stages of threat and flattened against the head in subsequent stages. The distinction between forward and backward ear movement may well correspond to the frowning (during concentration) and raising (during scanning) movements of the eyebrow discussed earlier. That is, during concentrated attention an individual may enhance the acuity of its auditory and visual sensory modalities bearing on the target by forward ear movement and frowning, respectively, although enhancement of the visual system may be considerably the lesser of the two effects. This may correspond to what has been referred to in the literature as the initial stages of threat. In both scanning movements and intense threat, by contrast, the individual is taking in as broad a spectrum of sensory data as possible. Again, this idea appears to be speculative, as it has not been substantiated by cited data.

The adaptive significance of both forward and backward ear movements seems identifiable. In the case of forward movement, it serves to enhance auditory acuity directly ahead of the individual. In the case of backward movement, it removes vulnerable and often prominent tissue from access by a potential antagonist, and it thus qualifies as a protective response in Andrew's schema. I am unaware if auditory functioning is impaired or peripherally enhanced while ears are flattened against the head.

Mouth. The final major component of the threat display considered here is the very important area of the mouth. A static gaping mouth is a feature of facial displays in an extremely large spectrum of animals. In cold-blooded taxa such as reptiles, the skin is largely immobile, and facial expressions are largely limited to ritualized intention movements of biting. In "primitive" primates and closely related nonprimate mammals, there is little or no displacement of the corners of the mouth during these ritualized movements and the teeth are conspicuously *exposed* (Andrew, 1964). Covering the teeth during threat displays is apparent in some more complex taxa such as lemurs (Andrew, 1964; Jolly, 1966). By the time one has reached Old and New World monkeys, the upper lip is typically rounded over the teeth during this display by constricting the upper *orbicularis oris* muscle; the profiles of both upper and lower teeth are obscured, but the dorsal side of the lower teeth and the tips of canines can occasionally be seen (Andrew, 1964; Redican, 1975; van Hooff, 1969).

The evolutionary ritualization of the open-mouth component in threat has been discussed most extensively by Andrew (1964, 1972). Opening the mouth is viewed as an intention movement of biting, as previously noted. He argued that rounding the lips is a response that accompanies the intense oral expiration involved in loud vocalizations of a relatively low frequency (roaring), via constriction of the entire *orbicularis oris*. However, Paul Ekman (Pers. comm.) has brought to my attention that there may be two separate muscle actions involved in the oral configuration of the primate mouth in threat: the upper lip is rounded via *orbicularis oris* but perhaps not the lower lip, which appears to be drawn down by *depressor labii inferioris* (as seen in Figure 10.2). The morphological correspondence between this configuration and the one during exhalation of intense vocalization must be carefully documented.

Andrew further suggested that rounding of lips (at least the upper lip, as we propose here) may regulate resistance to the flow of breath and thus prevent too rapid a collapse of the thoracic cavity. This proposal must remain hypothetical until data are presented.

It is generally believed that the vocal accompaniment to the display was selected against in many taxa because of its conspicuousness, but the gaping configuration of the mouth remained and became ritualized as a display. There is some evidence to suggest that the configuration of the mouth may have served to enhance or shape the resonant properties of vocalizations accompanying threat – which are still emitted, but at relatively low amplitude. In many mammals and birds, threat vocalizations are usually low in pitch. One of the factors affecting pitch, in mammals at least, is the size of the resonating chamber. Thus, larger animals make lower-pitched vocalizations; so pitch can serve as a cue for assessing body size of an opponent. The widespread incorporation of low-pitched vocalizations into threat displays can therefore be interpreted as a means of enhancing one's apparent size (Dawkins and Krebs, 1978). Piloerection, of course, can further enhance the effect. Conversely, the high-pitched sounds typically associated with fearful or submissive displays, as we shall see, may serve, together with body postures such as crouching, to diminish the apparent size of the emitter and thus help terminate or avert an attack. This is an example of Darwin's (1872, pp. 28, 50–65) well-known principle of *antithesis*, in which induction of opposite "states of mind" are said to elicit opposite, or antithetical, motor patterns. Ethologists often discuss one class of selection pressures, in the evolution of displays, as those leading to the divergence or distinctiveness of displays and thus to a greater efficiency thereof (e.g., Tinbergen, 1959). It seems reasonable that they and Darwin were referring to a common process. I note here with interest that K.R. Scherer (Giessen, West Germany) is currently studying the effects of various mouth configurations on the tonal properties of human vocal sounds.

Sequence of components. The common understanding of what is meant by a threat display, I believe, involves the full complement of the preceding components. However, we have seen that most of the components can be displayed virtually independently, or two or more may summate. At our present level of understanding, it seems reasonable to propose that, as arousal level increases, the following components become progressively involved: (1) stare, (2) frown, (3) brow-raising/ear-flattening, and (4) nostril-flaring/mouth-gaping. This sequence is based in part on the components that observers describe in mild versus severe threat displays and also on the fact that subsets proposed for higher levels of arousal often necessarily involve components for lower levels (e.g., if the mouth is gaping, the displayer can usually be assumed to have flattened its ears and be staring). Systematic data are not yet available, and particularly lacking are data involving correlations of independent measures of arousal level with particular display components.

Social contexts of threat displays. As might be expected, the social situations in which threat displays are seen are diverse. Perhaps the most frequent context mentioned is dominance–subordinance, or status interactions. Thus, for example, dominant stumptail macaques threaten lower-ranking individuals to prevent them from acquiring food or coming closer to the displayer (Bertrand, 1969). It is not at all clear, however, that frequency of displaying threats is a reliable index of dominance status; displacement, for example, is reported to be a more dependable measure (Kaufmann, 1967), where *displacement* is used in the sense of usurping another individual's location (e.g., near a food supply or at a vantage point) and is not to be confused with the ethological and psychoanalytic uses of the same term. Also, individuals high in a status hierarchy are often said to be relatively free from the strife that characterizes those lower in status, and one might accordingly expect a higher frequency of threats among the latter.

Another social context in which facial threat displays are often reported is that of sexual behavior, during which they can be directed at almost every conceivable class of target. Thus, an adult male patas monkey who is beginning to show sexual interest in another group member is much more likely to threaten individuals, even infants, who approach (K.R.L. Hall, 1968). Female vervets often lunge at and threaten males who have just dismounted (Struhsaker, 1967c). Female rhesus monkeys are observed to threaten distant males, which seems to incite the nearby consorting male to copulate (Altmann, 1962; see Cox and LeBoeuf, 1977, for an analysis of another mammal). This is the context that Figure 10.3 depicts; in this case, after innumerable threats had been directed at me I adopted a stoic posture and resolutely avoided eye contact with either the male or female. The female shortly thereafter began threatening nearby inanimate objects – the file cabinet, trashcan, sink, etc. As before, a brief threat was followed by turning around and looking (presumably not staring) at the male, back to the target, then again at the male, and so forth until the male responded and copulation ensued. In this same species, males may also engage in threat displays while in sexual consort. A male may threaten other individuals and repeatedly glance over his shoulder toward the female, who often responds by threatening in the same direction that the male is (Michael and Zumpe, 1970). Such are the contexts from which cost/benefit analyses of displays are made, provided that data such as frequency of copulation, birth and viability rates, etc., are available.

Other contexts of threat displays have emerged somewhat haphazardly from the literature. Eliciting circumstances include: (1) occasions when an animal approaches too closely or too swiftly to the displayer or to the latter's kin or consort, (2) the introduction of new members to a group or the proximity of another group, and (3) competition over food and other resources. Consequences include increased or maintained (i.e., rarely decreased) interindividual distance, flight, submission, and, far less frequently, overt attack. For the future documentation of such social contexts, I see a rather desperate need for the sort of data that Chalmers (1968, pp. 261–263) has provided on the black mangabey. He simply recorded the behavior of both the sender and percipient of a display in terms of three categories: attacks, approaches/remains with, and flees. In the case of the stare–threat display, he found that percipients of the display were far more likely to flee than either of the other two behavioral categories. Reciprocally, the displaying animals were twice as likely to remain with the target of the display as they were to attack, and on no observed occasions did the displayers flee after threatening. Not only do such data help sort out the antecedent and particularly the consequent events associated with displays, they also provide some insight into the displayer's presumed affective state, which is the topic to which we now turn.

Affect associated with threat display. It is perhaps unfortunate that the first display chosen for discussion has a relatively complex affective state associated with it, for we have not yet considered the displays of the affects from which the threat is said to be compounded: aggression and fear. It is not uncommon to encounter, even in the animal behavior literature, a presentation of the threat display as a purely aggressive signal. However, the classic ethological view posits a compound of aggression and fear – or attack and flight, which are their behavioral manifestations. Much of the formative theoretical work was done by European ethologists, in particular, Niko Tinbergen, studying bird displays (e.g., Moynihan, 1955; Tinbergen, 1952). These ethologists saw, in threat displays of birds, components of both attack (intention movements of advancing and pecking) and flight (intention movements of avoidance, escape, or retreat). We would do well to keep in mind Tinbergen's (1959; 1959a) distinction that threat displays occur when there is a conflict between the specific actions of attack and flight, not the more generalized ones of approach and avoidance (Tinbergen, 1959a). Thus, a brooding gull would not show a threat display when in conflict simply between leaving the nest and sitting on its eggs.

There are a number of finer points that merit brief scrutiny here. First, ethologists seem occasionally to refer to a simple *inhibition* of aggression as the underlying mechanism of threats, not a conflict between or compound of aggression and fear. Blurton Jones (1968) found that threats in one variety of bird occurred when full attack was simply prevented, either by a physical barrier or by the tendency to flee. A different sort of threat display in the same species of bird depended specifically on the tendency to flee. He concluded that some threats depend on: (1) a conflict among tendencies to attack, remain, and flee, (2) a conflict between tendencies for locomotion in different directions, or (3) a conflict between a strong tendency and any other that blocks it. This level of fine-tuned analysis has not been performed on nonhuman primate displays, and there is not a consensus on these issues. A second note is that the attack–fear theory has been challenged on neurophysiological grounds because threat, flight, and attack were separately elicited by electrical stimulation (Brown and Hunsperger, 1963; Maley, 1969), but the interpretation of that evidence is also in dispute (Andrew, 1972).

The substantiation in the primate literature for the attack–flight hypothesis is limited but plausible. For instance, Struhsaker (1967c) emphasized that threats in the monkeys he studied may occur in either an aggressive or defensive context. Moreover, one would hope to find distinct facial displays that reflect uncompounded anger and fear, and that is indeed the case. In the case of anger, it is the "tense-mouth" display, which is typically followed by chase, attack, or stealthy approach; in the case of fear, it is the grimace, together with other responses such as gaze aversion, flight, or crouching. (Both the tense-mouth display and the grimace will be considered later in greater detail.)

Tinbergen (1959a) reviewed three methods by which ethologists analyze motivation (structural, sequential, and situational), and we can employ them here to see if the threat display stands up to analysis as an anger–fear hybrid. According to a *structural* analysis, displays can reveal their complex origin if components of each underlying affect either: (1) alternate, (2) form a simultaneous mosaic, or (3) give rise to a compromise or blended movement or posture. By these structural criteria, the anger–fear hypothesis appears to have failed, as the threat display seems to satisfy none of those criteria, at least given our current understanding of the functional morphology of primate facial displays. By the remaining two analytic methods, however, there is more promise. That is, a *sequential* analysis should reveal that threat displays alternate with attack and flight (or associated displays). Moreover, the threat display should occur in a social *situation* that is intermediate between attack and flight situations. My position is that satisfying quantitative tests of these two criteria are not yet available, but descriptive accounts tentatively appear to support the compound anger–fear hypothesis.

Possible human homologs. It appears that the threat display per se is mentioned relatively rarely in the literature on human displays. Because the threat display develops late in ontogeny in nonhuman primates, relative to other displays (Redican, 1975), one would not expect it to be well documented in the child-ethology literature. Indeed, Blurton Jones (1972a), McGrew (1972), and Young and Decarie (1977), for example, cite it briefly or not at all, although frowning accompanying a stare was recorded in their human subjects in the context expected from the nonhuman primate literature. I am unaware of reliable data on open-mouth threat displays by human adults, and what little has come to my attention often involves intense concurrent vocalization or speech. (Imagine, for example, the facial configuration during an antagonistically expressed "Huh!" The mouth is in the appropriate position, and if a raised brow and perhaps a quick upward jerk of the head were to accompany the open mouth, we would not be far at all from the classic nonhuman primate display.) Given the widespread occurrence of some form of open-mouth threat display in such a wide variety of animals, its lack of documentation in the human literature is surprising. This is particularly so in view of the fact that many human ethologists have engaged in research with nonhuman primates. Perhaps the influence of ontogenetic experience is relatively great in this display. Humans are, after all, socialized rather sternly against biting as a way of resolving disputes. A cross-cultural perspective on this display would be welcome. In terms of primates, we have Kaufmann's (1966, p. 22) very interesting observation of rhesus monkeys: "The infants seemed to learn slowly the meaning of aggressive signals. Males threatened infants with direct, open-mouthed stares and head-bobbing, and occasionally a male hit an infant and briefly pinned it to the ground. The infants completely ignored this hostile behavior. . . ." This fits well with Redican's (1975) conclusion that the threat display appears relatively late in ontogeny, with the proposed sequence being: (1) affiliative displays (lipsmack, play face, and perhaps pout), (2) fearful displays (grimace and related displays), and (3) aggressive displays (threat, tense-mouth displays, and perhaps yawn). Given the late onset of the threat display and its probable lack of prepotent activating properties (cf. Sackett, 1966), the role of ontogenic experience in the development of the threat seems great in a species as behaviorally plastic as *Homo sapiens*.

Tense-mouth display

A display that has received relatively little attention, but is of some conceptual importance, is referred to as the *tense-mouth face* (van Hooff, 1969). In this display the eyes are fixed and staring; the jaws are close together with lips compressed and perhaps drawn slightly inward, thus bulging the lips; the position of the brow appears to be variable; and the ears are usually flattened against the head (Redican, 1975) (see Figure 10.4).

The associated motivational state is said to be almost exclusively anger. (*Anger* is too dangerously anthropomorphic for most primatologists to use without discomfort; I am using it here to refer to the emotional state of an animal whose overt behavior is attack or associated behaviors.) The display has been observed in the initiator of a chase, attack, or stealthy approach. It appears reasonable to interpret the components of the display as protective movements prior to an imminent physical conflict, which, in particular, involve a bite by the displayer.

The display is interesting on theoretical grounds because it lends indirect support to the compound-affect theory of the threat display. That is, one would hope to find a display that is associated primarily with anger

Figure 10.4. A tense-mouth display by an adult female rhesus monkey. Ears are flattened, brows raised, gaze fixed and staring, jaws close together, and lips compressed. Teeth are not prominently exposed, although this animal is highly disposed toward attack. Angry humans display a quite similar configuration. (Photograph copyright 1982 by William K. Redican)

if the compound theory were to be upheld, just as one would hope for a primarily fearful display, which is the next to be considered.

I am reasonably confident that students of human facial expression are familiar with this display in the human repertoire. I have a cherished newspaper clipping in my possession from the sports page of the *San Francisco Chronicle* (19 March 1974, p. 45) in which a classic tense-mouth face is displayed by a basketball player. He was being restrained by teammates after punching an opponent who, it was claimed, elbowed him unnecessarily. (The opponent had no comment.) Also, in Ekman et al.'s study of universals in human facial expression, an adult male of the South Fore of New Guinea was asked to show how he would look if he were "angry and about to fight," and the pictured response was remarkably similar to a tense-mouth face (e.g., Fig. 3c in Ekman and Friesen, 1975, p. 27). The position of the mouth in the nonhuman primate display corresponds well to the component associated with human anger, i.e., the "closed, lip-pressed-against-lip mouth" (Ekman & Friesen, 1975, p. 83), seen when engaging in physical violence.

Grimace

The grimace is a display that might well appear in response to the threat or tense-mouth displays just considered. The terminology for this display is less clear than for that of other displays: *grimace display* is redundant; *grimace* is a popular term often used to denote any sort of facial expression; and *fear grimace* is frequently employed, but its use gives rise to complications (e.g., it is often difficult to specify that an animal is fearful if independent observable indexes such as urination and defecation are absent). Tinbergen (1959) argued decades ago that displays are best described in terms of their form; their names "should be descriptive without any reference to either function or causation, for uncertainties in interpretation may lead to confusing changes of names as these interpretations change" (p. 6). In this chapter, as in my previous review (Redican, 1975), I have opted for the simplest term in part, I confess, for its linguistic convenience. Complex terms for displays seem rarely to attain widespread usage. The parsimony of a simple term is also attractive because the reader is free to make a more elaborate construct of it if he or she wishes. By contrast, van Hooff (1969, p. 40) prefers the more formally correct term *silent bared-teeth face*; the reader should be aware that van Hooff and I are referring to the same display.

Structural features. The structural features of the grimace appear to be relatively uniform in most taxa of nonhuman primates (Redican, 1975; van Hooff, 1969). The teeth are exposed prominently as the corners of the mouth and lips are retracted (see Figure 10.5); in more extreme forms, the ears may be flattened, the brows raised, and the head drawn back on the shoulder; however, these latter characteristics are not well studied. The most variable components are perhaps the degree to which the rows of teeth are separated and whether or not a vocalization (typically a screech) accompanies the display.

Visual orientation during the grimace typically consists of a rapid alternation toward and away from the other individual (e.g., Redican, 1975), which, it will be recalled, is antithetical to sustained visual orientation during threat. Miller (1967, p. 133) referred to the rapid glancing toward a frightening object as "repetitive peeking" (not necessarily ac-

Figure 10.5. A grimace by an adult female rhesus macaque. Teeth receive a prominent frontal exposure in this and related compound displays. Its role as an ancestor of the pleasurable human smile is now in question. (Photograph copyright 1982 by William K. Redican)

companied by a grimace). This orientation pattern is probably related to the very widespread pattern of looking away from a frightening or threatening object or individual, about which more will be said shortly.

Social contexts. The grimace is seen in three primary social contexts: agonism, sexual behavior, and greeting. Corresponding functions have been assigned to each (Redican, 1975).

In the context of *agonism*, an animal that is the target of an actual or impending attack is often seen to display a grimace; a relatively subtle event such as a close approach by another may also be a sufficient eliciting circumstance. Rowell (1966) found that as many as 97% of grimaces in a group of baboons were given by subordinate to dominant individuals.

In the agonistic context, the function of the grimace is commonly said to be appeasement, i.e., a potential or actual attack is averted or terminated as a consequence of the display. However, that functional interpretation has been established, at least in the primatological literature, in the virtual absence of empirical data. A very fundamental sort of data would do quite nicely, such as the proportion of times an attack is thwarted after the perception of the display.

The reader by this time must be aware of the dearth of empirical data in this area. A major contributing factor may be that the early foundations of research in displays were conducted in the classical, or European, school of ethology. This discipline places prime emphasis on meticulous unobtrusive observation, primarily in the natural habitat, and little or none on controlled experimental study. Consequently, significant inferences and judgments have often been made on the basis of relatively few observations, often involving no interobserver agreement procedures and little explication of sampling procedures. These interpretations (e.g., "the grimace is an appeasement gesture") have made their way into the literature and been widely accepted, but their reliability and validity need to be more systematically demonstrated. This subject will be discussed in more detail later.

The second major context in which the grimace appears is *sexual* or *copulatory behavior*. In this context, the grimace is consistently reported more often in male than in female nonhuman primates. Males of at least two species of the macaque genus not only grimace but emit a screech as well, the latter often during the last mount in a copulatory sequence – the one involving ejaculation (Altmann, 1962; Southwick, Beg, & Siddiqi, 1965; Tokuda, Simons, & Jensen, 1968). The reasons for the association of this display with copulation remain obscure, but its association with high-frequency vocalization is, as we shall shortly see, probably significant. As to why the male vocalizes prior to or during ejaculation remains open to speculation; it may well keep at a distance the competing males and juveniles who often harass copulating pairs at a moment unquestionably crucial to the transmission of genes to subsequent generations. The vocalization, at least in several male rhesus monkeys studied, is remarkably loud and sudden. Having been startled by it many times myself, I can testify to its probable efficacy on conspecifics; however, once again reproductive cost/benefit data are lacking.

The third principal context in which grimacing is observed is *greeting*, which one can readily appreciate as being similar to the agonistic context. Greeting can be generally defined as the set of behaviors occurring upon first meeting after separation, regardless of the positions in the status hierarchy of each individual (Andrew, 1964). Grimacing is seen in a subordinate animal approaching a dominant animal, in the converse situation (albeit rarely), or both may simultaneously grimace (Carpenter, 1940; van Lawick-Goodall, 1968). It is also not exclusively the approacher who grimaces, as the approachee may exhibit the display; in this case, it may border more closely on the agonistic context previously discussed.

Evolution of the grimace. The most careful elucidation of the evolution of this display was Andrew (1963, 1964), who proposed two contributing sets of factors: protective responses and vocalizations. In the first instance, he proposed that the basic movement of the mouth in grimacing is a protective response consequent to a noxious stimulus. He notes that mammals that are not as unspecialized as primates, such as the opossum, rely greatly on taste and smell in exploring the environment. Accordingly, they are said to have evolved expulsive responses to deal with noxious objects in the mouth: withdrawal of the mouth corners and lips, together with occasional protrusions of the tongue (see Figure 10.6). A relatively primitive primate, *Lemur catta*, grins not only when smelling scent marks of conspecifics but in response to a threat by dominant individuals (Jolly, 1966). An important issue here that remains to be quantified is the relationship of these movements to what in humans represents a disgust response. As can be seen in Ekman and Friesen (1975), for example, the movements of the human mouth during disgust are quite different from the expulsive movements described by Andrew, particularly because a human disgust display involves prominent upward movement of the upper lip and downward movement of the lower lip.

A second, and probably the more important, variable is the set of high-frequency vocalizations (screeching, screaming, geckering) that accompany many fear-inducing situations. Such vocal sounds are emitted concurrently with withdrawal of the mouth corners. During these vocalizations, the larynx is subjected to relatively intense vibratory stress, and Andrew suggested that constriction of the neck muscles, in particular the *platysma*, helps provide structural support encircling the vocal cords. Withdrawing the corners of the mouth immediately involves the neck muscles in a rigid tonus. The reader can readily demonstrate this by palpating the front of the neck and forming the mouth into a grimace. As in the case of the threat display, it is proposed that the threshold for vocalization during the grimace was raised through a process of evolutionary simplification until the display evolved into a primarily silent one.

As is evident by now, the primary emotional state associated with the grimace is fear. Just as classical ethologists posit an inhibition of attack by flight in an animal displaying the threat, the grimace is viewed as an

Figure 10.6. A grimace interspersed with tongue protrusion (Frame 3) and a barking vocalization (Frame 4) in an adult female rhesus macaque. The grimace is said to have evolved in part as a protective response to noxious stimuli, and tongue protrusion and withdrawal of the mouth are believed to facilitate expulsion of such noxious agents. Reproduced from S8mm film exposed at 18 fps; elapsed time .33 seconds. (Photographs copyright 1982 by William K. Redican)

inhibition of flight by a tendency to remain in place (e.g., van Hooff, 1969), with the usual precautions about the absence of data applying again.

Gaze aversion. Just as a direct stare was seen to be associated with the threat display, fear is often associated with gaze aversion, turning of the head, or both, and such responses are widely reported as responses to threat-stares. Once again, classical ethologists had much to do with the initial inquiry in this area. Tinbergen (1959a) described how he and a student, M. Moynihan, were puzzling over a phase of pair-formation displays by black-headed gulls in which both birds suddenly face away from each other. At that time, 1951, the prevalent interpretation of such movements was as a means of exposing a highly conspicuous structure, such as a patch of wing feathers. Walking back to camp one morning, Moynihan proposed, "Perhaps it is rather the other way around: perhaps the movements serve *to hide the face*" (Tinbergen, 1959a [1972, p. 113]). That insight led to an extensive body of work on what Chance (1962) called *cut-off movements*, one subset of which is gaze aversion or facing away (see also Coss, 1973).

The ethologists regard facing away as a movement that results from simultaneous tendencies to flee and stay or approach. Facing away took its place in a range of transitional behaviors that included turning the head alone, turning the whole body, and, finally, flight (Weidmann, 1955). It regularly occurred, for example, when a bird had usurped a cliff nest and stayed on it when its occupant returned (Cullen, 1957). In such cases, the usurper simply turned away and the antagonist was abruptly and strongly inhibited by "bringing about the disappearance of some of the stimuli that release aggression and withdrawal" (Tinbergen, 1959a [1972, p. 123]), i.e., the bird's beak.

In the case of nonhuman primates, turning the head or averting the gaze removes the set of threatening stimuli associated with direct eye contact, thus diminishing the likelihood of eliciting attack. Chance (1962) also suggested that turning away one's eyes in a social encounter cuts off incoming agonistic stimuli from further perceptual processing by the animal turning away. The arousal level is thus reduced by means short of withdrawal from the interaction. Fundamentally, avoiding visual contact is a means of avoiding social interaction (Altmann, 1967). Thus, the behavior affects both performer and percipient.

Examples of the occurrence of gaze aversion in ongoing social interactions in primates are numerous and are reviewed elsewhere (Argyle and

Cook, 1976; Exline 1972; Redican, 1975, p. 120; Thomsen, 1974). Avoiding visual contact or stares is a behavior ranked just below a grimace in intensity of submissiveness (Altmann, 1962, 1968b; Jay 1965). Stumptail macaques, for example, usually avoid looking in the eyes of a dominant animal and avert their gaze when looked at or stared at (Bertrand, 1969). Gorillas refrain from directly looking at human observers during low-intensity alarms, and submission or appeasment is generally associated with averting the gaze and turning the head from side-to-side (Schaller, 1963, 1965). It is said that a rhesus monkey will look in practically every direction other than that of a frightening object (Hinde and Rowell, 1962). I suspect, however, that careful measurement would reveal that primates rarely look far enough away to remove the frightening object or individual from the field of peripheral vision, as it is clearly advantageous to keep sensory inputs on the target operational.

*Human homologs.*There has probably been more speculation on the homologous relationship between the nonhuman primate grimace and a corresponding human expression than for any other category of display. The human expression in question is the smile, or at least one or more variants of it, as there are more than 180 forms of human smiling that are visually and anatomically distinct (Ekman and Friesen, 1978). The homologous contexts proposed in the primate literature are typically those involved with agonistic (submissive or appeasing) and greeting interactions. I am unaware of speculation on the remaining context in which primates may grimace, that of sexual behavior. In particular, the question might be asked whether human males grimace close to ejaculation. There are many other circumstances in which human displays similar to a grimace might occur, but descriptive data are too scanty to discuss them here beyond simple citation; e.g., the grimacing following "physiological" yawning and preceding sneezing (Andrew, 1972).

I shall now offer a more particular explanation as to why I, as a terrified adolescent, developed the facial configuration referred to in the incident recounted at the beginning of this chapter. I believe I was displaying a grimace in much the same way that a juvenile rhesus monkey does while approaching (or being approached by) an alpha male. One might also expect a human to grimace while anticipating a noxious or frightening event, such as when a vase is heading for the floor, when two cars appear destined to crash, or when two people are about to come to blows. I emphasize that the human expression I am referring to in these examples is what has been described as the human expression of fear (it lacks an ethological term) rather than a variant of the smile (see, e.g., Ekman and Friesen, 1975, Figures 18b or 19b).

In much of the primate literature (including Redican, 1975), however, there is speculation on a homology between the primate grimace and the human smile. For example, Andrew (1965, p. 91) wrote, "When a man maintains a fixed smile in response to the verbal attacks of a superior, or when he smiles on meeting a stranger, he is behaving defensively in the same way as his fellow primates." I propose, however, that the issue may be far less resolved than had been supposed. As Paul Ekman (Pers. comm.) pointed out, the human fear expression that is regarded here as homologous with the grimace involves action of the *risorius* (which draws the corner of the mouth laterally) and the *platysma* (which, among other actions, pulls downward on the jaw). The smile, however, involves action of the *zygomaticus major* (which draws the corner of the mouth backward and upward). That is, *the grimace and the smile are morphologically quite distinct sets of actions.* If there is a homologous link between them, it remains to be demonstrated anatomically. The distinction between the smile and grimace is underscored by a valuable observation by the psychotherapist Fritz Perls, founder of Gestalt therapy: "*A frightened person does not smile*" (in the film "Three approaches to Psychotherapy – II – Frederick Perls").

In accounting for the smile being displayed by humans in pleasurable circumstances, Andrew (1963, 1965) suggested that the primate grimace, originally a response to startling or fearful stimuli, evolved in humans to be associated also with much smaller (and sometimes pleasurable) changes in stimulation. That proposal remains largely untested, however, and there is need for not only a detailed specification of the nature of the stimulation but for a highly resolved measurement of the facial activity in question (see also van Hooff, 1969, pp. 17–20, for a discussion of Andrew's hypothesis).

A major contributor to recent speculation on the evolution of the human smile has been van Hooff (1972, 1976).[1] He distinguished two general forms of the human smile, one of which will be considered in the discussion of the play face and laughter. The human display that concerns us here is what van Hooff (1972) refers to as the *broad smile* (once again, however, it appears to be a *zygomaticus major* smile) that is

[1]If the reader does consult van Hooff's important 1972 paper, it will avoid considerable confusion if I point out that the grimacing human in the bottom-left terminus in one of the proposed phylogenetic lineages (Figure 13, p. 237) should have a raised, not a lowered, brow (see van Hooff, 1976, p. 179).

said to be associated with the "emphatic manifestation of a non-hostile, friendly attitude" (p. 232), such as during greetings and apologies. He traces this display to the primate grimace but places particular emphasis on the view that the grimace appears to be given in some highly developed taxa as a "reassuring signal or even as a sign of attachment" (p. 215), e.g., from a dominant to a subordinate individual. Van Hooff goes on to conclude: "Originally reflecting an attitude of submission, this display has come to represent non-hostility and finally has become emancipated to an expression of social attachment or friendliness, which is non-hostility *par excellence*. The situations in which the *silent bared-teeth* display [grimace] occurs have in common that a certain amount of uncertainty about the social relationship is overcome" (van Hooff, 1972, p. 235).

It should be noted that van Hooff's hypothesis involves a rather large evolutionary shift in motivation for the grimace: from fearfulness to attachment. This may indeed be shown to be the case, but for the present I choose a more parsimonious view. I did not greatly distinguish between a subordinate grimacing to a dominant animal and the converse, the former perhaps being termed *appeasement* and the latter *reassurance*. One must be vigilant lest one's conceptual categories (e.g., dominant–subordinate; sane–insane) begin to gain momentum over observational inputs. I see far less of a dichotomy between the affective states of grimacing dominant and subordinate animals than between what we conceptually make of the behaviors post facto. However, we would benefit from data on the use of the display by confident or high-status animals, for it is safe to say that because the grimace is predominantly conceived as a submissive display, its occurence among high-status animals has been probably underestimated.

In terms of homologous extrapolation of the grimace to the broad smile, we are at an impasse until the musculature involved in both displays has been explicated. What primatologists have commonly referred to as a human smile, occurring at such times as an apology, may *not* be what investigators in the human domain call a smile! For the present, a reasonable position to adopt is that the homology with the primate grimace is limited to fearful human expressions and that for the origins of the human *zygomaticus major* smile we may have to look elsewhere, such as the proposal to be considered later with reference to the play face and laughter. What is needed now is not only a forthright interdisciplinary effort to agree on nomenclature but also very detailed measurements of the movements of the mouth area during the primate grimace. Current descriptions of lip-corner "retraction" have been based generally on real-time observation and not on high-speed motion picture records or functional anatomy. Such data are urgently needed if we are to further our understanding of this important concern.

Open-mouth grimace

All but one of the displays described for nonhuman primates appear to intergrade with one or more other specific displays. (The exception is the yawn. There also has been little or no mention of displays intergrading with the tense-mouth display, but I suspect that is for wont of observational or experimental data.) A particularly common intergradation is a display that I shall refer to as the *open-mouth grimace*, which incorporates several categories described by van Hooff: the "staring bared-teeth scream face," the "frowning bared-teeth scream face" (van Hooff, 1969; later subsumed into one category in van Hooff, 1976), and probably the chimpanzee's "vertical bared-teeth display" (van Hooff, 1972).

Detailed consideration of the display will not be given here because we have already considered its apparent progenitors, the threat and grimace. The displayer's mouth is relatively wide open, but there is considerable vertical lip retraction so that the teeth are predominently displayed. As might be inferred from van Hooff's terminology, the brow may be raised or lowered; the direction of gaze is, respectively, staring or averted. High-pitched vocalizations are an almost invariable accompaniment.

The displaying animal is said to have a higher tendency to flee than is the case for the threat display. It is often given in response to a threat display or an overt attack, or in states of apparent discomfort or frustration (van Hooff, 1976): "In an agonistic context the staring version indicates that the animal is prepared to make a last stand; it functions as a defensive threat" (p. 170). In the case of the chimpanzee, van Lawick-Goodall (1971) specifically interprets the display as being on an affective continuum with the grimace.

Lipsmack display

Structural features. The displays considered to this point have been concerned primarily with agonistic interactions. The lipsmack display is perhaps the clearest example of an affiliative one. It also differs from the preceding displays insofar as it is a mobile display (in terms of mouth movements, that is), not a primarily static one. It is thus slightly more difficult to describe (see Figure 10.7). In its full form, it includes the following features (see Redican, 1975):

1. The lower jaw moves up and down (at varying velocities, depending on the context), but the teeth do not meet;
2. The lips are brought forward, and they part and close repeatedly;
3. The tongue is brought forward and back against the back of the teeth or between the two rows, but it infrequently protrudes far beyond the lips;
4. The ears are usually flattened and the brow raised;
5. The head may be tilted upward, bobbed repeatedly, or rotated slightly;
6. The gaze is typically oriented directly at the percipient.

As in the case of other displays, one or more of these components may be lacking during lipsmacking, depending, in part, on the intensity of arousal. In particular, Colmenares and Rivero (Pers. comm.) kindly furnished records of their observations of ear-flattening as a display feature among captive baboons. Ear-flattening typically accompanied lipsmacking, but by itself it also took place as a "pacificatory, inhibitory, cohesive, affinitive, associative and friendly gesture, present in the behaviour patterns of non-agonistic physical contact (patterns of greeting and appeasement) and of reduction of physical distance (greeting)." Thus, for example, if a high-ranking animal responded to an approach by flattening its ears, affiliative contact was likely to follow; if not, attack was likely.

Social contexts. In the clear majority of circumstances in which it is displayed, lipsmacking is thought to serve a pacificatory, appeasing, or submissive function. As Chalmers (1968) found in the case of black mangabeys, neither the displayer nor the percipient was seen to attack after a lipsmack display; the displayer remained about twice as often as it fled, and the percipient approached or remained in all cases. I will indulge in a bit of speculation and propose that the affiliative state of the displayer may be revealed by the fact that the lips are drawn *toward* the percipient of the display, whereas in the grimace the predominant movement is *away* from the percipient. Certainly this may be a spurious correlation, but the fundamental directions of major display components might well be significant.

The display has been recorded in at least four social contexts: grooming, copulation, greeting, and (paradoxically) agonism. It takes place in the initiator of grooming – the process of brushing through another's fur and removing particles of debris and skin. The groomer transfers particles to its mouth either directly or with the hand (*question*: is there any nutritional significance at all?), and the discovery and ingestion of a

Figure 10.7. A lipsmacking adult male rhesus monkey. The lipsmack is the most clearly affiliative display in the nonhuman primate facial repertoire, and it may be an ancestor of the human kiss. Note the progressive raising of the brow and flattening of the ears. The lips begin to pucker in the final frames. Reproduced from S8mm film exposed at 18 fps; elapsed time .33 seconds. (Photographs copyright 1982 by William K. Redican)

particle coincide with the intermittent onset of lip movements. During grooming, lip movements are relatively slow and are often not accompanied by other components such as ear-flattening.

Lipsmacking is observed during behaviors surrounding copulation in a wide range of circumstances and in both sexes. It occurs both during an approach and during copulation itself.

The display has been described as a form of greeting in several taxa. Indeed, it is said to be more frequently displayed than the grimace for this function in several taxa (Andrew, 1965). Introduction of a stranger to an established group is a particularly reliable elicitor of lipsmacking. Also, it often occurs during an affiliative approach toward an adult or especially an infant. For example, adult olive baboons "take the keenest interest in the newborn infant. They peer at its face, lip-smack and present to it if they 'catch its eye,' touch or try to touch it and groom it" (Rowell, Din, & Omar, 1968, p. 471).

In the agonistic context, the lipsmack is typically described as a submissive or appeasing display, much like the grimace again. For example, if a subordinate bonnet macaque (*Macaca radiata*) happens to make eye contact with a dominant animal, the former will often lipsmack (Rahaman and Parthasarathy, 1968). But dominant baboons (*Papio anubis*) lipsmack to subordinates far more often than the converse (Rowell, 1966). Thus, although interspecific comparisons confound the issue, it appears that lipsmacking is not a rigid index of position in a status hierarchy.

Paradoxically, there are several reports of animals lipsmacking as a form of threat or while the displayer is chasing or displacing the percipient. This phenomenon remains something of a mystery, pending further data, but one possibility is that the display may enlist the assistance of others in the aggressive effort, particularly if the displayer repeatedly turns and looks at others (K.R.L. Hall, 1967). It is also a remote possibility that it is an example of deception, a topic that we shall turn to shortly.

Evolution of lipsmacking. There are several possible evolutionary antecedents involved in this display. Perhaps the most apparent is its ritualization from the highly affiliative context of grooming to a wider range of social contexts. In addition, developmental experience may be important in shaping this display, for the grooming movements may converge with infantile behavior patterns involved with nursing (e.g., Andrew, 1963; Anthoney, 1968; Chevalier-Skolnikoff, 1973; 1974b). Both Chevalier-Skolnikoff and Redican independently focused on *anticipatory* nursing or nonnutritive sucking movements. Two processes may thus be involved: First, these sucking movements would be displayed by an infant to an approaching adult. Second, the infant might be perceiving them in an adult who is approaching to groom the mother or infant. Clearly there is again an unresolved question of developmental or causal sequence here, lacking an extensive body of ontogenic data that is admittedly difficult to obtain. But it is apparent that the sight of an infant is a supremely effective elicitor of lipsmacking by adults. If infants are frequently exposed to such displays with an affiliative association and if conditioning thereby plays an appreciable role in the development of this display, then its occurrence in such a wide variety of social contexts can be more fully appreciated.

Human homologs. This subject is almost unknown terrain, but there may be a few landmarks. Van Hooff (1972, 1976) believes the display to be virtually or completely absent in *Homo sapiens.* One might take note, however, of the "bottle movements" described for human infants by Polak, Emde, and Spitz (1964, p. 410) and adopt a more optimistic view: "Bottle movements we refer to as various movements of the mouth, tongue and lips, very often involving pursing of the lips and successive protrusion and withdrawal of the tongue accompanied by mouth opening and closing." Smiles were seen to occur at the approach of a human face, and the bottle movements tended to do so at the approach of a bottle. Also, I do not have the citation at hand, but I have been apprised of the fact that fathers whose spouses have recently given birth are apt to lipsmack at their newborns through nursery windows. A similarly fertile area for possible comparative work would be the close face-to-face (eye-to-eye?) lively behavior that adults often unabashedly engage in with infants – the "koochy-koo" category of behavior, for want of a lofty aphorism, the vocalizations of which require a lip configuration quite similar to the lipsmack. And let us not overlook the courtship context. There is certainly the possibility that a form of the lipsmack display could have converged with other factors (such as food-sharing and oral–olfactory sensory investigation) to shape the emergence of the human kiss. In a way, the mouth movements of a lipsmack are a series of kisses. (An aside: Do human raise their brows when they kiss?)

A final note with reference to this display is that even if it is not regularly documented in human nonverbal communication, some lipsmacking patterns are most certainly easily acquired with minimal practice. (Is it not commonly said, amidst the rubble of the nature–nurture dichotomy, that our evolutionary heritage makes some things easier to learn?) In an affectionate context, it is an endearing and compelling expression. And it has an orienting auditory component that most other human and nonhuman displays lack, which conceivably is functional in such a context.

Grin–lipsmack display

Again this is an intermediate display, between the grimace and the lipsmack, and it accordingly is treated here in passing. Van Hooff's (1969) terminology is the "teeth-chattering face." Indeed, the lips are retracted vertically and the lower jaw is moved rapidly up and down so the teeth often meet in a chattering fashion. There may also be a more discrete and rapid alternation between grimacing and lipsmacking. What appears to be a form of this intermediate display is often seen in macaque mothers (Bobbitt, Jensen, & Gordon, 1964; Hansen, 1966), in fathers (Redican, 1976) recently separated from infants to whom they are attached, or in such individuals as a form of retrieval display toward their infants.

Play face

Structural features. When monkeys and apes play, among taxa widespread throughout the primate order, they typically display a facial configuration referred to as the *play face* (in van Hooff's, e.g., 1976, terminology, the "relaxed open-mouth face") (see Figure 10.8). The display bears a striking resemblance to the threat display, but there are subtle differences.

Components of this display include a mouth that is usually wide open, with the mouth corners retracted only slightly. The upper lip may be tensed and curled over the upper incisors, but the extent of teeth exposure is a highly variable characteristic. The ears may or may not be flattened, and the eyelids are often lowered (see, e.g., van Hooff, 1976; Chevalier-Skolnikoff, 1974a, b). The display is typically interpreted as a set of ritualized intention and protective movements associated with play-biting, which is one of the foci around which play revolves. As was the case for the threat display, the configuration of the mouth may be involved with strong respiratory patterns.

A significant feature of the display is its associated vocal component, particularly, it seems, among chimpanzees and gorillas. Soft, repetitive guttural sounds or low-intensity panting noises are described during

Figure 10.8. A playful chimpanzee (*Pan troglodytes*) displaying the apparent evolutionary precursor to the human laugh and pleasurable smile. (Photograph courtesy of and copyright 1982 by Michael Lyster)

exhalation that "sound roughly like human laughter" (van Lawick-Goodall, 1968a, p. 244; see also Marler and Tenaza, 1977; van Hooff, 1973).

Some structural distinctions between the play face and the threat display have been proposed in a qualitative fashion. For example, van Hooff (1972, p. 217) proposed that they differ in terms of the "free and easy nature of the eye and body movements" during play and by the fact that the mouth corners are not drawn forward. (Whether they are drawn upward in play may be an important question to document, as we shall see.) Recalling the previous comments about the *lack* of behaviors being of potential communicative significance, the movements of the eyes during play would probably be found to be more frequent and more responsive to environmental stimuli. I suspect the *orbicularis oculi* musculature would also be less constricted in play. The Gautiers (1977) and

Chevalier-Skolnikoff (1974a, b) found that the eyelids are often partially or fully lowered during play. Chevalier-Skolnikoff (1974a, p. 25) also recorded a total absence of eye-to-eye contact during play in stumptail macaques. Although an absolute lack of such eye contact may not prove invariable (Redican, 1975, p. 154), this feature is an important example of the antithetical aspects of play and threat displays.

Certainly, it would be unwise to restrict one's attention just to facial features, as the postural and locomotor characteristics of threat and play are quite divergent: body tonus during threat is often tense and rigid; during play it is more relaxed, mobile, and spontaneous – described, for example, as "cutting up" (Carpenter, 1971) or "jaunty" (MacKinnon, 1971) behavior.

Social contexts. In the clear preponderance of instances, this display is seen during play. It also occurs quite readily when apes are tickled (e.g., van Hooff, 1969). It is not yet clear how efficient an elicitor of play the display is, as opposed to being an ongoing response during play sequences.

Human homologs. The comparative significance of this display has largely to do with the evolution of human laughter and, it now seems likely, a form of the smile. Considering the morphology, social contexts, and associated vocalization of the play face, the widespread consensus of its homologous relationship to the human *laugh* is compelling (e.g., Blurton Jones, 1969; Bolwig, 1964; Chevalier-Skolnikoff, 1974b; Darwin, 1872; van Hooff, 1969).

More controversial, and quite important, is the proposal of van Hooff (1972, 1976) and others that one of the fundamental categories of the human *smile* has also evolved from the play face. We saw earlier that van Hooff described the "broad smile" as a descendant of the grimace, a view disputed here. However, he conceives of a second form of smile as a "diminutive of the laugh, in which the mouth is only slightly opened and mouth-corner retraction is slight" (1976, p. 178). The laugh is viewed more specifically as an intermediate display or a convergence between the play face and the grimace. The evidence supporting this laugh-as-intermediate hypothesis, however, is fragmentary and open to varying interpretations. It consists, in part, in interpreting the grimace in certain "advanced" Old World monkeys as a reassuring, as distinct from sub-missive display, a view previously discussed as open to question (see also Andrew's and Hinde's comments in Hinde, 1972, p. 240).

Van Hooff's insightful description, however, of a form of *the smile as a low-intensity laugh* (i.e., play face) is an important one and quite plausible in view of the occasionally prominent teeth exposure in the play face. It would be further enlightening if the 180 documented human smiles were able to be categorized into broad typologies to determine if there is a correspondence with van Hooff's thesis, for primatologists have failed to discriminate among the many variants of the human smile.

Let us summarize the reconsideration proposed here of this admittedly complex topic. Primatologists and ethologists have traditionally traced the evolution of the pleasurable human smile to the nonhuman primate fear grimace. This view now seems incorrect. It is more likely, pending the collection of functional–anatomical data, that the nonhuman primate fear grimace corresponds to a homologous display in humans involving action of the *risorius* and *platysma*. The pleasurable human smile now appears to be a low-intensity laugh, both the smile and laugh being homologous to varying intensities of the play face in nonhuman primates that involve action of the *zygomaticus major*. Thus, the ancestor of the pleasurable human smile appears to be the play face, not the fear grimace.

Support for the hypothesis of the pleasurable smile as a diminutive laugh is found in a variety of sources. In Schaller's (1965, p. 361) account of his field study of mountain gorillas, he noted that "playing youngsters sometimes chuckled audibly with their mouths wide open and lips drawn back into a smile." Bolwig (1964) asserted many years ago that both smiling and laughter derive from the play face. His observations are often maddeningly idiosyncratic (many of the monkeys were his pets) but unflinchingly and uniquely detailed. "Sometimes when the animal [a baboon] has a drive to tease (not necessarily by biting), or its attention is taken by something it likes, small pulls at the corners of the mouth may be noticed, accompanied by a slight upwards pull of the corners of the eyes. The lips may or may not be slightly parted" (Bolwig, 1964, p. 181). Bolwig presented several photographic plates and line drawings as illustrations and made valuable observations on musculature involved in displays. His subjectivity is understandably vexing to empirical investigators, but the closeness of the relationship with his subjects gave rise to detailed observation and speculation that may prove to be fruitful terrain for hypothesis generation.

Likewise, some of the early reports of chimpanzee behavior are fascinating in terms of the link between the play face, laughter, and smiling. Consider, for example, Wolfgang Köhler's account:

There is a certain resemblance to our laughter in their rhythmic gasping and grunting when they are tickled, and probably this manifestation is, physiologically, remotely akin to *laughter*. And, during the leisurely contemplation of any objects which give particular pleasure (for example, little human children), the whole face, and especially the outer corners of the mouth, are formed into an expression that resembles our "smile." [Köhler, 1925, p. 318]

Consider next Sokolowsky's narrative:

Toward the public, on the other hand, the chimpanzee always behaved very shabbily. He took great joy in, so to speak, "wiping out" the human beings who were watching him. . . . A trace of mischievousness passed at times over his face. The corners of the mouth would be drawn wide open, the teeth bared, and the eyelids a little closed. His eyes had a glittering expression; one could see from the whole animal that this procedure gave him great joy. He was ready for every kind of mischief. It was one specialty of his to take hats from the heads of the ladies and gentlemen . . . . [Sokolowsky, 1908, p. 69]

Similarly, Robert and Ada Yerkes reported, in their landmark monograph:

Especially in the young chimpanzee it is possible to induce smiles, facial and vocal responses simulating laughter, evidences of good humor, and there are many and varied spontaneous manifestations of mischievousness and enjoyment. . . . [Yerkes & Yerkes, 1929, p. 295]

Perhaps the most persuasive of the early evidence for a chimpanzee homolog to smiling was pictorial: the series of photographs provided by Nadie Ladygin-Kohts (Kohts, 1935, reproduced in Yerkes, 1943, Plate 6). The series is remarkably unambiguous and leaves room for few descriptors other than "smile" for several expressions. There also appears to be a smooth gradient from the closed-lip smile to the open-mouth play face, particularly with regard to the direction of mouth-corner withdrawal and the configuration around the eyes.

Although this final example has little directly to do with smiling and laughter, it helps set the stage for related points of a more general nature. Passemard (1927, p. 247; also translated and quoted in Yerkes and Yerkes, 1929, p. 371) attempted to induce an adult male and female chimpanzee to leave an outer cage and enter an adjoining, smaller cage for the night. The two areas were joined by a horizontally sliding door; the male had seen it operated once or twice and had been placed in the outer cage for the first time that morning. The pair refused to transfer cages, regardless of a variety of contingencies. The male had been fasted since the morning, and Passemard decided to place a large jar of food in the smaller cage in an attempt to attract the pair:

> It was then that the following events occurred, events which I should have had difficulty in believing had I not myself observed them.... The two apes did not look at the food.... After they had both wandered about in the vicinity of the door, they settled down face-to-face, in a corner of the cage, eye fixed on eye, lips rather close, and emitted low sounds perceptible to us.... In an instant, the male, on three feet [*sic*] and with disconcerting assurance and calm, turned toward the door, pushed it open on the rails as far as it would go, then sat down on the lower rail – his feet braced against the stone frame, his back against the edge of the door. Then the female entered quietly and returned with abundant provisions; they shared the food, then the trick took place again. Our plan was discovered; we were defeated. [Passemard, 1927, p. 247][2]

At this point we cannot conclude with Passemard that the chimps seem to have engaged in "secret consultation." However, I retold this tale for several reasons. First, it illustrates the remarkable cognitive sophistication of the animal. Second, it gives an idea of the impressive amount of information, so to speak, that can be transmitted nonverbally (but it also raises the question of whether an information-exchange model is appropriate). Third, in conjunction with the other early narratives, it raises the question of what is to be done with these early observations. Primatologists have, for the most part, assiduously avoided them, undoubtedly because they entail complex internal cognitive and emotional states that seem to defy quantification or, more to the point, are almost painful to quantify. (An exception is Menzel's series of ingenious studies that bear an interesting relationship to Passemard's account; see Menzel, 1971, 1974; Menzel and Halperin, 1975.) But it seems reasonable now to say that if primatologists wish to revitalize their inquiries into nonverbal behavior and to establish significant inferential bridges to the body of human literature, then such complex affective states and cognitive processes must be more seriously dealt with. We have lost our ability even to entertain such observations as those cited here above (granted their severe methodological limitations) for fear of cries of anthropomorphism or sentimentality. In this light we need new methodologies, new vocab-

[2]The translation is primarily the Yerkes', but I have made a number of revisions. The original passage concluded: "...on partage, puis le manège se renouvelle. Notre plan est dévoilé, nous avons été mis en échec" (p. 248).

Figure 10.9. A yawning adult male rhesus monkey just prior to the peak of the display. The canines are remarkably developed in such noncarnivorous taxa, at least in males, in part suggesting that prominent canines evolved for display functions. (Photograph copyright 1982 by William K. Redican)

ularies, and new interpretive models to help stir the prevailing becalmed waters and to reassess the anthropomorphism issue.

Yawn

The yawn has had a varied reception as a communicative signal. Van Hooff, for example, in his several treatises on primate facial displays, omitted the yawn from consideration, as did Chevalier-Skolnikoff (1973) – both intentionally. In contrast, a recent doctoral dissertation (Deputte, 1978) has been entirely devoted to the display.[3]

Structural features. The features of the primate yawn are rather straightforward and closely parellel the human yawn (see Figure 10.9). Deputte (1978) distinguished three main characteristics in his study of yawning mangabeys and macaques: (1) opening of the mouth with progressive exposure and then reconcealment of both rows of teeth; (2) concommitant

---

[3]The sections of Deputte's dissertation quoted in this discussion are my translation.

raising of the head as the mouth is opened and then lowering as the mouth is closed; and (3) brief closure of the eyes in the first part of yawning and tight closure when the mouth is opened maximally, then progressive opening when the head is lowering and the mouth closing. The associated visual orientation when the eyes are open is difficult to specify.

Forms of yawning. In general, Redican (1975) sidestepped the issue of distinguishing between a physiological and affective yawn. The former was attributed simply to surplus CO_2 or insufficient O_2 in the cerebral arterial system. That widely held belief, however, may rest on controversial grounds (reviewed by Deputte, 1978, pp. 83–86). For example, the pause in breathing during the swallow that follows the yawn may in part counteract the oxygenation produced by the inhalation of the yawn.

Deputte's careful sequential analyses did, indeed, reveal two general categories of yawns: the "yawn of inactivity" (i.e., the physiological yawn) and the "yawn of emotivity" (i.e., the tension yawn). He proposed a physiological model that associates yawns with periods of transition from waking to sleeping, or during the downward phases of cyclic arousal. Affective yawns, which most concern us here, were seen *after* social interactions, most commonly among adult males. They were displayed by a stationary animal – standing, sitting, or reclining – and most often preceded rest, thus involving a decline in vigilance level. Both forms of yawning were said to have in common that they bring about relaxation via the stretching of the anterior part of the body: muscles of mastication, cutaneous receptors, and muscles of the neck and thoracic cage. (Also, one might add, a vigorous contraction of *orbicularis oculi* musculature takes place as well.) As Deputte acknowledges, concurrent physiological and ethological data would be invaluable in testing the hypotheses concerned with vigilance and relaxation. It may be of interest to note here that, although yawns usually emerge in an all-or-none fashion (the appropriate ethological term is *at typical intensity*), Deputte's analyses suggest that a sudden increase in arousal or vigilance should abort the yawn. This appears to be so, but straightforward experimentation should be able to generate supportive data on this point (e.g., by generating frightening stimuli at various stages of the yawn). Similarly, if CO_2/O_2 levels are of little consequence to yawning, then the administration of a highly oxygenated environment should not affect its frequency.

Social contexts. Two closely related social contexts have been described concerning yawning: (1) tension, conflict, or stress, and (2) threat (Redican, 1975). The former occasions include being stared at or being in the proximity of a human observer; the orientation of the yawn is typically away from the presumed percipient. The threat yawn is said to occur when the displayer is oriented directly *at* the percipient (K.R.L. Hall and DeVore, 1965; K.R.L. Hall, 1967), at least in taxa such as baboons, macaques, and mangabeys. Chalmers (1968) rated a yawn as just below a stare in intensity of agonism and found that animals yawning directly toward a percipient were less likely to flee than were those yawning away. Deputte (1978) found no perceptible effects of yawns on percipients. In contrast, Bolwig (1959) reported an increase in interindividual distance after he yawned while sitting amidst a group of baboons. (But given his lack of prominent canines, the display may have been interpreted as a threat.) Baulu (1973) established an experimental situation in which rhesus macaques could press a lever to show a 16-mm film loop of various social stimuli. One adult male "would often let go of the lever precisely at the time when the familiar high-ranking male would yawn and fully expose his canines" (p. 76.) What appears to be most needed in future research on the yawn are data on its social effects on percipients. I believe it is premature to conclude that it has no effect; such statements have historically often led to chagrin. The philosophically preferable position is, of course, that we have yet to observe an effect.

An integration of Deputte's hypotheses with available field literature is difficult because of the lack of precise data. Deputte (1978, p. 91) regarded the yawn as indicating "to potential receptors the end of an interaction of hierarchical (aggressive) or sexual nature." Thus, the process is an arousal-reducing rather than an arousal-increasing or constant one – the latter two being implicit in many descriptions in the existing literature. However, Deputte (1978, p. 91) also interpreted yawns as a "signal reinforcing the message. . . of identity as the 'alpha' " and assuring the status of the displayer, particularly when yawns are associated with other prominent "intimidation" activities. (A key stimulus here would appear to be the display of prominent canines, but Deputte deemphasizes their role.) It may well be that existing descriptions of primates yawning in conflict or in threat apply to animals, particularly high-status individuals, at a point when they are reducing their involvement in the social interaction, and the yawn in those contexts is thus an index of de-arousal. If so, Deputte's contribution is a significant one in furthering our understanding of this display. In this regard, it is with considerable interest that one reads the caption to a photograph of an adult male gelada yawning (*Theropithecus gelada,* an Old World monkey found in the highlands of Ethiopia), presented in a recent account of a field study of this remarkable animal (Mori, 1979, p. 89): "When being groomed, the leader sometimes gave a gaping yawn for tension reduction after he had become tense on the approach of an all-male group, or on return to his females after a ritual fight with the all-male group." As is the case with many similar interpretations in field and laboratory accounts, this statement appears to be intuitive and not inferred from quantified data. However, it does support Deputte's thesis.

On the basis of available evidence, it would seem unwise to completely abnegate the role of canine exhibition in the evolution of the display. It is the only primate display in which the canines are prominently exposed, and it is indeed a prominent exposure (as seen in Figure 10.9) in sexually dimorphic taxa.[4] Coss (1968) associated the display features of profiled canines with similar properties of tusks, horns, and claws in eliciting autonomic responses from a percipient. The remarkable development of primate canines is not a carnivorous adaptation (Napier and Napier, 1967), unlike the case for canids and felids, nor do they appear to be useful in predator defense (see the review by Shafton, 1976, p. 88). Rather, they are believed to have evolved exclusively for intraspecific fighting and displaying. The common observation that males, in sexually dimorphic taxa, are the predominant or exclusive displayers of the yawn and are also the ones who possess prominent canines seems too striking a correlation to ignore. Deputte argues that adult males take a relatively long time to awaken, and attributes sex and age differences (adults yawn more often) in frequence of yawning principally to the anabolic effect of androgens. There is no reason to believe, however, that a convergence of hormonal and social selective pressures did not take place.

[4]Sexually dimorphic taxa are those in which one sex is appreciably larger than the other. Where this is so among primates, the male is larger than the female and often possesses more developed weaponry such as canines. In monogamous (pair-bonded) primates, the two sexes are much more equal in size, social roles, and weaponry; the female may be slightly larger than the male (Napier and Napier, 1967). The important phenomenon in question here is called *sexual selection* (Darwin, 1871), which is a subcategory of natural selection whereby traits are selected that benefit males in intrasexual competition for females (the converse is not seen), who then choose among males for a mate or mates. In birds and mammals, these traits include horns, antlers, large canines, large body size, heightened aggressive capacity, and elaborate plumage and coloration. Sexual selection is more intense, therefore, in polygamous ("many mates") taxa, and sexual dimorphism is correspondingly more pronounced than in monogamous taxa, where sexual selection and dimorphism are both slight.

In passing, one takes note of the question that must have been posed by every child since the beginnings of social existence, and perhaps first formally recorded by Robert Burton (1577-1640) in *Anatomy of Melancholy* (Part I, Sect. 3, Memb. 3): "Why doth one man's yawning make another yawn?" It seems the question can also be asked of our primate relatives, for Deputte (1978) presented evidence that yawns are contagious among the monkeys he studied, particularly within individuals of similar age and social status. He interpreted this contagion as a synchronization of activities "due to the imposition of wake–sleep rhythms on different individuals and to the 'attention' that they devote to each other" (p. 90), with the process perhaps being facilitated by shared physiological states (e.g., a raise in ambient temperature). Thus, a yawning animal should, according to Deputte's analysis, be in a process of decreasing arousal. If observed by other animals and if the observers' arousal level becomes synchronized as a consequence (by a mechanism that has yet to be precisely explicated), the observers will also yawn. Accordingly, the yawn should be only a sufficient, not a necessary, factor in eliciting yawns from other group members. Watching somebody taking a nap, in other words, might also induce a state of declining arousal and trigger yawns. One would expect observed yawns to be a more powerful stimulus, however, because another's yawns might precipitate the observer attending to muscular tension in the facial muscles that can be dissipated by the yawn's stretch. In addition, one might expect observed stretches in general to be contagious, and yawns may thus be a particularly obvious example of the general behavioral synchrony of interactants.

I conclude this section with the same observation that began it: the yawn occupies a singular place in the repertoire of primate facial activity. Perhaps the dearth of consideration of it in the human literature attests to this uniqueness. It may well be more of a self-adaptor of a muscular stretch than a display, but future research attention on its sequential occurrence, effects on conspecifics, and concurrent measures of physiological arousal would go far in clarifying this issue. Lastly, a passage from Rudyard Kipling (*Under the Deodars: The Education of Otis Yeere*, 1888) is one on which might be built a formidable research enterprise: "The first proof a man gives of his interest in a woman is by talking to her about his own sweet self. If the woman listens without yawning, he begins to like her. If she flatters the animal's vanity, he ends by adoring her."

Table 10.2. *Correspondence between categories of human emotions and facial displays of nonhuman primates*

Category of human emotion	Nonhuman primate facial display	
	Monovalent	Bivalent
Fear/surprise	Grimace; open-mouth grimace	Threat display
Anger	Tense-mouth display	
Disgust	?	
Happiness	Play face and intention movements thereof (smiling)	
Sadness	Pout (?)	

10.6. Concluding remarks

This concluding section will offer a collection of random thoughts and suggestions that have arisen on various topics discussed in the preceding sections. Insofar as these remarks might be said to have a coherent theme, it is that primatologists and students of human nonvocal communication have much to offer each other.

Categories of affect in nonhuman primates

One of the most significant advances in recent research on human non-vocal communication has been the systemization of the fundamental categories of affect or emotion experienced by *Homo sapiens* regardless of culturally specific rules of display. Moreover, these basic categories are the components of which, in the view of both empiricists and clinicians, the compound or compound-complex affective states are constituted (e.g., depression as both anger and fear). A comparable systemization of nonhuman primate affect has not yet been elaborated; nor is there yet sufficient data to construct a satisfying schema. That would seem to be a highly commendable goal for the future, for it would be both a contribution to an understanding of human emotion as well as a major systematic advance in primatology, which has lagged far behind the human disciplines in this regard.

Table 10.2 supplies a sketchy and deliberately conservative outline of possible correspondence between the facial displays of nonhuman primates and the basic categories of human emotion (the ones for which there is unambiguous evidence of transcultural universality; see Ekman, 1973; Ekman and Oster, 1979). For other similar presentations, see Chevalier-Skolnikoff (1973) and van Hooff (1976). The employment of the concept of valency is based on Huxley's (1966) treatise on ritualization: *monovalent* displays arise from ritualized "singly-motivated intention-movements" (p. 251); *bivalent* displays arise from ritualized anger and fear motives, which can occur in alternation or combination; and *trivalent* displays arise from three motives: sexual attraction or arousal, anger, and fear. Presumably, the bivalent and trivalent (or higher-order) displays could conceivably be comprised of emotions or motives other than anger, fear, and sexual arousal, but these are the three most often studied in the history of ethology. This is particularly so in the case of courtship (e.g., Hinde, 1972, p. 177).

It is clear that there are several lacunae in Table 10.2. The lack of nonhuman primate display corresponding to a human category of emotion could conceivably mean: (1) that the category of human emotion is less basic than had been supposed or (2) that there have been insufficient observation or experimentation of human and nonhuman primates. At present, my inclination is toward the latter alternative. For example, very basic studies of facial disgust reactions in primates have not been done (e.g., with noxious gustatory or olfactory stimuli such as asafetida) and compared with human responses. A similar statement can be made regarding surprise, and it would be of particular interest to sort out whether surprise and fear are on close points of a continuum or are qualitatively distinct. Here, high-speed motion picture responses at the sudden onset of stimuli could be very profitably compared to varieties of grimaces in primates. Landis and Hunt (1939) presented some pioneering data on startle responses in apes and monkeys, but detailed facial responses still merit study. Baldwin and Teleki (1976, p. 33) also presented data on startle responses in gibbons, noting a raising of the brow and a frequent association of the startle response with the grimace. In this and every other category of basic emotion, careful comparisons must be made with the pioneering work of Ekman, Friesen, and associates (e.g., Ekman and Friesen, 1975, 1978) in their detailed measurement of human expressions.

Two other problematic areas in Table 10.2 are the categories of happiness and sadness. Insofar as playing monkeys can be said to be happy, the play face is the appropriate display for that category. But there are reasonable grounds for contesting that view, if play is regarded more as exercise than affect. (Here again, animal behaviorists have stuck close to the observable behavior in lieu of the internal state, just as classical ethologists focused on attack and flight in lieu of anger and fear.) We appear to be dealing with a very gradual transition in the primate order from the varieties of play displays seen in Old World monkeys such as baboons and macaques to the smile of chimpanzees observing little human children. This gradual transition is exactly what one would expect, but we would do well to note that when humans and monkeys are in quite comparable circumstances (e.g., being groomed), the former smiles and the latter does not. I suspect that much of what is involved in the human pleasurable smile is a reflection upon one's state via a cognitive system with capacities for significant internal representation – traits that are shared, at least to some degree, by gorillas, chimpanzees, and humans.

The situation is similar in the case of sadness, where a gradual elaboration in the primate order culminates in the remarkable chimpanzee. To the best of our current knowledge, a rhesus macaque recently separated from an object of attachment does not show a facial display of sadness, although it may emit a variety of vocal "distress calls." It seems ironic that *distress* is a term often used interchangeably with *sadness* in the human literature, and yet primatologists (albeit understandably) are reluctant to invoke the subject of sadness.

In the case of the chimpanzee, there has been speculation on a possible facial display corresponding to sadness. Van Hooff (1973, 1976) described a "stretched-pout whimper" with retracted corners of the mouth and lips curled outward and slightly protruded "in a manner that is also characteristic for a sulky or crying child" (1973, p. 113). He regarded it as intermediate between a grimace and pout, both structurally and in terms of its causal determinants. (That is, component analysis of social interactions showed it to be intermediate between the silent pout and bared-teeth scream, and it may therefore be a bivalent display.)

Pouting is a facial configuration not considered earlier in this chapter because of its close association with vocalization and because it appears to be primarily an infantile behavior, except in the chimpanzee. The eyebrows are raised, the mouth is slightly open, and the mouth corners and lips are brought prominently forward; a drawn-out clear-call (e.g., "coo") often accompanies the facial configuration. Infants of several taxa pout when away from the mother and it often immediately precedes the return of same. Adult chimpanzees may pout when shown attractive objects (van Hooff, 1969; van Lawick-Goodall, 1968, pp. 323–375). Marler and Tenaza (1977, p. 1011) offered a summation of the social circumstances of chimp pouting as follows: 'Upon detecting a strange object or sound; infant while searching for mother or her nipple; begging; after being rejected for grooming; after threat or attack; during juvenile "temper tantrums"; in other situations of "anxiety" or "frustration." ' The social contexts and morphology of this configuration or display need further clarification, but it would appear that there are reasonable grounds for associating it, and possibly the intermediate form van Hooff proposed, with a primal state of sadness. But much work remains to be done, for many of the social contexts of pouting point to an internal state of attraction rather than sadness.

Indeed, a considerable challenge is how to integrate positive or affiliative affect into existing schemata. Notably, in terms of primate displays, there is the lipsmack with which to contend. A valuable contribution was proposed by Zajonc (1971, p. 146), who distinguished the following levels of bonding. "*Attraction* emphasizes the individual's tendency to approach the given stimulus object, animate or inanimate. *Attachment* places stress on the temporal and more permanent aspects of emotional bonds. *Affiliation* is merely attachment or attraction of the individual to animate objects." Thus, in the case of many social animals, one can begin to distinguish between aggregations organized around simply feeding (e.g., reptiles converging to feed on prey) and the bonding of individuals within a social group (e.g., a group of adult females, an adult male, and young offspring organized into a "harem" of hamadryas baboons). Presumably, reptiles in the preceding context are not emotionally distressed on separation from their conspecific aggregation, whereas a member of the hamadryas group certainly is.

Beyond this fundamental sorting of positive motives, what are we to do with as complex a phenomenon as attachment? What, if anything, might it have to do with human love and affection? Robert Hinde, one of the most distinguished researchers in the development of mother-infant relations in primates, not long ago offered an exemplary characterization of human love as follows: (1) it is multiplex; (2) it is of long duration; (3) in the absence of the partner, the regaining of proximity is sought; (4) it is "well-meshed," i.e., the behavior of each partner is organized in relation to the ongoing behavior of the other; (5) anxiety (from strange objects or situations) is alleviated in the presence of the partner; and (6) actions conducive to the welfare of the partner are likely to be repeated (Hinde, 1976). This list could undoubtedly be elaborated, bringing us still farther afield, but the point that might be appreciated is that love can be approached in an empirical conceptual framework. This being so, it may be possible to integrate it more fully into the existing schemata of the emotions. It may well be that, in the case of the primate display of lipsmacking, for example, the underlying emotional complex is trivalent. If so, what are its components? Will it be possible to distinguish a universal, transcultural expression in *Homo sapiens* for affection or love? (One cannot overemphasize the point that investigators simply have *not yet looked* for such an expression cross-culturally; it is not the case that they looked and did not find it; P. Ekman, Pers. comm.)

Deception

A certain fictional prince, upon learning that his mother was lying in incestuous sheets with the man who had murdered the prince's father, cried "O villain, villain, smiling, damnèd villain!" and recorded an anguished perception of his mother in his notebook: "One may smile, and smile, and be a villain. At least I'm sure it may be so in Denmark" (W. Shakespeare, *The Tragedy of Hamlet Prince of Denmark*, 1600, 1.5.106; 108-09). The phenomenon of deception has been found to have considerably wider generality than Denmark, which would not have surprised that prince. Indeed, in one sense of the term, i.e., in interspecific relations, deceit is found throughout the animal kingdom (see, e.g., Eibl-Eibesfeldt, 1970, chap. 7; Wickler, 1968). Thus, some butterflies have evolved "eyespot" patterns that become visible when they unfold their wings at the approach of a potential songbird predator. The eyespot patterns so closely mimic the prominent eyes of raptorial predators (e.g., owls) that some even include small white dots that appear to be reflections of the sun on spherical eyes. Of course, these mimic eyespots function to startle potential predators of the butterfly that are themselves preyed upon by raptorial birds. That and countless other examples involve structural features, but there are also many examples of behavioral deceit. Female fireflies mimic the flashing pattern of another genus, and the attracted males are eaten by the females. One species of beetle has an anti-predator defense in which it supports itself on its head and sprays a noxious substance from its abdomen; another species of beetle in the same area performs the same motor activity even though it lacks the secretion (Dawkins, 1976).

By using *deceit* in these examples, I was referring, in a rather loose sense, to some form of discrepancy between the perceived signal and the state of displayer. That is, butterflies do not have large eyes; *Photuris* fireflies are not *Photinus* fireflies; and *Megasida* beetles are not *Eleodes* beetles. To be sure, intervening variables involving intentionality need not be invoked and would, indeed, be unparsimonious in these examples.

One of the more interesting areas of recent research in human nonvocal communication has been the display and detection of deceptive processes, predominantly those involving conscious intention (although the boundary between conscious and unconscious is admittedly fuzzy, as we shall see further). For example, Ekman and Friesen (1969a) found that deceptive subjects engaged more frequently in hand-shrug emblems and a self-adapting behavior involving manipulation of the face and less often in illustrator movements.

Primatologists have generally overlooked the topic of intraspecific deception, however. I believe a comparative perspective on this issue would be of value for several reasons. First, it may shed light on the evolution of defense mechanisms in humans (particularly denial and reaction–formation), although the psychotherapist Stewart Kiritz has cautioned me that defense mechanisms in a strict sense require invoking the concept of the unconscious. The examples I am about to discuss allow no such construct, but they presumably may be the substrate from which the more complex defense processes evolved. Second, the topic of deception bears upon a prevalent view of communication among primatologists that facial displays and vocalizations take place when the sender is in an emotional state. (Thus, a call does not *represent* "fig," but the animal may become highly aroused when it beholds a fig.) To my knowledge, there has been no attempt to inquire systematically about: (1) the converse of that proposition: Can a primate feel something and *not* express (display) it? and (2) a derivation of that proposition: Can a primate feel something and express (display) something else? The former I will refer to as *inhibition*; the latter, *dissembling*. The following are a few examples, in which inhibition and dissembling occasionally blend:

1. "Clearer evidence that a chimpanzee leader knows the sign value of his own behavior for his followers and responds accordingly is the ability of the animals to withhold response to a preferred object as long as a dominant animal is watching – or even to deliberately mislead others and then sneak back for the goal" (Menzel and Halperin, 1975, p. 654, note 7; see also Menzel, 1974).
2. In reference to a pet gibbon, Hahn (1972, p. 253) noted: "Once when I hit him he acted as if he had been badly hurt. Whenever I looked in his direction he limped pitifully, but when he thought himself out of sight the limp disappeared." But "he was not adept, as chimps are, in dissimulating..." (p. 252).
3. In her study of free-ranging mountain gorillas, Fossey (1972) found that "the most extreme form of fear was expressed by immediate cessation of all noise, both vocal and mechanical..." (p. 45).

4. Lucy, a chimpanzee taught American Sign Language and studied by Roger Fouts, was once found to have defecated on the floor of a room. When asked who had done it, Lucy replied first that a student had, then that Dr. Fouts had, and then finally signed "Lucy, sorry, Lucy" (Fouts, Pers. comm.). Other examples of deceit by this chimpanzee are discussed by Fouts and Mellgren (1976).

5. Bertrand (1969), in perhaps the most extensive discussion of the topic relative to primates, described feigned *indifference* in stumptail macaques of which there are two forms. In one form, "an animal pretends not to notice another animal or object of which it is afraid..." (p. 70). This is said to occur commonly. It may be accompanied by brief, repeated glances or displacement activities. In the other form, "the animal pretends to be uninterested by something it wants to have, or refrains from acting the way it wants to, until the opportunity arises" (p. 72). This is said to occur rarely. For example, a juvenile stole food, without looking at it, with the foot.

6. Bertrand (1969) also described feigned *interest* in stumptail macaques. An animal scrutinized or stared at may stare at another monkey, at an empty point in space, or "it may also look attentively at an object and manipulate it, or feign interest in its own body, scratching or grooming it conscientiously" (p. 72).

7. The Gautiers (1977, p. 956) noted: "Anyone who has seen a female monkey trying to touch an infant in the arms of its mother has surely been astonished by the subtlety of the behavior. The female grooms the mother with great attention, then surreptitiously slips her hand over the mother's abdomen in order to touch the infant's fur. All the while she pretends to continue grooming with one hand.... All primatologists have observations of this kind in their notebooks, but possessing only a very anthropomorphic vocabulary, they would rather remain silent about them."

8. It has often been recounted that chimpanzees may wait stoically, with a mouthful of water or quantity of spit, for an unsuspecting human to wander within range, at which time the human is victimized (e.g., Yerkes and Yerkes, 1929).

9. Chevalier-Skolnikoff (1976, p. 185) observed a young lowland gorilla hugging and looking into the eyes of a human while surreptitiously stealing the latter's watch.

10. A remarkable account of a gorilla at the San Francisco Zoo was kindly furnished by Lawrence Bingham, a psychologist studying behavior associated with parturition. Pogo, an adult female reared by humans early in life, had shown difficulty assimilating into the established social group of gorillas. After another female had given birth, the mother–infant pair was reintroduced to the group. On Day 1 of the reintroduction (Day 5 postpartum), Pogo threw several automobile tires at the pair. By Day 3, she had become functionally blind: she closed her eyes for most of the day and tumbled into objects and walls in an exaggerated fashion. (She had lived in that enclosure for at least six years and can be presumed to know the location of objects quite accurately.) After several days of this behavior, by which time the zoo staff had concluded she was blind, Bingham devised an ingenious test. She had been conditioned to associate the sound of "fig newton" with that highly desired food object. Accordingly, Bingham said "fig newton" when she was standing nearby. She covered her eyes with one hand, turned to Bingham, opened her eyes, and *looked* at him through the spaces between her fingers. As Bingham was being deceptive himself, he had no fig newtons and Pogo

resumed her previous activity. The functional blindness abated after several more days, during which time Bingham successfully replicated the preceding procedure.

11. A second account from this group also concerns Pogo. She had been playing with the silverback adult male of the group, Bwana, and cuffed him on the ear. Bwana chased her into the blockhouse, where evidently there was some form of agonistic exchange (judging from the intense vocalizations emitted). Pogo fled the blockhouse and ran to a tree where a large tractor tire was suspended on a rope. She grasped the tire, backed away from the blockhouse, and waited. When Bwana emerged at high velocity, she swung the tire and scored a direct hit. Bwana fell to the ground and lay sprawled on his back, immobile. Pogo showed several signs of distress and crept up to the still unmoving Bwana. When she came within range, he instantly reached up, grabbed her, and mayhem ensued.

I have presented these examples, even though they regrettably lacked detailed observation of facial activity, to demonstrate that it is at least reasonable both to regard intraspecific behavioral deception as a significant process among nonhuman primates and to begin orienting systematic observation and experimentation toward that process. In terms of *leakage* of primate facial activity during deceit, it is clear that very finely tuned measurements of muscular activity must be made, and concurrent physiological measures of arousal (e.g., heart rate and cardiac acceleration and deceleration) would indeed be helpful.

In researching deception, it would seem that there is a rare opportunity for an interdisciplinary exchange. Primatologists have not investigated the subject systematically, so they stand to gain much from the questions posed and methods used in research with humans. Conversely, investigators in the human domain might greatly profit from the recent theoretical orientation of evolutionary biologists toward deception. For example, Dawkins (1976, p. 70) speculated that *all* animal communication may contain an element of deception because of the conflict of interest inherent in interactions between individuals. (That is, each individual is said to be selected to maximize the chances of its own genes surviving.) Rather than a deliberate and conscious intention to deceive, Dawkins was referring to "an effect *functionally* equivalent to deception" (Dawkins, 1976, p. 68, emphasis added).[5] The example he gives is that if a bird emits a predator alarm call in the absence of a predator, nearby conspecifics would be frightened away, leaving the deceiver in custody of food or other resources: "All that is implied is that the [deceiver]

[5]This model of deception was more recently discussed by Dawkins and Krebs (1978, p. 302), at which time deceit was defined as the act of "deliberately misleading," and what appear to be different predictions and constraints were generated.

gained food at the other birds' expense, and the reason the other birds flew away was that they reacted to the [deceiver's] cry in a way appropriate" to the presence of a hawk (Dawkins, 1976, p. 68). Thus, Dawkins was employing ultimate or distal rather than proximate causation. In a characteristically insightful comment in the foreword to Dawkins' volume, Robert L. Trivers extended the line of reasoning thus:

> If (as Dawkins argues) deceit is fundamental to animal communication, then there must be strong selection to spot deception and this ought, in turn, to select for a degree of self-deception, rendering some facts and motives unconscious so as not to betray – by the subtle signs of self-knowledge – the deception being practised. [Dawkins, 1976, p. iv]

Trivers's proposal is consonant with that of Otte (1974, p. 401): "When knowledge of deceit is relegated to the subconscious, the likelihood that an individual will betray himself by visible [i.e., perceptible] changes might be reduced"; hence the fuzzy boundary between conscious and unconscious deceit just mentioned.

This biological model of deceit exclusively emphasizes interindividual dynamics. A component not yet integrated into the model is the role of unconscious processes in the sender's perception of *self*, which is the perspective long emphasized by psychoanalysts and psychodynamically oriented psychologists. Thus, a motive is said to become unconscious because its conscious perception engenders intense anxiety or other affect, e.g., as a threat to one's self-concept. It would appear that both the psychological and biological models would profit from a closer approximation to one another. At the present time, it is difficult to evaluate Dawkins et al.'s model of deceit because it has only recently been formulated and as yet lacks extensive empirical verification. Certainly one need not embrace Dawkins's proposal that the totality of animal communication involves an element of deceit in order to judge the model useful. (Indeed, I must comment that if all communication involves deceit, what are we to make of Dawkins's proposal?) His model requires substantial elaboration of the types of interactions subsumed (e.g., are human verbal utterances included?) and whether, in fact, such behaviors are necessarily selfish. Otte (1974), for example, discussed deceit without concluding that it pertains to all of animal communication, and he indeed took the position that most intraspecific signaling benefits both sender and percipient (i.e., is cooperative rather than selfish). If there is a concordance between an animal's emotional state at the time of signaling (which can be inferred from other indices) and the signal emitted, it remains to be explicated why the concept of deceit need be invoked. And there is the host of altruistic and reciprocally altruistic behaviors (Trivers, 1971) of which individuals, particularly human individuals, are capable – behaviors that I find difficult to incorporate into Dawkins's selfish–deceit model.

Judgment

An issue that has long held the interest of students of human communication is the judgment of forms of facial expression. Understandably, the topic has not been formally approached by primatologists, because a verbal response of the subject has been regarded as all but indispensable. But nonvocal instrumental responses could conceivably be worked into a research design utilizing nonhuman primates to assess such questions as: How do monkeys and apes themselves categorize displays? Do their judgments agree with our categories? What is the degree of interobserver agreement in judgment among primates? Thus, rewarding of correct operant responses in a sameness/difference paradigm might be employed. Moreover, the existence of the growing group of chimpanzees trained in American Sign Language, the use of symbols, or a computer interface opens up a limitless vista in research of this sort through two-way communication.

There is also the intriguing possibility of studying cross-species facial judgment in both directions. The successful judgment by humans of nonhuman primate displays would add strength to the existing evidence supporting the universality of a number of human facial displays. To my considerable surprise, a study of this sort was conducted in 1935 by Foley, who concluded that undergraduates did not accurately interpret photographs of six categories of facial configurations in chimpanzees, as provided by Kohts (see Kohts, 1935, and Yerkes and Yerkes, 1929, p. 280). However, Ekman (1973) quite effectively dismantled Foley's procedure and analysis and concluded, contrary to Foley, that human observers did accurately judge at least a few of Kohts's stimuli. As Ekman and Chevalier-Skolnikoff also noted (Ekman, 1973), there are major problems with Kohts's descriptors of the six categories. In my judgment, based on recent findings such as van Hooff's (1973) and Marler and Tenaza's (1977), the six descriptors of Kohts could be recategorized as shown in Table 10.3. Accordingly, one would expect little more than chaos from such a cross-taxonomic judgment study, and the study would bear replication with a more coherent set of stimuli. Because the chimpanzee has a repertoire of facial displays rivaling that of *Homo sapiens*

Table 10.3. *Recategorization of Kohts' descriptors*

Kohts' term	Proposed term
Quietude	Interest
Sadness	Low-intensity silent pout
Laughter	Play face
Weeping	Open-mouth grimace
Anger	Higher-intensity play face
Excitement	Full silent pout

and because it has appreciably greater mobility of the lips (particularly in vertical retraction), one might also use a model more remotely related to the human with a more fundamental display repertoire, such as the rhesus macaque. For example, I recently showed slides of rhesus facial displays to a group of graduate students in clinical psychology, and they showed a remarkably high accuracy in associating affect with the depicted displays. Indeed, they even associated both fear and anger with the threat display. I mention this not as data but as a suggestion that such research might be feasible.

As noted, cross-taxonomic judgment research might also work in both directions. Might we not ask chimps to judge *human* displays, at least those chimps skilled in two-way communication? The techniques used in the human cross-cultural work are not beyond the mastery of chimpanzees (e.g., having the subject point to the picture of a human who is "angry and is about to fight"), and one could hardly conceive of more convincing evidence of universality if chimpanzees were successful.

The nature of communication

An issue not discussed previously in this chapter is the fundamental nature of communicative processes. Because of its enormity, no complete discussion is here contemplated. Rather, I hope to acquaint the reader with a perspective on communication that has been recently developed and that both diverges and converges with the models of communication implicit in this chapter.

As is undoubtedly apparent to the reader, the traditional view of communication via displays that is shared by ethologists and animal behaviorists of many persuasions places emphasis on the emotional or motivational substrates of the displays. As Dawkins and Krebs (1978) observed, this model posits a fundamentally cooperative interchange during communication: Signals should be efficient, unambiguous, and informative in order to benefit *both* sender and percipient (e.g., the sender can avert tissue damage and the percipient can reliably predict the behavior of the sender). Recently, several evolutionary biologists developed a model that is potentially quite different. The emphasis in this approach is on maximizing either: (1) "inclusive fitness" of the displayer, (i.e., the displayer is selected to maximize the reproduction of its own genes and identical genes found in relatives) or (2) the chances of the displayer's genes surviving into the future. The choice of these alternatives depends on whether one regards the unit of natural selection to be the individual or the gene, respectively. Thus, in one recent controversial formulation of an evolutionary view (Dawkins & Krebs, 1978), communication is regarded as a selfish, not cooperative, process (where a selfish act is regarded as one that enhances the fitness of the actor to the detriment of the recipient). The reader may be now somewhat prepared for the definition of communication offered by Dawkins and Krebs (1978, p. 285): "As an inevitable byproduct of the fact that animals are selected to respond to their environment in ways that are *on average* beneficial to themselves, other animals can be selected to subvert this responsiveness for their own benefit. This is communication" (emphasis added). Thus, a signaling animal acts such that the percipient behaves or changes in a way that benefits the signaler: "Communication [is] a means by which one animal makes use of another animal's muscle power" (Dawkins & Krebs, 1978, p. 283). More particularly, Dawkins (1978) declared that signals are means by which the central nervous system of one animal controls the muscles of a second. (One wonders what became of the emotions and the autonomic nervous system.) Rather than a transmittal of information, the process of communication is likened more closely to manipulation, persuasion, propaganda, or advertising (Dawkins and Krebs, 1978, p. 304).

As can be swiftly appreciated, such a formulation is highly provocative and is sure to engender a lively exchange. It seems to hinge crucially on Dawkins's premise that the unit of selection is the gene, not the individual. Precise citation is again important here, so I quote the first sentence of Dawkins and Krebs (1978, p. 282): "It is reasonable for us to picture an animal as a machine designed to preserve and propagate the genes which ride inside it (Dawkins 1976). As a means to this end it will often manipulate objects in its world, pushing them around to its own advantage" via such processes as communication. Thus, the "animal is a

gene's way of making another gene" (Dawkins, 1978), which brings to
mind the view that novelist and philosopher Samuel Butler proffered a
century earlier: "A hen is only an egg's way of making another egg"
(1878, p. 134).

I expect that one wave of criticism is likely to emerge from logicians
(with theologians raising a clamor right behind them), for Dawkins seems
to have reified the gene as an actor, a sort of homunculus within the
organism. Juxtaposed to such a view, Cartesian dualism seems pallid.
Moreover, a more basic assumption of the model of Dawkins and others
is the existence of linkages between specific genes and specific behaviors; otherwise, there is said to be nothing upon which natural selection
can act. Given the formidable problems linking even such a definable
trait as intelligence with specific genes, how much greater is the difficulty of contending with behaviors such as selfishness and altruism!
This point does not necessarily refute such models, of course, but rather
points to enormous gaps of evidence needed to support the theoretical
enterprise.

However, one need not embrace the gene-as-selection-unit view in
order to find some merit in the recent evolutionary emphasis on assessing the cost/benefit outcomes of communicative events, and some sophisticated methodologies have begun to emerge to quantify such
contingencies. We already noted, for example, that high-intensity vocalizations might be interpreted in terms of costs and benefits, as measured
by success in mating and propagating offspring. Such issues have certainly captured the attention of animal behaviorists, and they are among
the subjects most discussed today in the discipline. And surely there can
be a sensible integration of the best of both the proximate (i.e., displays
reflecting affect) and ultimate (i.e., displays as a selection mechanism)
views.

Future work in primatology

In addition to the suggestions scattered throughout this paper, I will
present here a few general and specific propositions with regard to
future research in the area of primate facial displays and its interface
with human research.

Terminology. First, there is the matter of terminology. Progress in the
field will be impeded unless there is some consolidation and agreement
on display nomenclature. As an example, the number of terms applied

to what is referred to here as the grimace is truly sobering. In an early study (Rosvold, Mirsky, & Pribram, 1954), "teeth baring or grimacing" was even used as a defining feature of threatening. Van Hooff's terminology has been the most precise, but it is often cumbersome to use. It is no doubt overly optimistic to hope for a widespread consensus on terminology, considering the present gaps in data, but it is absolutely essential that authors meticulously describe the facial activity that corresponds to the terms employed.

Muscular Coding. There is also a need for descriptions of facial displays constructed in terms of units of facial muscle movement. Once again, investigators of human expressions have far outstripped primatologists. This would seem to be a paradox, considering the long history of primate morphological work associated with phylogenetic lineages, dentition, locomotion, and so forth. Now that we have Seiler's *Die Gesichtsmuskeln* ["The facial muscles"] (1976), which hopefully will be translated into English and French, and the multivolume series by W. C. O. Hill, *Primates: Comparative Anatomy and Taxonomy*, (Edinburgh University Press, 1953 et seq.; Hill, 1969), primatologists have little excuse for further delay. It need hardly be stressed how important muscular coding would be in providing firm bases for cross–taxon comparisons (especially with humans), in standardizing the nomenclature for primate facial displays, in clarifying the intergradations of displays, and in discovering subtle facial movements previously overlooked. In particular, we might be able to pinpoint the subtle differences between a look, a stare, and even a glimmer in the eye; to determine if there actually is a primate disgust reaction shown in the face; to distinguish among the various play faces, smiles, and grimaces discussed here and in the literature; to determine and quantify the shifts in displays as intensity rises (e.g., when are the brows and ears shifted? does movement of one necessarily involve the other?); to determine if our descriptions have been too gross (e.g., primate brow movement is almost universally described as a simple raising or lowering, thus neglecting the *corrugator* convergence during frowning; and are the inner and outer aspects of the brow capable of independent action, as in *Homo sapiens*?); and even to measure the elusive smile of chimpanzees and gorillas.

Electromyography, electrical stimulation, and behavioral elicitation under controlled and definable circumstances are all methods available to primatologists. Electrical stimulation of muscle units and assemblies would also enable researchers to generate stimuli with which to study percipients' responsiveness (e.g., by making transparency or motion picture records during electrical stimulation that would subsequently be used as eliciting stimuli). In this regard, it is pertinent to note here that motion picture stimuli appear to be more potent than still stimuli (e.g., Adamson, Romano, Burdick, Corman, & Chebib, 1972; Baulu, 1973). Baulu offered a detailed description of a particularly effective technique of presenting motion picture stimuli, and noted that his rhesus subjects gave no indication of extinction after five months. There is also a recent brief report of the effective use of color video recordings (Plimpton and Rosenblum, 1978).

If an operant response is a part of the research design, I recommend that the display of the visual stimuli be highly contingent on the response; that is, for example, that stimuli be shown only when the animal is actively depressing a lever. Redican, Kellicutt, and Mitchell (1971) used a technique in which a single, brief lever–press would produce a 5–second presentation of a stimulus (a slide of a conspecific facial display). A relatively low response rate was obtained. Moreover, once the lever was depressed, the subject was free to wander away from the stimulus and not attend to it. It would appear that the more direct the contingency between response and stimulus duration the better.

Excellent treatments of human facial muscle movement are available as guides to primatologists (Hjortsjö, 1970; Ekman and Friesen, 1976, 1978). It is evidently *not* needless to say that the systemizing of muscular involvement in primate facial displays must be a careful procedure. It can potentially retard development in this area if investigators simply estimate or infer the muscles believed to be involved or if they do not clearly state the criteria by which these judgments are made. Thus, for example, Marler and Tenaza's (1977, p. 1015) "interpretations of muscle involvement are based on examination of photographs and on Andrew, 1963, and van Hooff, 1967 [1969 in the present bibliography]." But I was unable to find a clear statement of Andrew's own criteria, other than a citation of Huber (1931) for the illustrated directions of contraction by nine muscles in a "generalised primate" (Andrew, 1963, p. 9, Figure 1), and Huber's anatomical treatise was largely structural, not functional. Van Hooff's explication of musculature was made only *en passant*. Clearly, this is an opportune time to develop a systematic manual of facial movements associated with display components in nonhuman primates.

Empirical data. Perhaps the major task facing primatologists in this area is to provide quantifiable evidence for many of the qualitative deductions and inferences that have become so widely established in the literature. How do we know that threat displays avert tissue damage? What are the data that lead us to conclude that a grimace arrests ongoing or potential attacks, or that the lipsmack serves a reassuring function?

It seems a paradox that animal behaviorists, skilled as they are in many forms of meticulous observation, seem to state what should be conclusions as observations. Rather, quantitative data should be collected and assessed to determine if a null hypothesis should be rejected. This very basic model is often eschewed in this area.

A significant contributing variable to the present state of the discipline is undoubtedly historical. Classical ethologists do not make use of the model described here, for which experimental psychologists have such an allegiance. It would be quite a mistake to believe that ethologists are unaware of the issue. Tinbergen (1959a [1972, p. 118]) remarked: "Selective observations are admittedly difficult to make because they frequently involve split-second appraisals of the behaviour of two animals. Observers vary greatly in their ability to do this; and there is no doubt that wishful thinking might all too easily affect an observer's judgment." Thus, the very fundamental question of reliability is raised. After briefly commending the value of replicability and controllability, Tinbergen concluded (with, I assume, undisguised sarcasm), "It is possible [in a controlled study] to make statements that can be tested and compared, for instance: 'A stuffed gull in breeding plumage: beginning of the breeding period; placed for 10 minutes at a distance of 50 cm from the nest; releases in 10 presentations 12 pecking and 5 retreat reactions.' " If my interpretation of Tinbergen's comments is correct, he has certainly underestimated the potential value of the experimental method. Moreover, such a view overlooks the expansive question of how to conduct systematic, empirical, quantifiable, noninterventive observations (as distinct from controlled experimental manipulation) that are objective, reliable, and valid. The failure to quantify properly decades' worth of observation has led to the current situation in which we must now disentangle impressions and observations of limited generality from rigorous principles of behavior.

The ideal future studies of nonhuman primate facial displays will employ not only careful and quantified description, observation, and experimentation, but pay due regard to the social contexts of the displays and the potential ultimate costs and benefits of display behavior. I see that future as optimistic and exciting, for in very few areas of primatology have I seen such a rich potential for a synthetic and integrative understanding of the evolutionary bases of human behavior.

Acknowledgments

I dedicate this chapter to the memory of the late Daniel D. Cubicciotti III, a gifted and singularly promising primatologist and cherished friend. *Stella fieret etiam illustrior.* I am grateful to acknowledge the late Robert Howard, master psychotherapist and teacher, for his careful reading of the manuscript and for his inspiring and humble wisdom. I am also appreciative of the many ever-stimulating conversations I have shared with Professor Ron Schusterman that contributed importantly to this chapter. Professor Paul Ekman's editorship was extraordinarily scholarly, patient, and generous, and I have greatly valued this interchange between human and primate research disciplines. And I offer a bouquet of thanks to Blossom Young and Wanda Matsubayashi for their unfailingly cheerful and skilled help in the preparation of the typescript. Suzanne Chevalier-Skolnikoff very kindly offered comments on the final draft, which were appreciated.

11. Measuring the ability to recognize facial expressions of emotion

MAUREEN O'SULLIVAN

When the first edition of *Emotion in the Human Face* was published in 1972, little could be said about individual differences in the ability to recognize facial expressions of emotion. Although a number of such tests had been proposed (e.g., Langfeld, 1918b; O'Sullivan, Guilford, & de Mille, 1965; Wedeck, 1947), no coherent or extensive research literature existed at that time. Since then, several tests of the ability to recognize facial emotional behavior have been proposed (Buck, 1976; Rosenthal, Hall, DiMatteo, Rogers, & Archer, 1979). These newer tests, along with the older ones, provide a sufficient "critical mass" so that the methodological issues involved in measuring individual differences in recognizing facially expressed emotion may be meaningfully explored.

In this chapter the methodological requirements of a good test of the ability to recognize facial expressions of emotion using the psychometric principles of construct validity and reliability will be discussed. Although Petrinovich (1979) pointed out the conceptual overlap of hypothesis testing and construct validation, procedures within the two endeavors are quite different. Measures acceptable for use in a single experiment rarely meet the requirements of a psychometrically sound "test." This distinction between a *measure* (an operational definition of a variable) and a *test* (a technique for reliably and validly assessing differences among individuals) is important. A measure is usually only interpreted by researchers within its particular experimental paradigm. Investigators are usually aware of its shortcomings and are seeking to improve it or to understand its function better. When a measure is published as a test, however, the user clientele is greatly enlarged and may include less-sophisticated consumers. People seeking solutions to practical problems of selection, placement, and assessment may select an instrument based on little other than its name. The requirements for calling a measure of the ability to recognize facial expressions of emotion a test (in the psychometric sense) need to be clarified, which is the aim of this chapter.

11.1. Measure selection

Since 1914, more than 50 different measures of the ability to recognize facial expressions of emotion have been suggested. We have selected eight of these for analysis because they illustrate various methodological difficulties. In selecting these measures from the large number available, four criteria were used. The first criterion was to represent the most often used testing paradigm, namely, presenting a photograph of a facial expression and asking observers to choose a verbal label that describes it. The measure selected to represent this paradigm from the many available is the one reported by Tomkins and McCarter (1964).

The second criterion was to reflect the variety of test formats available, with respect to both stimulus and response. Based on this criterion, three measures were selected: (1) the Brief Affect Recognition Task (BART) (Ekman & Friesen, 1974b), which uses a tachistoscopic stimulus presentation; (2) Faces (O'Sullivan et al., 1965), which uses an unusual response format; and (3) Social Relations (O'Sullivan et al., 1965), which has both unusual stimuli and an unusual response format. These three measures were chosen because their creators intended their procedures to assess individual differences and because their psychometric descriptions were available to the author.

The third criterion for selection was whether a measure was currently being used either in research or clinical practice. On this basis, two measures, the Communication of Affect Receiving Ability Test (CARAT) (Buck, 1976) and the Profile of Nonverbal Sensitivity test (PONS) (Rosenthal et al., 1979), were selected. These tests also use unusual stimuli and testing procedures and could be included under the second criterion as well. Of the measures selected, only these two have actually been published for use as tests. The other six instruments were not thought to be sufficiently well validated by their developers and were reported only as attempts to solve the many problems in this domain.

The fourth criterion for inclusion was to represent early efforts of historical interest. To meet this criterion, two quite different measures were selected. Langfeld's (1918b) use of the Rudolf sketches was selected as the first investigation explicitly to study individual differences in people's ability to recognize facial expressions of emotion. Although Feleky (1914) previously reported the responses of subjects to her photographs of emotion expression, her interest was to determine general reactions to the photographs and not to examine individual variations in responses to them. The second test selected for historical reasons was Buzby's (1924) measure based on the Piderit profile. This measure was selected because it uses a schematic, not a realistic, face. Although schematic faces have not been used often in research in recent years, such stimuli offer a frequently ignored advantage, that of experimental control.

The measures to be discussed in this chapter have in common the attempt to assess how well different people can recognize or identify facial expressions of emotion. The face has been used as a stimulus in many other types of tests, which will not be reviewed for a number of reasons:

1. The face is embedded in more complex material, including verbal and other nonverbal stimuli, as in the Affective Sensitivity Scale (Kagan, Warner, & Schneider, 1977); Missing Cartoons and Expression Grouping (O'Sullivan & Guilford, 1975); the Social Interpretation Task (Archer & Akert, 1977); and the Behavior Postdiction Test (Cline,1964).
2. The face is used to assess memory for faces, not the differential ability to recognize emotion (Moss, Hunt, Omwake, & Bonning, 1972; Messick & Damarin, 1963).
3. The face is used to determine whether more attention is paid to the face or the voice, not whether people varied in their accuracy at recognizing facial expressions of emotion (e.g., Bugental, Kaswan & Love, 1970; Shapiro, 1968).
4. The face is used to assess perceptual functioning (Mooney, 1956).
5. The face is used to assess personality characteristics (Szondi, 1947).
6. The face is used to assess responses to different racial groups (Harrison, Ekman, & Friesen, 1971).

11.2. Description of measures

The Primary Affect Measure

We will refer to the Tomkins–McCarter (1964) measure as the *Primary Affect Measure*. It consists of 69 black-and-white photographs mounted on 3-by-5-inch index cards. These photographs show the posed expressions of people of both sexes, ranging in age from young to old (an example of these photographs is shown in Figure 7.1). Eight affects and a neutral expression were depicted. Seven photos each were chosen for fear, surprise, interest, and anger; eight photos each for neutrality, enjoyment, contempt, and shame; and nine photos for distress. The response alternatives are nine sets of four or five words. Each set reflects various aspects of the intended affect, e.g., one set includes "distressed," "sad," "lonely," and "pained"; another set contains "angry," "mad," "furious," "aggressive," and "hostile." (Additional information about this measure is given in Table 11.1.)

Table 11.1. *Comparison of eight measures of the ability to recognize facial expressions of emotion*

Factor	Rudolf sketches (Langfeld, 1918b)	Piderit profile (Buzby, 1924)	Faces (O'Sullivan et al., 1965)	Social Relations (O'Sullivan et al., 1965)	BART (Ekman & Friesen, 1974b)	Primary Affect Measure (Tomkins & McCarter, 1964)	CARAT (Buck, 1976)	PONS Face Alone (Rosenthal et al., 1979)
Number of emotions	14	6	—	—	6 + neutral	8 + neutral	—	—
Number of stimuli for each emotion	2 to 16	1	—	—	10	7–9	—	—
Method of stimulus presentation	Sketches	Profile drawings	Black/white photographs	Cartoon drawings	Black/white tachistoscopic photos	Black/white photos	Tv heads and shoulders	Tv heads
Eliciting circumstance	Pose	—	Pose and muscle movements	—	Pose and muscle movements	Pose	Slide viewing	Acting
Number of stimulus persons	1	—	2	—	10	11	25	1
Judgment task	Free Verbal label; label match	Verbal label	Photo match	Sketch-statement match	Verbal label	Verbal group match	Video-Situation match; pleasantness rating	Video-Statement match
Number of response alternatives	∞	18	4	3	6	9	4; 9	2

Accuracy criterion	Artist's intention	Theoretical description; expert judges	Poser; author; item analysis	Author; item analysis	Poser; author; judges	Poser; author; judges	Reality; self-report	Poser; author; judges
Number of items	105	6	30	24	70	69	32	20
Relative difficulty of stimulus versus response	Stimulus	Equal	Equal	Stimulus	Stimulus	Stimulus	Stimulus	Equal
Reliability (KR 20 or alpha)	—	—	.37	.29	.41–.67	—	.56	.39

Although a number of other scores were generated from this instrument so as to test Tomkins's affect theory, individual differences in recognizing emotion were assessed using two different sets of error scores. One set of error scores was based on the number of times that a given affect was wrongly ascribed to a photo expressing some other affect. The second set of error scores was the number of times an observer failed to recognize a particular affect in a photo selected to show that affect. Tomkins and McCarter suggested that the scores for each observer be used to generate a profile they called the *Affect Sensitivity Contour*.

Brief Affect Recognition Task

The Brief Affect Recognition Task (BART) measures "a person's accuracy in decoding six emotions" (Ekman & Friesen, 1974b, p. 221). It consists of 70 black-and-white slides of facial expressions selected to represent neutral faces and six basic emotions – happy, sad, fear, anger, surprise, and disgust. Ten different men and women were photographed under carefully controlled studio conditions. Head size and head tilt were kept constant. Brightness and contrast were also adjusted for similarity across photographs. Each of the photographs was judged as the intended emotion by more than 70% of judges when presented for 10 seconds. In BART the slides are presented tachistoscopically (at 1/60th of a second) to make identifying the expression more difficult and to simulate micromomentary or fleeting expressions of emotion (Haggard & Isaacs, 1966). There are seven BART scores, one for total accuracy and one for accuracy in judging each of the six emotions (see Table 11.1).

To control for tachistoscopic proficiency, the Facial Interpretation Test (FIT) was devised. It consists of 24 black-and-white slides of men and women whose eyes and mouths are in various combinations of open or closed. These stimuli are presented at various tachistoscopic speeds (from 1/30th to 1/125th of a second). Scores on FIT are used to adjust scores on BART by controlling the influence of tachistoscopic proficiency.

Faces

Faces is one of 23 measures constructed by O'Sullivan and her colleagues (1965) to assess the ability to understand the thoughts, feelings, and intentions of others as they are manifested in behavioral or nonverbal cues. The measures were designed to reflect six factors of behavioral cognition hypothesized by the Structure of Intellect model (Guilford, 1967). In Faces, the observer indicates cognition or understanding of a given facial expression by choosing the one of four alternative photographs of facial expressions with the same emotional or intentional meaning (see Figure 11.1). The given photographs were chosen from the Marjorie Lightfoot series (Engen, Levy, & Schlosberg, 1957). The four alternative photographs were selected from the Frois-Wittmann (1930) series. Faces consists of two separately timed parts with 15 items per part. A correction for guessing (a percentage of omitted items) is applied. This test, which is similar in format to a vocabulary test, was designed to bear the same relationship to social intelligence or understanding other people that the vocabulary test bears to general or verbal intelligence (i.e., to be highly correlated).

Social Relations

Social Relations is another of the behavioral cognition tests (O'Sullivan et al., 1965). Each item consists of two schematic faces looking at each other. Each face has an emotional expression. Observers indicate that they understand the feeling shown by one of the two faces (indicated by an arrow) by choosing one of three verbal statements (see Figure 11.1). The correct answer is appropriate not only for the expression on the indicated face but also for the other face with which it is interacting. Social Relations consists of two separately timed parts of 12 items each. A correction for guessing is applied (see Table 11.1). Social Relations was hypothesized to measure a different intellectual ability than Faces, although both are measures of a more general "behavioral cognition" skill.

Profile of Nonverbal Sensitivity

The Profile of Nonverbal Sensitivity (PONS) was designed by Rosenthal and co-workers (1979) to measure nonverbal sensitivity, or the ability to recognize nonverbal cues in 11 channels – face alone, body alone, randomly spliced speech, content-filtered speech, and seven combinations of these single channels. In this chapter the face alone score will be emphasized. The test stimuli are videotaped segments of 2-second duration showing one young woman simulating reactions to different emotional and social situations, such as comforting a lost child or talking about her divorce. The total PONS consists of 220 items, each having a nonverbal stimulus followed by two verbal statements of social situa-

FACES   Which man's face expresses the same feeling or intention as the woman's?

SOCIAL RELATIONS

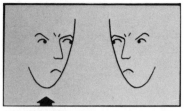

1. I didn't like that movie very much.
2. What a bore!
3. Who does he think he is, anyway?

RUDOLF SKETCH

PROFILE OF NONVERBAL
SENSITIVITY

1. Admiring nature
2. Helping a customer

PIDERIT PROFILE

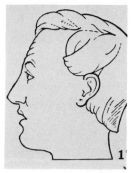

Figure 11.1 Stimuli and items from five measures of facial expression recognition. (Faces and Social Relations from *Behavioral cognition tests* by M. O'Sullivan and J. P. Guilford. 1965. Copyright 1965 by M. O'Sullivan. Reproduced by permission. Profile of nonverbal sensitivity from *Sensitivity to nonverbal communication* by R. Rosenthal, J. A. Hall, M. R. DiMatteo, P. L. Rogers, & D. Archer. Baltimore: Johns Hopkins University Press, 1979. Copyright 1979 by The Johns Hopkins University Press. Reproduced by permission)

tions (see Figure 11.1). There are 20 items in which the face alone is the nonverbal stimulus. The situations on which both the nonverbal and verbal stimuli are based were chosen to reflect two dimensions: pleasant–unpleasant and dominance–submission. The number of correct items are summed for a total raw score; a fraction of omitted items is added to the raw score for a "credited" score. This is similar to the correction for guessing used in Faces and Social Relations

Communication of Affect Receiving Ability Test (CARAT)

The 32 items in CARAT (Buck, 1976) are black-and-white videotape segments of about 25-second duration showing the head and shoulders of 25 individuals watching slides of four types: unusual, unpleasant, sexual, and scenic. The videotape segments were recorded as the subjects viewed the slides and reported verbally how pleasant or unpleasant they felt on a 9-point rating scale (see Table 11.1). These videotapes were then shown without sound to observers who judged which slide type was being watched and rated how pleasant the stimulus person was feeling.

The aim of CARAT is to measure ' "nonverbal receiving ability" or the ability to accurately decode the affective state of another person based on...nonverbal behaviors' (Buck, 1976, p. 162). The test yields two scores: (1) number of slide categories judged correctly and (2) the correlation between the stimulus person's self-ratings of pleasantness and the observer's ratings of the stimulus person's pleasantness.

Piderit profile

Buzby's (1924) measure using the Piderit profile consists of six profiles selected from the series suggested by Boring and Titchener (1923) in their adaptation of the Piderit model. In 1888, Piderit suggested that facial expressions could be demonstrated using a model with interchangeable brows, eyes, noses, and mouths. Boring and Titchener's adaptation consisted of a white cardboard profile with nine interchangeable mouths, five eyes, two noses, and four brows (see Figure 11.1). They suggested many possible combinations of these face parts and offered descriptions of the emotions expressed by the total faces, based largely on Wundt's theory of feelings. The six faces selected by Buzby were presumed to express anger, dismay, horror, disdain, disgust, and bewilderment. He showed each of the six faces to 716 university students and asked them to identify the facial expressions by choosing one affect term from a list of 18. Buzby also examined group differences in accuracy. He found that the women in his sample did slightly better than the men and that beginning students performed better than psychology graduate students.

Rudolf sketches

Using the Rudolf (1903) series, Langfeld (1918b) selected 105 sketches of facial expressions (see Table 11.1), which were presented to subjects to describe in their own words. The correct answer was determined by the title given to the sketch by the artist who drew it. The Rudolf series were realistically drawn depictions (see Figure 11.1) of a bearded actor posing a variety of emotional and attitudinal expressions. In the sketches, head tilt and position were used to convey the intended feeling as well as the more usual muscle changes of the face. The Rudolf series is of interest also because sketches from it were used by both Allport (1924) and Guilford (1929) in early attempts to study the impact of training on the ability to recognize facial expressions of emotion.

11.3. Construct validity

A continuing problem in measuring individual differences in the ability to recognize facial expressions of emotion is the widespread confusion between face validity (which is not validity at all) and construct validity. *Face validity* refers to the seeming validity of a measure; it appeals to observers. A face valid measure *looks* as if it should measure the ability to recognize facial expressions of emotion. Merely using photographs of facial expressions in a measure, however, does not guarantee that the measure reflects the ability to interpret or understand the expressions shown. The test may *look* valid (i.e., have face validity) and be interesting on this basis to both researchers and observers, but this consumer appeal bears little relationship to psychometric validity. To demonstrate *construct validity*, that is, that a measure reflects the ability to recognize facial expressions, a more complex validation procedure is necessary. The investigator subjects the instrument to a series of experiments in which the ideas underlying the measure and the measure itself are subjected to scrutiny and the possibility of rejection. Attempts have been made to describe and label some of the levels at which such scrutiny is undertaken. One of the more useful is the test validation paradigm suggested by Nunnally (1967). This paradigm was modified by O'Sullivan and Hager (1980) for a review of person perception measures, and this modification will be used to organize this discussion. In this model, three aspects of validation are differentiated: (1) conceptualization; (2) reification; and (3) elaboration. These aspects, or stages, will be discussed separately and sequentially, although the validation of an instrument may occur at all three stages simultaneously or the order in which different aspects of validation is achieved may vary.

11.4. Stage one: conceptualization

The conceptualization phase of test validation is frequently overlooked. In establishing test validity, the researcher's first responsibility is to define clearly the construct or constructs of interest lexically, logically, and methodologically. In lexically clarifying ideas or constructs, a clear terminology must be provided. In logically clarifying ideas, conceptual linkage to existing or new theory must be indicated and elaborated. Further, the relationship of the measures to the construct must be clarified. In methodologically clarifying the construct, alternative methods of measuring it must be provided and similarities and differences with existing measures indicated.

An evaluation of the adequacy of the conceptualization phase is primarily nonstatistical. It involves evaluating the completeness, coherence, and complexity of the proposed construct as well as a judgment about the likelihood that a proposed measure or measures will reflect that construct. Eventually, however, the value of a construct and its measures is tested statistically in studies at the reification and elaboration stages.

In discussing the conceptualization of the eight measures summarized in Table 11.1, the explanations of the measures' creators are relied on where available. Frequently, such conceptualizations are incomplete or unclear. In these instances, an evaluation of the implied construct and its measures is based on examination of the test and what is known from studies with it.

Lexical distinctions

In describing a construct, it is essential to be clear about the terms used in naming it. A variety of terms have been used to describe the ability to recognize emotions and it is unclear whether similar constructs are intended by these different terms or whether different terms reflect different constructs. In the literature, the term *decoding facial expression* is used frequently. *To decode* means to "convert from code into ordinary language; to identify the constituent significant elements" (*Webster's Third New International Dictionary, decode*). This definition, when applied to the recognition of facial expressions, implies that there is an underlying code of the face. This may not be meant by those who use this term, but the issue is unclear.

Other terms in the domain include *receiving ability*, as in the Communication of Affect Receiving Ability Test (CARAT) and *sensitivity*, as in the Profile of Nonverbal Sensitivity (PONS). In common parlance, *receiving* is used to mean acting "as a container or receptacle for." In information theory, *receiving* has another, though more technical, definition. Which usage is intended by CARAT's creator is unclear. *Sensitivity* is defined as "the capacity of a person to respond emotionally to changes in his interpersonal or social relationships" (*Webster's Third New International Dictionary, sensitivity*). The elements of emotional response and social change contained in this definition may or may not be what is intended by the creators of PONS.

Both *receiving* and *sensitivity* are different from terms like *recognize*, *interpret*, and *judge*, which are often used as synonyms for them. *Recognize* is defined as "to recall knowledge of; make out as or perceive to be something previously known" (*Webster's Third New International Dictionary, recognize*). Terms such as *interpret* or *judge* are close in meaning to *recognize* but connote more complex intellectual processes.

Depending on what the test creator intends to measure, one or more of these terms may be appropriate. The exact sense in which a particular term is used, however, is rarely clarified. One of the few exceptions is the work of O'Sullivan et al. (1965), whose terminology, generated by Guilford's Structure of Intellect model, is precise, although unfamiliar. (Faces, for example, is intended to assess "cognition of behavioral units"; Social Relations measures "cognition of behavioral relations.")

At a lexical level, then, the domain is cluttered with a variety of terms ranging from the indefinite (e.g., *receiving*) to the recondite (e.g., *cognition of behavioral units*). For the purposes of this chapter, all the measures are presumed to be attempts to assess the ability to recognize facially expressed emotional behavior. Some test creators might argue about the inclusion of their measure in such a category. For example, PONS is intended to measure sensitivity to nonverbal communications of various sorts. In this chapter, however, only the Face Alone score from this measure will be discussed. Others might argue with the term *ability*, feeling that it implies too much cognitive processing. Certainly, under-standing facial expression can occur at a nonsemantic, kinesthetic level (Miller, Levine, & Mirsky, 1973), as occurs with animals, or in an empa-thetic response, as occurs with people (Lipps, cited in Taguiri, 1968). In the measures we are considering, however, the nature of the tasks de-mands cognitive processing. An item for which there is a right answer implies that an ability is involved in recognizing or generating that right answer. Recognizing facial expressions in social interactions may involve functions other than abilities, such as personality traits and mood states. As operationalized in the eight measures we are considering, ability is certainly involved. The ability, however, is probably what has been called social intelligence rather than verbal or general intelligence.

Logical distinctions

The particular label to be applied to a construct (i.e., the lexical distinc-tion) may be the last decision made. Early decisions include determining exactly what one intends to measure. Intrinsic to the logical explanation of one's construct is a consideration of the stimuli and responses used to measure it. Often researchers end up measuring what it is possible to measure and not what they want to measure. Availability of stimuli and economy of test format often decide the kind of test produced. Unfortu-nately, expedient decisions early in test development often cause years of wasted effort late in test development.

In the conceptualization phase of test validation, the test developers describe their constructs clearly and fully, if possible by referring to the writings of others. At this stage, the theoretical bases for the construct are clearly explained. Among the tests we are considering, the Primary Affect Measure, Faces, and Social Relations are adequate in this regard. The Primary Affect Measure was intended to measure the abilities to recognize specific affects and this effort was related to Tomkins's well-articulated theory of emotion. Faces and Social Relations were based on Guilford's detailed theory of human intelligence. The relationship of these tests to a theory of intelligence was explained; however, the rela-tionship with theories of emotion was only sketchily indicated.

Although the creators of PONS refer to a number of emotion theories in a footnote (Rosenthal et al., 1979, p. 29), the bases for selecting the particular dimensions used in their instrument (positive–negative and dominance–submission) are not clearly explained. In the case of BART, which has not been published as a test by Ekman and Friesen, its rationale is not readily available. Their work, however, owes much to Tomkins's theory of emotion as well as his Primary Affect Measure. The CARAT measure stems from a research program on communication skills in monkeys and its relation to a theory of human emotion has not been explicated.

In addition to clarifying constructs logically at a theoretical level, other, more specific aspects of the construct must be clarified conceptually before test construction begins: What kind of ability is being measured? What stimulus characteristics are appropriate for the intended construct? What kind of response alternatives relate logically to the intended construct? These aspects of conceptual clarification will be discussed in the following sections.

General ability versus specific abilities

A major distinction at the logical level is whether the construct of interest involves a general ability or a set of specific abilities. If the hypothesis is that there is a general ability to recognize all kinds of facial expressions of emotion, the type of measures produced will be different than if the hypothesis is that there is differential accuracy depending on the particular emotions involved. Tomkins and McCarter are quite explicit in their attempt to measure differential accuracy, and the Primary Affect Measure, with its separate scores for each emotion and no total score, reflects this intent well. Ekman and Friesen also intended to measure differential accuracy in recognizing different emotions, and BART has both affect-specific scores and a total score. The total score has been used (O'Sullivan, Micklewright, Ekman, Jones, and Friesen, 1975), to demonstrate the relative ineffectiveness of a total score when compared with affect-specific scores. At a conceptual level, the creators of both the Primary Affect Measure and BART argue well for the logical distinctions on which their tests are based, referring to both emotion theory and field and laboratory work to buttress their arguments.

At the other end of the general–specific continuum are those test creators, such as O'Sullivan and her colleagues, whose intention was to measure a general ability to recognize facially expressed emotion. The O'Sullivan and Guilford tests (Faces and Social Relations) were based on a hypothesis of social intelligence that includes more than the ability to recognize emotion. The tests were designed to reflect the understanding of the thoughts, feelings, and intentions of other persons. In actuality, most of the stimuli are affective ones. The behavioral cognition tests are relatively early measures in this area. Although some effort was made to represent a variety of emotions and to reference the emotion theories available at the time that the tests were produced, this was not done systematically and no subscores are provided for different affects. These tests may reflect the constructs suggested by Guilford's model of intelligence, but they need further work at the conceptualization level if they are to be considered adequate measures of the ability to recognize facial expression.

The status of CARAT and PONS with respect to their positions on the logical continuum of general versus specific abilities is less clear. In CARAT, two separate scores are provided. The first yields a total accuracy score based on guessing correctly which of four types of slides the stimulus person is watching. Because this first score is a total accuracy score (over the 32 items of the test), it implies an attempt to measure a general ability to recognize facial expressions of emotion. On the other hand, four different types of slides are shown to the target person, suggesting that different emotional responses were expected to the slides. (Otherwise, what is the reason for selecting these four types of slides rather than some other ones?) If the four types of slides elicit different emotional facial behaviors, why are four different accuracy scores not reported? The second score for CARAT is the correlation between the pleasantness ratings of the target person and the pleasantness ratings of the observer. The relevance of pleasantness–unpleasantness in the affect domain is unexplained by Buck, its existence as a construct in the research of others is unreferenced, and the manner in which the stimuli of CARAT represent or sample this domain is unclarified. Further, the relationship of this second (pleasantness) score to the first (accuracy) score is unclear. Are they both measures of the same general ability or do they reflect two different specific abilities? The status of CARAT with respect to its position on the general–specific continuum is thus difficult to determine.

The position of PONS with respect to what it is measuring in the affect domain is also unclear. Because only a single score is given for each of the channels, e.g., Face Alone, it would seem that the PONS creators are hypothesizing a general ability to recognize emotion in each channel across all emotions sampled. In constructing PONS, they attempted to represent three dimensions in their stimuli: pleasant–unpleasant, dominance–submission, and intensity. As previously mentioned, a footnote containing 21 references is the only theoretical justification provided for these dimensions. Many of those referenced represent different points of view about emotion theory. Because all are included in the same footnote, it is unclear to which theories the PONS creators subscribe and to which they do not. At some point, intensity as a dimension of interest was dropped and not discussed further. Because intensity is an affect dimension that was found in a number of emotion studies (see Table 3.4) and dominance–submission was not, it is unclear why it was dropped from the PONS data analysis. Although the PONS creators do analyze their instrument in terms of pleasantness-unpleasantness and dominance–submission to demonstrate the validity of calling their stimuli by those names, they do not assign scores to individuals on these dimensions. Therefore, the relevance of these dimensions to differences in how people perceive facial expressions of others, as well as the relevance of these dimensions to the test creators' conception of what is involved in recognizing facial expressions of emotion, is unclear.

At a logical level, then, half of the measures discussed (the exceptions being the Primary Affect Measure, BART, and the behavioral cognition measures) are deficient in clarifying whether they are measures of a general recognition ability or measures of affect specific recognition abilities. Further, three-fourths of the measures (the exceptions being BART and the Primary Affect Measure) are inadequate in specifying the bases for sampling the affect domain.

Stimulus characteristics

In addition to clarifying whether general or specific abilities are hypothesized, test constructors must consider the appropriateness of their stimuli for the construct of interest. In this domain a great deal of attention has been paid to certain kinds of stimulus characteristics, such as whether expressions are posed or spontaneous. Less attention has been given to the adequacy of the stimuli as reflections of the intended construct. In this section these issues will be considered along with such questions as: Does the face show emotion? Should the facial expression be posed or spontaneous? Should the face be schematic or realistic? What difficulty level is appropriate? How are facial expressions sampled? What is the effect of lip movements on facial expressions of emotion?

Facial Emotion. If a measure is to assess the ability to recognize facial expressions relevant to emotion, the stimuli presented to observers should contain facial expressions of emotion. This is not always the case. The face contains information other than that pertaining to emotion (Ekman,

1978, 1979). A photograph of a facial expression shows a person of recognizable age, sex, and condition of health. It is also likely that observers make inferences concerning social class, intelligence, marital status, and personality characteristics based on the hair style, skin color, attractiveness, age, sex, and other aspects of the facial configuration. The face, then, may occasion judgments about many aspects of the person in addition to what emotion is being expressed at a given moment.

The adequacy of a photograph in depicting emotion must be considered carefully (see Chapter 2). One accuracy criterion usually used is the emotion intended by the poser (as in PONS, Faces, the Rudolf sketches and the Primary Affect Measure). Another accuracy criterion is observers' ratings of the emotion in the stimulus (as in BART, PONS, the Buzby measure using the Piderit profile, and the Primary Affect Measure). These procedures suffer from several deficiencies:

1. The poser may not succeed in showing the desired emotion.
2. The poser may exhibit facial expressions that are not truly expressions of emotion, although they may be easily identified within a culture. For example, lowered eyelids may frequently be identified as love within a culture, but it is unlikely that love is universally expressed by lowered eyelids.
3. The observers may agree in their ratings because of similarity in their responses, including their agreement about stereotypic depictions of emotion, or response biases based on their similarity with one another or the stimulus person.

The question of what is in the face (i.e., emotion or other relevant information) is of particular importance with the stimuli used in CARAT. It is presumed, not demonstrated, that the stimulus persons in this test show facial affect cues while watching slides. This may not be the case. Merely looking at slides may not be a sufficient stimulus to rouse emotion. Harper, Wiens, and Matarazzo (1979), using a methodology similar to CARAT, improved Buck's design by demonstrating that observers do assign different affect labels to different slides. The question still remains, however, as to whether the slides actually arouse emotions in those viewing them similar to the emotions they depict. Further, there is no evidence that even if viewers are affectively aroused, a corresponding facial expression will be shown. People may be affectively aroused and not show it on their faces. Buck, Baron, Goodman, & Shapiro (1980), using Newtson's unitization technique, demonstrated that something discernibly different occurs during the CARAT items. Whether this "something" is emotion was not addressed by Buck and co-workers. Without some kind of facial measurement (Ekman & Friesen, 1978 and Chapter 9) to demonstrate that the stimulus faces contain affective cues, it cannot be assumed that differences in accuracy on this test reflect differences in the ability to recognize emotion. Observers may arrive at the correct answer by means of stereotypic judgments based on the age, sex, or physiognomy of the face, through the use of response sets such as assumed similarity (Cline, 1964; Cronbach, 1955) or through nonemotional facial cues related to facial tonus, lip movements, or attempts to mask or control emotion.

Posed versus spontaneous expressions. In selecting facial stimuli, the issue of whether to use posed or spontaneous expressions has been hotly debated. Experimentalists and most emotion theorists argue that spontaneous expressions are the only "true" expressions of facial emotion and therefore such stimuli are the only ones of merit. Spontaneous facial expressions present many problems, however. Not all people express emotion equally well; many individuals have idiosyncratic methods of expressing emotion as a result of personal, familial, or culturally learned display rules (see Chapter 7). Situations in which spontaneous facial expressions are usually recorded (e.g., the laboratory) are often unusual and artificial. If the stimulus person is aware of being photographed, facial expressions may not be spontaneous (see Chapter 7). Even if the stimulus person is unaware of being photographed, the laboratory situation may not encourage natural or usual emotional response. In interacting with scientists or other authorities, subjects will attempt to act in appropriate ways (Milgram, 1974; Rosenthal, 1966) so that emotion expression may be masked or controlled. Additionally, there are only a relatively few universal emotions and only some of these can be ethically stimulated in the laboratory. The base rate of naturally occurring, fully articulated expressions of basic emotions is so low that obtaining clear depictions of them is probably an impossible task. (Of the tests being discussed, only CARAT uses unposed facial expressions, and it is unclear whether its facial expressions are affective in nature.) For all these reasons, the use of only spontaneous expressions of emotion is neither desirable nor likely. Another alternative, posed expressions, has much to recommend it, provided certain safeguards are followed. Increased knowledge about the face, based in large part on observation of spontaneous, naturally occurring facial expressions, has made possible a number of methods of measuring the face (Ekman, 1982). These measurement techniques can be used to ascertain whether or not emotional facial behavior has occurred and what emotion is shown in a given photograph. Such facial scoring provides a kind of stimulus criterion validity that is important in this area (Archer & Akert, 1977). Additionally, posers can be instructed, not to act or pose a specific emotion, but rather to move certain muscles so as to effect the desired emotional expression. In this way, experimental control may be exerted on the stimuli and the relationship between the elements of the facial expression and the responses of observers may be analyzed and used as a guide in item selection.

Schematic versus realistic faces. Earlier (Chapter 2) it was argued that drawings or other representations of human faces should not be used in experimental studies of human facial emotion. In constructing individual difference measures, another point of view may be espoused. General laws of facial affect are best sought with lifelike stimuli, and in pursuing this goal, facial photographs and motion pictures of faces are preferable. In validating tests, however, a variety of measures is necessary. Once the elements of facial affect displays have been isolated in laboratory and field work using the most realistic stimuli possible, then approximations of these stimuli may be used to provide the variety in testing forms necessary for construct validation. If a test with photographed faces correlates highly with a test of schematic faces, the investigator may have more confidence that what is reflected in both tests is the ability to recognize faces, not merely the ability to recognize photographed faces. For this reason, in test construction, schematic faces (such as those used in the Piderit profile or in Social Relations) should not be discarded out of hand but should be examined in conjunction with more immediately appealing and realistic-seeming faces such as those in PONS, CARAT, BART, or the Primary Affect Measure. The degree of abstraction of the schematic faces should also be considered. Such faces may vary from the highly abstract, such as those used in Social Relations (see Figure 11.1), to the relatively realistic depictions of the Rudolf series. They may also be moderate in degree of abstraction, such as the schematized profile of the Piderit series or the front-face version of the Piderit model suggested by Guilford and Wilke (1930) and used by Guilford and his students (Hendricks, Guiford, & Hoepfner, 1969) 40 years later.

Difficulty level. Another aspect of selecting photographs for use in an individual differences measure is the difficulty level of the emotion expressed. Many studies indicate that clear, unambiguous expressions of basic human emotions such as happiness, sorrow, anger, and fear are recognized by most of the people rating them regardless of the culture of the observers or the stimulus persons (see Chapter 7). When stimuli are this "easy" to recognize, they are useless in an individual differences test. Everyone who takes such a test will score highly and no discrimination among test takers will be possible. If an attempt is made to increase the difficulty of the emotion shown by making it more subtle or more complex, often there is no agreement among judges that the "subtle" emotion is there. What results, instead, are photographs showing facial expressions idiosyncratic to the person depicted.

An ingenious solution to this problem was tried by Ekman and Friesen with BART. The basic stimuli of BART are easily recognized photographs. Ekman and Friesen manipulated the difficulty of the items by presenting them very rapidly (1/60th of a second) using tachistoscopic presentation. A similar attempt to manipulate stimulus difficulty level is the 2-second presentation of the PONS faces. At longer exposure times, the PONS creators found that the facial expressions were too easily identified, resulting in inadequate score variance.

Context. It is impossible to present people without a context. Feleky (1914), in her pioneering work, was photographed wearing a variety of clothing and positioned vis-à-vis the camera in a variety of body and head tilt positions. All the variations other than the facial expressions are extraneous to the task of recognizing facial emotion and a potential source of error variance in the test scores. Frois-Wittmann (1930), whose photographs are used in Faces, attempted to solve this limitation by photographing himself without visible clothing. A seemingly naked man, however, provides yet another and potentially confounding context for interpreting a given facial expression. An angry face on a clothed man might be seen as less intense than an angry face on a naked one, or vice versa. Similarly, the impact of differently colored backgrounds needs to be assessed. Silverthorne, Gibson, Micklewright, & O'Connell (1975), for example, demonstrated that facial expressions are labeled differently depending on the background color against which they are shown.

Sampling. In selecting stimuli for a test, another concern is the adequacy of the sampling (see Chapter 2). If only a single stimulus person is shown (as in Faces, PONS, and the Rudolf series), the test is necessarily limited, both by the ability of that stimulus person to express all emotions equally well and by the idiosyncratic responses of observers to that particular stimulus person. If the same person is shown repeatedly, it is likely that a gestalt of that person may build up in the minds of observers.

Insofar as this gestalt is correct, it will increase an observer's score; insofar as it is incorrect, it will decrease an observer's score. The capacity to form a correct gestalt of another person may be an important social skill. In the context of measuring accuracy in judging facial expressions of emotion, however, it is a confounding variable. In a related vein, most current psychometric theories presume that each item is an independent measure of the construct of interest. Using the same stimulus person repeatedly lessens the likelihood of such independence. It is preferable to sample persons as well as emotions.

Rosenthal (1982) argued that because the reliability of scores based on decoding a single encoder "sending" many scenes (as in PONS) is similar to the reliability of many encoders sending the same scene, it matters little whether one poser or many posers is used. Rosenthal's analysis suffers from a logical flaw. Demonstrating that two scores have the same reliability does not constitute proof that they sample or measure the same construct. For example, height and weight have similarly high levels of reliability. They are not the same construct. The issue is not whether the same poser is more or less reliable than many posers but whether the domain of interest, that of recognizing facial expressions, is well sampled.

Speech movements. Another aspect of selecting stimuli is whether the stimuli include speech-related actions. Both CARAT and PONS, for example, use moving faces, filmed during the occurrence of speech. In addition to the possible confounding of lip reading, further difficulties are that the same muscles are used in speech as in some facial affect configurations and that some conversational signals, such as brow raisings and lowerings, also occur in facial emotions (Ekman, 1979). This may make recognition of emotion cues more difficult or may require different skills than recognizing emotional cues with no other moving signals on the face. Recognizing emotion as it occurs during speech may be a valuable social skill; recognizing emotion as it occurs in a face with moving lips and no audible speech is a skill of value to deaf people. It may have no generalizability of value for those with normal hearing. Recognizing emotional cues during speech may require different skills than recognizing emotional cues with no other moving signals on the face.

Response alternatives

Although stimulus characteristics are important to consider in devising a measure, the response alternatives to be used must also be examined carefully to ensure that they reflect the construct of interest. The entire testing experience of the test taker, stimulus and response, must be scrutinized. A particular photograph may constitute a difficult or an easy item, depending on what the test taker is asked about it. For example, if a test taker is shown a photograph of a smiling face and then is asked whether it shows happiness or anger, the item is an easy one. If the test taker is shown the same photograph and then asked whether it shows contentment or satisfaction, the task is far more difficult. The difficulty lies not in the facial expression (the stimulus), which is simple in itself, but rather in the semantically subtle distinction between contentment and satisfaction (the response).

Empirical evidence regarding the impact of the response alternative in recognizing facial expressions can be found in two distinct lines of inquiry. Studies of hemispheric specialization (Gazzaniga, 1970) lend support to the contention that different intellectual processes may be involved in different identification techniques: verbal labeling seems to be a left hemisphere function, while photograph or figure matching seems to be a right hemisphere function. Extrapolating from these studies of hemispheric specialization to measures of recognizing facial expressions, two different results might be expected: when verbal labels are used to describe facial expressions (as in BART, the Rudolf and Piderit series, CARAT, and the Primary Affect Measure), individuals with intact left hemispheres are likely to be superior; when a nonverbal task like facial matching is used (as in Faces), individuals with intact right hemispheres are more likely to be superior.

A second source of evidence may be found in the results of factor analytic studies. O'Sullivan and Guilford (1975) found that behavioral cognition tests using words were more likely to stress verbal intelligence factors than tests using only nonverbal stimuli (i.e., photographs, drawings, cartoons, or sounds), which were more likely to define other than verbal factors. A test like Faces, in which the response involves matching photographs, might tap the same general ability domain as tests requiring the use of verbal labels, such as BART or the Primary Affect Measure, but other sources of variance are also involved.

In addition to the distinction between verbal and nonverbal response modes, the kind of verbal response requested will influence the kind of ability measured. In CARAT, one of the two scores is based on the test taker's accuracy in guessing which of four slide types the stimulus person is watching. Buck presumes that "receiving" the affect message is sufficient information to enable judges to determine which slide is being watched. Different people, however, react differently to the same stimuli. Selecting which slide is being watched probably involves not only interpreting facial expressions of emotion (the intended aim of the measure) but also determining what kind of stimulus would produce such an expression in this type of person. This task is far more complicated than merely "receiving affect," the construct of interest. Although CARAT may reflect important social skills, the complexity of its response task would suggest that interpreting facial expressions of emotion is a small part of what it measures.

Social Relations and PONS are similar to one another in that relatively simple nonverbal stimuli are presented and the understanding of these stimuli is tested by asking that one of several verbal statements be chosen. In PONS, the task is to choose a description of a social situation such as "getting a divorce" or "comforting a lost child." Choosing the correct answer probably entails not only recognition of the given facial expression (the construct of interest) but also some knowledge of what is an appropriate facial expression in a given social situation. Fields and O'Sullivan (1976) found that PONS did not correlate significantly with either BART or behavioral cognition tests emphasizing recognition of faces or hand gestures but did correlate significantly with a cartoon test based on making predictions about what is culturally appropriate in middle-class America. Similarly, Rosenthal et al. (1979) showed that PONS scores for different cultural groups increase with increasing similarity of the groups' languages and customs to those of the United States. Although they interpret this finding as evidence for the cultural relativity of nonverbal messages, it could equally well indicate that PONS scores reflect an understanding of what behaviors are culturally appropriate in certain situations. Although PONS may measure social intelligence, social ability, or other person-perception skills, it is doubtful that it is a test primarily of sensitivity to nonverbal cues.

In Social Relations (see Figure 11.1), the test task is even more complicated than in PONS. In choosing the correct alternative statement, the test taker must consider two facial expressions at the same time, as well as their interactive effect on one another. This complicated judgment is far removed from the simple verbal labeling used in most tests of the ability to recognize facial expression. At this point, it is premature to say whether tasks like those in Social Relations and PONS reflect how people process facial expressions in ordinary social exchange. But it is essential that test makers and test users be aware that their test stimuli are not the only nor necessarily the most important aspect of their test (see Table 11.1). The test task is determined by both the stimulus and the response.

Methodological distinctions

After clarifying the construct, logically, the test creator then produces or suggests several alternative measures for it. By specifying differing measurement techniques, an investigator demonstrates the generality of the construct beyond a single method. If only a single measure of a construct is available, it is unclear whether score variance is specific to that set of observations or will permit inferences about a more general construct, inferences that can be derived independently from other measures and other kinds of observations.

In ordinary test construction practice, the researcher conceives and produces several different methods or tests that are expected to measure the same construct. O'Sullivan and her colleagues (1965) hypothesized that, although both Faces and Social Relations used facial affective stimuli, each measured a different ability because of the different tasks the observer had to perform. They provided three additional tests of the ability hypothesized to be measured by Faces and two additional tests of the ability presumed to be measured by Social Relations. These two clusters of tests did indeed load on separate factors, providing some support for their constructs over and above the scores of a single test (Cronbach, 1970). None of the other test creators have provided alternative measures of their constructs.

Alternatively, a researcher can indicate techniques developed by others that might measure the same construct. Most of the investigators whose techniques are reviewed here did not indicate other researchers' measures that might be alternatives to their own. This practice highlights the different approaches to test construction taken by experimentalists and psychometricians. By analogy, if an experimentalist developed the Wechsler Adult Intelligence Scale, no mention would have been made of the earlier, related Stanford–Binet.

A third approach to specifying alternative measures is to elicit different responses to the same stimulus set. Buck (1976), for example, used a single set of stimuli to generate two decoding accuracy scores. If these scores are measures of the same construct, they should correlate with one another. If they are measures of different constructs, as Buck, Savin, Miller, and Caul (1972) suggest, validity must be established for each score separately in the same manner as for the whole test. The current status of these scores as measures of the same or different constructs is unclear. Buck (1976) reported low correlations between the two scores (about .30) for a precursor of CARAT, but nothing on CARAT itelf. The PONS creators (Rosenthal et al., 1979) examined relationships among longer and shorter versions of their measure and among variations in stimulus presentation. These studies, however, do not seem motivated by the need to clarify underlying constructs because suggestions for other methods of measurement did not follow from them.

A fourth approach to specifying alternative measures concerns the items of a single test. In providing different items for a test, a test constructor implies that each item is an alternative measure of the construct. Therefore, the items of a test measuring a single construct should be highly correlated with one another. This relationship among the items of a test is known as the measure's *internal consistency*. Although usually used to describe a measure's reliability, an internal consistency coefficient may also be regarded as evidence of validity insofar as it reveals whether the items of a test are measuring the same construct. Although high internal consistency is neither a necessary nor sufficient demonstration of validity, low internal consistency undermines the presumption that a single construct is being measured.

In summary, most of the facial expression tests are inadequate in the conceptualization phase of test validation. Lexically, distinctions are largely absent. Logically, distinctions are poorly or incompletely made. (With the exception of BART and the Primary Affect Measure, the tests lack an adequate theoretical rationale relative to a theory of emotion or the bases on which stimuli or responses were chosen.) Methodologically, all the instruments, except the behavioral cognition measures, lack alternative ways of measuring their construct.

11.5. Stage two: reification

The second phase of test validation involves demonstrating empirically that different measures of the construct are significantly correlated with one another, i.e., have congruent validity. This phase has been termed *reification* because, without demonstrating congruence of measures presumed to measure the same construct, it is unclear whether a stable, measurable construct exists. High correlations among differing measures of the same construct provide some evidence that the construct does in fact exist. In this sense the construct is reified. It is reflected in the scores of its correlated measures. (In the conceptualization stage, alternative measures are described. In the reification stage, the actual correlations among measures are obtained.)

Despite the importance of this step in validating a test, few investigators perform it. Faces and Social Relations were correlated with other tests from the Guilford laboratory and the factor analytic relationships among these measures were replicated in a number of studies in the United States (Hendricks et al., 1969; Tenopyr, 1967) and Europe, (Jung, 1972; Rombouts, 1978). The historical tests of Langfeld and Buzby, as well as the Primary Affect Measure, have no reported evidence of congruent validity.

A few studies did examine the relationships among PONS, CARAT, and some behavioral cognition tests other than Faces and Social Relations. These studies were disappointing in terms of providing congruent validity for the tests of recognizing facial expressions of emotion. Harper et al. (1979) found no significant correlation between their CARAT-like decoding tasks and some behavioral cognition tests other than Faces and Social Relations. Fields and O'Sullivan (1976) examined the relationships among BART, four behavioral cognition tests, PONS, SIT (Archer & Akert, 1977), and Chapin's Social Insight Test (Gough, 1965). Except for the correlations among the behavioral cognition tests, only one other significant correlation was found. Buck reported no congruent validity studies with CARAT. The creators of PONS (Rosenthal et al., 1979) report the correlations of total PONS scores with four nonverbal decoding tasks including CARAT, CARAT-like measures, and judgment of still photographs. Their conclusions regarding these studies are: "In summary, the median correlation of the PONS total with the four other measures of nonverbal decoding for adults was .28" (p. 244). This conclusion, although technically accurate, does not indicate the range of correlations, from -.01 to .58. This variability may be caused by the unreliability of the other measures, the differences in the constructs measured, the differences in how well the same construct is assessed, or some combination of these factors.

These congruent validity studies with PONS refer to correlations obtained with the total PONS, not the Face Alone score. No studies have been reported concerning the validity of the channel scores on this measure. The original purpose of PONS was to provide a measure that would yield different channel scores: for the face alone, the body alone, etc. When the 11 "channels" of PONS are factor analyzed, however, only four factors result, and the PONS creators describe one of these as a "decoding facial cues" factor (Rosenthal et al., 1979, p. 89). This may be misleading because the scores correlating highest with this factor involve the full figure with Face Alone correlating fifth highest. Because Face Alone stimuli are part of the Full Figure stimuli, it seems more parsimonious to regard this as a Full Figure factor to which reading the face contributes, not the other way around. On this basis, the utility of the PONS Face Alone score as a test of recognizing facial expression of emotion must be questioned.

Even the congruent validity of scores derived from the same test has been inadequately examined and reported. For example, as already noted, only a low correlation between two subscores of CARAT was reported. Because this finding was not amplified by Buck, it is unclear whether or not this is desirable in terms of his construct conceptualization.

The importance of obtaining congruent validity on seemingly similar measures is well illustrated in a study by Mullaney (Pers. comm.). Four groups of 20 to 30 police trainees labeled rapidly presented facial expressions of emotion (a task based on BART procedures). In each group, those with the two highest and two lowest scores were chosen as posers of similar facial expressions, which were videotaped. The same groups of trainees then judged the poses of their classmates. The scores on this test showed either a zero or a negative correlation with scores on the briefly presented slides. In both tests, the task was similar, labeling facial affect, but differences in method (e.g., manner of stimulus presentation, accuracy of the emotions depicted, and acquaintance with the stimulus persons) significantly changed the results.

11.6. Stage three: elaboration

In the conceptualization phase of test validation, the researcher defines the construct and specifies its measures. In the reification stage, congruence among alternative measures is sought. In the elaboration stage, the construct of interest is more fully examined and its meaning explored through consideration of its relationships with other constructs. The elaboration stage proceeds along two fronts. In one, the researcher seeks to demonstrate discriminant validity, to show that this construct and its measures is different from other measures and constructs in predicted ways. The other aspect of elaboration validation is to demonstrate convergent validity, that is, to show that the construct of interest and its measures is positively related to similar or theoretically relevant constructs.

Discriminant validity

An important achievement in discriminant validity is the demonstration that the measurement of the ability to recognize facial expressions of emotion is more than the measurement of general intellectual or verbal ability. Rosenthal and his colleagues (1979) accomplished this by finding relatively low median correlations between PONS total score and various measures of intellectual ability. Similarly, a number of researchers (i.e., O'Sullivan & Guilford, 1975; Rombouts, 1978) showed that Faces and Social Relations define unique factors not related to factors defined by verbal intelligence tests or tests of the ability to understand figural, spatial, or artistic material.

A third example of the search for discriminant validity may be found in the development of BART. In studies with an early version of BART, Ekman and Friesen (Pers. comm.) found that the measure correlated significantly with a measure of tachistoscopic proficiency. Because tachistoscopic proficiency was a confounding variable for the construct of interest, the BART authors devised the Facial Interpretation Task (FIT). Scores from this separately administered test were used to correct BART scores statistically. Following this procedure, the correlation with tachistoscopic proficiency dropped to zero.

A fourth example of discriminant validity would consist of showing that subscores of a test, intended to measure different constructs, are in fact not highly correlated with one another. If the two CARAT subscores are intended as measures of different constructs, then their low intercorrelation is evidence of this. If they are intended to be alternate measures of a general decoding ability, then their low intercorrelation does not support that hypothesis. Similarly, if PONS subscores are to be used as scores of different channels, then a factor defined by several supposedly different channel scores does not provide the requisite discriminant validity.

Convergent validity

Most validity studies emphasize the second aspect of elaboration validation, convergent validity, in which correlations with related variables are sought or the predicted effects of experimental treatments are examined.

Convergent validity differs from congruent validity in that measures of related, but different, constructs are examined. In the reification stage, two measures of the ability to recognize facial expressions are correlated to determine their similarity. In the elaboration phase, a test of the ability to recognize facial expressions of emotion might be correlated with a measure of another construct, such as counselor effectiveness. By examining the relationships among measures of facial expression recognition and measures of counselor effectiveness, the elements similar to both constructs may be elaborated and better understood. In the reification stage, congruent validity refers to the coherence of measures of the same construct (i.e., recognizing facial expressions of emotion). In the elaboration stage, convergent validity refers to the coherence of theoretically or logically related, but different, constructs.

Without evidence of conceptualization or reification validation, validation efforts made exclusively at the elaboration stage may be misleading. D.T. Campbell and Fiske (1959) wrote, "Before one can test the relationships between a specific trait and other traits, one must have some confidence in one's measure of that trait" (p. 100). If an instrument has no demonstrated relationship with a construct, correlations of such an instrument can be interpreted only cautiously and with great difficulty.

A recent example of interpreting elaboration validation in the absence of conceptualization or reification validation was found in a study by Sabatelli, Buck, and Dreyer (1980). Their hypothesis was that there is differential accuracy in recognizing emotions expressed by strangers (i.e., as in CARAT) and by friends (i.e., dating partners in a CARAT-like experimental situation). Their hypothesis was not supported. As a failure to establish convergent validity for CARAT, this study is worth reporting. As a test of the stated hypothesis, however, the study is misleading. Because there is no evidence at the conceptualization or reification stage that CARAT measures the ability to recognize facial expressions of emotion, there is no real test of the stated hypothesis. The results obtained might be a result of a deficiency in the hypothesis or a deficiency in measuring either of the variables involved in it.

Convergent relationships among measures of different constructs may be examined in two ways: (1) relationships among constructs may be predicted a priori or (2) a variety of measures may be intercorrelated without guiding theory. Relationships discovered using the second approach must be replicated and tied to explanatory concepts if they are to be used as validity evidence.

Several variables and paradigms can be used in elaboration validation. Gender has frequently been related to the ability to recognize facial expressions of emotion (Hall, 1978). As evidence of construct validity, however, gender differences are unsatisfactory. The sexes differ in many regards and a correlated measure could be reflecting any of these differences and not the construct of interest. An examination of why the sexes differ on a particular measure might contribute to validating and illuminating the construct (Westbrook, 1974), but this is rarely done.

Groups with contrasting characteristics have also been used as a validating criterion for some measures. Shannon (1970) found predicted differences in BART scores among schizophrenic, depressed, and nonpsychiatric patients. The PONS measure was extensively studied using the contrasting groups approach. The groups examined by the PONS creators include: mothers of preverbal children versus nonmothers of the same age; friends and acquaintances of the PONS stimulus person versus strangers; alcoholics and other psychiatric patients versus normal people; and deaf and blind people versus nonhandicapped individuals. In a related vein, the differing total PONS scores of various occupational groups were examined, although these studies were concerned with the validity of the total PONS score and not the Face Alone score, which is the focus of this chapter.

Personality correlates are often studied, but only rarely have significant findings resulted. An ill-advised but common practice has been to report significant correlations based on a single small sample (e.g., Harper et al., 1979). Correlations in small samples ($N < 30$) present a number of problems. The impact of a single deviant score is great; score distributions depart markedly from normality; the distribution of the variables correlated is often asymmetrical; the range of score variation in the population is usually not reflected in the sample; the central tendency of distributions may vary from sample to sample; and the impact of measurement error is increased. Post hoc personality correlates based on small samples should be replicated before they are reported or used as validity evidence.

Physiological correlates (e.g., GSR and heart rate) were also explored (Buck et al., 1972; Lanzetta & Kleck, 1970), but relationships were not consistent. In part, this may reflect the low reliability of both the facial expression and the physiological measures and, in part, the lack of coherent theory surrounding such relationships. Additionally, the comments made about personality correlations with small samples apply to physiological correlations as well.

Ratings by self, friends, supervisors, teachers, etc., have been used as validation criteria in other fields of psychological testing for years. Among the facial expression tests, only PONS creators used this method of convergent validation, and as noted already, these studies were performed for the total PONS score, not for any of the channel scores. Some of the behavioral cognition measures had significant correlations with behavior ratings (Osipow & Walsh, 1973; O'Sullivan, Fields, & Carney, 1979; Shipe, Prato, Rosser, & Sidhu, 1976) but not the two tests considered in this chapter.

Experimental manipulation of conditions that influence the ability to recognize facial expressions is a compelling means of construct validation that is seldom used. Allport (1924) and Guilford (1929) demonstrated that instruction relevant to the testing materials increased scores on their measures. It is unclear whether an increase generally in the ability to recognize facial expressions resulted. Mann (Pers. comm.) examined the effects of training on a measure like BART, and Rosenthal and his colleagues (1979) examined the effects of both practice and training on total PONS scores. O'Sullivan et al. (1975) manipulated mood with alcohol and marijuana and studied the effect on BART scores. Such manipulations usually have the intrinsic merit of a previous empirical base or a theory-related prediction of the effect. As such, they are a preferred method of construct and instrument validation.

11.7. Reliability

In addition to demonstrating that a test measures what it is intended to measure (its validity), a test creator must demonstrate that the test is reliable, that its scores are consistent either over time, over parallel forms of the test, over parts of the test, or over items of the test. A test may be reliable and not valid. A person's weight may be measured quite reliably, but the validity of this score as a measure of intelligence is questionable. On the other hand, it is difficult for a test to be valid if it is not first reliable. A test that does not correlate with itself has little chance of correlating with other measures, which is important to establish its validity. Although many kinds of reliability coefficients have been proposed, only two general classes of reliability will be considered here: test–retest reliability and estimates of internal consistency or homogeneity.

Test–retest reliability

If a test–retest reliability coefficient is reported, the author is suggesting that an examinee's scores on the test should remain constant over time. With respect to the measures we are considering, this is tantamount to saying that the ability to recognize facial expressions of emotion is a trait ability not a state ability. Such may not be the case. Schiffenbauer (1974) and O'Sullivan and her colleagues (1975) found that scores in recognizing facial expressions were influenced by the emotional state of the examinee. Theoretically, mood is expected to vary over time. The reliability of a mood measure would not be assessed with a test–retest reliability coefficient. Insofar as mood affects scores on a facial expression measure, test–retest reliability is not the best coefficient to use. If test–retest reliability is thought to be important for theoretical purposes (i.e., to demonstrate that the ability is not merely state-dependent), then the mood of the subject should be measured on both testing occasions and its effect on the scores examined. Buck (1976) found that the pleasantness score on CARAT had a test–retest reliability of -.18. The test–retest reliability for the slide accuracy score on CARAT was at least moderate. This suggests that the pleasantness score is more susceptible to examinee's mood or to some other aspect of the examinee's functioning. In any event, this finding with CARAT highlights a possible difficulty in using test–retest reliability coefficients with facial expression measures.

Internal consistency

The second major class of reliability coefficients is estimates of internal consistency. The test creator attempts to show that different parts of the test are measuring the same construct. This is done by demonstrating that there is high correlation among the parts of the test. Several subtypes of internal consistency coefficients may be used. One type of internal consistency reliability, split-half reliability, can be determined if a test has separately administered and scored parts, for example, two halves. The scores on these halves may be correlated and then corrected for test length by the Spearman-Brown formula. (The Spearman-Brown extension, when used with split-half scores, is based on two premises: (1) the actual length of the test is twice as long as each half and (2) test length is positively related to reliability.) If no separately timed or administered parts are available, test halves may be "constructed" by scoring all the odd items of a test for an odd item score and all the even items for an even item score. Such "half" scores may also be correlated and extended by the Spearman-Brown formula to obtain an internal consistency reliability estimate.

A second set of internal consistency estimates are derived essentially by intercorrelating all possible split halves of items and adjusting the average intercorrelation obtained in this way for the number of items averaged over. Coefficient alpha and the Kuder–Richardson formula 20 (KR-20) are examples of this method. (Coefficient alpha is the more general formula because KR-20 can only be used when test items are scored dichotomously, as with right or wrong answers.) Although it has been done, alpha and KR-20 estimates should not be further extended by the Spearman–Brown formula. For example, the PONS Face Alone score has a reported "effective" reliability of .88. This is remarkably high for a 20-item test. It was obtained by extending the KR-20 reliability of the 20-item Face Alone score by the Spearman–Brown formula, as though it were based on 220 items. This would be appropriate if the Face Alone score contained 220 items, the number of items in the total PONS. Since the Face Alone score is not based on 220 items, but only 20, its actual internal consistency reliability is closer to .40 than to .88.

A third technique for determining internal consistency reliability uses analysis of variance procedures. This is sometimes called *Hoyt reliability*. The variance in scores resulting from differences among examinees minus an error term, such as the interaction between examinees and items, is divided by the error term. This ratio is interpreted like other internal consistency coefficients, although the actual numerical value of the coefficients will vary. Analysis of variance procedures for determining reliability offer the advantage of specifying the sources of variance, whether from examinees, items, administration, or interactions of these variables.

One cannot refer to *the* reliability of a given measure. A test creator presents reliability estimates for a test. Such estimates will vary from subject group to subject group, from experimental condition to experimental condition. If the range of the estimates provided is relatively narrow and relatively high, i.e., coefficients about .70, then a test user may feel some confidence regarding the reliability of such scores when used in other situations with other subjects.

Test length

The number of items in a test bears a direct relationship to its reliability. If one can assume that all the items of a test sample the same domain of behavior, the longer the test, the more reliable it will be. This relationship is the basis for the Spearman–Brown extension mentioned earlier. As can be seen in Table 11.1, most of the facial expression measures contain relatively few items. Even tests with a moderately large number of items (i.e., 25 or more) are usually subdivided so that subscores for separate affects are based on as few as 7 items. The likelihood is low that a small number of items chosen from the large array possible will be highly redundant with one another. It is not surprising, therefore, that the reliabilities of the resulting instruments are, for the most part, too low for practical use.

Reliabilities of facial expression tests

As Table 11.1 indicates, the reliability estimates reported for the facial expression measures are not impressive. The authors of Faces and Social Relations considered their reliabilities too low to publish them as tests, although other behavioral cognition measures were made available for use by researchers. The low reliability of Faces is probably due to its low difficulty level. The restricted range of its scores reduces the range of obtainable correlation coefficients. With stimuli of more appropriate difficulty, this photo-matching format might be a useful one. The reliability of Social Relations, like many of the tests, might be improved if the number of items in it were increased.

In terms of reliability, BART looks most promising. Each part of this test contains only 10 items. By doubling the number of items in each affect subtest to 20, the effective reliability could be increased from approximately .50 to approximately .67.

Although the internal consistency reliability reported for CARAT (.56) is adequate for an experimental measure (see Table 11.1), it is unclear whether this reliability holds for the current measure or is based on an earlier version that was 50% longer. As noted earlier, one of the reported test–retest reliabilities for this measure was surprisingly low -.18. Although the reliability of the total PONS, based on 220 items, is highly satisfactory, the reliability of the PONS Face Alone score (estimated $r =$ .40) is inadequate.

11.8. Conclusions and suggestions for future research

In this chapter the methodological issues involved in devising tests of the ability to recognize facial expressions of emotion were discussed. These issues were illustrated with reference to the strengths and weaknesses of several measures in the domain. Many of these measures contain promising and exciting test ideas, which could be further developed. In conclusion, specific directions for improving some of these measures and developing new ones will be indicated.

At the conceptualization level of validation, the most obvious need is for a clear statement of the theory underlying the measures. A measure can be valid only if the theory on which it is based is valid. At a technical level, theoretical clarity is a boon to test construction. Without clear ideas, clear tests will not eventuate. When theory predates test construction, test development proceeds in a more logical manner. For example, starting with Guilford's theoretical conception of "cognition of behavioral units," O'Sullivan and her colleagues were able to indicate theoretically, before producing any tests at all, what stimuli and what responses were likely to be appropriate for such measures.

Similarly, the Primary Affect Measure and BART offer good models of how to select stimuli appropriate to a construct. Stimuli selection in these measures was guided by theory, providing a more coherent method of sampling facial expressions. By specifying beforehand the affects of interest, the domain was limited and, therefore, could be more efficiently sampled.

The lack of theoretical justification for the selection of stimuli for both PONS and CARAT make it difficult to assess the adequacy of these and similar measures. For example, CARAT was developed from a series of experiments on communication among monkeys. The relationship between that body of knowledge and recognizing emotion in humans needs to be explicated. The theoretical ambiguities inherent in PONS need to be clarified before this interesting measure can be properly understood. For example, what is the purpose of this test? At its inception, the aim of the PONS creators seemed to be to measure differential accuracy in different nonverbal channels. Little has been done, however, to validate these channel scores separately, so their status as separate scores and representatives of separate constructs is unclear. The relationships among accuracies in different nonverbal channels are useful topics to consider.

In terms of promising stimuli types, CARAT and the historical tests using the Rudolf sketches and the Piderit profile deserve further attention. Although CARAT is unique in being the only measure discussed in this chapter that uses spontaneously occurring facial behavior, it suggests that other measures might be devised using laboratory-based stimuli. (As noted earlier, however, such stimuli should not be taken at face value. What is in the face should be validated using either judges' ratings of the emotion in the face or a facial measurement procedure.) The Piderit profile might also serve as a useful heuristic tool. Such schematic faces, despite their current lack of appeal, offer the valuable advantage of experimental control. The ease with which schematic faces may be manipulated, in combination with current knowledge of the face, suggests that they might be useful in generating a variety of test items. Similarly, drawings such as those in the Rudolph series might be produced if guided, not by artistic expressiveness, but by current knowledge of affect-appropriate facial muscle changes.

In terms of validating response alternatives, PONS offers a good model of a careful, sophisticated, and organized manner in which to proceed. Although the bases for the choice of pleasant–unpleasant and dominance–submission as dimensions of affect are inadequately specified, the PONS creators did a good job in examining their response alternatives in the light of these dimensions. Judges' ratings of the relevance of the dimensions to the response alternatives were sought and the differential functioning of these dimensions, statistically, was examined. The PONS creators' use of situational descriptions rather than affect labels is also a creative contribution to the domain of usable response alternatives. Other kinds of response alternatives and stimulus–response combinations may be found in the behavioral cognition tests. In addition to the photo-matching response used in Faces and the verbal statements used in Social Relations, the other 21 behavioral cognition tests employ a variety of stimuli and responses that could be adapted for use in measures of the ability to recognize facial expressions of emotion. These include drawn faces paired with nonsemantic vocalizations, cartoon characters in social situations, and facial expressions mixed with hand gestures and body postures.

In terms of reification validation, all the measures should be extensively examined vis-à-vis one another and other tests in the domain. Congruent validity studies with PONS, CARAT, and BART were done but are only beginning attempts in this stage of validation. Often, however, measures having test formats very similar to the target test are used. It is more appropriate to use tests with dissimilar testing methods to demonstrate more convincingly the existence of the underlying construct. At a technical level, almost all the tests need to be lengthened. Most of the facial expression measures correlate so poorly with themselves (i.e., have insufficient reliability) that it is unlikely that they will correlate significantly with other measures. By increasing the number of items in each test, assuming that items of similar type could be added, the reliability of measures could be increased. Researchers should also attempt to develop more than a single measure of their construct.

At the elaboration stage of validation, PONS can serve as a model of how to proceed. Rosenthal and his colleagues examined almost every variable that could logically be related to PONS and they did this in many samples of Americans and other nationalities. They explained inconsistencies and discrepancies well and followed initially promising leads with further research. Their selection of variables shows creativity (mothers of preverbal children), theoretical common sense (verbal intelligence), and interest in broad applicability (effective counselors, cultural differences, deaf and blind people). Their studies reported results only on total PONS scores. What also needs to be reported is the relationship of variables such as these to the Face Alone score and the other channel scores derived from this measure.

Buck also examined a number of interesting variables (such as physiological arousal) as they relate to CARAT performance and BART was examined in terms of the effect of alcohol and marijuana on its scores. Additional experimental studies of this sort are needed.

Among current measures of the ability to recognize facial expressions of emotion, many show ingenuity, sophistication, and promise of validity. At this point, theoretical elaboration and explanation of underlying constructs are needed, as well as intensive exploration of the relationships among these various measures.

12. Asymmetries in facial expression

JOSEPH C. HAGER

Psychologists began studying differences between the two sides of the face in the 1930s. Early researchers reported intriguing findings but failed to arouse much enthusiasm, and this line of inquiry became dormant after 1950. Recently, interest has revived because research on cerebral hemispheric specialization for processing facial information and emotion has provided a new conceptual basis for studying facial asymmetry. Research on asymmetry can help us to understand what information is available in the face, how the face transmits this information, and what organic or neural processes give rise to it.

Methodological problems have weakened many studies of facial expression asymmetry, as can be seen by inspecting Tables 12.1–12.4, which summarize the studies reviewed here. Some problems, such as inadequate sampling of stimulus persons, were discussed in previous chapters (see especially Chapter 2) and will not be elaborated further here. In this chapter other methodological problems, which are unique to studies of facial expression asymmetry, will be discussed and the substantive issues and findings in this field will be critically integrated.

Studies of asymmetries in facial expression have addressed three general issues: how each side expresses a person's character and personality, whether one side represents the identity of the whole face better than the other, and whether expressions of emotion are greater on one side. Studies of asymmetry in the expression of personality and identity historically have provided methods and ideas for studies about asymmetry of emotion expression. These issues are related because observers' judgments about personality, identity, and emotion may be interdependent. For example, an expression of emotion may influence judgments of character and identity. Secord, Dukes, and Bevan (1954) illustrated this relationship with their finding that people with smiling faces tend to be - perceived as friendly and easygoing. Conversely, information about personality or identity may influence judgments about emotion. For example, a stereotype about fat people (e.g., jolly) could bias an observer's perception of such a person's emotional state. These mutual influences may make observers' judgments imprecise indicators of any single characteristic.

A different problem with observers' judgments is that using them to assess a person's characteristics does not indicate the source of information that provides the basis for the judgments. None of the asymmetry studies of personality or identity and only a few of emotion expression have examined these sources. Because specification of the basis for judged asymmetry is a fundamental issue and a serious deficiency in most studies, it will be discussed in the following section before turning to each substantive area.

12.1. The sources of facial information (sign vehicles)

In his semiotic analysis of the face, Ekman (1978) grouped the bases or sources of facial information into four kinds of sign vehicles: static, slow, rapid, and artificial. Static sign vehicles include the bony structure and skin pigmentation, which change only very slowly and infrequently, if at all. The slow sign vehicles, such as skin texture, fatty deposits, bags, and pouches, change with age. Rapid sign vehicles change quickly and are produced by the activity of facial muscles and the autonomic nervous system. Artificial sign vehicles are alterations or disguises of natural sign vehicles with cosmetics or surgery. Ekman discussed how these sign vehicles are sources for 18 different types of facial information such as personality, identity, beauty, gender, and kinship. This concept of sign vehicles attempts to distinguish sources of information from the inferences that an observer makes.

Evidence from orthodontists and plastic surgeons who have studied the symmetry of relatively permanent facial features suggests that static and slow sign vehicles may be asymmetrical. They agree that asymmetry is usually not noticed by observers but that some degree, even a substantial degree, of facial asymmetry is normal (e.g., Gorney & Harries, 1974; J. R. Thompson, 1943). For example, several researchers reported that the sizes of both bony and soft tissues are asymmetrical and lateralized. Burke (1971) found that in a group of children the maxillary skin surface area tended to be greater on the left side. He also found other asymmetries in surface areas that were not consistent across children. Other researchers (Letzer & Kronman, 1967; Mulik, 1965; Vig &

Hewitt, 1975) found that the maxillary region of the bony skull tends to be larger on the left side in children. In adults, the larger skeletal maxillary region seems to shift to the right side (Shah & Joshi, 1978; Woo, 1931), but this shift may reflect differences in measurement methods or population samples rather than age.

Rapid sign vehicles may also be asymmetrical. Researchers reported that facial movements can be more frequent, stronger, or better coordinated on one side than on the other (see Section 12.4 for details). Reports of normal asymmetry in pupil size, blushing, and other facial autonomic behaviors could not be found.

Little is known about the symmetry of artificial sign vehicles. Hair parting and combing and application of some cosmetics (e.g., to emphasize moles or hide blemishes) are typically asymmetrical.[1] On the other hand, Janzen (1977) argued that making smiles symmetrical is an important objective of orthodontic treatment. The symmetry of artificial sign vehicles may depend on the sign vehicles they alter.

The asymmetry of sign vehicles could produce differences in the information observers obtain from each side. Determining the sign vehicle on which observers base their judgments is an important goal because sign vehicles are the link between such judgments and the organic processes that cause asymmetry. For example, many recent researchers hypothesize that asymmetrical neural processes cause differences in how observers judge each side of the face (e.g. Sackeim, Gur, & Saucy, 1978; Stringer & May, 1979), but they do not specify the sign vehicles for this information, i.e., what in the face reflects asymmetrical neural processes. Clearly, finding that observers receive different information from the two sides of the face does not establish neural processes as the cause of asymmetrical sign vehicles. These researchers must show that a sign vehicle controlled by neural processes underlies the asymmetry of information received by observers. In contrast, some investigators identified asymmetries in potential sign vehicles (e.g., Chaurasia & Goswami, 1975; Ekman, Hager, & Friesen, 1981). However, researchers have yet to show that these asymmetries produce differences in how observers judge each side of the face, although such a relationship is plausible.

---

[1]Moles may be related embryologically to neural tissue and pimples may be affected by stress, so it could be important to know if moles and pimples are lateralized. Cosmetic alterations of the face and head could reflect the physical asymmetry of the face, i.e., an attempt to make the face either more symmetrical or asymmetrical, an attempt to produce sign vehicles on one side of the face rather than the other, or some other underlying asymmetrical tendency on the part of the actor. Further research should explore these issues.

Determining the asymmetrical sign vehicle is the first step in identifying the processes that give rise to this asymmetry. Asymmetries in rapid sign vehicles are most likely the result of asymmetries in neural function, although Ekman (1980) pointed out that the physical actions and sizes of muscle and fat tissue may affect the movements of muscles asymmetrically. The sizes of muscles were found to be lateralized which may be genetically determined (Papadatos, Alexiou, Nicolopoulos, Mikropoulos, & Hadzigeorgiou, 1974). On the other hand, neural processes probably do not directly control static and slow sign vehicles, although they may do so indirectly by influencing determinants of bone and tissue growth (e.g., muscle activity and hormones). Other factors such as genetics (Fogh-Andersen, 1942), injury to the face and head (Churchill & Igna, 1962), or disease processes (Dorchy, Baran, & Richard, 1976) are more likely to underlie asymmetries of slow and static sign vehicles.

In addition to clarifying causes of asymmetry, identification of the asymmetrical sign vehicle can help in evaluating the veracity of observers' judgments about each side of the face. For example, information about emotion is transmitted by rapid sign vehicles (Ekman & Friesen, 1975). Slow and static facial properties are not appropriate for conveying veridical information about quickly changing emotional states, but these properties are mistaken as sign vehicles for emotion information by some observers (Ekman & Friesen, 1975). Judgments about emotion are spurious inferences if they depend on static or slow cues rather than rapid sign vehicles. If an asymmetrical static or slow sign vehicle were the basis for differences between the sides of the face in judgments about emotion, the conclusion that the face expresses information about emotion asymmetrically would be equally false.

In the next three sections of this chapter, the discussion will show that assessment of differences in the information available in the two sides of the face is often based only on observers' judgments of each side. The judgment studies of personality, identity, or emotion expression that will be analyzed indicated that some judgments are a function of the facial side viewed, but they did not show what sign vehicles are responsible for the judged asymmetry. For example, all the studies in the next section used judgments to assess the asymmetry of personality expression, and no attempt was made to link these judgments with sign vehicles. We do not know whether facial movements frozen by the camera, muscle tone, physiognomic facial properties, permanent wrinkles, or merely hair styles underlie the results obtained. Judgment studies of the symmetry of other facial expressions have similar problems (see Chapters 2 and 4 for a discussion of judgment versus measurement studies).

12.2. Facial expression of character and personality

Table 12.1 is a summary of studies that examined differences between the two sides of the face in transmitting information about personality. Like other tables in this chapter, it reports methodological features and major findings. The tables contain information not in the text but useful for evaluating the studies.

W. Wolff (1933, 1943) took still photographs of faces and made prints, both normally and by turning the negative over to print images reversed right for left (mirror reversed). He cut these prints down the midline and rearranged the halves to produce faces in which each side was an image of the other. Thus, two composite pictures were made for each person, one using the original right and its reverse and one using the original left and its reverse. Figure 12.1 shows an example of Wolff's stimuli. Wolff showed these composite pictures one at a time to observers. The observers gave their impressions of the pictures, usually by free response, but sometimes by checking adjectives. Observers judged both themselves and others. Subjects who judged their own pictures sometimes did not recognize themselves and tended to give more extreme judgments than others gave. Wolff reported that observers' impressions of others varied depending on whether the right or the left composite picture were judged. He claimed that the right side is "full of vitality, sensual, smiling, frank, active, brutal, social or full of emotion" but that the left side "is described as being in a state of rigor, dead, concentrated, reticent, passive, ethereal, demonic, solitary and masklike" (1933, p. 175). Wolff concluded that the right side of the face expresses individual aspects of the personality and the left side expresses unconscious wish images and collective or species characteristics. These conclusions were based on a qualitative analysis of observers' responses and were illustrated by case reports. Wolff did not present statistical evidence to support his conclusions or to show the strength of these effects.

Lindzey, Prince, and Wright (1952) tried to test Wolff's conclusions by using a more structured technique and a quantitative analysis. They used Wolff's method of constructing composite photographs and had observers view those of themselves and others. The stimulus persons' judgments of their own composites were free responses and were classified by the investigators into groups of synonyms for analysis. Judg-

Table 12.1. *Methods and results for studies of asymmetrical expression of character and personality*

Method	W. Wolff (1943)	Lindzey et al. (1952)	Seinen & Werff (1969)	Stringer & May (1979)	Karch & Grant (1978)
Task	Give impressions of own and others' faces	Describe own face and rate faces of others	Rate own face	Select whether right or left face of others of same sex shows more	Rate others' faces
Number of stimulus persons	Not reported	20 Young men	70 Young people	12 Men; 12 women	11 Right-handed men
Type of stimuli	Composite still photos	Composite still photos	Half-faces	Composite video images	Composite still photos
Eliciting circumstances	Not reported	Not reported	Not reported	Talk about their TV image as they view it	Neutral expression
Number of scales or adjectives supplied for rating	Not reported	7	17	10	9
Number of judges	Not reported	20 Men and women	70	37 Men for men; 33 women for women	26
Analysis	Qualitative	T-Test	Qualitative	Binomial	MANOVA
Results	Consistent asymmetries across persons; right more vital and emotional, left passive and dead	Right more vital, less passive; trend for right more intelligent	Right more favorably judged	Each side transmits different information consistently across persons	Left judged differently than right on seven scales

Note: All studies used observers' judgments to assess asymmetry. No study specified sign vehicles for the judgments. None of these studies is subject to the perceptual bias problem because they used both normal and mirror-reversed stimuli.

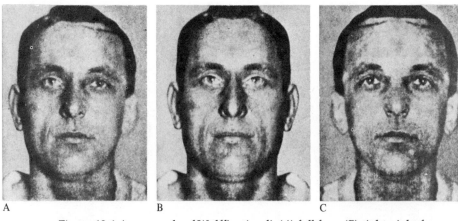

A   B   C

Figure 12.1 An example of Wolff's stimuli: (A) full face; (B) right–right face; (C) left–left face. (From W. Wolff, *The expression of personality*. New York: Harper & Row, 1943. Reproduced by permission of the publisher)

ments about others were made by rating the faces on seven adjective scales. Observers' judgments of their own right- and left-composite pictures did not differ. Judgments of others' pictures on a vital–passive scale were significantly different, with the right side judged more vital, just as Wolff claimed. Judgments of intelligence nearly reached significance, also in the direction predicted by Wolff. Because they thought this pattern of results could be attributed to chance, Lindzey and his co-workers concluded that "observers did not show any significant differences in their judgments" of the composite pictures (1952, pp. 83–84). This explanation and conclusion, however, seem unsatisfactory for their promising findings.

Stringer and May (1979; Stringer, 1979) produced composite pictures using a sophisticated video system, which permitted television images rather than still photographs to be used as stimuli. They electronically matched the pictures and sides of the face for size, intensity, and grayness. Stimulus persons were men and women who were judged only by same sex observers. These judges saw both composite pictures simultaneously without knowing which was the right or left. They decided, if they could, whether the right or left composite corresponded more to each of 10 adjectives. Three polar pairs of these adjectives reflected Jungian psychological types. One adjective of each pair (i.e., receptive, intuitive, feeling) was attributed significantly more often to the left than to the right composites for both men and women. However, the opposite adjective in each pair was not reliably attributed more to the right than to the left. The other four adjectives, which were selected from their previous research, also showed some significant differences. For the adjective *tired* more right composites were selected for men, but more left, for women. In general, the results were consistent with Stringer and May's predictions, which were based on ideas about cerebral hemispheric specialization for personality types. Some of the adjectives in this experiment were the same as, or synonyms of, adjectives in Wolff's and Lindzey et al.'s studies, but the results of these studies did not consistently agree. For example, judgments on the adjective *active* were not significantly different between sides, in contrast to Lindzey et al.'s study. *Pleasant* was attributed significantly more often to left composites, in contradiction to Wolff, but *strong* was attributed more to right composites for both men and women, consistent with Wolff's ideas. These inconsistencies in findings could be a result of the differences in tasks or stimuli. Stringer and May's stimuli provided many more rapid sign vehicles to observers than the still photographs of other researchers.

Karch and Grant (1978) selected 11 of 37 men as stimuli, based on their impressions of symmetry, a choice that could have biased their results. They made composite pictures like Wolff's and had observers rate them on nine bipolar adjective scales. The left-composite photos were rated harder, stronger, more masculine, excitable, active, healthy, and more toward bad on a good–bad scale. Again, some of these results are consistent with Wolff's ideas or with the results of other studies (e.g., good–bad), but others are contradictory (e.g., active–passive, strong–weak).

Seinen and Werff (1969) had subjects rate the right and left sides of their own faces on 17 five-point adjective scales. Rather than prepare composite pictures, they covered half of the face so that only one side could be seen at a time. They reported that subjects rated the right side of their own face more favorably (i.e., more sympathetic, impulsive, and gay) and their left side more negatively (i.e., more distrustful, hard, aloof). However, no quantitative analysis was reported to support these conclusions. A control study was conducted to show that these results were not an artifact of the placement of normally oriented half-faces in the visual field. Judgments of mirror-reversed half-faces were correlated with judgments of the normally oriented half-face. The direction of correlation was consistent with Seinen and Werff's conclusion that position of the half-face did not confound their results, but these correlations were not significant, indicating that the ratings were not reliable. Thus their findings are too dubious to warrant comparison with other studies.

326   J. C. Hager

Taken together, the studies of personality expression indicate that observers judge the two sides of the face differently. There are several important qualifications to this conclusion. First, it is not clear whether the information available in each side of the face is consistent across people, i.e., lateralized. Even though a particular study might have found consistent asymmetry across stimulus persons in regard to some judgments, these specific findings were rarely replicated in another study. Researchers have not often requested the same or similar judgments that were in another study, but when they did, results were inconsistent. One reason for this inconsistency may be that the eliciting circumstances (see Chapter 2) for stimulus pictures might have varied across studies. Some circumstances might have produced rapid sign vehicles in stimulus faces, but in other studies the face might have shown only static and slow signs. The most promising judgments for use in future research appear to be those reflecting the liveliness, vitality, or expressiveness of the face.

A second qualification is that the differences obtained between the two sides of the face were small even when significant. This could indicate that asymmetries are slight and difficult to detect, that only a few people have the same asymmetry, or that many people have asymmetry but the side that provides the information changes from person to person. Knox (1972; see Section 12.4 for a summary) provided evidence that bears on these alternatives. She showed that asymmetries were common but not consistent across people. This finding suggests that data be analyzed within each stimulus person as well as across persons.

Another qualification is the generalizability of the results obtained with composite pictures or half-faces to normal faces. These artificial faces may change the sign vehicles and provide different information from that in each side of a normal face. To clarify this issue, researchers could study how judgments of each side relate to judgments of the whole face. Also, rather than presenting each side in isolation, the investigator could present a normal face and ask observers to judge each side one at a time or to compare the sides with each other.

A final qualification is that no study has related the judgments made about either side of the face to the stimulus person's actual personality. This issue bears on whether the cues that observers use to make judgments are valid sign vehicles for personality or are merely mistaken for them. Exploring what sign vehicles underlie these judgments is one approach to clarifying the validity of the judgments.

12.3. Facial identity

W. Wolff (1933) claimed that his studies of facial expression of personality indicated that the right half of the face "roughly agrees with the impression caused by the original, merely intensifying the latter" but that the impression given by the left half "cannot be traced in the original" (p. 173). In 1943, he produced some evidence to support this proposition, noting that the percentage of subjects who recognized their own or others' composite pictures was greater for the right composite (p. 154). These differences were not significant.

McCurdy (1949) and Lindzey et al. (1952) experimentally tested Wolff's ideas (see Table 12.2 for summaries). They hypothesized that right composites would be judged as more similiar to original faces than left composites. Photographs of a face and its composites were presented simultaneously to observers who judged which composite was more like the original. For most faces, one composite or the other was chosen significantly more often. In both studies, significantly more right than left composites were selected as more closely resembling the original face. McCurdy also found that judges could reliably rank faces on the degree of asymmetry between sides of the face. He did not find support for his hypothesis that these rankings would be related to a measure of neuroticism, the Bell Adjustment Inventory. Lindzey et al. had judges rank the faces on degree of asymmetry and found that these ranks were highly correlated to asymmetry as measured by a planimeter. In contrast to McCurdy, they found that the degree of facial asymmetry was positively related to a measure of neuroticism, clinical psychologists' rankings of "effectiveness of adjustment." This discrepancy between studies might be the result of differences in measures of neuroticism or to the measurement of different sign vehicles, which might have been produced by varying eliciting circumstances.

In these two studies, observers' judgments of which side more resembled the whole face could reflect either different identity information available in each side (transmitted by static, slow, or rapid sign vehicles) or the observers' biases for one side regardless of any differences in information. Gilbert and Bakan (1973) pointed out that the right side of the face might be judged as more similar to the whole face because observers perceive this side in their left visual field with their right cerebral hemisphere. Because the right hemisphere is more specialized for processing facial information (for a review see Ellis, 1975), the right side of the face simply could be more salient for observers. To test this

Table 12.2. *Methods and results for studies of asymmetry of facial identity*

Method	W. Wolff (1933–1943)	McCurdy (1949)	Lindzey et al. (1952)	Gilbert & Bakan (1973)[a]	Bennett et al. (1980)[b]
Type of stimuli	Composite still photos	Composite still photos and normal whole face	Composite still photos and normal whole face	Composite still photos and normal and mirror-reversed whole face	Composite still photos
Mirror image to control for artifacts?	No[c]	No	No	Yes	No[c]
Number of stimulus persons	Not reported	42 Young women	20 Young men	20 Men and women	40 Men and women in one study; 28 in the other
Eliciting circumstance	Not reported	"Natural" pose	Not reported	Not reported	Request to relax muscles[d]
Number of judges	Not reported	4 Groups of from 17 to 23 men and women each	20 Men and women	41 normal, 41 mirror	169 first study; 108 second
Analysis	Qualitative	Binomial	Binomial	Proportions to Z	Chi-square
Results	Right resembles whole face more	Right selected more often	Right selected often	Side selected more often corresponded to side of the whole face in the left visual field	Which composite was selected depended on level of acquaintance, but the direction was opposite in each study

Note: The task in all studies except Wolff's was to select whether the right or left composite was more like the whole face. Wolff reached his conclusions about identity based largely on the similarity between personality judgments of the right face and the whole face, but he also said that people recognized their own and others' right composites better. All studies used observers' judgments to assess asymmetry. No study specified sign vehicles for identity.
[a] Three studies were reported with similar method and results. Only the first is summarized.
[b] The authors conducted two studies varying stimulus persons, eliciting circumstances, and technical preparation of stimuli.
[c] Composites were compared with respondent's previous experiences with the real face, not with pictures of the whole face.
[d] The authors think differences in lighting between their two studies (strobes versus floods) might have affected ability to relax muscles.

hypothesis, Gilbert and Bakan used the same method as previous researchers, except that composite pictures were compared with a mirror-reversed image of the original face as well as with the normal face. Their data showed that right composites were judged to be more similar to the normal face, but left composites were judged to be more similar to the mirror image of the normal. This finding indicates that the side of a face judged more similar to the whole face depends on which of its sides appears in the left visual field and thus is processed by the right cerebral hemisphere. Although cerebral specialization accounts for some of this similarity phenomenon, Gilbert and Bakan suggested that other biases such as perceptual scanning strategies (Walker-Smith, Gale & Findlay, 1977) may contribute.

The findings of McCurdy and Lindzey et al. might have been wholly or partly caused by observers' perceptual biases, but ambiguities that cloud interpretation remain. Although Gilbert and Bakan showed that observers tend to use the side of the face in the left visual field to identify the whole face, perceptual bias due to hemispheric specialization cannot explain why, for some faces in each of these studies, the side in the right visual field was judged to be more like the whole face. Also, the demonstration of bias does not clarify whether the two sides of the face provide the same or different information about identity or whether rapid, slow, or static sign vehicles transmit this information. All of these researchers had observers judge unfamiliar faces (except for self-judgments). Observers who were familiar with the stimulus persons may have overcome perceptual biases and may have been sensitive to possible differences in the identity information available in each side. Observers of unfamiliar faces, however, must rely on the resemblance of physical configurations of the face to make their identity judgments, but they may use different characteristics or sign vehicles to judge the identity of familiar faces (e.g. messages about emotion, personality, etc.). Benton (1980) argued that recognition of familiar faces and discrimination of unfamiliar faces are fundamentally different and are associated with different patterns of hemispheric activity. His conclusion implies that observers use different criteria for identity judgments based on whether the stimulus person is familiar or unfamiliar.

Bennett, Giannini, and Delmonico (1980) conducted two studies bearing on this issue. They prepared a different set of composite pictures for each study and showed them to observers who knew the stimulus persons either well or slightly. The observers reported which composite looked more like the stimulus person's usual appearance. In both studies, the side that the observers more often chose depended significantly on their level of acquaintance, but the direction of the relationship was different in each study. They are now investigating the reasons for this shift, but whatever the reasons, their findings suggest that observers use different characteristics or strategies to identify people depending on their familiarity with the stimulus person.

The demonstration of observers' bias in the perception of facial identity raises the problem of bias in perceiving other aspects of facial expression. Mita, Dermer, and Knight (1977) showed such a bias in the preference for normally oriented versus mirror-reversed photographs of faces. Intimate friends of the stimulus person preferred a normal oriented face, but the stimulus person preferred the mirror-reversed image. The researchers concluded that people prefer orientations of images to which they have been exposed more often. The processes underlying this preference may be the cerebral specialization previously discussed.[2]

Perceptual biases like those that affect identity judgments may also affect the measurement of asymmetry in emotion expression, which will be discussed in the next section. R. Campbell (1978) studied observer bias in the perception of intensity of emotion expression. She prepared composite photographs of faces in which one side came from a relaxed face and the other half came from a smiling face. Half of the composite faces had the smile on the right, half on the left. Both normally oriented and mirror-reversed images of these composites were prepared. Observers saw two faces sequentially and tachistoscopically where one face had the smile on the left, the other on the right. Observers selected which face "looked happier." They chose the face with a smile in the left visual field significantly more often. This finding indicates that smiles were rated as more intense when they were perceived by the right cerebral hemisphere.[3]

Reuter-Lorenz and Davidson (1980) also reported a bias in perceiving emotion expressions. They tachistoscopically presented simultaneously a neutral expression in one visual field and an emotional facial expression in the other. Subjects pressed a button to indicate on which side the emotion expression appeared. Happy and sad expressions were identi-

[2]Bennett et al. (1980) asked stimulus persons to indicate their preferences for their own composite pictures. In both studies, they tended to pick more left than right composites. This result is consistent with Mita et al. but suggests that hemispheric specialization underlies this "mere exposure" effect because these composite faces were unfamiliar stimuli to the subjects.
[3]Several studies suggest that the right hemisphere is specialized for recognizing emotion expressions (e.g., Ley & Bryden, 1979; Suberi & McKeever, 1977).

fied as emotion expressions equally well when they appeared in the left visual field, but happy expressions were identified better when the expressions appeared in the right visual field. Reaction time data showed a pattern similar to identification accuracy. The finding that happy expressions were better perceived in the right visual field apparently contradicts Campbell's findings, but there are several important differences in these two studies including the kind of stimuli used, stimulus presentation time, the tasks, and the dependent measures.

Although the studies of asymmetries in the perception of faces have left many issues unresolved, they have established that perceptual bias can occur. Although this bias may confound measurement of actual asymmetry in expression, the more conditions diverge from those of experiments that have shown this effect (e.g., very brief exposure, no opportunity for scanning the entire face, and global judgments of intensity) the less tenable perceptual bias becomes as an explanation of perceived asymmetry. When the face is seen in only the normal orientation, a direct test of bias in the judgment or measurement of asymmetry is not possible. Other indirect evidence can help to assess the effect of possible bias. For example, showing that measured asymmetry changes in different conditions, expressions, or groups of people indicates that any perceptual bias is small compared with the effects of these variables on the asymmetry.

12.4. Facial expression of emotion

Asymmetry of emotion expression has attracted more interest than other areas of research on facial asymmetry. Darwin (1872) described qualitatively the asymmetry of emotion expressions such as sneering, sardonic smiling, and disdain. He thought that asymmetry was a natural aspect of expression conveying part of the message and that the side of greater movement was the one more in view of the observer. Darwin did not conceive of asymmetries as occurring more often on one side than the other or as being related to cerebral hemispheric specialization. Recent research has emphasized the laterality of asymmetries, i.e., a similar asymmetry consistent across people and situations, and its connection with hemispheric specialization. Tables 12.3 and 12.4 contain summaries of these studies of emotion expression and facial movements.[4]

[4]Abrams (in press) studied expressive asymmetries relying heavily on schematic faces, but following the general policy of this book to not discuss research that uses drawings rather than more lifelike stimuli, we have omitted a discussion of his work. His study is, however, subject to many of the same criticisms raised in this section.

Table 12.3. *Methods and results for studies of asymmetries in emotion expression using a judgment approach*

Method	Knox (1972)	Sackeim et al., (1978)	R. Campbell (1978)[a]	R. Campbell (in press)
Number of stimulus persons	24 Women psychiatric patients	14	9 Right-handers	24 Left-handers
Number of stimuli	A right and left half-face for each woman plus a mirror-reversed image of each half	70 Right and 70 left composites plus 70 neutral faces	9 Right and 9 left composites of both smiling and "relaxed" faces	24 Right and 24 left composites of both smiling and "relaxed" faces
Type of stimuli	Half-face photos	Still composite photos	Still composite photos	Still composite photos
Eliciting circumstances	Show happy and how they really felt	Requested actions except for happy, which was spontaneous	Request to "smile for the camera" and "relax"	Request to "smile for the camera" and "relax"
Type of movement specified?	No	No	Yes	Yes
Number of judges	15/Each picture	20–24/Stimulus, 86 total	24	14
Sign vehicles	Not specified	Not specified: 6 expressions and neutral	Not specified	Not specified
Task of judge	Select one of six affects and rate the faces of other people	Rate each photo on intensity of expression	Select which smile composite is happier or which relaxed composite is more miserable	Select which smile composite is happier or which relaxed composite is sadder
Results	Judgments are affected by side viewed, but this effect depended on the stimulus person	Left composites rated more intense except for happy	More left composites selected as happier, and as more miserable	More left composites selected as happier, but more right composites selected as sadder

[a]The results of this study for the "relaxed" face, but not for "smiles," were replicated in a similar study that used ratings rather than binary choice.

A study by Sackeim, Gur, and Saucy (1978) illustrates the focus of current research interest and the problems inherent in this field. Table 12.3 summarizes their study and others that used a judgment approach to assess emotion expression asymmetry. They prepared right and left composites as Wolff had of faces that typically showed several muscles contracting. Observers judged on rating scales how intensely the composite faces expressed emotion. The left composite pictures were judged as more intense than the right composites in five of the six emotion categories. They concluded that "emotions are expressed more intensely on the left side of the face" (p. 434).

Ekman (1980) criticized the study by Sackeim et al. for not distinguishing carefully enough the type of facial movements they studied. The type of facial movement is an important issue because different types may have different upper motor neuron innervations. Neurologists are familiar with patients who have pyramidal tract lesions that disrupt their ability to move muscles voluntarily but may not affect involuntary emotional movements (Tschiassny, 1953). Other patients with nonpyramidal lesions may show abnormal involuntary emotional expressions but retain voluntary control of their muscles (S. A. K. Wilson, 1924; Monrad-Krohn, 1924). Clearly, movements that have different neural pathways may have different patterns of asymmetry. Some neurologists reported that although patients may show symmetrical involuntary movements, they may have quite asymmetrical voluntary movements (Tschiassny, 1953; S. A. K. Wilson, 1924).

Ekman noted that Sackeim et al. failed to make a distinction between at least two types of facial movements involved and that there was a difference in judged asymmetry between these two types. Ekman explained that the expressions judged as more intense on the left were not genuinely emotional expressions but rather were deliberately produced movements, carefully directed by the photographer who gave instructions to move particular muscles, such as "raise your upper lip" (Ekman & Friesen, 1976a). Sackeim et al. did not find left composites more intense for the one expression (happy) that spontaneously occurred during the repartee of the photographic session rather than at the request for a movement (Ekman, 1980).

Specifying the type of facial movement is crucial to asymmetry studies because different types of movement may have different neural substrates, but there are many cross-cutting, overlapping approaches to categorizing expressions. The voluntary–involuntary distinction is related to others such as spontaneous–deliberate, conscious–unconscious, and intentional–habitual, but the exact relationship among these similar dimensions is unclear in the literature. A second set of distinctions pertains to the issue of control of movement: inhibited, modulated, directed, and transformed (see Ekman and Friesen, 1975, for a discussion of control and deceit). Movements may be inhibited to prevent them from becoming visible, modulated to increase or decrease their intensity, directed in a deliberate attempt to move particular muscles, or transformed to a different appearance by adding contractions of other muscles.

Another way to categorize facial movements is by their function. For example, Ekman and Friesen (1966) discussed five communicative functions of facial movements: *emblems*, which are learned symbolic gestures whose meaning can be expressed in a word or two, such as brow raises in greetings (Eibl-Eibesfeldt, 1972); *illustrators*, which accompany speech and illustrate nonverbally what is said by providing emphasis, punctuation, etc.; *manipulators*, which are related to activities that help satisfy bodily needs or manage emotion and include such behaviors as wetting the lips and grinding the teeth; *regulators*, which are signals that help to manage the flow of the interaction; and *affect displays*, which are important aspects of emotional processes, at least some of which are universal and biologically based. Many researchers studying facial expression have not carefully distinguished natural, uncontrolled affect displays from other related movements such as masked or modulated affect expressions, simulations of emotion expressions, and symbolic movements used as references to emotion.

Most situations in which facial expressions are observed elicit various or ambiguous types of facial movements. Common situations used by researchers to elicit facial behaviors include conversation and posing an emotion. The types of facial movement that occur during conversation are especially varied. For example, although expressions occurring during conversation are spontaneous in the sense that they have not been requested, the speaker can initiate deliberate movements. Many facial movements, such as illustrators, which accompany speech, are overlearned habits that may rely on voluntary or involuntary pathways or a combination of the two. Movements that signal emotion may be either spontaneous emotional expressions or emblems referring to the emotion but not involving emotional experience (Ekman & Friesen, 1969b).

Posing an emotion expression is another problematic eliciting circumstance because subjects can adopt a variety of performance strategies, which may involve different neural pathways. Ekman, Roper, and Hager (1980) noted that when people were asked to pose an emotion or were shown a picture of an emotion expression to imitate, they could use at least two methods to solve the problem. Subjects could self-induce the emotion described or pictured and allow the expression to emerge, as in, what is called in theater, Stanislavski or method acting. Alternatively, subjects could deliberately produce each movement without emotion, in theatrical terms, acting mechanically with an external approach. Situations like conversation and posing an emotion are poor choices of circumstances to observe one specific type of facial movement because they elicit various types of movements, which may have different neural substrates.

Another circumstance that creates ambiguity about the type of movements produced is when subjects know or suspect that their face is being scrutinized. Once aware of observation, subjects may become self-conscious and alter their facial behaviors. Studies have shown that self-awareness of facial behavior changes other responses (e.g., Cupchik & Leventhal, 1974) and that observation by others alters facial behavior (Ekman, 1972; Friesen, 1972; Kleck, Vaughan, Cartwright-Smith, Vaughan, Colby, & Lanzetta, 1976). It is possible that even naturally symmetrical movements may become asymmetrical if subjects exercise some form of control. They may change the symmetry of movements by altering their expressions according to display rules, which are habits for managing expressions (Ekman, 1972). They may become embarrassed and produce an expression that changes the symmetry of other movements. Subjects are aware of scrutiny whenever they are asked to perform movements, have electrodes attached for recording facial EMG, or are obviously being videotaped. In studies of natural, spontaneous movements, self-consciousness and the operation of display rules can be minimized by recording subjects' behaviors in a manner that does not draw attention to the observation.

Ambiguity about the type of movement can be reduced by choosing eliciting circumstances carefully. Some circumstances are conducive to eliciting a particular type of spontaneous movement, although other types of spontaneous movements and deliberate movements can occur as well. For example, Ekman, Friesen, and Ancoli (1980) videotaped subjects as they viewed emotion-eliciting humorous and stressful films, which produced strong physiological responses. These subjects were not aware that their faces were being videotaped, and they viewed the films alone. Even under these carefully planned circumstances, not every movement was part of an uncontrolled emotional expression. The absence of an audience probably tended to reduce the influence of social display rules on muscle movements, but these rules can operate habitually even when a person is alone. Some expressions were inappropriate for the type of film viewed. For example, smiles appeared during the negative films, perhaps as an habitual mask for concealing negative affect or as embarrassed amusement about the stress and the negative affect aroused. Some of the facial movements measured were not specific to a single emotion, including movements involved in yawning, breathing, wetting the lips, and self-stimulation. Emotion expressions were identified by referring to theories about what movements reflect emotion (Ekman & Friesen, 1978). These emotion expressions were predictably related to other responses such as self-report of emotion, but the other facial movements were not. This study indicates that even a carefully chosen circumstance can elicit many types of movements and that care is needed to distinguish among them.

Although it is difficult to elicit and identify natural, spontaneous expressions, it is easier to elicit nonemotional, deliberate movements. Ekman, Roper, and Hager (1980) wanted to study deliberate facial movements and used a method that would tend to elicit only this type of movement. To minimize subjects' use of an emotion-generating strategy, they created a facial imitation test requiring subjects to imitate elementary facial movements or their combinations rather than to pose an emotion. Most of these movements had no emotional meaning for subjects to use to generate the emotion as an aid in making the movement.

Lynn and Lynn (1938, 1943) were the first investigators to examine the symmetry of a facial expression of emotion appropriate to carefully chosen eliciting circumstances. They measured the movement(s) involved in smiling in a humorous situation. Table 12.4 summarizes their studies and others which used a measurement research design. In their first study, three experimenters observed subjects' spontaneous smiles in real time during administration of visual tests. Lynn and Lynn remarked that their procedure induced "a prevailing spirit of good-natured levity" and "the necessary involuntary smiling" (1938, p. 295). They defined a subject's *facedness*, or *smiledness*, as the dominant side of the face showing the greater intensity of smiling. The experimenters imagined a line from the mouth corners to the outside eye corners and called the side on which the line shortened more the dominant side (as determined in real time). If a person's smile was not clearly greater on one side, that person was categorized as having an "evenness" of facial expression. The three experimenters agreed unanimously that 26% of the 398 subjects were either right- or left-faced and that 31% were even-faced. Disagreements were usually over whether the subject was symmetrical or asymmetrical rather than right- or left-faced. The subjects unanimously scored as asymmetrical were evenly divided on the side of facedness, 50 right and 55 left. The perceptual bias problem is a possible weakness in the scoring used by the Lynns, even though any such bias was not strong enough to yield a significant difference in the number of right- and left-faced subjects. A bias to score one side as dominant could have cancelled out an actual, but overlooked, dominance on the other side.

Unfortunately, Lynn and Lynn did not specify the anatomical basis for the smile movement they studied. They did not realize that smiles can be produced by several muscle contractions or combinations of muscles and that different activities might have been included as smiles. Smiles typically involve the *zygomatic major* muscle but may also be produced by the *zygomatic minor* and *caninus*. The *risorius* and buccinator muscles may elevate the lip corners as well. Specifying the anatomical basis for movements identifies the sign vehicles involved precisely. Using anatomy to identify the action is also important to avoid confusion when comparing activities observed in different faces. Individual differences in bony structure, fatty deposits, points of attachment, etc., make recognizing the same action across people difficult without relying upon the anatomy of the movements (Ekman & Friesen, 1976a).

In their second study, the Lynns (1943) used a new method of measuring asymmetry (Lynn, 1940). Subjects' faces were filmed surreptitiously as they viewed humorous movies. Using tracings of faces in these films, the experimenters measured in millimeters the distance each lip corner moved during smiling. This procedure minimized perceptual bias problems because the measurements were objective and were made independently on each side. They noted that one corner initially traveled faster than the other. Measurements were taken at the moment when the slower corner caught up to the speed of the other. It is not clear how often this measurement was of the maximum excursion of lip corners because the Lynns note that "the slower mouth corner usually catches up with and often passes the mouth corner which led at first" (1943, p. 259). Also unclear is when measurements were taken if the slower corner did not catch up or if both corners were equally fast. The distances were entered into a formula for a "smiledness quotient," or the difference between the right and left distances divided by their sum. This measure was normally distributed and showed again "an approximately equal distribution of subjects with right- and left-smiledness" (p. 261). This distribution was, however, slightly skewed to the left-faced side.

Table 12.4. *Methods and results for studies of asymmetries in emotion expression using a facial measurement approach*

Method	Lynn & Lynn (1938)	Lynn & Lynn (1943)	Chaurasia & Goswami (1975)	Ekman Hager & Friesen (1981)	Borod & Caron (1980)	Moscovitch & Olds (1979)[a]	Schwartz et al. (1979)
Number of stimulus persons	398	82	300 Right-30 left-handers	36 Children, 36 women	52	20 Right-14 left-handers	20 Right-handers
Number of stimuli	398	82	330 × 6 Actions	Varied with subjects and conditions	459	Not reported; 5 minutes of tape	20 Sessions × 60 questions
Type of stimuli	Live action	Films	Live action	Video records	Video records	Video records	Real time data
Eliciting circumstances	Vision tests inducing involuntary smiling	Humorous movies with subjects unaware of observation or camera	Requested imitations of 5 specific movements plus smiling in conversation	Either emotion-arousing situations or requested movements	Request to pose expressions	Conversation	Think about answers to different types of questions; posing EMG
Measurement	Visual	Visual	Visual	Visual	Visual	Visual	—
Number of scorers or judges	3 Scorers	At least 1 main and 1 reliability scorer	1 Experimenter	1 Main scorer and 2 reliability scorers	3 Scorers	2 Scorers	—
Reliability data?	Only agreements used	Yes	No	Yes	Yes	Yes	—
Did scorer know hypothesis?	No hypothesis	No hypothesis	Yes	Yes	Yes	Yes	—
Perceptual bias problem?	Yes	No	No	No	Yes	Yes	—

Sign vehicles	Smiles	Smiles	5 Movements plus smiles	Specific movements identified with facial measurement	Not specified; 9 expressions	Not specified	Not specified; electrode placed over corrugator and zygomatic areas
Type of movement specified	Yes	Yes	Yes	Yes	No	No	No
Anatomy specified?	No	No	No	Yes	No	No	No
Task of scorer or judge	Determine which side smiles more strongly	Measure distance traveled by lip corners	Assess dominance of each movement	Score each movement for asymmetry	Rate each stimulus on 15-point scale for asymmetry	Rate each expression for asymmetry	—
Results	All scorers agree that 26% are asymmetrical (50 right, 55 left) and 31% are symmetrical	Coefficient normally distributed with similar numbers of right and left dominant	Right-handers: 97% asymmetrical, 39% right, 59% left; left-handers: 97% asymmetrical, 73% right, 23% left	Requested movements more asymmetrical with left stronger; spontaneous movements not lateralized	All expressions more intense on left side	Right-handers consistently stronger on left, replicating their other other studies; no consistent pattern in left-handers	Greater activity on left side

---

[a]The authors conducted several studies with similar results. Only the last is summarized here.

Chaurasia and Goswami (1975) examined the symmetry of several deliberate facial movements in addition to smiling. They observed spontaneous smiles during conversation and asked subjects to perform five movements on each side of their face: lateral mouth corner movements, winking, platysma contraction, raising the upper lip, and vertical wrinkling of the forehead. The exact anatomical basis for each of these movements was not specified. The dominant side of the face was determined in real time based on "fine performance, convenience and uniform rapidity of movements" (p. 155). Movements that did not show dominance were scored as ambilateral. This scoring appears to have been subjective, without explicit rules. They found that 97% of the 330 subjects manifested a dominant side rather than ambilaterality when the separate performances of the five deliberate movements were combined into an index. Each movement showed a similarly high percentage of dominance. The authors stated that "the side of spontaneous smile corresponded uniformly to the dominant side of the face" (p. 155). Whether these smiles were associated with happiness, embarrassment, or a social convention is unknown. Facial dominance was related to handedness. Right-handers had significantly more left than right facial dominance, but left-handers had significantly more right than left facial dominance. This pattern was the same for each of the five movements individually and might have been the same for spontaneous smiling although the report is unclear. The perceptual bias problem could have influenced scores, but any such effect must have been weak because dominance changed between right- and left-handers.

R. Campbell (1978) photographed right-handed people as they relaxed and when they were instructed to "smile for the camera." Nine of 24 stimulus persons were selected on an unknown basis. Her report did not indicate whether this selection may have introduced an artifact. Composite pictures similar to Wolff's were made of each person's relaxed face and smiling face. Observers saw pairs of one person's right and left composite smiling face or right and left composite relaxed face. Observers judged whether the right or left composite of the smiling face looked happier or which composite of the relaxed face looked "more miserable" (p. 335). Campbell (see Table 12.3) found that more left than right composite pictures were selected for both the smiling and relaxed faces. In a study of left-handed stimulus persons using an identical procedure, Campbell (in press) found again that more left composites of smiling faces were judged as happier but that more right composites of smiling faces were judged as sadder. The lack of a relationship between handedness and the side of the face judged as happier indicated to Campbell that cerebral hemispheric specialization did not underlie asymmetry of the smiling expression. Conversely, the shift in which composite was judged sadder indicated that cerebral specialization created asymmetries in the relaxed face. There are two problems with these conclusions. The judgments of *miserable* in the first study may be different from the judgments of *sad* in the second. More importantly, the sign vehicles for the judgments were not specified. About the relaxed face, Campbell speculated that muscle tone was greater on the same side as the preferred hand, making the contralateral side relatively more relaxed. Thus, the face may not actually have been relaxed, but Campbell did not specify whether particular muscles or all muscles had an asymmetrical tone. As discussed previously, other facial properties besides muscle tone or contractions could have been the sign vehicles for these judgments.

Campbell (1979) conducted another study in which each composite picture of 18 right-handers was rated separately on a five-point scale running from sad to neutral to happy. Right and left composites of smiling faces were not rated as significantly different, but left composites of relaxed faces were rated as more miserable. She interpreted these results to reflect the greater asymmetry of the relaxed face in contrast to the smiling face.

Borod and Caron (1980) requested subjects to pose facial expressions to convey nine messages such as mild greeting, disgust, grief, and flirtation. They did not explain the rationale for choosing these messages, but some of the messages pertain to emotion (e.g., horror) and others pertain to social conventions (e.g., greeting, flirtation). Subjects heard short sketches describing a situation in which each of these expressions might be appropriate. Apparently, these sketches were intended to put subjects in the mood to express each message. Subjects also saw a photograph of the expression they were to produce. Posing these expressions may have elicited a variety of types of facial movements, and the researchers had no way to distinguish among them. Three judges reliably rated the degree of asymmetry in these expressions and which side was of greater intensity. This data, summed over all expressions, indicated that the left side of the face had more intense expression than the right. Perceptual bias could have affected the results of this study because judges saw only the normally oriented face. There was no condition in which the pattern of asymmetry scores changed, so the affect of bias cannot be assessed.

Moscovitch and Olds (1979) conducted several studies in which they observed the facial expressions of people conversing. They presented no evidence that these conversations elicited any emotion, even though in one subjects talked about their emotions. The authors assumed that talking about emotion would elicit a reexperience of emotion, but there is no reason to believe that this occurred. Even if expressions related to emotion were observed, they could either reflect an emotion experience or be a symbolic reference to the emotion. The researchers had no way to distinguish between these different types of movement. They noted whether each expression occurred unilaterally on the left or right side or was bilateral. Although they were not explicit, apparently the individual movements in each expression were scored rather than a blend of movements, but scoring rules were not reported. Scoring reliability was reported in only one study, but all the studies showed that unilateral movements more often occurred on the left side of the face. Again, because there was no condition in which this pattern of asymmetry changed, assessing whether perceptual biases affected reliability or findings is not possible.

The Moscovitch and Olds report raises other issues about studying asymmetry in facial movement. First, their dependent measure was the number of unilateral, rather than asymmetrical, movements. Unilateral movements might be a different kind of phenomenon than asymmetrical movements. Whereas some asymmetry may be attributed to peripheral factors (Ekman, 1980), unilateral movements are less subject to this explanation. Alternatively, unilaterality can be considered an extreme form of asymmetry. In observations of facial movement, close inspection of movements that initially appear unilateral often reveals a trace or slight evidence of the movement on the other side. Moscovitch and Olds probably did not distinguish extreme asymmetries from unilateralities because the large number of unilateralities they reported far exceeds the rate noticed by other researchers (Ekman, Hager, & Friesen, 1981).

A second issue raised by this study is the effect of speech upon the symmetry of facial movements, an issue distinct from the types of movement that occur during conversation. Moscovitch and Olds were apparently the first investigators to score the symmetry of movements while the subject was talking. They did not score movements integral to those involved in speaking: rather, they scored other movements that occurred during speech. There are two ways in which speech could influence the symmetry of facial movements. The speech movements in the mouth area could change the apparent symmetry of other movements in the mouth area by physical action. This effect could occur whether the speech movements themselves were symmetrical or asymmetrical.[5] Second, the neural activity involved in speaking could potentiate or inhibit movements on one side of the face. Typically, one side of the cerebral cortex is dominant for speech. When this side is more active during speech, movements controlled by that side could be potentiated or movements controlled by the other side could be inhibited.[6]

Schwartz, Ahern, and Brown (1979) studied the symmetry of facial activity using facial electromyography (EMG). They attached surface EMG electrodes to subjects' left and right *zygomatic* and corrugator muscle areas. In an "involuntary" condition, subjects heard questions having different emotional contents, i.e., happiness, excitement, neutral, sadness, and fear. In a "voluntary" condition, subjects were asked to generate expressions of these emotions. The EMG activity in response to these questions and to the request for poses was the dependent variable. Schwartz et al. claimed that the results supported their hypothesis that "positive emotions elicit relatively greater right muscle output while negative emotions elicit relatively greater left muscle output" (1979, p. 568). However, the evidence adduced to support this hypothesis is weak. The hypothesized effect of an interaction between positive–negative emotion and left–right side was found only for the *zygomatic* placement in the involuntary condition but not for the corrugator placement nor for either placement in the voluntary condition. They did not analyze this one significant interaction. Inspection of the cell means indicates that it resulted from negative questions eliciting more output on the left side and positive questions failing to elicit any significant difference. Their analysis of EMG output for the corrugator placement in the voluntary condition showed greater output on the left side regardless of question type. Thus, their data show that all the laterality effects observed were a result of greater output on the left side, but that sometimes lateralization did not occur.[7]

[5]One of my students, Tim Feener, observed 100 television celebrities as they conversed. He scored the symmetry of mouth activity during speech and found that about half of these people consistently used one side more than the other. Twice as many people showed greater involvement of the right side of the mouth in speaking than the left. Preliminary results of a study conducted by Ronald von Gelder and myself corroborated these findings.
[6]Kimura (1973) used a similar explanation for her findings that the right hand made more free movements during speech than nonspeech but that the frequency of these movements by the left hand did not change. This explanation is similar to that for the relationship between direction of eye movement and hemispheric activation (Bakan, 1969; Kinsbourne, 1972; for a critical review see Ehrlichman & Weinberger, 1978).
[7]In a recent study, Sirota and Schwartz (1980) reported that muscle activity during positive emotion was greater on the right. Detailed information to evaluate this study is not yet available, but it was similar to the Schwartz et al. study and appears subject to the same criticisms.

Conceptual problems plague interpretation of the Schwartz et al. study. Although they implied that emotion was elicited by their questions and requests for expressions, as in the Borod and Caron study, emotion might or might not have been generated when subjects posed expressions in the voluntary (deliberate) condition. After the involuntary condition, subjects rated each question on how much emotion they experienced in response to it. Analysis of these ratings indicated that subjects reported experiencing the appropriate emotion to each question. However, demand characteristics are a plausible explanation of this finding because an appropriate emotion rating for each question is obvious. On reading these questions, it is difficult to imagine that subjects actually experienced any emotion to them. For example, one question for sadness was "Make up a sentence using the words *extremely discouraged.*" The questions may have elicited cognitive processes related to memories of emotion, but they probably did not elicit the kind of emotional processes studied by the Lynns and Ekman et al. Also uncertain is whether facial activity in the involuntary condition was spontaneous or deliberate. Some activity such as concomitants of effortful cognitive processing might have been spontaneous; other activity might have been deliberate. For example, one question presumed to elicit spontaneous excitement was: "Visualize your face. What part of your face is most expressive of emotions such as excitement?" Pilot research (Hager, 1975) showed that subjects deliberately produce facial movements in response to such questions as an aid to finding the answer. Although this was an attempt to study two types of facial movements, the tasks used probably elicited both types in each condition and made distinguishing between types impossible.

Schwartz et al. raised the issue of whether the pattern of asymmetry varies with expressions of different emotions. As previously noted, they did not produce evidence that the activity of muscles would shift from one side to the other depending on whether the emotion question was positive or negative. Following their suggestion, Sackeim and Gur (1978) conducted a post hoc analysis of the Sackeim et al. (1978) data. They showed only that the negative expressions were judged as stronger on the left more often than positive emotions. They did not show, as they imply, that positive expressions were judged as stronger on the right. Taken together, these studies suggest that some expressions are lateralized on the left and others are not. This finding could be attributed to the difference between types of movements (as explained previously, the only positive expression was spontaneous and the others were deliberate) rather than positive versus negative emotion.

Related to this issue is whether asymmetry of an expression depends on the muscles involved in it. Studies of individual muscle movements (e.g., Chaurasia and Goswami, 1975; Ekman, Hager, & Friesen, 1981) suggested that the requested movements of some muscles were more strongly lateralized than others. Studies using global judgments of intensity of expressions having more than one muscular movement cannot determine which of the individual movements underlie judged asymmetry. This disadvantage implies that each movement in an expression should be scored for asymmetry separately.

Ekman, Hager, and Friesen (1981) were the first investigators to explore possible differences in the symmetry of deliberate facial movements versus spontaneous emotional expressions.[8] Rather than using global judgments of emotion to assess asymmetry in sign vehicles, they measured the sign vehicles directly with a new facial measurement technique, FACS (Ekman & Friesen, 1978), which identified each individual muscle movement. These movements were then scored as symmetrical or asymmetrical with greater intensity on the left or the right side. Contraction of *zygomatic major* was scored on the faces of 30 children both when they deliberately imitated this movement as requested by the experimenter and when they spontaneously smiled at an experimenter's jokes and praise. Other studies showed that spontaneous actions of *zygomatic major* observed in an appropriate eliciting circumstance are associated with positive affect (e.g., Ekman, Friesen, & Ancoli, 1980). A total of 114 deliberate and 78 spontaneous emotional movements were examined. Asymmetrical movements were significantly more frequent in deliberate imitations than in spontaneous smiles. Deliberate asymmetrical movements were more frequently greater on the left than on the right side. This laterality of movement was not apparent for spontaneous smiles. Deliberate contractions of other muscles beside *zygomatic major* were also examined to see whether they followed the same pattern. Children's deliberate imitations of five other muscle contractions (total of 106 movements) were as frequently asymmetrical as deliberate smiles, and these asymmetrical movements were more often greater on the left than the right.

[8]Remillard, Andermann, Rhi-sausi, and Robbins (1977) studied patterns of facial movement asymmetry in temporal lobe epileptics. Although interesting, most of their material does not bear directly on the issues discussed in this chapter because their subjects were brain-damaged patients. However, 25 normal controls were observed while smiling with amusement and while smiling deliberately on request. Although this issue was not examined, inspection of their data (p. 114) shows the same pattern of results as in the Ekman et al. study. Unfortunately, there were far too few events scored asymmetrical for significant findings to emerge. This pattern was not the same for epileptics.

Ekman et al. extended their examination of spontaneous emotional expressions to a sample of 36 women who expressed both positive and negative emotions. They scored 110 spontaneous actions of *zygomatic major* videotaped while the women watched a humorous film. Again, few of these smiles were asymmetrical, and those that were were as often greater on the right as on the left. The women spontaneously made 24 negative emotional movements in response to a stressful film. As in the case of other spontaneous movements, the asymmetrical movements were as likely to be greater on one side as on the other, but the incidence of asymmetry was higher than in other spontaneous conditions. The small number of negative movements made these findings tentative. Perceptual biases could not have accounted for the Ekman et al. results because the pattern of scoring changed with the type of movement.

Although Ekman et al. found that asymmetries of spontaneous emotional movements were not lateralized across subjects, there was evidence that asymmetries of both spontaneous and deliberate movements were consistent within subjects. In an unpublished analysis, they found that if a subject showed more than one asymmetry, he or she tended to have the stronger contractions on a particular side. Chaurasia and Goswami (1975, p. 158) presented compatible data for deliberate movements. Lynn and Lynn's (1943) test–retest reliabilities for their "smiledness quotient" (about .6) supported their assumptions about consistency in "facedness." This issue of individual differences in asymmetrical behaviors deserves further exploration because it may be related to important personality dimensions as indicated by the Lynns' studies.

Another approach to the relation between consistency of asymmetries and personality was taken by Knox (1972, in a thesis supervised by Ekman). She had observers judge photographs of faces of depressed psychiatric patients at admission and discharge (see Table 12.3). These patients were asked to show how they really felt and also to make a happy expression regardless of their real feelings. They were probably self-conscious about this task and embarrassment or display rules might have affected these expressions. Knox showed only one side of the face at a time to observers. Mirror-reversed images of the half-faces were also presented in order to control for possible artifacts stemming from consistently presenting each side in its normal orientation. No such artifacts were detected. Observers selected which one of six emotions best described the expression of each half-face. They also rated the face on three nine-point scales indicating the intensity of muscular contraction in the emotion expression, the conflict present in the face, and how posed versus spontaneous the expression looked. These judgments reflect aspects of both emotion and personality expression. Observers' judgments were affected by the side of the face observed, but this effect depended on the stimulus person. Even though most patients were judged differently depending on whether their right or left face was viewed, the direction of judged asymmetry was not consistent across patients. For example, muscle contractions on the right side of some faces were rated as more intense than on the left, but for an equal number of patients, this pattern was reversed. The judgments in this study were not about the intensity of emotion expression, and they represent another approach to determining asymmetry of emotion expressions.

Some researchers who studied the symmetry of emotion expressions and facial movements were relatively clear about what type of movement they examined (i.e., Lynn and Lynn, Campbell, Chaurasia and Goswami, and Ekman et al.). These studies indicated that the pattern of asymmetry is different when people are requested to perform specific movements as opposed to when they spontaneously react to emotion-eliciting circumstances. The types of movements these situations tend to elicit may be described as deliberate nonemotional and spontaneous emotional movements, respectively. Spontaneous emotional movements appear to be less asymmetrical than deliberate movements. Ekman et al. found that spontaneous smiles were less asymmetrical than deliberate imitative smiles. Tokizane (cited in Kohara, n.d.) also reached the conclusion that emotional expressions are symmetrical, but intellectual expressions are often asymmetrical.

A second conclusion is that deliberate movements that are asymmetrical more often have greater excursion on the left than the right side, but asymmetrical movements in spontaneous emotion expressions do not show this pattern. Deliberate contractions of *zygomatic major* (which produces smiling) were stronger on the left side more often than on the right (Ekman, Hager, & Friesen, 1981). R. Campbell (1978) found that left composites of people deliberately smiling for the camera were judged as more intense than right composites. This result is consistent with the Ekman et al. finding if the cues for these judgments were the smiling movements frozen in the picture. Like deliberate smiles, other deliberate movements show laterality with the left side dominant. Chaurasia and Goswami (1975) found that five deliberate movements were better performed on the left. Ekman et al. found that asymmetrical deliberate contractions of five muscles besides *zygomatic major* were greater in intensity on the left more frequently than on the right. Sackeim et al.

(1978) found that left composites of deliberately composed expressions were judged as more intense than right composites. Like the judgments in Campbell's study, the Sackeim et al. results are consistent with the studies of movements if the muscle contractions in these pictures were the sign vehicles for the judgments of intensity.

In contrast to deliberate movements, emotion expressions that occur spontaneously and are appropriate to an emotion-arousing situation have not been found to be lateralized. Lynn and Lynn (1938, 1943) and Ekman, Hager, & Friesen (1981) found that asymmetrical smiles occurring spontaneously in pleasant situations were not greater on one side more frequently than on the other. Sackeim et al. (1978) unwittingly provided support for this conclusion when they found that right and left composite pictures of spontaneous, happy smiles were not judged significantly different in intensity. Some researchers argued that *zygomatic* muscle activity during positive emotion is stronger on the right, but their own evidence does not support this position and contradicts other data. Only Ekman et al. reported data on spontaneous emotional movements other than smiling. Although few in number, these other movements showed no laterality. In spite of the fact that these studies did not reveal laterality in spontaneous emotional movements, it is possible that measures more sensitive to asymmetry may detect laterality that cannot be observed visually.

The studies by Borod and Caron, Moscovitch and Olds, and Schwartz et al. showed that asymmetrical expressions tended to be greater on the left than the right side of the face. Unfortunately, the type of facial movements involved in the expressions was not specified. Because other researchers indicated that the type of movement affects asymmetry, this deficiency seriously impairs interpretation of these studies. The eliciting circumstances in these studies suggest that few, if any, spontaneous emotional expressions were observed. Tomkins (1979) noted that virtually every emotional expression of adults is transformed to some degree so that the innate expression is rarely observed. This view suggests that extreme care and much effort are needed to create situations conducive to eliciting spontaneous emotional expressions. The results of these studies may be attributed to the sampling of movements corresponding to more deliberate, controlled, learned, cognitive neural processing rather than unlearned, spontaneous emotional processing.

12.5. Summary

The two sides of the face differ to some degree in physical properties such as the shape of bony structures, skin surface area, tissue shapes, strength and coordination of muscle contractions, wrinkle patterns, etc. Any of these asymmetrical properties may underlie differences in the information that can be obtained from each side. One side of the face could provide more information about a particular characteristic or it could provide different information. In this chapter emphasis has been placed on the value of studying the relation between asymmetrical properties and the information they provide. Studies in which observers judge each side of the face in respect to certain characteristics are useful for determining whether the two sides of the face provide different information. Such studies showed that observers judge the two sides of the face differently in respect to the intensity of emotion expression and some personality characteristics. However, like the judgment approach to studying the accuracy of inferences about emotion (Chapter 4), judgments reflecting asymmetry in personality, identity, or emotion expression do not show which facial properties observers use as sign vehicles or cues for their inferences. Determining the sign vehicle for an observer's judgment can help the researcher to decide whether the judgments are accurate and truly reflect characteristics of the stimulus person or are spurious inferences. If the judgments are spurious, concluding that the face expresses this information asymmetrically would be an error. Identifying the sign vehicles responsible for asymmetrical transmission of information is also a first step to understanding the organic basis or underlying cause of the asymmetry.

Rather than assessing the asymmetry of expression through observers' judgments, some researchers measured the asymmetry of sign vehicles, using several measurement methods. Three groups of researchers scored the symmetry of specific movements using visual inspection of the strength of muscular contraction. This scoring was in terms of unilaterality (Moscovitch & Olds, 1979) and the degree of asymmetry (Ekman, Hager, & Friesen, 1981; Lynn & Lynn, 1943). Others visually scored the asymmetry of muscular contraction in the whole expression (Borod & Caron, 1980). Scores were also based on the rapidity and coordination of specific movements rather than on their strength (Chaurasia & Goswami, 1975). Electromyography was used to measure electrical activity of muscles in specific areas of the face (e.g., Schwartz et al., 1979). Although EMG has an uncertain relation to the visible movements of muscles, its units of measurement are smaller and enable finer distinctions in activity than visible measurement. Also, EMG readings are typically averaged over many seconds, whereas visible measurements are usually taken only at the moment of greatest contraction. The placement of an electrode on the surface of the skin rather than in a muscle may pick up the activity of several muscles and not allow distinctions that can be made visually (Ekman, Schwartz, and Friesen, in preparation). Ekman and Schwartz found a linear relationship between EMG readings and the visual intensity scoring of Ekman and Friesen's FACS during voluntary movements. However, they found that this relationship was not the same when subjects anticipated making the movements. Also, EMG activity could indicate inhibition of movement as well as actual movement. Tasks for future research include determining the relationships among these different measurement methods and exploring others, such as which side contracts or reaches maximum excursion first.

There are several advantages to measuring the symmetry of specific muscle movements. An expression may be asymmetrical because the contractions of muscles are greater on one side or because more muscles are contracted on one side. All or only some of the muscular contractions in an expression may be asymmetrical in strength. The muscles that are asymmetrical may be the same or different when they are involved in different expressions (e.g., brow movements in fear versus surprise versus skepticism). The muscles that most often contract asymmetrically may change from person to person or remain constant so that some movements are consistently more asymmetrical than others. If so, then asymmetry of an expression may depend partly on the muscles involved. These issues can be resolved only through measuring asymmetry of specific muscle contractions. Measurement may be more sensitive than observer judgments because judges may not be able to detect the asymmetries in an expression as well as a technician trained in facial measurement.

Whether a researcher decides to use observers' judgments or facial measurement to assess expressive asymmetries, perceptual bias may be a problem. Observers may perceive the two sides of the face differently because each side tends to be perceived by a different cerebral hemisphere or because they look at one side of the face longer, more closely, etc. Perceptual bias has made the findings about asymmetry of identity information difficult to interpret. Researchers measured or controlled such perceptual bias by using mirror-reversed images, in addition to the normally oriented face, as stimuli. When half-faces are used as stimuli rather than composites, they should be presented in a mirror-reversed orientation so that the position of the half-face is counterbalanced. Studies that compare composite pictures with the original face should also compare them with the mirror image of the original. Probably, naive observers' global judgments under restricted viewing conditions are more influenced by perceptual bias than the careful, objective measurements made by skilled observers.

Determining whether facial movements are asymmetrical is only one aspect of studying the symmetry of emotion expression. There are many types of facial movement beside those involved in emotion. These different types of movements are often mistaken for or confused with one another. Posing an emotion and conversing are two of the most problematic elicitors because many types of movement can occur and it is hard to distinguish among them. Researchers can maximize their opportunity to observe a particular type of movement by choosing eliciting circumstances carefully. Some situations are conducive to eliciting only one type of movement, but eliciting only genuine, spontaneous emotional movements may be difficult. Researchers who have been relatively careful about choosing elicitors have produced evidence to indicate that the pattern of asymmetry varies with the type of movement. This point is important for researchers studying the relation between asymmetry and cerebral hemispheric specialization. Various types of movement probably involve different neural pathways, which may correspond to different patterns of hemispheric specialization.

Although asymmetry in facial expressions is an old issue, research in this area appears barely to have begun. There are many specific issues that need to be clarified empirically. An important step in studying asymmetry in expressions of character and personality is to determine whether judgments about the whole face and its sides actually reflect the person's personality or are based merely on stereotypes or other irrelevant factors (Ekman, 1978; Secord, 1958; R. L. Terry, 1972). Studying asymmetry of the expression of identity is complicated by the observer's bias to favor the side of the face in the left visual field as an identifier. However, Wolff's original observation that the identity of the person is expressed more by the right than the left side has yet to be proved or disproved. To clarify this issue conceptually, researchers should consider what factors or characteristics underlie identity judgments. Studies of the expression of emotion should determine whether the pattern of asymmetry varies with the many different types of movement, the different muscles involved in the expressions, different emotions (e.g., positive versus negative), or different persons (e.g., right- versus left-handers). How the measures of asymmetry are related to higher neural activity and cerebral specialization is unknown. For example, more intense muscle contractions on one side may indicate either better-directed control on that side or inhibition of movement on the other side. No one has shown whether observers detect asymmetries in real-life interaction or whether these asymmetries have any signal value. Asymmetries in facial movement may give cues about whether a person is deliberately trying to deceive others with their expression or whether the emotion expressed is genuine. Asymmetry inherent to some emotion expressions may be peculiar to those that are not universal and biologically based.[9]

Acknowledgments

I thank Paul Ekman for his critical comments and suggestions on drafts of this chapter, Richard Davidson for his comments on a previous draft, and Tamara Sturak for her editorial help.

[9]Paul Ekman suggested the possibility of this relationship.

13. Affect theory

SILVAN S. TOMKINS

In this chapter I will present a brief account of the historical development of my interest in affect and of the theory that emerged from that interest. Then some of the major features of that theory are described: the nature of affect as amplification; what and where the primary affects are; the role of each of the primary affects; and how the affects are innately activated. Finally, some of the more recent developments and modifications of my theory will be presented. I will exclude entirely the most recent application of the theory to the study of personality, called *script theory* (Tomkins, 1979).

My awareness of the centrality of affect began in the early 1940s when the field of affect was in deep trouble and disrepute. Judgments of affect from photographs of the face appeared to lack any consistency or validity, and the role of affect was presumed to be either trivial or disorganizing. Freud had misidentified aggression as a drive, and anxiety, first, as the result of repressed sexuality and, finally, as a danger signal – an essentially cognitive interpretation of a primary affect. Murray's "needs" incorporated affects along with cognitions and acts in a complex that did not encourage the recognition of affect as an independent central motivation mechanism. Thus, fear was studied as harmavoidance, shame as infavoidance. Furthermore, consciousness as such was in disrepute, caught in the cross fire between the "unconscious" and "behavior." Behaviorism had seized center stage in American psychology. Despite every apparent reason against the importance of affect, my intuition was that it was important. Thus, in the design of the Tomkins–Horn Picture Arrangement Test (Tomkins and Horn, 1943), affect was one of the central variables measured, using figures with faces drawn as happy,

The modifications in theory presented here are taken from my book, *Affect, imagery, consciousness*, Vol. 3, New York: Springer, 1982.

sad, or angry. Yet, in the book on that test, I could find no persuasive theoretical rationale for what I had done.

The road to discovery was, with respect to theory, circuitous, and with respect to evidence, accidental. In the late 1930s I had been seized with the fantasy of a "humanomaton" – a human machine – an early version of what was later called *computer simulation*. While pursuing this line of theorizing I was captured by Wiener's early papers on cybernetics. This project of a "humanomaton" led to the conception of multiple assemblies of varying degrees of independence, dependence and interdependence, and control and transformation of one assembly by another. It was this general conception that, one day in the late 1940s, resulted in my first understanding of the role of the affect mechanism as a separate but amplifying coassembly.

The second critical discovery occurred when my son was born in 1955 while I was on sabbatical leave. I observed him daily, for hours on end. I was struck with the massiveness of the crying response. It included not only very loud vocalization and facial muscular responses, but also large changes in blood flow to the face and engagement of all the striate musculature of the body. It was a massive total-body response, which, however, seemed to center on the face. Freud had suggested that the birth cry was the prototype of anxiety, but my son didn't seem anxious. What, then, was this facial response? I labeled it *distress*. In the following months, I observed intense excitement on his face as he labored to shape his mouth to try to imitate the speech he heard. He would struggle minutes on end and then give up, apparently exhausted and discouraged. I noted the intensity of his smiling response to his mother and to me, and again I became aware that nothing in psychoanalytic theory (or any other personality theory at this time) paid any attention to the specificity of enjoyment as contrasted with excitement.

The first public presentation of this model was at a colloquium at Yale University in the early 1950s under the title "Drive Theory is Dead," delivered with fear and trembling in the stronghold of Freudian and Hullian drive theory. To my surprise, it was well received. In 1954, at the 14th International Congress in Montreal, it was presented as "Consciousness and the unconscious in a model of the human being" (Tomkins, 1955) and was later expanded and published as *Affect, imagery, consciousness* (Tomkins, 1962, 1963, 1982).

13.1. Affects and drives

I view affect as the primary innate biological motivating mechanism, more urgent than drive deprivation and pleasure, and more urgent even than physical pain. That this is so is not obvious, but it is readily demonstrated. Consider that almost any interference with breathing will immediately arouse the most desperate gasping for breath. Consider the drivenness of the tumescent, erect male. Consider the urgency of desperate hunger. These are the intractable driven states that prompted the answer to the question, "What do human beings really want?" to be: "the human animal is driven to breathe, to sex, to drink, and to eat." Yet this apparent urgency proves to be an illusion. It is *not* an illusion that one must have air, water, and food to maintain oneself and sex to reproduce oneself. What *is* illusory is the biological and psychological source of the apparent urgency of the desperate quality of the hunger, thirst, breathing, and sex drives.

Consider these drive states more closely. When someone puts their hand over my mouth and nose, I become terrified. But this panic, this terror, is in no way a part of the drive mechanism. I can be terrified at the possibility of losing my job, of developing cancer or of losing my spouse. Fear or terror is an innate affect, which can be triggered by a wide variety of circumstances. Not having enough air to breathe is one of many such circumstances. But if the rate of anoxic deprivation becomes slower, as, for example, in the case of wartime pilots who refused to wear oxygen masks at 30,000 ft, then there develops, not a panic, but a euphoric state; and some of these men met their deaths with smiles on their lips. The smile and its feedback are the affect of enjoyment, in no way specific to slow anoxic deprivation.

Consider more closely the tumescent male with an erection. He is sexually excited, we saw. He is indeed excited, but no one has ever observed an excited penis. It is a man who is excited and who breathes hard, not in the penis, but in the chest, the face, the nose, and the nostrils. But such excitement is in no way peculiarly sexual. The same excitement can be experienced, without an erection, from mathematics – beauty bare – to poetry, to a rise in the stock market. Instead of these representing sublimations of sexuality, it is rather that sexuality, in order to become possible, must borrow its potency from the affect of excitement. The drive must be assisted by affect as an *amplifier* if it is to work at all. Freud, better than anyone else, knew that the blind, pushy, imperious Id was the most fragile of impulses, readily disrupted by fear, by shame, by rage, by boredom. At the first sign of affect other than *excitement*, there is impotence and frigidity. The penis proves to be a paper tiger in the absence of appropriate affective amplification.

The affect system is, therefore, the primary motivational system because without its amplification, nothing else matters, and with its amplification, anything else *can* matter. It thus combines urgency and generality. It lends its power to memory, to perception, to thought, and to action no less than to the drives.

The relationship we have postulated between the drive system and the affect system must also be postulated between both of these and nonspecific amplifying systems, such as the reticular formation. This and other amplifier circuits serve both motivational and nonmotivational systems. The words "activation" and "arousal" have tended to confound the distinction between amplification from affects and the nonspecific amplification of any neural message, be it a sensory, motor, drive, or affect message. *Amplification* is the preferable, more generic term, because it describes equally well the increase or decrease in gain for any and every kind of message or structure. Analogic amplification is now restricted to the affect system. The terms *activation* and *arousal* should be abandoned because of their affective connotations.

It is clear from the work of Sprague, Chambers, and Stellar (1961) that is possible, by appropriate anatomical lesions, to produce a cat that is active by virtue of intact amplifier structure but shows little affect and, conversely, to produce a cat that is inactive and drowsy but responds readily with affect to mild stimulation.

Both drives and affects require nonspecific amplification, but the drives have insufficient strength as motives without concurrent amplification by both the affects and the nonspecific amplification. Their critical role is to provide vital information of time, of place and of response, i.e., where and when to do what, when the body does not know how to otherwise help itself. When the drive signal is activated, we learn first when we must start and stop consummatory activity. We become hungry long before our tissues are in an emergency state of deficit, and we stop eating, due to satiety, long before the tissue deficit has been remedied.

But there is also the information of place and of response – where to do what. When the drive is activated it tells us a very specific story – that the "problem" is in the mouth in the case of hunger, farther back in the nose and throat and chest if it is an oxygen drive, in the urethra if it is the urination drive, at the anal sphincter if it is the defecation drive. This information has been built into the site of consummation, so the probability of finding the correct consumatory response is very high. That this information is as vital as the message *when* to eat can be easily demonstrated:

Let us suppose that the hunger drive were "rewired" to be localized in the urethra and the sex drive localized in the palm of the hand. For sexual satisfaction the individual would first open and close his hand

and then reach for a wide variety of "objects" as possible satisfiers, cupping and rubbing his hand until orgasm. When he became hungry, he might first release the urethra and urinate to relieve his hunger. If this did not relieve it, he might use his hands to find objects that might be put inside the urethra, depending on just how we rewired the apparatus. Such an organism would be neither viable nor reproductive. Such specificity of time and place of the drive system, critical though it is for viability, is, nevertheless, a limitation on its general significance for the human being.

It is the affects, rather than the drives, that are the primary human motives. This primacy is demonstrated, first, by the fact that the drives require amplification from the affects, whereas the affects are sufficient motivators in the absence of drives. For example, one must be excited to be sexually aroused, but one need not be sexually aroused to be excited. It is quite sufficient to motivate any man, to arouse either excitement or joy or terror or anger or shame or contempt or distress or surprise.

Second, in contrast to the specificity of the space–time information of the drive system, the affect system has those more general properties, which permit it to assume a central position in the motivation of man. Thus, the affect system has generality of time rather than the rhythmic specificity of the drive system. Because the drive system is essentially a transport system, taking material in and out of the body, it must impose its specific temporal rhythms, strictly. One cannot breathe only on Tuesday, Thursday and Saturday, but one could be happy on Tuesday, Thursday and Saturday and sad on Monday, Wednesday, and Friday.

In contrast to the necessary constraints of a system that enjoys few degrees of freedom in transporting material in and out of the body, there is nothing inherent in the structure of the affect mechanism to limit its activation with respect to time. One can be anxious for just a moment or for half an hour, for a day, for a year, or a lifetime, or never, or only occasionally now, though much more frequently some time ago, or conversely.

There are structures in the body that are midway between the drive and affect mechanism. Thus the pain receptors on the back of my hand are as site-specific as any drive. If I were to place a lit cigarette on the skin of my hand, I would experience pain. But the pain mechanism is similar to the affect mechanism in its time generality. There is nothing in the nature of pain receptors that requires that they be stimulated rhythmically or that they ever be stimulated and nothing that would prevent them from being stimulated whenever the person had an accident.

The affect system also permits generality or freedom of object. Although one may satisfy hunger by Chinese, American or Italian food, it must be some variety of edible object. Not so with any affect. There is literally no kind of object that has not been linked to one or another of the affects. In masochism man has even learned to love pain and death. In Puritanism he has learned to hate pleasure and life. He can invest any and every aspect of existence with the magic of excitement and joy or with the dread of fear or shame or distress.

Affects also are capable of much greater generality of intensity than drives. If I do not eat, I become hungrier and hungrier. As I eat I become less hungry. But I may wake mildy irritable in the morning and remain so for the rest of the day. Or, one day I may not be at all angry until quite suddenly something makes me explode with rage. I may start the day moderately angry and quickly become interested in some other matter and so dissipate my anger.

Not only are both intensity and duration of affect capable of greater modulation than is possible for drives, but so is their *density*. By affect density I mean the product of intensity times duration. Most drives operate within relatively narrow density tolerances. The consequence of too much variation of density of intake of air is loss of consciousness and possible death. Compared with drives, affects may be either much more casual and low in density or much more monopolistic and high in density. By virtue of the flexibility of this system, humans are able to oscillate between affect fickleness and obsessive possession by the object of their affective investments.

Not only may affects be widely invested and variously invested, but they may also be invested in other affects, combined with other affects, to intensify or modulate them and to suppress or reduce them. Neither hunger nor thirst can be used to reduce the need for air, as a child may be shamed into crying or may be shamed into stopping his crying.

The generality of time, object, intensity, and density of the affect system are not the *consequence* of learning but rather the structural, innate features of the affect system that make learning possible. In contrast to the drive system with its insistence on air, food, and water, it is *possible* to live a lifetime without ever experiencing fear or joy because the affect mechanism has these structural degrees of freedom that the drive mechanism lacks. Further, in contrast to the customary antithesis between the innate and learned motives, I base the possibility of learning on just these very general features built into the structures and programs of the affect system.

The basic power of the affect system is a consequence of its freedom to combine with a variety of other components in what may be called a *central assembly*. This is an executive mechanism upon which messages converge from all sources, competing from moment to moment for inclusion in this governing central assembly. The affect system can be evoked by central and peripheral messages from any source and, in turn, it can control the disposition of such messages and their sources.

The affect system provides the primary blueprints for cognition, decision, and action. Humans are responsive to whatever circumstances activate the varieties of positive and negative affects. Some of these circumstances innately activate the affects. At the same time, the affect system is also capable of being instigated by learned stimuli and responses. The human being is thus urged by nature and by nurture to explore and to attempt to control the circumstances that evoke his positive and negative affective responses. It is the freedom of the affect system that makes it possible for the human being to begin to implement and to progress toward what he regards as an ideal state – one that, however else he may describe it, implicitly or explicitly entails the maximizing of positive affect and the minimizing of negative affect.

13.2. Innate affect activators

I turn now to an examination of the specific affects I have postulated, how they are activated and some of the consequences of that theory of activation.

I now distinguish nine innate affects.[1] The positive affects are as follows: first, *interest* or *excitement*, with eyebrows down and stare fixed or tracking an object; second, *enjoyment* or *joy*, the smiling response; third, *surprise* or *startle*, with eyebrows raised and eyes blinking. The negative affects are the following: first, *distress* or *anguish*, the crying response; second, *fear* or *terror*, with eyes frozen open in fixed stare or moving away from the dreaded object to the side, with skin pale, cold, sweating, and trembling, and with hair erect; third, *shame* or *humiliation*, with eyes and head lowered; fourth, *contempt*, with the upper lip raised in a sneer; fifth, *disgust*, with the lower lip lowered and protruded; sixth, *anger*, or *rage*, with a frown, clenched jaw, and red face. These facial and skin

[1]Data from the Polarity Scale (Tomkins & Izard, 1965) revealed that differential magnification of contempt was correlated with normative ideology and that disgust was correlated with humanistic ideology. Originally, contempt and disgust were treated as variants of a unitary response, thus making for eight affects in the original theory, rather than nine.

responses are not meant to represent an exhaustive description of the primary affects but rather a representative sample of the more prominent features.

If these are innately patterned responses, are there also innate activators of each affect? Consider the nature of the problem. The innate activators must include the drives as innate activators but *not* be limited to drives as exclusive activators. The neonate, for example, must respond with innate fear to any difficulty in breathing but must also be afraid of other objects. Each affect had to be capable of being activated by a *variety* of unlearned stimuli. The child had to be able to cry at hunger or loud sounds as well as at a diaper pin stuck in his flesh. Therefore, each affect had to be activated by some general characteristic of neural stimulation, common to both internal and external stimuli and not too stimulus-specific like a releaser. Next, the activator had to be correlated with biologically useful information. The young child must fear what is dangerous and smile at what is safe. The activator had to "know the address" of the subcortical center at which the appropriate affect program is stored, not unlike the problem of how the ear responds correctly to each tone. Next, some of the activators had to be capable of nonhabituation, whereas others had to be capable of habituation, otherwise a painful stimulus might too soon cease to be distressing and an exciting stimulus never be let go – such as a deer caught by a bright light. These are some of the characteristics built into the affect mechanism's activation sensitivity. The most economical assumption on which to proceed is to look for communalities among these varieties in the characteristics of the innate activators of each affect. This I have done, and I believe it is possible to account for the major phenomena with a few, relatively simple, assumptions about the general characteristics of the stimuli that innately activate affect.

I account for the differences in affect activation by three general variants of a single principle – the density of neural firing, or stimulation. By density, I mean the number of neural firings per unit of time. The theory posits three discrete classes of activators of affect, each of which further amplifies the sources that activate them. These are *stimulation increase, stimulation level,* and *stimulation decrease.* Thus, there is a provision for three distinct classes of motives: affects about stimulation that is on the increase, about stimulation that is steady, about stimulation that is on the decrease. With respect to density of neural firing, or stimulation, then, the human being is equipped for affective arousal for every major contingency. If internal or external sources of neural firing suddenly increase, he will startle or become afraid, or become interested, depending on the suddenness of the increase in stimulation. If internal or external sources of neural firing reach and maintain a high, constant level of stimulation, which deviates in excess of an optimal level of neural firing, he will respond with anger or distress, depending on the level of stimulation. If internal or external sources of neural firing suddenly decrease, he will laugh or smile with enjoyment, depending on the suddenness of the decrease in stimulation.

The general advantage of affective arousal to such a broad spectrum of levels and changes of level of nerual firing is to make the individual care about quite different states of affairs in different ways. It should be noted that, according to my views, there are both positive and negative affects (startle, fear, interest) activated by stimulation increase; only negative affects are activated by a continuing, unrelieved level of stimulation (distress, anger); and only positive affects are activated by stimulation decrease (laughter, joy). This latter, in my theory, is the only remnant of the tension reduction theory of reinforcement. Stimulation increase may, in my view, result in punishing inasmuch as it activates the cry of distress or anger, depending on how high above optimal levels of stimulation the particular density of neural firing is. A suddenly reduced density of stimulation is invariably rewarding, whether, it should be noted, the stimulation reduced is itself positive or negative in quality. Stated another way, such a set of mechanisms guarantees sensitivity to whatever is new, to whatever continues for any extended period of time, and to whatever is ceasing to happen. In Figure 13.1, I have graphically represented this theory.

Thus, any stimulus with a relatively sudden onset and a steep increase in rate of neural firing will innately activate a startle response. As shown also in Figure 13.1, if the rate of neural firing increases less rapidly, fear is activated, and if the rate increases still less rapidly, interest is innately activated. In contrast, any sustained increase in the level of neural firing, as with a continuing loud noise, would innately activate the cry of distress. If it were sustained and still louder, it would innately activate the anger response. Finally, any sudden decrease in stimulation that reduced the rate of neural firing, as in the sudden reduction of excessive noise, would innately activate the rewarding smile of enjoyment.

Such a neural theory must be able to account for how the "meaning" in such neural messages operates without the benefit of a homunculus who "appraises" every message before instructing the individual to become interested or afraid. It is clear that any theory of affect activation

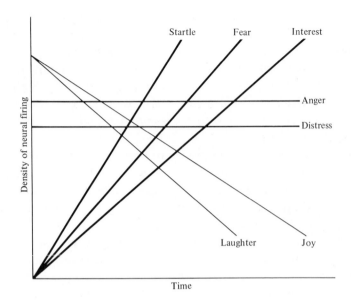

Figure 13.1 Model of the innate activators of affect.

must be capable of accounting for affect that is triggered in either an unlearned or a learned fashion. Certainly the infant who emits his birth cry upon exit from the birth canal has not "appraised" the new environment as a vale of tears before he cries. Equally certain he will later learn to cry at communications telling of death of a beloved person and this does depend on meaning and its appraisal. It is my view that theories (e.g. Arnold or Lazarus) that postulate such appraisal as a necessary condition for affect activation are more embarrassed by unlearned activation than my theory is embarrassed by the learned activation of affect, which I propose can activate affect *only* through the general profiles of neural firing I have postulated. Thus, the novelty of information adequate to trigger interest and the final laughter to a new joke depends on the rate of acceleration of information in the first case and in the rate of deceleration in the second case. If we hear the same information a second time, there is a sense in which it may be appraised as essentially a repetition, but because we now see it coming, there is neither interest nor enjoyment because the gradients of neural firing are now much flatter because compressed, than when the information was first received. Similarly with the startle response, a pistol shot is adequate as an unlearned activator but so is the sudden appearance of a man with two heads. In such a case I would suggest that the rate of neural firing from the conjoint muscular responses of the double-take and the very rapid recruitment of information from memory to check the nature of the apparent message also have the requisite square-wave profile of neural firing called for in my model. In short, "meaning" operates through the very general profiles of acceleration, deceleration, or level of neural firing as these are produced by either cognitive, memorial, perceptual, or motor responses. Any such responses singly or in concert can, through their correlation between meaning and the profiles of neural firing, "innately" fire innate affect programs by stimuli, or responses that are themselves learned may.

13.3. Role of the specific affects

Let us consider now some of the consequences of the affect theory for each of the specific primary affects. We shall begin with startle, fear, and interest, which differ, with respect to activation, only in the rate at which stimulation or neural firing increases.

Startle

Startle appears to be activated by a critical rate of increase in the density of neural firing. The difference between startle (or surprise in its weaker form) and interest is a difference in the steepness of the gradient of stimulation. The same stimulus, therefore, may evoke surprise or interest, depending on the steepness of the rise of stimulation (which in turn depends on numerous factors, prominent among which is the degree of unexpectedness). Thus, a gun shot will evoke startle rather than interest. An unexpected tap on the shoulder by someone who is not seen will also evoke startle rather than interest. In the case of the gun shot, the suddenness of increase of stimulation was primarily in the auditory stimulus itself.

The general function of the startle response we take to be that of a circuit breaker, or interrupter mechanism, which resets the central assembly. This mechanism is similar in design and function to that in a radio or television network that enables special announcements to interrupt any ongoing program. It is ancillary to every other affect because it orients the individual to turn his attention from one thing to another. Whether, having been interrupted, the individual will respond with interest, fear, joy, distress, disgust, shame, or anger will depend on the nature of the interrupting stimulus and on the interpretation given to it.

The experience of surprise itself is brief and varies from an essentially neutral quality in its milder form to a somewhat negative quality in its more intense form as the startle response. Whatever its quality, positive or negative, it is frequently confused with the affect that immediately follows it. The surprise of seeing an unexpected love object is an overall positive experience. The surprise of seeing a dreaded person is an essentially negative experience. In its intense form, it is an involuntary massive contraction of the body as a whole, which momentarily renders individuals incapable of either continuing whatever they were doing before the startle or of initiating new activity for the duration of the startle response.

If startle, fear, and interest differ with respect to activation only in the rate at which stimulation or neural firing increases, then we can account for the unstable equilibria that there seem to be among them. First, it would illuminate the familiar sequences of startle, fear, interest. The same object that first startles quickly passes over into fear and then, somewhat less quickly, is transformed into interest or excitement.

Fear

Study of the fear affect has led to the conclusion that the fear experience in infancy should have minimal aftereffects upon repetition. D. M. Levy (1960) found that in the first six months of life, infants did not cry upon seeing the same doctor about to give them an injection for the second time in their life. Even as late as a year of age, if the interval between inoculations exceeded two months, there was no memory cry. There was a rising frequency of memory cries with age, starting with 1% at six months of age and rising to 20% at a year. There is nothing in the visual stimulus of doctor or needle that would innately activate fear, according to our model. Because memory and recognition are primitive in the first year we should expect fear to be limited to only those stimuli that produce the requisite density of neural firing. The pain of the needle does cause crying, but the sight of the needle again produces no apparent affect.

Our second conclusion about fear is that we should expect a great variety of sudden internal events to be capable of activating fear. These include the feedback of sudden muscular contractions, as in avoidance responses, the rapidly accelerating construction of future possibilities via imagery or cognition, the rapid change of rate of any internal organ or system, such as the heart, circulatory system, respiration, endocrine system, and so on.

Thus it follows that any radical change of the internal environment by drugs can either increase or decrease the threshold for fear by increasing or decreasing the general neural rate of firing. We would suggest that the time-honored effect of alcohol on the release of inhibitions occurs through its relaxation of the skeletal musculature and of the blood vessels lying close to the skin. The muscles relax and the face becomes warm and tingles from vascular relaxation. The combined effect is to reduce radically the possibility of activating fear. A warm bath is similarly disinhibiting, and hydrotherapy has been used successfully to control acute anxiety through essentially similar mechanisms.

Interest

With respect to interest and excitement, while it is sufficiently massive a motive to amplify and make a difference to such an already intense stimulation as that from sexual intercourse, it is also capable of sufficiently graded, flexible innervation and combination to provide a motive matched to the most subtle cognitive capacities. Rapidly varying perception and thinking is thereby combined with varying shades of interest and excitement, which wax and wane appropriately with the operation of the analyzer mechanisms. The match between excitement and the drives is a different match from that between excitement and cognition. Because the latter is a process that is much more rapid, and much more variable in time, it necessarily requires a motivational system that is matched in speed, gradation and flexibility of arousal, combination, and reduction. It must be possible to turn excitement on and off quickly, to grade its intensity, and, above all, to combine it with everchanging central assemblies. In contrast even with other affects, such as fear and anger, interest must have both more and less inertia. It must not necessarily remain activated too long once aroused, but it must also be capable of being sustained indefinitely if the object or activity so demands it.

Interest is also a necessary condition for the formation of the perceptual world. In learning to perceive any new object, the infant must attack the problem over time. Almost any object is too big a bite to be swallowed whole. If it is swallowed whole it remains whole until its parts are decomposed, magnified, examined in great detail and reconstructed into a new more differentiated object. There is thus created a variety of problems in early perception. The object must be perceived in some detail, but it must also be perceived in its unity. Attention must steer a middle course between extreme distractibility from one aspect of an object to some other aspect of an adjacent object, and extreme stickiness and compelled attention to the same object, as in the case of a deer caught and immobilized by a light or an animal fascinated by the eyes of a cobra. Attention must stick long enough both to achieve detail and to move on to some other aspect of the object, not to every competing stimulus in the field. In order to make such graded and differential sampling possible, there must be the continuing support of interest or excitement to the *changing* sampling of the object.

In order to shift from one perceptual perspective to another, from the perceptual to the motor orientation and back again, from both the perceptual and the motor to the conceptual level and back again, and from one memory to another, one must, at the very least, maintain a continuing interest in all of these varying transactions with what is the same object. Without such an underlying continuity of motivational support, there could indeed be no creation of a single object with complex perspectives and with some unity in its variety.

Interest is also a necessary condition for the physiological support of long-term effort. Excitement lends more than spice to life. Without zest, long-term effort and commitment cannot be sustained, either physiologically or psychologically. What constitutes a clogging of the zest for work can be transformed into a major stasis when the individual, through sudden changes in circumstances, comes face to face with the awareness that he cannot fulfill himself in his work. When the individual knows what he wants but must renounce his central aims, this crisis has dramatic physiological consequences. (See Alexander and Portis, 1944).

Distress

In comparison with startle and fear, the affect of distress appears to be based, not on an increase of density of stimulation, but rather on an absolute level of density of stimulation or neural firing, which deviates in excess of an optimal level of neural firing. Thus, pain characteristically produces crying in the infant. The suddenness of pain is not the critical feature of the activation of distress. Either sudden or prolonged pain is equally capable of activating distress. Thus, a sudden stab of pain elicits a sudden scream of distress, and prolonged pain ordinarily produces prolonged crying. In contrast to fear, it is the total quantity or density of stimulation through crying. It is the quantity rather than the quality of stimulation that appears to be critical.

Distress–anguish is a fundamental human affect primarily because of the ubiquity of human suffering. Anxiety, by contrast, is properly an emergency affect. When life and death hang in the balance, most animals have been endowed with the capacity for terror. This is appropriate if life is to be surrendered only very dearly. The cost of terror is so great that the body was not designed for chronic activation of this affect. A human being who responds as if there were justification for being chronically terrorized would properly be diagnosed as ill.

It seems very likely that the differentiation of distress from fear was required in part because the coexistence of superior cognitive powers of anticipation, with an affect as toxic as fear, could have destroyed man if this were the only affect expressing suffering. What was called for was a less toxic, but still negative, affect, which would motivate human beings to solve disagreeable problems without too great a physiological cost or too great a probability of running away from the many problems that confront the human being and which would permit anticipation of trouble at an optimal psychic and biological cost. Such, we think, is the human cry of distress.

If distress is activated by a general continuing level of nonoptimal neural stimulation, then we can account for the fact that such a variety of stimuli, from both internal and external sources, can produce the cry of distress in the infant and the muted distress response in the adult. This variety ranges from the low-level pains of fatigue, hunger, cold, wetness, loud sounds, and overly bright lights to the cry itself as a further stimulus.

The crying response is the first response the human being makes upon being born. The birth cry is a cry of distress. It is not, as Freud supposed, the prototype of anxiety. It is a response of distress at the excessive level of stimulation to which the neonate is suddenly exposed upon being born.

The general biological function of crying is, first, to communicate to the organism itself and to others that all is not well, doing this for a number of alternative distressors; second, to motivate both the self and others to do something to reduce the crying response with a degree of toxicity that is tolerable for both the organism that cries and for the one who hears it cry.

Because the cry is an auditory stimulus, it can be heard at a distance, which provides a considerable safety factor for the otherwise helpless infant. It is also a much more distinctive stimulus for purposes of communication than are the various thrashing-about movements of which the neonate is capable. It is conceivable that, in the absence of the auditory cry, the human mother would be quite as unable to detect the distress of the neonate as is the chick's mother when she sees but is prevented from hearing the cry. This is also likely because of the number of alternative ways in which the cry can be activated. A mother who could detect distress if a diaper pin were sticking into the infant might be unable to do so if the infant were distressed at being alone, in the absence of a distress cry, since much of the thrashing about of the infant is very similar whether the infant is happy or unhappy.

What the distress cry gains in specificity as a distinctive communication, it sacrifices somewhat because it is a sign of so many possible different distressors. When a mother hears an infant cry, she characteristically does not know what it is crying about. It might be hungry, or cold, or in pain, or lonely. She must try each of these in turn to find out, and even then the test does not always remove the ambiguity. Because infants will stop crying for many reasons, quite unrelated to what started them, the mother may easily misdiagnose the nature of the distressor. For example, an infant who is hungry may stop crying upon being picked up but start again when it is put down. The mother at this point cannot be sure whether the child is crying from hunger or loneliness.

The degree of ambiguity is a necessary consequence of the generality of activation of the distress response. In lower forms, the cries are more specific in nature. It is an unanswered question of how specific the cries of the human neonate may be.[2]

Although the number of alternative activators of the cry creates some ambiguity concerning its significance, it is this multiplicity of activators that makes the cry a response of such general significance. It enables general suffering and communication of such suffering. It is as important for the individual to be distressed about many aspects of its life, which continue to overstimulate it, and to communicate this as it is to be able to become interested in anything that is changing.

Although the communication of distress to the mother is primary during infancy because of the infant's helpless dependency, the signifi-

---

[2]One method of answering such a question would be to record a sample of the cries of a neonate during its first week. Then, at moments when the infant was not crying, subject it to a distributed series of playbacks of its past cries and record the fresh crying that the infant emitted in response to hearing itself cry. The infant should cry to the sound of its own cry, because the cry is a quite contagious response. One could then examine the degree of correlation between each cry used as a stimulus and the contagious response to that cry. If the neonate does emit distinctively different cries, then it might respond differentially to its own distinctive cries; therefore the variance between pairs of cries should exceed that within pairs of cries.

cance of communication of distress to the self increases with age. Just as the human drive signal is of value in telling the individual when he is hungry and when he should stop eating, so the distress cry is critical in telling the individual himself when he is suffering and when he has stopped suffering. Awareness that all is not well, without actual suffering, is as unlikely as would be the awareness of the threat of a cigarette burning the skin that had no pain receptors. This is to say that, over and above the motivating qualities of pain or of the distress cry, there are important informational characteristics that are a consequence of their intense motivating properties. The cry not only has information for the self and others about a variety of matters needing alleviation, but it also motivates the self and others to reduce it.

Both the nonoptimal level of stimulation and the distress cry may be masked or reduced in awareness or in general by competing stimulation, which is more intense and more sharply increasing in intensity, and by the affects of startle, fear, or excitement, which may be activated by such competing stimulation. Despite such competition, the coupling of distress and its activators enjoys the competitive advantage of endurance in its claim upon consciousness. Both the activator and the distress cry are long-term motivators, requiring no novelty to keep the individual in a perpetual bind.

Anger

Anger is the other affect that is activated by the absolute density level of stimulation. It is our assumption that anger is activated by a higher density level of stimulation than is distress. Hence, if a source of stimulation, say pain, is adequate to activate distress and both pain and distress continue unrelieved for any period of time, the combination of stimulation may reach the level necessary to activate anger. This is also why frustration may lead to anger. Further, either distress alone or pain alone might be sufficiently dense to activate anger. Thus, a slap on the face is likely to arouse anger because of the very high density of receptors on the surface of the face. In contrast, a stab of pain elsewhere in the body may lack both the requisite density and the duration to activate more than a cry of distress. This principle would also account for the irritability produced by continuous loud noise that tends to recruit widespread muscle contraction, which, added to the distress affect, could raise the density of stimulation to that necessary for anger. The role of distress and anger in the mother-infant relationship is complex. The infant's crying is capable of innately activating the distress of the mother, and so enlisting the aid of the mother and strengthening commitment to her child. But this very combination of the loud crying of distress of the child and the evoked distress of the mother is also quite capable of innately activating anger sufficient to attenuate the tie to the infant and, in the extreme case, lead the mother to destroy the child.

Joy

In contrast to stimulation increase and stimulation level, there is also the affect that operates on the principle of stimulation reduction. The *smile of joy* is based on such a mechanism. The smile of joy is innately activated in our view by any relatively steep reduction of the density of stimulation and neural firing. Thus, sudden relief from such negative stimulations as pain, fear, distress, or agression will produce the smile of joy. In the case of pain, fear, and distress, the smile of joy is a smile of relief. In the case of sudden anger reduction, it is the smile of triumph. The same principle operates with the sudden reduction of pleasure, as after orgasm or the completion of a good meal, there is often the smile of pleasure. Further, the sudden reduction of positive affect, such as excitement, also activates the smile of joy, in this case usually the smile of recognition or familiarity. In all of these cases, it is the steepness of the gradient of stimulation reduction that is critical. A gradual reduction of pain may pass into indifference. A gradual reduction of distress, similarly, may provide no secondary reward of joy. For a steep gradient reduction in density of stimulation to be possible, it is, of course, necessary that there be a prior level of high density of stimulation. This means that a reduction of weak pain stimulation that is sudden enough may nonetheless not involve a sufficient reduction in density of stimulation to activate the smiling response. Under such conditions, whatever reward value there may be in the cessation of pain stimulation is not enhanced by the incremental reward of the smiling response. Further, it means that many familiar objects in the environment may be too familiar to evoke enough, even momentary, excitement to evoke the smile of joy at the recognition of the familiar and the reduction of very weak interest. In order to enjoy seeing someone or something familiar, one must first have been sufficiently interested so that the sudden reduction of this interest will constitute a sufficient change in density of stimulation to evoke the smiling response.

This theory of activation of the smiling response enables us to account for phenomena as disparate as the joy of relief from pain and the joy of the infant at the sight of the mother. The mother's face is one of the few objects in the environment with sufficient variation in appearance to produce both excitement at its sudden appearance and the smile at the sudden reduction of this excitement when the face is recognized as a familiar one. This would account for the smile, observed by other investigators, such as Piaget, at the sudden perception of familiar toys or at somewhat expected and somewhat unexpected "effects" produced by the child's own efforts.

The second principle of activation of the smiling response is based on our theory of memory. Simply stated, the visual sight of a smiling face can be learned to become a "name", i.e., a message capable of retrieving from memory a specific trace at a specific address. In this case, it retrieves the stored memory of how the individual experienced the feedback from the muscles of his own face when he smiled in the past. This retrieved past experience can also become a "name" of a stored program, which translates these perceived "awarenesses" into their equivalent motor messages, i.e., a set of impulses that instruct the facial muscles to contract in such a way that the feedback from the contracted facial muscles is equal to the experienced set that initiated this motor translation.

We do not wish at this point to enlarge on subtle distinctions, except to note that the conscious experience of the smile of another face may activate retrieved awareness of one's own past smiles, which may then either retrieve a stored program in the manner just indicated or directly innervate the innate program of the smiling response via the subcortical centers. The difference in these two routes would be that in the former case a "learned" smile would be activated and in the latter it would be an "unlearned" smile.

We are attempting here to distinguish learning that utilizes preformed programs from learning and memory that may produce identical responses on a purely learned basis, which bypasses the innate programs while it mimics them. It is, in part, the difference between the "Oh!" of surprise and the same "Oh" of an actor reading his lines. In either event, and by either route, the smile of another person is capable of evoking the empathic response. Such mimesis is quite different from the activation by sudden stimulation reduction and somewhat confounds the empirical investigation of the smiling response.

The third way in which the smiling response may be activated is through memory, or learning. It is not necessarily the case that any experience that produced the smile of enjoyment in the past will be capable of activating the same affect upon being recalled. Emotion remembered in tranquility need be no more motivating than the toothache that has just stopped aching, which can be recalled with relative calm. Any affect requiring any degree of uncertainty for activation is all but impossible to repeat exactly, even when the circumstances, in fact or in memory, are duplicated exactly. No joke is ever quite as funny on repetition. Although the smile is an affect that can be emitted to the familiar, it also depends on stimulation reduction, which, apart from pain, distress, or anger, requires some novelty if excitement is to be activated sufficiently so that its reduction constitutes an adequate stimulus for the smile.

How then is memory, or anticipation, likely to evoke the smile of enjoyment? Any recollection, or anticipation, that produces a present affect sufficiently intense and suddenly reduced either through remembered, imagined, or anticipated consequences may evoke the smile of joy. Such would be the case if I anticipated meeting someone who excited me and whom I had not seen for many years. If this generated present excitement, the shock of recognition, in visualizing such a reunion, might sufficiently reduce the excitement so that the smile of joy might be evoked. Similarly, if the recollection of such a meeting first arouses excitement that is suddenly reduced, the smile of joy may be activated in what may be called "postication." If the anticipated or posticipated encounter generates fear, distress, or shame that is reduced in the imagination by appropriate counteractive measures, one may smile in joy. The crushing retort to the insufferable opponent, even when it occurs too late for the battle proper, may bring joy to the heart of the defeated, whose anger is suddenly reduced by the imagined discomfiture of the adversary. The recollection of past defeat in attempting problem solving, which may occasion present distress or shame, can evoke the smile of joy if suddenly there is an expectation of a solution and with it a rapid reduction of the distress or shame. The same smile of joy may occur in the midst of difficulties if the individual simply imagines to have heroically solved the problem.

Smiling creates a *felicité à deux* similar to and also different from that created by the enjoyment of sexual intercourse. In sexual intercourse, the behavior of each is a sufficient condition for the pleasure of each individual for himself and at the same time for the pleasure of the other. This dyadic interaction is inherently social inasmuch as the satisfaction of the self is at the same time the satisfaction of the other.

In the smiling response, as we see it first between the mother and her child, there is a similar mutuality, except that it is on the affect level rather than through mutual drive satisfaction, and it operates at a distance rather than requiring body contact. The difference in this respect is as profound a change in the structure of motivation as was involved in the development of perception with the appearance of distance receptors compared with proximity receptors.

Because the infant will smile at the face of the mother and thereby reward itself, and because the mother will in turn smile at the smile of the infant and thereby reward herself, concurrent smiling is mutually rewarding from the outset. Later, when the child's development is sufficiently advanced, both parties to this mutual enjoyment are further rewarded by the awareness that this enjoyment is shared enjoyment. This is mediated through the eyes. Through interocular interaction both parties become aware of each other's enjoyment and of the very fact of communion and mutuality. Indeed, one of the prime ways in later life that the adult will recapture this type of communion is when he smiles at another person, who smiles back at him and at the same time the eyes of each are arrested in a stare at the eyes of the other. Under these conditions one person can "fall in love with" another person. The power of this dyadic posture is a derivative of an earlier unashamed fascination-and-joy smile. The power of the earlier experience is essentially innate: the match between the stimulus characteristics of the human face and the conditions necessary for innately arousing the reciprocal affects of interest and joy biologically equips the infant, no less than the mother, to be joyous in this way.

More often than not, mutual awareness of each other's smile will include visual awareness of each other's face, including the smile but with the eyes as figure against the rest of the face as ground. One may look at the other's eyes, but with limited awareness. Because socialization ordinarily places restrictions on the direct intent stare into the eyes of another, adult communion ordinarily excludes prolonged interocular interaction as being excessively intimate. Despite this exclusion there is a deeply rewarding sense of communion made possible by mutual awareness of each other's face in mutual smiling. Awareness of mutuality is achieved without interocular interaction even though this exclusion somewhat attenuates the intimacy of this experience.

The general biological significance of social responsiveness and therefore of any affect supporting such characteristics is manifold. First, because the human infant is the most helpless of animals, it is important that he attract the care of the mother. This is guaranteed first by the distress cry, which creates an *infelicité à deux* and prompts the mother to attend to the punishment the infant is experiencing because the cry as heard will activate the cry in anyone who hears it. It is as unpleasant to hear as the stimulus that activates it in the infant. In addition to the cry as a motive urging both the infant and the mother to *do* something, there is the positive reward of the shared smile, which will make it more likely that after the crisis signaled by the cry is past the mother will continue to interact with and stimulate the child. Because the infant must learn how to become a human being from other human beings, his development necessarily requires much interaction, which must begin relatively early with the mother. For this to happen and for it to be frequently repeated, both parties must be continually rewarded by each other's presence.

Second, mutual social responsiveness between mother and child not only helps guarantee the survival of an otherwise relatively helpless animal but also makes possible the continuing reproduction of the species.

Social responsiveness in animals is, of course, by no means a necessary condition for the reproducibility of a species. Yet in some species of animals, social responsiveness is one of the techniques by which the group resists extinction. Animals requiring cooperation in order to cope successfully with predators, animals with a low reproductive rate, animals with relatively helpless infants for a protracted developmental period, and especially animals with heavy developmental dependence on learning from each other will require motivational systems that punish alienation and isolation. Every consideration critical to guaranteeing that the infant survive to reproduce is necessary for the preservation of the species, but this also requires, over and above individual survival, group competence in dealing with predators, with scarcity of food, with disruption of the group by individualistic motives, and with a low reproductive rate. Humans are among those animals whose individual survival and group reproduction rests heavily on social responsiveness, and the mutual enjoyment of each other's presence is one of the most important ways in which social interaction is rewarded and perpetuated.

The smiling response and the enjoyment of its feedback along with the feedback of concurrent autonomic and hypothalamic responses make possible a kind of human social responsiveness that is relatively free of drive satisfaction, of body site specificity of stimulation, and of specific motor responses other than that of the smile itself.

The smiling response as an independent source of reward frees the individual from the requirement of specific body contact and stimulation as a necessary condition of positive reward. In order to enjoy human interaction he no longer requires the breast in his mouth or the vagina to receive his penis. This is not to say that all positive affects can dispense with body contact. The love evoked in the child by cuddling, hugging, and kissing, as well as by feeding, is vitally important, especially for the very young infant. We do not wish to minimize the importance of body contact, body stimulation, and the satisfaction of hunger for the very young nor to minimize the importance of sexual intercourse for the adult as a source of both pleasure and the evoking of the affects of excitement and joy or love. We do wish to distinguish, however, the consequences of freeing positive affect from necessary dependence on the contact receptors.

The cat must have his fur rubbed to enjoy his own purring. In the infant monkey it is clear that the positive affect is closely tied to the clinging response and the reassuring contact, but it is also clear that it is developing in the direction of joy in the presence of the mother independent of contact. The biological importance of clinging for an arboreal infant whose mother necessarily has to use her arms to swing and support herself is obvious. In the case of birds, the critical response is following rather than clinging, because here it is also important that the infant not be separated from the mother. But since these birds are reared on the ground and not carried on the body of the mother, the imprinted response of the following of the earliest object seen, which is usually the mother, guarantees both some freedom of movement for the mother on the ground as well as the relative proximity of the infant bird.

In the case of the human infant there is a radical change in the biological requirements of the mother–child relationship. There is no clinging (although right after birth and for a short period thereafter the grasping reflex is powerful enough to sustain the weight of the infant) and there is clearly no possibility of following. This does not rule out the possibility that body contact initiated by the mother might not be of great importance as an activator of the smiling response. The smiling response, like the following response of some birds, is primarily mediated through what the infant sees rather than through what he feels through body contact. Body contact is one of the important ways in which distress is reduced in infancy, and because the sudden reduction of distress can be a stimulus to the smiling response, body contact in this way may become a stimulus to the smiling response. The body of the mother, of course, becomes the focus of a complex affect and drive matrix because it can activate both excitement and joy and can reduce fear, distress, and shame, as well as satisfy hunger and thirst.

But the restriction of positive or negative affects to body contact would seriously impair the social, intellectual, and motor development of the child. The child must be free to explore the world and yet to feel safe in doing so. To the extent to which he must have body contact to feel joy and love, the infant is not free to satisfy his curiosity in the world about him. He would also be restricted in the kind of social responsiveness which would be possible for him. Thus to be a few feet away from the mother or any other familiar person, to engage in conversation, or to engage in any of the adult variants of human communion, for example, to lecture, to act, to perform before an audience, all of these would constitute frustration unless the smiling–enjoyment response could be emitted to visual stimuli that were at some distance from the child.

The equation of oral interests with every type of human dependence and interdependence has masked the critical role both of the face and of the distance receptors in human communion. Both the face and tongue are organs of exquisite subtlety of expressiveness. We do not think it accidental that Freud sat behind the patient so that facial interaction was minimized. He shared the almost universal taboo on intimate facial interaction and overweighted the role of the mouth as an instrument of hunger, in symbolizing all human communion. We are arguing that the smile in response to the human face makes possible all those varieties of human communion that are independent of eating and of touching another.

The purely social wishes of the human being are diverse. They are derivatives of numerous affects complexly organized to create addictions to particular kinds of human communion. Although the smile of joy is perhaps the central affect in such a matrix, it is by no means the exclusive base of social responsiveness. Humans characteristically are excited by other human beings as well as made joyous by them. They are, on the negative side, distressed, frightened, ashamed, and angered by the deprivation of human interaction as well as by a variety of inappropriate responses from other human beings.

Social enjoyments are so diverse partly for the same reason that the objects of human excitement are so diverse. Anything that can capture the interest of a human being can also produce the smile of joy. Among this larger set of interests is a very large subset of social interests and enjoyments. Every time and in every manner in which one human being has excited another, either party independently or both can become candidates for social enjoyment. Add to this all the possible transformations that the imagination of an intelligent animal permits and the outcome is a very broad spectrum of social enjoyments.

Although I argued for the existence of nine innate affects, the theory of the innate activators of affect omitted shame, contempt, and disgust. I do not believe these three are innate affects in the same sense as the six already described. They have motivating, amplifying properties of affects but have somewhat different characteristics and mechanisms.

Contempt, disgust, and shame

Contempt and disgust are innate defensive responses, which are auxiliary to the hunger, thirst, and oxygen drives. Their function is clear. If the food about to be ingested activates contempt, the upper lip and nose are raised and the head is drawn away from the apparent source of the offending odor. If the food has been taken into the mouth, it may, if disgusting, be spit out. If it has been swallowed and is toxic, it will produce nausea and be vomited out, either through the mouth or nostrils. The early warning response via the nose is contempt; the mouth or stomach response is disgust. If contempt and disgust were limited to these functions, we should not define them as affects but rather as auxiliary drive mechanisms. However, their status is somewhat unique in that contempt, disgust, and nausea also function as signals and motives to others as well as to the self of feelings of rejection. They readily accompany a wide spectrum of entities that need not be tasted, smelled, or ingested. Contempt and disgust appear to be changing more in status from drive-reducing acts to acts that also have a more general motivating and signal function, both to the individual who emits it and to the one who sees it.

Just as contempt and disgust are drive auxiliary acts, I posit shame as an innate *affect auxiliary* response and a specific inhibitor of continuing interest and enjoyment. Like disgust, it operates only after interest or enjoyment has been activated and inhibits one or the other or both. The innate activator of shame is the incomplete reduction of interest or joy. Such a barrier might arise because one is suddenly looked at by one who is strange, or because one wishes to look at or commune with another person but suddenly cannot because he is strange, or one expected him to be familiar but he suddenly appears unfamiliar, or one started to smile but found one was smiling at a stranger. The response of shame includes lowering the eyelid, lowering the tonus of all facial muscles, lowering the head via a reduction in tonus of the neck muscles, and a unilateral tilting of the head in one direction.

Shyness, shame, and guilt are identical as affects, though not so experienced because of differential coassembly of perceived causes and consequences. Shyness is about strangeness of the other; guilt is about moral transgression; shame is about inferiority, but the core affect in all three is identical, though the coassembled perceptions, cognitions, and intentions may be vastly different.

Biologically, disgust and contempt are drive auxiliary responses that have evolved to protect the human being from coming too close to noxious-smelling objects and to regurgitate these if they have been ingested. Through learning, these responses have come to be emitted to biologically neutral stimuli, including, for example, disgusting and dirty thoughts. Shame, in contrast, is an affect auxiliary to the affect of interest–excitement. Any perceived barrier to positive affect with the other will evoke lowering of the eyelids and loss of tonus in the face and neck muscles, producing a head hung in shame. The child who is burning with excitement to explore the face of the stranger is nonetheless vulnerable to shame just because the other is perceived as strange. Characteristically, however, intimacy with the good and exciting other is eventually consummated. In contrast, the disgusting other is to be kept at a safe distance permanently. The reason for distinguishing disgust more sharply from contempt than I had done before, arose primarily from data in connection with my ideological polarity theory, which I shall now describe briefly.

13.4. Polarity theory

I have been concerned for some time with a field I have called the *psychology of knowledge*, an analog of the sociology of knowledge. It is a concern with the varieties of cognitive styles, with the types of evidence that the individual finds persuasive and, most particularly, with his ideology. I have defined *ideology* as any organized set of ideas about which humans are at once most articulate, ideas that produce enduring controversy over long periods of time, that evoke passionate partisanship, and about which humans are least certain because there is insufficient evidence. Ideology therefore abounds at the frontier of any science. But today's ideology may tomorrow be confirmed or disconfirmed and so cease to be ideology. In a review of 2,000 years of ideological controversy in western civilization, I have detected a sustained recurrent polarity between the humanistic and the normative orientations appearing in such diverse domains as the foundations of mathematics, the theory of aesthetics, political theory, epistemology, theory of perception, theory of value, theory of child rearing, theory of psychotherapy, and personality testing.

The issues are simple enough. Is man the measure, an end in himself, active, creative, thinking, desiring, loving force in nature? Or must man realize himself, attain his full stature, only through struggle toward, participation in, and conformity to a norm, a measure, an ideal essence basically prior to and independent of man? This polarity appeared first in Greek philosophy between Protagoras and Plato. Western thought has been an elaborate series of footnotes to the conflict between the conception of man as the measure of reality and value versus that of man and nature as alike unreal and valueless in comparison to the realm of essence that exists independently of space and time. More simply, this polarity represents an idealization of man – a positive idealization in the humanistic ideology and a negative idealization in the normative ideology. Human beings, in Western civilization, have tended toward self-celebration, positive or negative. In Oriental thought another alternative is represented, that of harmony between man and nature.

I have further assumed that the individual resonates to any organized ideology because of an underlying ideo-affective posture, which is a set of feelings that is more *loosely* organized than any highly organized ideology.

Some insight into these ideological concepts held by an individual may be obtained through use of my *polarity scale*. The polarity scale assesses the individual's normative or humanistic position on a broad spectrum of ideological issues in mathematics, science, art, education, politics, child rearing, and theory of personality. Following are a few sample items from the scale. The normative position will be A, the humanistic B. The individual is permitted four choices: A, B, A and B, and neither A nor B.

1. A. Numbers were discovered.   B. Numbers were invented
2. A. Play is childish   B. Nobody is too old to play.
3. A. The mind is like a mirror. B. The mind is like a lamp.
4. A. If you have had a bad   B. If you have had a bad experience
      experience with someone,   with someone, the way to
      the way to characterize   characterize this is that it leaves
      this is that it leaves a bad   a bad taste in the mouth
      smell.

I have assumed that the ideo-affective posture is the result of systematic differences in the socialization of affects. For example, the attitudes toward distress in the items above could be a consequence of the following differences in distress socialization. When the infant or child cries, the parent, following his own ideo-affective posture and more articulate ideology, may elect to convert the distress of the child into a rewarding scene by putting his arms around the child and comforting him. He may, however, amplify the punishment inherent in the distress response by putting himself into opposition to the child and his distress. He will require that the child stop crying, insisting that the child's crying results from some norm violation and threaten to increase the child's suffering if he does not suppress the response. "If you don't stop crying, I will really give you something to cry about." If the child internalizes his parent's ideo-affective posture and his ideology, the child has learned a very basic posture toward suffering, which will have important consequences for resonance to ideological beliefs quite remote from the nursery and the home. This is exemplified by the following items from the polarity scale: "The maintenance of law and order is the most important duty of any government" versus "Promotion of the welfare of the people is the most important function of a government."

The significance of the socialization of distress is amplified by the differential socialization of all the affects, including surprise, enjoyment, excitement, anger, fear, shame, contempt, and disgust. I have outlined elsewhere (Tomkins, 1979) a systematic program of differential socialization of each of these affects, which together produce an ideoaffective posture that inclines the individual to resonate differentially to ideology. In the preceding example, excitement and enjoyment are implicated along with distress, anger, shame, fear, contempt, and disgust, as it is the relative importance of the reward of positive affects versus the importance of the punishment of negative affects that is involved in law and order versus welfare.

What is less obvious is that similar differences in ideoaffective posture influence such remote ideological options as the following items from the polarity scale: "Numbers were invented" versus "Numbers were discovered"; "The mind is like a lamp which illuminates whatever it shines on" versus "The mind is like a mirror which reflects whatever strikes it"; "Reason is the chief means by which human beings make great discoveries" versus "Reason has to be continually disciplined and corrected by reality and hard facts"; "Human beings are basically good" versus "Human beings are basically evil." The structure of ideology and the relationships among the socialization of affects, the ideoaffective postures, and ideology are more complex than can be discussed here. I wish to present just enough of this theory to enable the reader to understand the relationship of the theory to the face.

I have assumed that the humanistic position is one that attempts to maximize positive affect for individuals and for all their interpersonal relationships. In contrast, the normative position is that norm compliance is the primary value and that positive affect is a *consequence* of norm compliance, not to be directly sought as a goal. Indeed, the suffering of negative affect is assumed to be a frequent experience and an inevitable consequence of the human condition. Therefore, in any interpersonal transaction, the humanist self-consciously strives to maximize positive affect insofar as it is possible.

The first hypothesis concerning the face is that humanists would smile more frequently than the normatively oriented, both because they experienced the smile of enjoyment more frequently during their socialization and because they internalized the ideoaffective posture that one should attempt to increase positive affect for the other as well as the self. The learned smile does not always mean that the individual *feels* happy. As often as not, it is a consequence of a wish to communicate to the other that one wishes him to feel smiled upon and to evoke the smile from the other. It is often the oil that is spread over troubled human waters to extinguish the fires of distress, hate and shame. It was known from previous investigations with the stereoscope (Tomkins & Izard, 1965) that when one presented humanists and normatives with two pictures of the same face (one of which was smiling and one of which was not), the humanists tended to suppress the nonsmiling face significantly more often than did the normatives. Vasquez (1975) confirmed that humanist subjects actually smile more frequently while talking with an experimenter than do normative subjects. There is, however, no such difference when subjects are alone, displaying affect spontaneously.

The second hypothesis is that humanists would respond more frequently with distress and normatives would respond more frequently with anger. The rationale for this is that when an interpersonal relationship is troubled, the humanist will try to absorb as much punishment as possible and so display distress rather than anger; anger being more likely to escalate into conflict is a more blaming extrapunitive response than distress. It was assumed that the normative subjects would more frequently respond with anger because they are more extrapunitive, more pious and blaming, and less concerned with sparing the feelings of others, as their internalized models did not spare their own feelings. This hypothesis was not confirmed, but neither was it reversed. This failure may have arisen because the differences in polarity scale scores were not as great as I would have wished. In part, this was a consequence of a strong humanistic bias among college students at the time of testing and because of the reluctance of known normatives to volunteer for testing. This is consistent with prior research, including my own, which indicates that volunteers are more sociophilic and friendly.

The third hypothesis is that humanists would more frequently respond with shame and that normatives would respond less frequently with shame but more frequently with disgust and contempt. The rationale is that shame represents an impunitive response to what is interpreted as an interruption to communion (as, e.g., in shyness) and that it will ultimately be replaced by full communication.

In contrast, contempt and disgust are responses to a bad other and the termination of intimacy with such a one is assumed to be permanent unless the other one changes significantly. These hypotheses were confirmed for shame and disgust but not for contempt. Humanistic subjects, although displaying affect spontaneously, did respond more frequently with shame responses than did normative subjects, whereas normative subjects displayed significantly more disgust responses than did humanistic subjects.

In conclusion, it was predicted and confirmed that humanistic subjects respond more frequently with smiling to the good other and with shame if there is any perceived barrier to intimacy. The normative subjects smile less frequently to the other and emit disgust more frequently to the other who is tested and found wanting. The differences represent a correlation between cognition and affect, as affect is displayed on the faces of those who differ significantly in what they believe about the world in which they live.

13.5. Major changes in my theory of affect

The theory presented in *Affect, imagery, consciousness* (Tomkins, 1982) has since been developed and modified in four essential ways. First, the theory of affect as amplification I now specify as analogic amplification. Second, I now believe that it is the skin of the face, rather than the musculature, that is the major mechanism of analogic amplification. Third, a substantial quantity of the affect we experience as adults is pseudo-, backed-up, affect. Fourth, affect amplifies not only its own activator but also the response to both that activator and to itself.

Analogic amplification

The theory of affect as amplification was flawed by a serious ambiguity. I unwittingly assumed a similarity between electronic amplification and affective amplification, such that in both there was an increase in gain of the signal. If such were the case, what was amplified would remain essentially the same except that it would become louder. But affects are separate mechanisms, involving bodily responses quite distinct from the other bodily responses they are presumed to amplify.

How can one response of our body amplify another response? It does this by being similar to that response, but also different. It is an analog amplifier. The affect mechanism is like the pain mechanism in this respect. If we cut our hand, saw it bleeding, but had no innate pain receptors, we would know we had done something that needed repair, but there would be no urgency to it. Like our automobile that needs a tune-up, we might well let it go until next week when we had more time. But the pain mechanism, like the affect mechanism, so amplifies our awareness of the injury that activates it that we are forced to be concerned, and concerned immediately. The biological utility of such analogic amplification is self-evident. The injury, as such, in the absence of pain, simply does not hurt. The pain receptors have evolved to make us hurt and care about injury and disease. Pain is an analog of injury in its inherent similarity. Contrast pain with an orgasm, as a possible analog. If, instead of pain, we always had an orgasm to injury, we would be biologically destined to bleed to death. Affect receptors are no less compelling. Our hair stands on end and we sweat in terror. Our face reddens as our blood pressure rises in anger. Our blood vessels dilate and our face becomes pleasantly warm as we smile in enjoyment. These are compelling analogs of what arouses terror, rage, and enjoyment.

These experiences constitute one form of affect amplification. A second form of affect amplification occurs also by virtue of the similarity of their profiles, in time, to their activating trigger. Just as a pistol shot is a stimulus that is very sudden in onset, very brief in duration, and equally sudden in decay, so its amplification affective analog, the startle response, mimics the pistol shot by being equally sudden in onset, brief in duration, and equally sudden in decay. Therefore, affect, by being analogous in the quality of the feelings from its specific receptors as well as in its profile of activation, maintenance, and decay, amplifies and extends the duration and impact of whatever triggers the affect. Epileptics do not startle, according to Landis and Hunt (1939). Their experienced world is different in this one fundamental way. If epileptics had in addition lacked fear and rage, their world would have become even more different than the usual humanly experienced world.

They experience a pistol shot as sudden but not startling. A world experienced without any affect at all because of a complete genetic defect in the whole spectrum of innate affects would be a pallid, meaningless world. We would know that things happened, but we could not care whether they did or not.

By being immediately activated and thereby coassembled with its activator, affect either makes good things better or bad things worse, by conjointly simulating its activator in its profile of neural firing and by adding a special analogic quality, which is intensely rewarding or punishing. In illustrating the simulation of an activating stimulus, e.g., a pistol shot by the startle response, which was equally sudden in onset, equally brief in duration, and equally sudden in decay, I somewhat exaggerated the goodness of fit between activator and affect to better illustrate the general principle. Having done so, let me now be more precise in the characterization of the degree of similarity in profile of neural firing between activator and affect activated. I presented a model of the innate activators of the primary affects in which every possible major general neural contingency innately activates different specific affects. As I explained earlier, increased gradients of rising neural firing activate interest, fear, or surprise as the slope of increasing density of neural firing becomes steeper. Enjoyment is activated by a decreasing gradient of neural firing; distress is activated by a sustained level of neural firing, which exceeds an optimal level by an as yet undetermined magnitude; and anger is also activated by a nonoptimal level of neural firing but one that is substantially higher than that which activates distress. Increase, decrease, or level of neural firing are in this model the sufficient conditions for activating specific affects. Analogic amplification, therefore, is based upon one of these three distinctive features rather than all of them. It so happens that the startle simulates the steepness of the gradient of onset, the brief plateau of maintenance, and the equally steep gradient of decline of profile of the pistol shot and its internal neural correlate, but that is not the general case. Analogic simulation is based on the similarity to the adequate activator, not on all of its characteristics. Thus, it is the decay alone of a stimulus that is simulated in enjoyment. If one places electrodes on the wrist of a subject, permits fear to build, and then removes the electrodes suddenly, we can invariably activate a smile of relief at just that moment. This amplifies (or makes more so) the declining neural stimulation from the reduction of fear. Therefore, enjoyment amplifies by simulating decreasing gradients of neural stimulation. Interest, fear, and surprise amplify by simulating increasing gradients of neural stimulation. Distress and anger amplify by simulating maintained level of simulation.

Locus of analogic amplification

The second modification in my theory concerns the exact loci of the rewarding and punishing amplifying analogs. From the start, I emphasized the face and voice as the major loci of the critical feedback experienced as affect. The voice I still regard as a major locus and shall discuss its role in the next section.

The significance of the face in interpersonal relations cannot be exaggerated. It is not only a communication center for the sending and receiving of information of all kinds, but because it is the organ of affect expression and communication, it is necessarily brought under strict social control. There are universal taboos on looking too directly into the eyes of the other because of the likelihood of affect contagion, as well as escalation, because of the unwillingness to express affect promiscuously, and because of concern lest others achieve control through knowledge of one's otherwise private feelings. Humans are primarily voyeuristic, not only because vision is their most informative sense, but because the shared eye-to-eye interaction is the most intimate relationship possible between human beings. There is, in this way, complete mutuality between two selves, each of whom simultaneously is aware of the self and the other. Indeed the intimacy of sexual intercourse is ordinarily attenuated, lest it become too intimate, by being performed in the dark. In the psychoanalytic myth, the crime of the son is voyeuristic by witnessing the "primal scene" and Oedipus is punished, in kind, by blindness.

The taboo on the shared interocular experience is easily exposed. If I were to ask you to turn to another person and stare directly into their eyes while permitting the other to stare directly into your eyes, you would become aware of the taboo. Ordinarily we confront each other by my looking at the bridge of your nose and your looking at my cheek bone. If our eyes should happen to meet directly, the confrontation is minimized by glancing down or away, by letting the eyes go slightly out of focus, or by attenuating the visual datum by making it background to the sound of the other's voice, which is made more figural. The taboo is not only a taboo on looking too intimately but also on exposing the taboo by too obviously avoiding direct confrontation. These two strategies are taught by shaming the child for staring into the eyes of visitors and then shaming the child a second time for hanging his head in shame before the guest.

Only the young or the young in heart are entirely free of the taboo. Those adults whose eyes are caught by the eyes of the other in the shared interocular intimacy may fall in love on such an occasion or, having fallen in love, thereby express the special intimacy they have recaptured from childhood.

The face now appears to be still the central site of the affect responses and their feedback, but I have now come to regard the skin, in general, and the skin of the face, in particular, as of the greatest importance in producing the feel of affect.

In *Affect, imagery, consciousness* (Tomkins, 1982, p. 244), I described the affect system as consisting of 13 components, beginning with the innate affect programs and including affect motor messages. My statement that I regard the face and voice as the central site of affect responses and their feedback must not be interpreted to mean that the whole affect system and its supporting mechanisms are found in the face. Analogically, one might argue for the importance of the thumb and fingers in human evolution without specifying that there is a forearm, biceps, body, and brain to support the thumb.

Further, it is now clear, as it was not then, that the brain is sensitive to its own synthesized chemical endorphins, which serve as analgesics and thus radically attenuate pain and all the negative affects recruited by pain on both innate and learning bases.

My original observations of the intensity of infantile affect, of how an infant was, for example, seized by his own crying, left no doubt in my mind that what the face was doing with its muscles and blood vessels as well as with its accompanying vocalization was at the heart of the matter. This seemed to me to be the major phenomenon, not an "expression" of anything else. I then spent a few years in posing professional actors and others to simulate facial affect. A correlation of +.86 was obtained (Tomkins & McCarter, 1964) between the judgments of trained observers as to what affects they saw on the faces of these subjects as presented in still photographs and what we had intended these sets of muscular responses to represent. This success was gratifying, after so many years of indifferent and variable findings in this field, but it was also somewhat misleading in overemphasizing the role of innately patterned facial muscular responses in the production of affect. I was further confirmed in these somewhat misleading results by the successes of Paul Ekman and Carroll Izard. Ekman, Sorenson, and Friesen (1969), using some of my photographs, were able to demonstrate a wide cultural consensus, even in very primitive remote preliterate societies. Izard

(1969), using different photographs but the same conceptual scheme, further extended these impressive results to many other literate societies.[3] The combined weight of all these investigations was most impressive, but I continued to be troubled by one small fact. The contraction of no other set of muscles in the body had *any* apparent motivational properties. Thus, if I were angry, I might clench my fist and hit someone, but if I simply clenched my fist, this would in no way guarantee I would bcome angry. Muscles appeared to be specialized for action and not for affect. Why then was the smile so easily and so universally responded to as an affect? Why did someone who was crying seem so distressed and so unhappy? Further, from an evolutionary point of view, we know that different functions are piled indiscriminately on top of structures that may originally have evolved to support quite different functions. The tongue was an organ of eating before it was an organ of speech. The muscles of the face were also probably involved in eating before they were used as vehicles of affect, though we do not know this for a fact. It is, of course, possible that the complex affect displays on the human face evolved primarily as communication mechanisms rather than as sources of motivating feedback. My intuition was, and still is, that the communication of affect is a secondary spin-off function rather than the primary function. This is not, however, to minimize its importance as communication.

The primary importance of motivating feedback over communication would appear to have been the case with a closely related mechanism, that of pain. The cry of pain does communicate but the feeling of pain does not. It powerfully motivates the person who feels it in much the same way that affect does. That someone else is informed of this is, however, not mediated by the pain receptors in themselves, but by the cry of distress that usually accompanies it. I, therefore, began to look at affect analogs such as pain and sexual sensitivity and fatigue for clues about the nature of the motivating properties of the affect mechanisms.

I soon became aware of a paradox: three of the most compelling states to which the human being is vulnerable arise on the surface of the skin. Torture via skin stimulation has been used for centuries to shape and compel human beings to act against their own deepest wishes and values. Sexual seduction, again via skin stimulation, particularly of the genitals,

[3]Izard's results were not quite as good as Ekman's, for, I think, two reasons: first, his photograph selection was guided primarily by empirical criteria rather than theoretical choice, i.e., if subjects agreed that a face showed interest, it was retained, despite the fact that the clue to such consensus might be that the subject was depicted staring at some object. Second, the critical distinction between innate and backed-up affect was not observed in Izard's picture selection.

has also prompted human beings to violate their own wishes and values. Finally, fatigue to the point of extreme sleepiness appears to be localized in the skin surrounding the eyes. This area will sometimes be rubbed in an effort to change the ongoing stimulation and ward off sleepiness. But in the end, it appears to be nothing but an altered responsiveness of skin receptors, especially in the eyelids, that makes it impossible for the sleepy person to maintain the state of wakefulness. He cannot keep his eyes open, though he may be powerfully motivated to do so. I then found further evidence that the skin, rather than "expressing" internal events, did, in diving animals, lead and command widespread autonomic changes throughout the body in order to conserve oxygen for the vulnerable brain. When the beak of a diving bird is stimulated by the water as it dives for fish, this change produces profound general changes, such as vasoconstriction within the body as a whole. Investigators somewhat accidentally discovered that similar changes can occur in a human being by putting his face in water (without total immersion of his body). Then I examined (at the suggestion of my friend Julian Jaynes) the work of Beach (1948) on the sexual mechanism in rats. Beach, examining the structure of the penis under a microscope, found that sensitive hair receptors of the skin of the penis were encased between what resembled the interstices of a cog wheel when the penis was flaccid. When there was a blood flow that engorged the penis, the skin was stretched smooth and the hairs of the receptors were no longer encased, but exposed, and their exquisite sensitivity changed the animal from a state of sexual quiescence to one of total sexual arousal. The relevance of such a mechanism for an understanding of the affect mechanism now seemed very clear. It had been known for centuries that the face became red and engorged with blood in anger. It had been known that in terror the hair stood on end and the skin became white and cold with sweat. It had long been known that the blood vessels dilated and the skin felt warm and relaxed in enjoyment. The face as penis would be relatively insensitive in its flaccid condition, its specific receptors hidden, encased within surrounding skin. When, however, there were massive shifts in blood flow and temperature, one should expect change in the positioning of the receptors, and pursuing the analogy to its bitter end, the patterned changes in facial muscle responses would serve as self-masturbatory stimulation to the skin and its own sensitized receptors. The feedback of this set of changes would provide the feel of specific affects. Although autonomic changes would be involved, the primary locus would now be seen to be in specific receptors, some as yet to be discovered. Changes in hotness, coldness, and warmth would undoubtedly be involved, but there may well be other, as yet unknown, specific receptors, which yield varieties of experience peculiar to the affect mechanism.[4] One implication of such a shift in theory is to render contemporary experimentation with the feedback of voluntarily simulated facial muscle responses as an inadequate test of the dynamics of the innate affect mechanism.

There have been a number of experiments in which an attempt has been made to test my theory of the significance of the face in the experience of emotion. These generally utilized voluntary simulation of facial affective responses. The most recent of these experiments is that of Tourangeau and Ellsworth (1979), whose subjects were required to simulate facial affective responses voluntarily and to hold these responses for a couple of minutes during which they observe a affect-evoking film. Not surprisingly, the voluntary responses were found to be ineffective in producing the experience of emotion.

This experiment is, however, seriously flawed in several respects. Voluntary simulation does not guarantee the generation of the appropriate full-blooded sensory feedback. Not only are the requisite vocal responses and the autonomic changes mediated by the endocrine, cardiac, and respiratory systems, bypassed in voluntary mimicry of the facial affective response, but no less important is the frozen, static quality of the simulation they used. Thus a smile is a sequence of motor responses as is a startle, as is a cry of distress, and as is a sudden fear response. When a static holding of the facial musculature in a fixed pattern selected from an organized series of responses with distinctive features of rate and distance is used, the affective response is not simulated nor is the learned simulation of the innate response. In a true voluntary simulation of a smile, in which, let us say, the individual uses his face to lie to the other, to pretend a friendliness he does not feel, his dissimulation succeeds only to the extent that the rate of the smile and the distance over which the mouth is moved approximate the innate smile. To the extent to which either of these parameters is not exactly simulated, the face fails to dissimulate affect and is diagnosed as a fake smile. How much more faked it would seem if it were simply held static for a period of time.

---

[4] It would suggest that thermography would be one major avenue of investigation. I pursued this possibility about 10 years ago and was disappointed at the relative inertia of the temperature of the skin. It may, however, be that advances in the state of the art in recent years may permit a more subtle mapping of the relationships between changes in skin temperature and affect.

Indeed, as I have argued elsewhere (Tomkins, 1975), voluntary facial behavior is also used as a symbol. The paradox of such use is that such symbolism rests on assumed and generally true consensus about what an innate facial response is. The information in such symbolic use of the face is to be found in the direction and magnitude of the *deviation* of the simulated response from the innate response. Thus a smile that is either faster or slower and/or more or less wide than an innate smile tells the other than one is really *not* amused. A surprise response that is slower than an innate surprise tells the other that one does not believe what the other is saying, i.e., that it is too surprising. One becomes uncomfortable in the presence of eyebrows that go up too slowly when one wanted to provoke astonishment at the tall tale one is trying to tell the other. The longer they remain up, as in this experiment, the more certain it becomes that the other is not surprised but is disbelieving.

I question the value of the Tourangeau and Ellsworth (1979) study apart from its irrelevance as a test of my theory. To explain why, I must first discuss the relationship of artificial intelligence and computer simulation of cognitive processes which it is generally recognized, are concerned with quite different domains. Artificial intelligence is concerned with the production of smart programs to do clever things. Whether it does this in the same way as a human being thinks is irrelevant as whether an aeroplane has feathers. It *flies*. Whether it flaps its wings is of no consequence. It is an engineering triumph in its own right, as is any program conceived as artificial intelligence. Within the field of artificial intelligence, the invidious comparison is *between* artificial intelligences, hardware as well as software. Thus an adding machine is a very poor computer and one computer is not as smart as the next generation computer. One chess program is better than another chess program, but both programs may be better or worse than any specific chess player.

In computer simulation of intelligent behavior, there should be nothing artificial. Ideally, one would require a program to simulate human errors as well as successes. The relevance of the distinction between artificial intelligence and computer simulation to the evaluation of the usefulness of testing voluntary muscular facial responses is this: the fruitfulness of artificial intelligence is in the utility of the achieved programs. These are technological inventions that justify themselves in many ways. The fruitfulness of computer simulation is more theoretical. It is a way of both producing and testing models of human cognition – of problem solving – that includes problem solution as a special case. What we hope to learn from such models is how the brain really works. We are not necessarily interested in its stupidity or in its cleverness because human condition is as vulnerable to error as to final output – the correct "response". I would suggest that the hypothesis tested in the Tourangeau and Ellsworth study has *no* utility as an example of artificial affect and very little utility as a simulation of a complex series of affective responses because it does not use the appropriate neural pathways, the appropriate muscular *series* of responses, or the appropriate full sensory feedback of innate affect responses but rather a frozen moment in the wrong modality and, as such, is a failure at simulation of innate affect. It is an exercise, not in affect simulation, but in artificial affect, without the possible benefits of its analog in artificial intelligence.

Although all investigators have the prerogative to test any hypothesis they consider worthwhile, they must take great care to present their material independent of other theories that have not been proven to be related. Tourangeau and Ellsworth erred in this respect when they stated that, "Even if there are reafferent loops and even if the proprioceptive feedback along voluntary and involuntary pathways is recognizably different, the theories *ought* to predict generally positive correlation" (page 1528, italics added).

Why should they have linked their hypothesis with mine? Primarily, I think, because it was more testable and more *easily* tested than mine would have been. Thus, in defense of what they did and in criticism of the difficulty of designing a more crucial test, they said: "In the second place, the qualifications render the theory much *less* testable. If the only influential facial expression is one that results from an involuntary natural response and if the facial muscles can be bypassed intracranially, the causal role of the face becomes inaccessible to *any* sort of definitive *test*" (page 1522, italics added).

There is a reliable and infinite difference between a theory being much less testable and being inaccessible to any sort of definitive test. The authors appear to have been victimized by their own affect in the course of writing that paragraph, growing more confident as they progressed in the defense of their procedure as they concluded their argument. I sympathize with anyone who attempts to deal with the complexities of the affect mechanism under controlled laboratory conditions. My theory, although difficult, is not impossible to test.

What is one to make of an experiment in which one opposes intense innate affect (evoked by films designed to do so) with the countervailing effects of artificially manipulated voluntary muscular contractions on the face? Consider the logic of this in an extreme case. Suppose I ask you to put a smile on your face and then stab you. Would anyone suppose that the simulated "smile" would in any way compete with the instigated terror?

The difference between innate affect triggered either by films, real life, or by thoughts and images and the voluntarily innervated simulations and transformations of these responses is fundamental. It is a difference whose importance must not be attenuated in the interest of easier experimental designs.

The importance of this difference has been further amplified by the revisions of my theory (Tomkins, 1982), which assign a primary role to blood flow, temperature, and altered sensory thresholds on the skin of the face in contrast to a more secondary role to the facial musculature. These changes were not published when Tourangeau and Ellsworth did their study, but, as noted, their study tests neither version of my theory.

It is my assumption that facial affective responses are neither necessary nor sufficient conditions for the concious experience of affect. They are not sufficient because these responses may or may not be admitted into the central assembly, depending on competing messages, which may succeed in prior entry and exclude affect messages from the face. In the same manner, even extreme pain messages may be excluded, e.g., in combat owing to intense concentration, which limits competing pain messages. Neither are they necessary conditions for the experience of affect, which can be produced by messages retrieved from memory in the absence of facial feedback. Just as a proofreader's error is based on memory–guided imagery rather than on sensory feedback and just as one can play blind–folded chess utilizing memory–generated arousal imagery, so affect imagery, which was originally facial and vocal, can be retrieved from memory and experienced as affect.

Backed-up affect

The third modification of the theory concerns the role of breathing and vocalization of affect. I have not changed my opinion that each affect has as part of its innate program a specific cry of vocalization, subserved by specific patterns of breathing. Rather, it is the implications of this aspect of the theory that took some years to understand. The major implications, which I now understand, concerns the universal confusion of the experience of backed-up affect with that of biologically and psychologically authentic innate affect. An analog may help in illustrating what is at issue. Let us suppose that all over the world human beings were forbidden to exhale air but were permitted and even encouraged to inhale air, so that everyone held their breaths to the point of cyanosis and death. Biologists who studied such a phenomenon (who had also been socialized to hold their breath) would have had to conclude that the breathing mechanism represented an evolutionary monstrosity devoid of any utility. Something similar to this has, in fact, happened to the affect mechanism. Because the free expression of innate affect is extremely contagious and because these are very high-powered phenomena, all societies, in varying degrees, exercise substantial control over the unfettered expression of affect, and particularly over the free expression of the cry of affect. No societies encourage or permit individuals to cry out in rage, excitement, distress, or terror whenever and wherever they wish. Very early on, strict control over affect expression is instituted, and such control is exerted particularly over the voice in general, whether used in speech or in direct affect expressions. Although there are large variations among societies and between different classes within societies, complete unconditional freedom of affect vocalization is quite exceptional. One of the most powerful effects of alcohol is the lifting of such control so that wherever alcohol is taken by large number of individuals in public places, there is a typical raising of the noise level of the intoxicated, accompanying a general loosening of affect control.

There are significant differences in how much control is exerted over voice and affect from society to society, and Lomax (1968) showed a significant correlation between the degree of tightness and closure of the vocal box as revealed in song and the degree of hierarchical social control in the society. It appears that more permissive societies also produce voice and song in which the throat is characteristically more relaxed and open.

If all societies, in varying degrees, suppress the free vocalization of affect, what is it that is being experienced as affect? It is what I have called *pseudo*– or backed–up, affect. It can be seen in children who are trying to suppress laughter by swallowing a snicker, by a stiff upper lip when trying not to cry, or by tightening their jaw trying not to cry out in anger. In all of these cases, one is truly holding one's breath as part of the technique of suppressing the vocalization of affect. Although this is not severe enough to produce cyanosis, we do not, in fact, know what are the biological and psychological prices of such suppression of the innate affect response. I would suggest that much of what is called stress is indeed back-up affect and that many of the endocrine changes reported by Frankenhaeuser (1979) are the consequence as much of backed-up affect as of affect per se. It seems at the very least that substantial psychosomatic disease might be one of the prices of such systematic suppression and transformation of the innate affective responses. Further, there could be a permanent elevation of blood pressure as a consequence of suppressed rage, and this would have a much longer duration than an innate momentary flash of expressed anger. Some years ago, French (1941) and the Chicago psychoanalytic group found some evidence for the suppressed cry of distress in psychosomatic asthma. The psychological consequences of such suppression would depend on the severity of the suppression, and I have spelled out some of these consequences elsewhere (Tomkins 1971, 1975). Even the least severe suppression of the vocalization of affect must result in some bleaching of the experience of affect and, therefore, some impoverishment of the quality of life. It must also produce some ambiguity about what affect feels like because so much of the adult's affect life represents, at the very least, a transformation of the affect response rather than the simpler, more direct and briefer innate affect. Such confusion, moreover, occurs even among theorists and investigators of affects, myself included.[5] The appearance of the backed-up, the simulated, and the innate is by no means the same. Although this may be generally recognized so that typically we know when someone is controlling an affect or showing a pretended affect, with anger the matter is quite confused. Because of the danger presented by the affect and the consequent enormous societal concern about the socialization of anger, what is typically seen and thought to be the innate is in actuality the backed-up. Finally, it is upon the discontinuity of vocalization of affect that the therapeutic power of primal screaming rests. One can uncover repressed affect by encouraging vocalization of affect, the more severe the suppression of vocalization has been.

Stimulus and response amplification

For several years I maintained that although affect has the function of amplifying its activator it does not influence the response to the activator or to itself. I portrayed the infant who was hungry as also distressed but saw the infant as in no way pushed in one direction or another in behavioral response to its hunger and distress. I was concerned to preserve the independence of the response from its affective precursor. It

[5]By this reasoning, the finding that observers across cultures will agree in identifying affect from facial expression does not tell us whether the faces utilized depicted innate or backed-up affect nor whether observers recognized the difference between the two. In these studies both controlled and innate responses were used as stimuli, but observers were not questioned about the difference between the two. It is my prediction that such an investigation would show a universal confusion just about anger, in which backed-up anger would be perceived as innate and innate anger would not be recognized as such.

seemed that to postulate a tight causal nexus between the affect and its response would to limit severely the apparent degrees of freedom that the human being appears to enjoy and to come dangerously close to reducing both affect and the human being to the level of tropism or instinct. It seems to me now that my concern was somewhat phobic and resulted in my overlooking a powerful connection among stimulus, affect, and response. I now believe that the affect connects both its own activator and the response that follows by imprinting the latter with the same amplification it exerts on its own activator. Thus, a response prompted by enjoyment will be a slow, relaxed response in contrast to a response prompted by anger, which will reflect the increased neural firing characteristic of both the activator of anger as well as the anger response itself. What we, therefore, inherit in the affect mechanism is not only an amplifier of its activator but also an amplifier of the response that it evokes. Such a connection is in no way learned, arising as it does simply from the overlap in time of the affect with what precedes and follows it. It should be noted that by the response to affect I do not intend any restriction to observable motor responses. The response may be in terms of retrieved memories or constructed thoughts, which might vary in acceleration if amplified by fear or interest, in quantity if amplified by distress or anger, or in deceleration of rate of information processing if amplified by enjoyment. Thus, in some acute schizophrenic panics, the individual is bombarded by a rapidly accelerating rush of ideas, which resist ordering and organization. Such individuals will try to write down these ideas as an attempt to order them, saying upon questioning that if they could separate and clarify all of these too fast, overwhelming ideas, they could cure themselves. Responses to the blank card in the TAT by such schizophrenics concern a hero who is trying to put half of his ideas on one half of the card and the other half on the other side of an imaginary line dividing the card into two.

The great German philospher, Immanuel Kant, likened the human mind to a glass that imprinted its shape on whatever liquid was poured into the glass. Thus, space, time, causality, he thought, were constructions of the human mind imposing the categories of pure reason upon the outside thing-in-itself, whose ultimate nature necessarily forever escaped us. I am suggesting that he neglected a major filtering mechanism, the innate affects, which necessarily color our every experience by producing a unique set of categorical imperatives, which amplify not only what precedes and activates each affect but also the further responses that are prompted by affect.

Conclusions

A number of promising areas for the study of facial expression and emotion remain almost totally unexplored. There is theory about the relevance of facial expression and styles of controlling emotional expression to personality disorders and psychosomatic disease (Ekman & Friesen, 1975; Izard, 1972; Plutchik, 1980; Tomkins, 1962, 1963) but almost no empirical work. Unstudied also is the relationship, real or perceived, between facial expression and intelligence, an important issue for the assessment of IQ (Haviland, 1975). Similarly, there has been little work on the moment-to-moment interrelationship between the facial expressions of two or more persons engaged in an interaction; the exception being Gottman's (1979) studies of marital interaction. Now that there are tools for measuring facial behavior directly, rather than just relying on observers' judgments when viewing the face, work should begin on these issues.

In the 1970s work began on integrating the study of facial expression with the examination of changes in other systems during emotion. There is little excuse any longer for examining the face independently. Body movement should be considered as well as the face, as well as measures of voice and speech, not just the visually perceived behaviors. A few studies have begun to look at the interrelationship between facial activity and autonomic nervous system changes. The face can be used to determine for a particular subject which emotion is experienced when, no longer making the simple, and usually false, assumption that any one experimental treatment is likely to produce only one emotion in any one person and necessarily that same emotion across people. There is no reason, of course, to focus just on the autonomic nervous system; central nervous system changes must be studied too.

Developmental studies of facial expression are now one of the most rapidly progressing areas of research on the face. Fortunately, many of these studies are showing care in description, consideration of vocalization and other motor behavior in addition to the face, and examination of the interaction between infant and caregiver, rather than focusing on only one participant in the situation.

Another newly developing area of research is the role of facial action as conversational signal. Much of the facial behavior observed in social life is not emotional; rather, it is composed of facial gestures (such as the wink), illustrations of what is being said, emphasis marks, and other forms of punctuation. These are important phenomena in their own right, and additionally, the conversational signals must be identified if investigators are not to consider them mistakenly as part of the emotional expressions.

A number of studies have been published in the 1970s that show that the measurement of facial expression can have practical social implications. Savitsky, Izard, Kotsch, & Christy (1974) found that an instructor in a learning task delivered less punishment to victims who looked angry rather than joyful. Fried (1976) showed that pupils learned more from a teacher who showed positive rather than negative emotional expressions while giving a lesson. Ekman, Liebert, et al (1972) found that children who looked happy rather than sad while watching televised violence subsequently showed more aggressive as compared with altruistic behavior. Also, Vasquez (1975) found that subjects scoring high on "humanism" smiled more often during conversation than "nonhumanist" subjects.

In a sense, this book can have no concluding chapter. We by no means have all the answers. Much has been learned. New methods are now available. An astounding number of questions relevant to a full understanding of emotion can now be addressed through a study of facial expression.

References

Abelson, R. P., & Sermat, V. Multidimensional scaling of facial expressions. *Journal of Experimental Psychology*, 1962, *63*, 546–554.

Abrams, K. H. Coordinated movement in children's faces, and what parents know about it. In M. R. Key & D. Presiosi (Eds.), *Nonverbal communication today: Current research*, in press.

Adamson, J. D., Romano, K. R., Burdick, J. A., Corman, C. L., & Chebib, F. S. Physiological responses to sexual and unpleasant film stimuli. *Journal of Psychosomatic Research*, 1972, *16*, 153–162.

Ainsworth, M. The development of infant–mother attachment. In B. Caldwell & H. Ricciuti (Eds.), *Review of child development research* (Vol. 3), pp. 1–94. Chicago: University of Chicago Press, 1973.

Alexander, F., & Portis, S. A psychosomatic study of hypoglycaemic fatigue. *Psychosomatic Medicine*, 1944, *6*, 195–205.

Allport, F. H. *Social psychology*. Boston: Houghton Mifflin, 1924.

Altmann, S. A. A field study of the sociobiology of rhesus monkeys, *Macaca mulatta*. *Annals of the New York Academy of Sciences*, 1962, *102*, 338–435.

Altmann, S. A. The structure of primate social communication. In S. A. Altmann (Ed.), *Social communication among primates*, pp. 325–362. Chicago: University of Chicago Press, 1967.

Altmann, S. A. Primates. In T. Sebeok (Ed.), *Animal communication: Techniques and results of research*, pp. 466–522. Bloomington: Indiana University Press, 1968. (a)

Altmann, S. A. Sociobiology of rhesus monkeys. III. The basic communication network. *Behaviour*, 1968, *32*, 17–32. (b)

Ancoli, S. *Psychophysiological response patterns to emotions*. Doctoral dissertation, University of California, San Francisco, 1979. *Dissertation Abstracts International*, 1979, *40*, 2887B. Order No. 79266-12.

Ancoli, S., Kamiya, J., & Ekman, P. *Psychophysiological differentiation of positive and negative affect*. Paper presented at the Annual Meeting of the Biofeedback Association of America, Colorado Springs, 1980.

Andrew, R. J. The origin and evolution of the calls and facial expressions of the primates. *Behaviour*, 1963, *20*, 1–109.

Andrew, R. J. The displays of the primates. In J. Buettner-Janusch (Ed.), *Evolutionary and genetic biology of primates* (Vol. II), pp. 227–309. New York: Academic Press, 1964.

Andrew, R. J. The origins of facial expressions. *Scientific American*, 1965, *213*(4), 88–94.

398

Andrew, R. J. The information potentially available in mammal displays. In R. A. Hinde (Ed.), *Non-verbal communication*, pp. 179–206. Cambridge University Press, 1972.

Anthoney, T. R. The ontogeny of greeting, grooming and sexual motor patterns in captive baboons (superspecies *Papio cynocephalus*). *Behaviour*, 1968, *31*, 358–372.

Archer, D., & Akert, R. M. Words and everything else: Verbal and nonverbal cues in social interpretation. *Journal of Personality and Social Psychology*, 1977, *35*(6), 443–449.

Argyle, M., Alkema, F., & Gilmour, R. The communication of friendly and hostile attitudes by verbal and nonverbal signals. *European Journal of Social Psychology*, 1971, *1*(3), 385–402.

Argyle, M., & Cook, M. *Gaze and mutual gaze*. Cambridge University Press, 1976.

Arnold, M. B. *Emotion and personality*. New York: Columbia University Press, 1960.

Asch, S. E. *Social psychology*. Englewood Cliffs, N.J.: Prentice-Hall, 1952.

Atz, J. W. The application of the idea of homology to behavior. In L. R. Aronson et al. (Eds.), *Development and evolution of behavior: Essays in memory of T. C. Schneirla*, pp. 53–74. San Francisco: Freeman, 1970.

Averill, J. R., Opton, E. M., Jr., & Lazarus, R. S. Cross-cultural studies of psychophysiological responses during stress and emotion. *International Journal of Psychology*, 1969, *4*, 88–102.

Baerends, G. P. Specialisations in organs and movements with a releasing function. *Symposia of the Society for Experimental Biology*, 1950, *4*, 337–360.

Bakan, P. Hypnotizability, laterality of eye movement and functional brain asymmetry. *Perceptual and Motor Skills*, 1969, *28*, 927–932.

Baker, C. *Observations on non-manual behaviors in American sign language discourse*. Doctoral dissertation, University of California, Berkeley, 1982.

Baldwin, L. A., & Teleki, G. Patterns of gibbon behavior on Hall's Island, Bermuda: A preliminary ethogram for *Hylobates lar*. In D. M. Rumbaugh (Ed.), *Gibbon and siamang* (Vol. 4), pp. 21–105. Basel: Karger, 1976.

Baulu, J. *Responses of rhesus monkeys* (Macaca mulatta) *to motion picture stimulation: A preliminary study*. M.S. thesis, University of Georgia, Athens, 1973.

Beach, F. A. *Hormones and behavior*. New York: P. B. Hoeber, 1948.

Bell, C. *The anatomy and philosophy of expression as connected with the fine arts* (4th ed.). London: John Murray, 1847.

Bell, S. M., & Ainsworth, M. D. S. Infant crying and maternal responsiveness. *Child Development*, 1972, *43*, 1171–1190.

Bennett, H. L., Giannini, J. A., & Delmonico, R. L. *Facial asymmetries: Recognition judgments by oneself and others*. Unpublished manuscript, University of California, Davis, 1980.

Benton, A. L. The neuropsychology of facial recognition. *American Psychologist*, 1980, *35*, 176–186.

Berman, H. J., Shulman, A. D., & Marwit, S. J. Comparison of multidimensional decoding of affect from audio, video and audiovideo recordings. *Sociometry*, 1976, *39*(1), 83–89.

Bertrand, M. The behavioral repertoire of the stumptail macaque. *Bibliotheca Primatologica*, 1969, *11*, xii + 273 pp.

Birdwhistell, R. L. The kinesic level in the investigation of the emotions. In P. H. Knapp (Ed.), *Expression of the emotions in man*, (Pt. II), Chap. 7. New York: International Universities Press, 1963.

Birdwhistell, R. L. *Kinesics and context*. Philadelphia: University of Pennsylvania Press, 1970.

Black, H. Race and sex factors influencing the correct and erroneous perception of emotion. *Proceedings of the 77th Annual Convention of the American Psychological Association*, 1969, 4, 363–364.

Blackwelder, R. E. *Taxonomy: A text and reference book*. New York: Wiley, 1967.

Blurton Jones, N. G. Observations and experiments on causation of threat displays of the great tit (*Parus major*). *Animal Behaviour Monographs*, 1968, 1, 75–158.

Blurton Jones, N. G. An ethological study of some aspects of social behaviour of children in nursery school. In D. Morris (Ed.), *Primate ethology*, pp. 437–463. Garden City, N. Y.: Anchor, 1969.

Blurton Jones, N. G. Criteria for use in describing facial expressions in children. *Human Biology*, 1971, 41, 365–413.

Blurton Jones, N. G. Categories of child–child interaction. In N. G. Blurton Jones (Ed.), *Ethological studies of child behaviour*, pp. 97–127. Cambridge University Press, 1972. (a)

Blurton Jones, N. G. Non-verbal communication in children. In R. A. Hinde (Ed.) *Non-verbal communication*. pp. 271–296. Cambridge University Press, 1972. (b)

Blurton Jones, N. G., & Konner, M. J. An experiment on eyebrow-raising and visual searching in children. *Journal of Child Psychology and Psychiatry*, 1971, 11, 233–240.

Bobbitt, R. A., Jensen, G. D., & Gordon, B. N. Behavioral elements (taxonomy) for observing mother–infant–peer interactions in *Macaca nemestrina*. *Primates*, 1964, 5(3–4), 71–80.

Bolwig, N. A study of the behaviour of the chacma baboon, *Papio ursinus*. *Behaviour*, 1959, 14, 136–163.

Bolwig, N. Facial expression in primates with remarks on a parallel development in certain carnivores: (A preliminary study on work in progress). *Behaviour*, 1964, 22, 167–192.

Boring, E. C., & Titchener, E. B. A model for the demonstrations of facial expressions. *American Journal of Psychology*, 1923, 34, 471–485.

Borod, J. C., & Caron, H. S. Facedness and emotion related to lateral dominance, sex, and expression type. *Neuropsychologia*, 1980, 18, 237–241.

Boucher, J. D. Facial displays of fear, sadness and pain. *Perceptual and Motor Skills*, 1969, 28, 239–242.

Boucher, J. D. *Facial behavior and the perception of emotion: Studies of Malays and Temuan Orang Asli*. Paper presented at the Conference of Psychology and Related Disciplines, Kuala Lumpur, 1973.

Boucher, J. D., & Ekman, P. *A replication of Schlosberg's evaluation of Woodworth's scale of emotion*. Paper presented at the Western Psychological Association Meeting, Honolulu, 1965.

Boucher, J. D., & Ekman, P. Facial areas and emotional information. *Journal of Communication*, 1975, 25(2), 21–29.

Bowlby, J. *Attachment and loss*, Vol. 1: *Attachment*. New York: Basic Books, 1969.

Brannigan, C. R., & Humphries, D. A. Human nonverbal behavior, a means of communication. In N. G. Blurton Jones (Ed.), *Ethological studies of child behavior*. Cambridge University Press, 1972.

Brazelton, T., Tronick, E., Adamson, L., Als, H., & Wise, S. Early mother–infant reciprocity. *Parent–infant interaction*. New York: Elsevier North-Holland, 1975.

Brown, J. L. *The evolution of behavior*. New York: Norton, 1975.

Brown, J. L., & Hunsperger, R. W. Neuroethology and the motivation of agonistic behaviour. *Animal Behaviour*, 1963, *11*, 439–448.

Bruner, J. S., & Tagiuri, R. The perception of people. In G. Lindzey (Ed.), *Handbook of social psychology* (Vol. 2), pp. 634–654. Reading, Mass.: Addison-Wesley, 1954.

Buck, R. Nonverbal communication of affect in children. *Journal of Personal and Social Psychology*, 1975, *31*, 644–653.

Buck, R. A test of nonverbal receiving ability: Preliminary studies. *Human Communications Research*, 1976, *2*(2), 162–171.

Buck, R. *Measuring individual differences in the nonverbal communication of affect: The slide viewing paradigm.* Paper presented at the meeting of the American Psychological Association, San Francisco, 1977.

Buck, R., Baron, R., Goodman, N., & Shapiro, B. Unitization of spontaneous nonverbal behavior in the study of emotion communication. *Journal of Personality and Social Psychology*, 1980, *39*(3), 522–529.

Buck, R., & Duffy, R. *Nonverbal communication of affect in brain-damaged patients.* Paper presented at the meeting of the American Psychological Association, San Francisco, 1977.

Buck, R., Miller, R. E., & Caul, W. F. Sex, personality, and physiological variables in the communication of affect via facial expression. *Journal of Personality and Social Psychology*, 1974, *30*(4); 587–596.

Buck, R., Savin, V. J., Miller, R. E., & Caul, W. F. Nonverbal communication of affect in humans. *Proceedings of the 77th Annual Convention of the American Psychological Association*, 1969, *4*, 367–368.

Buck, R., Savin, V. J. Miller, R. E., & Caul, W. F. Communication of affect through facial expressions in humans. *Journal of Personality and Social Psychology*, 1972, *23*, 362–371.

Bugental, D., Kaswan, J., & Love, L. Perception of contradictory meanings conveyed by verbal and nonverbal channels. *Journal of Personality and Social Psychology*, 1970, *16*, 647–655.

Bugental, D., Kaswan, J., Love, L. & Fox, M. Child versus adult perception of evaluative messages in verbal, vocal and visual channels. *Developmental Psychology*, 1970, *2*(3), 367–375.

Bugental, D., Love, L., & Gianetto, R. Perfidious feminine faces. *Journal of Personality and Social Psychology*, 1971, *17*(3), 314–318.

Bugental, D., Love, L., Kaswan, J., & April C. Verbal–nonverbal conflict in parental messages to normal and disturbed children. *Journal of Abnormal Psychology*, 1971, *77*(1), 6–10.

Burke, P. H. Stereophotogrammetric measurement of normal facial asymmetry in children. *Human Biology*, 1971, *43*, 536-548.

Burns, K. L., & Beier, E. G. Significance of vocal and visual channels in the decoding of emotional meaning. *Journal of Communication*, 1973, *23*, 118–130.

Butler, S. *Life and habit*. London: Trübner, 1878.

Buzby, D. E. The interpretation of facial expression. *American Journal of Psychology*, 1924, *35*, 602–604.

Campbell, D. T., & Fiske, D. W. Convergent and discriminant validation by the multi-trait–multimethod matrix. *Psychological Bulletin*, 1959, *56*, 81–105.

Campbell, F. W., & Gubisch, R. W. Optical quality of the human eye. *Journal of Physiology*, 1966, *186*, 558–578.

Campbell, R. Asymmetries in interpreting and expressing a posed facial expression. *Cortex*, 1978, *14*, 327–342.

Campbell, R. *Cerebral asymmetries in the interpetation and expression of a posed expression.* Unpublished doctoral dissertation, University of London, 1979.

Campbell, R. Left-handers' smiles: Asymmetries in the projection of a posed facial expression. *Cortex,* in press.

Campos, J. J., Emde, R. N., Gaensbauer, T., & Henderson, C. Cardiac and behavioral interrelationships in the reactions of infants to strangers. *Developmental Psychology,* 1975, *11*(4), 589–601.

Campos, J. J., Hiatt, S., Ramsay, D., Henderson, C., & Svejda, M. The emergence of fear on the visual cliff. In M. Lewis & L. Rosenblum (Eds.), *The development of affect,* pp. 149–182. New York: Plenum, 1978.

Camras, L. Facial expressions used by children in a conflict situation. *Child Development,* 1977, *48,* 1431–1435.

Camras, L. Facial behavior in mother-child interaction. In W. V. Friesen & P. Ekman (Eds.), *Analyzing facial action.* Book in preparation.

Carpenter, C. R. A field study in Siam of the behavior and social relations of the gibbon *(Hylobates lar). Comparative Psychology Monographs,* 1940, *16*(5), 1–212.

Carpenter, C. R. *Primate behavior and ecology.* Paper presented at the AAS–NSF Faculty Seminar, University of California, Berkeley, November 15–16, 1971.

Chalmers, N. R. The visual and vocal communication of free living mangabeys in Uganda. *Folia Primatologica,* 1968, *9,* 258–280.

Chalmers, N. R., & Rowell, T. E. Behaviour and female reproductive cycles in a captive group of mangabeys. *Folia Primatologica,* 1971, *14,* 1–14.

Chance, M. R. A. An interpretation of some agonistic postures; The role of "cut-offs" acts and postures. *Symposia of the Zoological Society of London,* 1962, *8,* 71–89.

Chapman, A. J., & Wright, D. S. Social enhancement of laughter: An experimental analysis of some companion variables. *Journal of Experimental Child Psychology,* 1976, *21,* 201–218.

Charlesworth, W. R., & Kreutzer, M. A. Facial expression of infants and children. In P. Ekman (Ed.), *Darwin and facial expression: A century of research in review,* pp. 91–168. New York: Academic Press, 1973.

Chaurasia, B. D., & Goswami, H. K. Functional asymmetry in the face. *Acta Anatomica,* 1975, *91,* 154–160.

Chevalier-Skolnikoff, S. Facial expressions of emotion in nonhuman primates. In P. Ekman (Ed.), *Darwin and facial expression: A century of research in review,* pp. 11–89. New York: Academic Press, 1973.

Chevalier-Skolnikoff, S. The primate play face: A possible key to the determinants and evolution of play. *Rice University Studies,* 1974, *60,* 9–29. (a)

Chevalier-Skolnikoff, S. The ontogeny of communication in the stumptail macaque *(Macaca arctoides). Contributions to Primatology,* 1974, *2,* x + 174 pp. (b)

Chevalier-Skolnikoff, S. The ontogeny of primate intelligence and its implications for communicative potential: A preliminary report. *Annals of the New York Academy of Sciences,* 1976, *280,* 173–211.

Churchill, J. A., & Igna, S. The association of position at birth and handedness. *Pediatrics,* 1962, *29,* 303–309.

Cicchetti, D., & Sroufe, L. A. An organizational view of affect: Illustration from the study of Down's Syndrome infants. In M. Lewis & L. Rosenblum (Eds.), *The development of affect,* pp. 309–350, New York: Plenum, 1978.

Cline, V. B. Interpersonal perception. In B. A. Maher (Ed.), *Progress in experimental personality research* (Vol. 1). New York: Academic Press, 1964.

Cline, V. B., Atzet, J., & Holmes, E. Assessing the validity of verbal and nonverbal cues in accurately judging others. *Comparative Group Studies,* 1972, *3,* 383–394.

Clutton-Brock, T. H. Primate social organisation and ecology. *Nature*, 1974, *250*, 539–542.

Colby, C. Z., Lanzetta, J. T., & Kleck, R. E. Effects of the expression of pain on autonomic and pain tolerance responses to subject-controlled pain. *Psychophysiology*, 1977, *14*(6), 537–540.

Coleman, J. C. Facial expressions of emotion. *Psychological Monograph*, 1949, *63* (1, Whole No. 296).

Coss, R. G. The ethological command in art. *Leonardo*, 1968, *1*, 273–287.

Coss, R. G. The cut-off hypothesis: Its relevance to the design of public places. *Man–Environment Systems*, 1973, *3*, 417–440.

Cox, C. R. & LeBoeuf, B. J. Female incitation of male competition: A mechanism in sexual selection. *American Naturalist*, 1977, *111*, 317–335.

Cronbach, L. J. Processes affecting scores on "understanding of others" and "assumed similarity." *Psychological Bulletin*, 1955, *52*, 177–193.

Cronbach, L. J. *Essentials of psychological testing* (3rd ed.). New York: Harper & Row, 1970.

Crook, J. H. The socio-ecology of primates. In J. H. Crook (Ed.), *Social behaviour in birds and mammals*, pp. 103–166. London: Academic Press, 1970.

Crook, J. H., & Goss-Custard, J. D. Social ethology. *Annual Review of Psychology*, 1972, *23*, 277–312.

Crouch, W. W. Dominant direction of conjugate lateral eye movements and responsiveness to facial and verbal cues. *Perceptual and Motor Skills*, 1976, *42*, 167–174.

Cullen, E. Adaptations in the kittiwake to cliff-nesting. *Ibis*, 1957, *99*, 275–302.

Cullen, J. M. Some principles of animal communication. In R. A. Hinde (Ed.), *Non-verbal communication*, pp. 101–125. Cambridge University Press, 1972.

Cunningham, M. R. Personality and the structure of the nonverbal communication of emotion. *Journal of Personality*, 1977, *45*, 564–584.

Cupchik, G., & Leventhal, H. Consistency between expressive behavior and the evaluation of humorous stimuli: The role of sex and self-observation. *Journal of Personality and Social Psychology*, 1974, *30*, 429–442.

Daanje, A. On locomotory movements in birds and the intention movements derived from them. *Behaviour*, 1950, *3*, 49–98.

Darlington, P. J., Jr. Nonmathematical concepts of selection, evolutionary energy, and levels of evolution. *Proceedings of the National Academy of Sciences*, U. S. A., 1972, *69*, 1239–1243.

Darwin, C. *The expression of the emotions in man and animals*. London: John Murray, 1872.

Darwin, C. *The descent of man, and selection in relation to sex* (2 vols.). (Reprinted from the edition of John Murray, London, 1871.) New York: International Publication Services, 1969.

Dashiell, J. F. A new method of measuring reactions to facial expression of emotion. *Psychology Bulletin*, 1927, *24*, 174–175.

Davis, R. C. The specificity of facial expressions. *Journal of General Psychology*, 1934, *10*, 42–58.

Davson, H. *The physiology of the eye* (3rd ed). New York: Academic Press, 1972.

Dawkins, R. *The selfish gene.* New York: Oxford University Press, 1976.

Dawkins, R. *The Danz Lecture.* Paper delivered at the annual meeting of the Animal Behavior Society, Seattle, June 19–24, 1978.

Dawkins, R., & Krebs, J. R. Animal signals: Information or manipulation? In J. R. Krebs & N. B. Davies (Eds.), *Behavioural ecology: An evolutionary approach*, pp. 282-309. Oxford: Blackwell Scientific Publications, 1978.

Decarie, T. Affect development and cognition in Piagetian context. In M. Lewis & L. Rosenblum (Eds.), *The development of affect*, pp. 149–182. New York: Plenum, 1978.

DePaulo, B., Rosenthal, R., Eisenstat, R., Finkelstein, S., & Rogers, P. Decoding discrepant nonverbal cues. *Journal of Personality and Social Psychology*, 1978, *36*(3), 313–323.

Deputte, B. [*Study of yawning in two species of Cercopithecidae*, Cercocebus albigena albigena *GRAY and* Macaca fascicularis *RAFFLES: Research on causal and functional factors; A consideration of socio-bioenergetic factors.*] Thèse présentée devant l'Université de Rennes, France, pour obtenir le titre de Docteur en Troisième Cycle, February 1978. v + 111 pp.

Dewsbury, D. A. *Comparative animal behavior*. New York: McGraw-Hill, 1978.

Diamond, R., & Carey, S. Developmental changes in the representation of faces. *Journal of Experimental Child Psychology*, 1977, *23*, 1–22.

Dickey, R. V., & Knower, F. H. A note on some ethnological differences in recognition of simulated expressions of the emotions. *American Journal of Sociology*, 1941, *47*, 190–193.

Dorchy, H., Baran, D., & Richard, J. Association of asymmetric crying faces, malformation of the ear, and pulmonary agenesis. *Acta Paediatrica Belgica*, 1976, *29*, 255–256.

Drag, R. M., & Shaw, M. E. Factors influencing the communication of emotional intent by facial expressions. *Psychometric Science*, 1967, *8*, 137–138.

Duchenne, B. *Mechanisme de la physionomie humaine; ou, analyse electrophysiologique de l'expression des passions*. Paris: Baillière, 1862.

Duncan, J., & Laird, J. D. Cross-modality consistencies in individual differences in self-attribution. *Journal of Personality*, 1977, *45*(2), 191–206.

Dunlap, K. The role of eye-muscles and mouth-muscles in the expression of the emotions. *Genetic Psychology Monograph*, 1927, *2*, 199–233.

Dusenbury, D., & Knower, F. H. Experimental studies on the symbolism of action and voice: I. A study of the specificity of meaning in facial expression. *Quarterly Journal of Speech*, 1938, *24*, 424–435.

Ehrlich, P. R., Holm, R. W., & Parnell, D. R. *The process of evolution* (2nd ed.). New York: McGraw-Hill, 1974.

Ehrlichman, H., & Weinberger, A. Lateral eye movements and hemispheric asymmetry: A critical review. *Psychological Bulletin*, 1978, *85*, 1080–1101.

Eibl-Eibesfeldt, I. *Ethology, the biology of behavior*. New York: Holt, Rinehart and Winston, 1970.

Eibl-Eibesfeldt, I. Similarities and differences between cultures in expressive movements. In R. A. Hinde (Ed.), *Nonverbal communication*. Cambridge University Press, 1972.

Eisenberg, J. F., Muckenhirn, N. A. & Rudran, R. The relation between ecology and social structure in primates. *Science*, 1972, *176*, 863–874.

Ekman, P. Communication through nonverbal behavior: A source of information about an interpersonal relationship. In S. S. Tomkins & C. E. Izard (Eds.), *Affect, cognition, and personality*, chap. XIII, pp. 390–442. 1965. (a)

Ekman, P. Differential communication of affect by head and body cues. *Journal of Personality and Social Psychology*, 1965, *2*(5), 725–735. (b)

Ekman, P. Universals and cultural differences in facial expressions of emotion. In J. Cole (Ed.), *Nebraska Symposium on Motivation*, 1971 (Vol. *19*). Lincoln: University of Nebraska Press, 1972.

Ekman, P. Cross-cultural studies of facial expression. In P. Ekman (Ed.), *Darwin and facial expression: A century of research in review*, pp. 169–222. New York: Academic Press, 1973.

Ekman, P. Biological and cultural contributions to body and facial movement. In J. Blacking (Ed.), *The anthropology of the body*. London: Academic Press, 1977.

Ekman, P. Facial signs: Facts, fantasies, and possibilities. In T. Sebeok (Ed.), *Sight, sound and sense*, pp. 124–156. Bloomington: Indiana University Press, 1978.

Ekman, P. About brows: Emotional and conversational signals. In M. von Cranach, K. Foppa, W. Lepenies, & D. Ploog (Eds.), *Human ethology*. Cambridge University Press, 1979.

Ekman, P. Asymmetry in facial expression. *Science*, 1980, *209*, 833–834.

Ekman, P. Methods of measuring facial action. In K. R. Scherer & P. Ekman (Eds.), *Handbook of methods in nonverbal behavior research*. Cambridge University Press, 1982.

Ekman, P., & Bressler, J. In P. Ekman, Progress report to National Institute of Mental Health, Bethesda, Md.: 1964.

Ekman, P. & Friesen, W. V. Progress report to National Institute of Mental Health, Bethesda, Md., 1965.

Ekman, P., & Friesen, W. V. Head and body cues in the judgment of emotion: A reformulation. *Perceptual and Motor Skills*, 1967, *24*, 711–724. (a)

Ekman, P., & Friesen, W. V. *Origin, usage and coding: The basis for five categories of nonverbal behavior*. Paper presented at the Symposium on Communication Theory and Linguistic Models, Buenos Aires, 1967. (b)

Ekman, P., & Friesen, W. V. Nonverbal behavior in psychotherapy research. In J. Shlien (Ed.), *Research in psychotherapy* (Vol. 3). Washington, D.C.: American Psychological Association, 1968.

Ekman, P., & Friesen, W. V. Nonverbal leakage and clues to deception. *Psychiatry*, 1969, *32*(1), 88–105. (a)

Ekman, P., & Friesen, W. V. The repertoire of nonverbal behavior – Categories, origins, usage and coding. *Semiotica*, 1969, *1*, 49–98. (b)

Ekman, P., & Friesen, W. V. Constants across cultures in the face and emotion. Journal of Personality and Social Psychology, 1971, *17*(2), 124–129.

Ekman, P., & Friesen, W. V. Detecting deception from the body or face. *Journal of Personality and Social Psychology*, 1974, *29*(3), 288–298. (a)

Ekman, P., & Friesen, W. V. Nonverbal behavior and psychopathology. In R. J. Friedman & M. M. Katz (Eds.), *The psychology of depression: Contemporary theory and research*. Washington, D. C.: Winston & Sons, 1974. (b)

Ekman, P., & Friesen, W. V. *Unmasking the face: A guide to recognizing emotions from facial clues*. Englewood Cliffs, N. J.: Prentice-Hall, 1975.

Ekman, P., & Friesen, W. V. Measuring facial movement, *Environmental Psychology and Nonverbal Behavior*, 1976, *1*(1), 56–75. (a)

Ekman, P., & Friesen, W. V. *Pictures of facial affect*. Palo Alto, Ca.: Consulting Psychologists Press, 1976. (b)

Ekman, P., & Friesen, W. V. *Facial Action Coding System (FACS): A technique for the measurement of facial action*. Palo Alto, Ca.: Consulting Psychologists Press, 1978.

Ekman, P. & Friesen, W. V. Felt, false and miserable smiles. *Journal of Nonverbal Behavior*, 1982, in press.

Ekman, P., Friesen, W. V., & Ancoli, S. Facial signs of emotional experience. *Journal of Personality and Social Psychology*, 1980, *39*(6), 1125–1134.

Ekman, P., Friesen, W. V., & Ellsworth, P. *Emotion in the human face*. Elmsford, N.Y: Pergamon Press, 1972.

Ekman, P., Friesen, W. V., & Malmstrom, E. J. *Facial behavior and stress in two cultures*. Unpublished manuscript, Langley Porter Neuropsychiatric Institute, San Francisco, 1970.

406   *References*

Ekman, P., Friesen, W. V., O'Sullivan, M., & Scherer, K. Relative importance of face, body, and speech in judgments of personality and affect. *Journal of Personality and Social Psychology.* 1980, *38*, 270–277.

Ekman, P., Friesen, W. V., & Scherer, K. Body movement and voice pitch in deceptive interaction. *Semiotica.* 1976, *16*(1), 23–27.

Ekman, P., Friesen, W. V., & Simons, R. Manuscript in preparation. 1982.

Ekman, P., Friesen, W. V., & Tomkins, S. S. Facial Affect Scoring Technique (FAST): A first validity study. *Semiotica,* 1971. 3(1), 37–58.

Ekman, P., Hager, J. C., & Friesen, W. V. The symmetry of emotional and deliberate facial action. *Psychophysiology,* 1981, *18*(2), 101–106.

Ekman, P., Liebert, R. M., Friesen, W. V., Harrison, R., Zlatchin, C., Malmstrom, E. J., & Baron, R. A. Facial expressions of emotion while watching televised violence as predictors of subsequent aggression. In G. A. Comstock, E. A. Rubinstein, & J. P. Murray (Eds.), *Television and social behavior* (Vol. 5: *Television's effects: Further Explorations*). Washington, D.C.: Government Printing Office, 1972.

Ekman, P., & Oster, H. Facial expressions of emotion. *Annual Review of Psychology,* 1979, *30*, 527–554.

Ekman, P., Roper, G., & Hager, J. C. Deliberate facial movement. *Child Development,* 1980, *51*, 886–891.

Ekman, P., & Rose, D. In P. Ekman, Progress report to National Institute of Mental Health, Bethesda, Md., 1965.

Ekman, P., Schwartz, G. E., & Friesen, W. V. Manuscript in preparation. 1982.

Ekman, P., Sorenson, E. R., & Friesen, W. V. Pan-cultural elements in facial displays of emotions. *Science,* 1969, *164*(3875), 86–88.

Ellis, H. D. Recognizing faces. *British Journal of Psychology,* 1975, *66*, 409–426.

Ellsworth, P., & Tourangeau, R. On our failure to disconfirm what nobody ever said. *Journal of Personality and Social Psychology,* 1981, 40(2), 363–369.

Emde, R. N., Gaensbauer, T. J., & Harmon, R. J. Emotional expression in infancy: A biobehavioral study. *Psychological Issues Monograph,* 1976, Series 10, Monograph 37.

Engen, T., Levy, N., & Schlosberg, H. A new series of facial expressions. *American Psychologist,* 1957, *12*, 264–266.

Ermiane, R., & Gergerian, E. [*Atlas of facial expressions.*] *Album des expressions du visage.* Paris: La Pensée Universelle, 1978.

Exline, R. V. Visual interaction: The glances of power and preference. In J. K. Cole (Ed.), *Nebraska Symposium on Motivation,* 1971 (Vol. 19), pp. 163–206. Lincoln: University of Nebraska Press, 1972.

Feleky, A. M. The expression of the emotions. *Psychological Review,* 1914, *21*, 33–41.

Fernberger, S. W. Six more Piderit faces. *American Journal of Psychology,* 1927, *39*, 162–166.

Fernberger, S. W. False suggestion and the Piderit model. *American Journal of Psychology,* 1928, *40*, 562–568.

Fields, B., & O'Sullivan, M. *Convergent validation of five person perception measures.* Paper presented at the meeting of the Western Psychological Association, Los Angeles, April 1976.

Fifteenth International Congress of Zoology. *International code of zoological nomenclature.* London: Trust for Zoological Nomenclature, 1964.

Fogh-Andersen, P. *Inheritance of harelip and cleft palate.* Copenhagen: Nyt Nordisk Forlag, 1942.

Foley, J. P., Jr., Judgment of facial expression of emotion in the chimpanzee. *Journal of Social Psychology,* 1935, VI(1), 31–54.

Ford, F. R. *Diseases of the nervous system in infancy, childhood, and adolescence* (5th ed.). Springfield, Ill.: Thomas, 1966.

Fossey, D. Vocalizations of the mountain gorilla (*Gorilla gorilla beringei*). *Animal Behaviour*, 1972, *20*, 36–53.

Fouts, R. S., & Mellgren, R. L. Language, sign, and cognition in chimpanzee. *Sign Language Studies*, 1976, *13*, 319–346.

Fraiberg, S. Blind infants and their mothers: An examination of the sign system. In M. Lewis & L. A. Rosenblum (Eds.), *The effect of the infant on its care-giver*, pp. 215-232. New York: Wiley, 1974.

Frankenhaeuser, M. Psychoendocrine approaches to the study of emotion. In H. Howe, (Ed.), *Nebraska Symposium on Motivation*, 1978, (Vol. 26). Lincoln: University of Nebraska Press, 1979.

French, T. M., Alexander, F. Psychogenic factors in bronchial asthma. *Psychosomatic Medicine*, 1941, Monograph No. 2.

Fried, E. *The impact of nonverbal communication of facial affect on children's learning.* Unpublished doctoral dissertation, Rutgers University, 1976.

Friesen, W. V. *Cultural differences in facial expression in a social situation: An experimental test of the concept of display rules.* Unpublished doctoral dissertation, University of California, San Francisco, 1972.

Frijda, N. H. The understanding of facial expression of emotion. *Acta Psychologica*, 1953, *9*, 294–362.

Frijda, N. H. Facial expression and situational cues. *Journal of Abnormal Social Psychology*, 1958, *57*, 149–154.

Frijda, N. H. *Emotion and recognition of emotion.* Paper presented at the Third Symposium on Feelings and Emotions, Loyola University, Chicago, October 10–12, 1968.

Frijda, N. H. Recognition of emotion. In L. Berkowitz (Ed.), *Advances in experimental social psychology* (Vol. 4). pp. 167–223. New York: Academic Press, 1969.

Frijda, N. H., & Philipszoon, E. Dimensions of recognition of emotion. *Journal of Abnormal Social Psychology*, 1963, *66*, 45–51.

Frois-Wittmann, J. The judgment of facial expression. *Journal of Experimental Psychology*, 1930, *13*, 113–151.

Fujita, B. *Encoding and decoding of spontaneous and enacted facial expressions of emotion.* Unpublished doctoral dissertation, University of Oregon, Portland, 1977.

Fulcher, J. S. "Voluntary" facial expression in blind and seeing children. *Archives of Psychology*, 1942, *38*(No. 272).

Gaulin, S. J. C., & Konner, M. On the natural diet of primates, including humans. In R. J. Wurtman and J. J. Wurtman (Eds.), *Nutrition and the brain* (Vol. 1), pp. 1–86. New York: Raven Press, 1977.

Gautier, J.-P., & Gautier, A. Communication in Old World Monkeys. In T. A. Sebeok (Ed.), *How animals communicate*, pp. 890–964. Bloomington: Indiana University Press, 1977.

Gazzaniga, M. S. *The bisected brain.* New York: Academic Press, 1970.

Geldard, F. Some neglected aspects of communication. *Science*, 1960, *131*, 1583–1588.

Gesell, A. *The embryology of behavior.* New York: Harper, 1945.

Gewirtz, J. L., & Boyd, E. F. Mother–infant interaction and its study. *Advanced Child Development Behavior*, 1976, *11*, 141–163.

Gilbert, C., & Bakan, P. Visual asymmetry in perception of faces. *Neuropsychologia*, 1973, *11*, 355–362.

Gitter, A. G., & Black, H. *Perception of emotion: Differences in race and sex of perceiver and expressor.* (Tech. Rep. 17). Boston University, 1968.

Gladstones, W. H. A multi-dimensional study of facial expressions of emotions. *Australian Journal of Psychology*, 1962, *14*, 95–100.

Goffman, E. *Behavior in public places*. New York: Free Press of Glencoe, 1963.

Goldberg, H. D. The role of "cutting" in the perception of motion pictures. *Journal of Applied Psychology*, 1951, *35*, 70–71.

Goodenough, F. L. The expression of the emotions in infancy. *Child Development*, 1931, *2*, 96–101.

Goodenough, F. L. Expression of the emotions in a blind–deaf child. *Journal of Abnormal and Social Psychology*, 1932/1933, *27*, 328–333.

Goodenough, F. L., & Tinker, M. A. The relative potency of facial expression and verbal description of stimulus in the judgment of emotion. *Journal of Comparative Psychology*, 1931, *12*, 365–370.

Gorney, M., & Harries, T. The preoperative and postoperative consideration of natural facial asymmetry. *Plastic and Reconstructive Surgery*, 1974, *54*, 187–191.

Gottman, J. *Marital interaction: Experimental investigations*. New York: Academic Press, 1979.

Gough, H. C. A validational study of the Chapin Social Insight Test. *Psychological Reports*, 1965, *17*, 355–368.

Graham, J. A., & Argyle, M. The effects of different patterns of gaze combined with different facial expressions on impression information. *Journal of Human Movement Studies*, 1975, *1*, 178–182.

Grant, N. G. Human facial expression. *Man*, 1969, *4*, 525–536.

Greenspan, S., Barenboim, C., & Chandler, M. J. Empathy and pseudoempathy: The affective judgments of first- and third-graders. *Journal of Genetic Psychology*, 1976, *129*, 77–88.

Guilford, J. P. An experiment in learning to read facial expression. *Journal of Abnormal and Social Psychology*, 1929, *24*, 191–202.

Guilford, J. P. *The nature of human intelligence*. New York: McGraw-Hill, 1967.

Guilford, J. P., & Wilke, M. A new model for the demonstration of facial expressions. *American Journal of Psychology*, 1930, *42*, 436–439.

Guthrie, R. D., & Petocz, R. G. Weapon automimicry among mammals. *American Naturalist*, 1970, *104*, 585–588.

Hager, J. C. *The describing expressions task*. Unpublished manuscript. Human Interaction Laboratory, University of California, San Francisco, 1975.

Hager, J. C., & Ekman, P. Methodological problems of Tourangeau and Ellsworth's study of facial expression and experience of emotion. *Journal of Personality and Social Psychology*, 1981, *40*(2), 385–362.

Haggard, E. A., & Isaacs, K. S. Micro-momentary facial expressions as indicators of ego mechanisms in psychotherapy. In L. A. Gottschalk & A. H. Auerbach (Eds.), *Methods of research in psychotherapy*. New York: Appleton-Century-Crofts, 1966.

Hahn, E. Gibbons in interactions with man in domestic settings. *Gibbon and Siamang*, 1972, *1*, 250–260.

Hall, J. *Gender effects in encoding nonverbal cues*. Unpublished manuscript. The Johns Hopkins University, 1977.

Hall, J. Gender effects in decoding nonverbal cues. *Psychological Bulletin*, 1978, *85*, 845–857.

Hall, K. R. L. The sexual, agonistic and derived social behaviour patterns of the wild chacma baboon, *Papio ursinus*. *Proceedings of the Zoological Society of London*, 1962, *139*, 283–327.

Hall, K. R. L. Social interactions of the adult male and adult females of a patas monkey group. In S. A. Altmann (Ed.), *Social communication among primates*, pp. 261–280. Chicago: University of Chicago Press, 1967.

Hall, K. R. L. Behaviour and ecology of the wild patas monkey, *Erythrocebus patas*, in Uganda. In P. Jay (Ed.), *Primates: Studies in adaptation and viability*, pp. 32–119. New York: Holt, Rinehart and Winston, 1968.

Hall, K. R. L., & DeVore, I. Baboon social behavior. In I. De Vore (Ed.), *Primate behavior: Field studies of monkeys and apes*, pp. 53–110. New York: Holt, Rinehart and Winston, 1965.

Hamilton, M. L. Imitative behavior and expressive ability in facial expression of emotion. *Developmental Psychology*, 1973, *8*(1), 138.

Hanawalt, N. G. The role of the upper and the lower parts of the face as the basis for judging facial expressions: II. In posed expressions and "candid camera" pictures. *Journal of General Psychology*, 1944, *31*, 23–36.

Hansen, E. The development of maternal and infant behavior in the rhesus monkey. *Behaviour*, 1966, *27*, 107–149.

Harper, R. G., Wiens, A. N., & Fujita, B. *Individual differences in encoding–decoding of emotional expression and emotional dissimulation*. Paper presented at the meeting of the American Psychological Association, San Francisco, 1977.

Harper, R. G., Weins, A. N., & Matarazzo, J. D. The relationship between encoding–decoding of visual nonverbal emotional cues. *Semiotica*, 1979, *28*, 171–192.

Harrison, R. P., Ekman, P., & Friesen, W. *The Drawn Affect Recognition Test*. Unpublished test, University of California, San Francisco, 1971.

Hastorf, A. H., Osgood, E. E., & Ono, H. The semantics of facial expressions and the prediction of the meanings of stereoscopically fused facial expressions. *Scandinavian Journal of Psychology*, 1966, *7*, 179–188.

Haviland, J. Looking smart: The relationship between affect and intelligence in infancy. In M. Lewis, (Ed.). *Origins of infant intelligence*. New York: Plenum, 1975.

Hebb, D. O. Emotion in man and animal: An analysis of the intuitive processes of recognition. *Psychological Review*, 1946, *53*, 88–106.

Heider, K. *Affect display rules in the Dani*. Paper presented at the meeting of the American Anthropology Association, New Orleans, 1974.

Heinroth, O. Beiträge zur Biologie, namentlich Ethologie und Psychologie der Anatiden. *Verhandlungen des Internationalen Ornithologischen Kongresses*, (Berlin, 1910) 1911, 589–702.

Hendricks, M., Guilford, J. P., & Hoepfner, R. *Measuring creative social intelligence*. (Rep. No. 42). Los Angeles: University of Southern California, Psychological Laboratory, 1969.

Hiatt, S., Campos, J., & Emde, R. *Fear, surprise, and happiness: The patterning of facial expression in infants*, Paper presented at the meeting of the Society for Research in Child Development, New Orleans, 1977.

Hill, W. C. O. On the muscles of expression in the gelada *Theropithecus gelada* (Rüppell) (Primates, Cercopithecidae). *Zeitschrift für Morphologie der Tiere*, 1969, *65*, 274–286.

Hinde, R. A. (Ed.) *Non-verbal communication*. Cambridge University Press, 1972.

Hinde, R. A. *Contributions from primatology to the study of human social development*. Address delivered at the Department of Psychiatry and Program in Human Biology, Stanford University, April 12, 1976.

Hinde, R. A., & Rowell, T. E. Communication by posture and facial expression in the rhesus monkey. *Proceedings of the Zoological Society of London*, 1962, *138*, 1–21.

Hinde, R. A., & Tinbergen, N. The comparative study of species-specific behavior. In A. Roe & G. G. Simpson (Eds.), *Behavior and evolution*, pp. 251–268. New Haven, Conn.: Yale University Press, 1958.

Hjortsjö, C. H. *Man's face and mimic language*. Lund, Sweden: Student-Litteratur, 1970.

Hoffman, M. L. Empathy, its development and prosial implications. In H. Howe (Ed.), *Nebraska Symposium on Motivation*, 1977, (Vol. 25), pp. 169–217. Lincoln: University of Nebraska Press, 1978.

Honkavaara, S. The psychology of expression. *British Journal of Psychology*, 1961, 32 (Monograph Supplements).

Howell, R. J., & Jorgenson, E. C. Accuracy of judging emotional behavior in a natural setting – A replication. *Journal of Social Psychology*, 1970, 81(2), 269–270.

Huber, E. *Evolution of facial musculature and facial expression*. Baltimore: The Johns Hopkins University Press, 1931.

Hulin, W. S. & Katz, D. The Frois–Wittmann pictures of facial expressions. *Journal of Experimental Psychology*, 1935, 18, 482–498.

Hunt, W. A. Recent developments in the field of emotion. *Psychological Bulletin*, 1941, 38(5), 249–276.

Huxley, J. S. The courtship-habits of the Great Crested Grebe (*Podiceps cristatus*) with an addition to the theory of sexual selection. *Proceedings of the Zoological Society of London*, 1914, 35, 491–562.

Huxley, J. Introduction to "A discussion on ritualization of behaviour in animals and man." *Philosophical Transactions of the Royal Society of London*, Series B, 1966, 251(772), 249–271.

Izard, C. E. The emotions and emotion constructs in personality and culture research. In R. B. Cattell (Ed.), *Handbook of modern personality theory*. Chicago: Aldine, 1969.

Izard, C. E. *The face of emotion*. New York: Appleton-Century-Crofts, 1971.

Izard, C. E. *Patterns of emotions: A new analysis of anxiety and depression*. New York: Academic Press, 1972.

Izard, C. E. *Human emotions*. New York: Plenum, 1977.

Izard, C. E. On the ontogenesis of emotions and emotion–cognition relationships in infancy. In M. Lewis & L. A. Rosenblum (Eds.), *The development of affect*, pp. 389–413. New York: Plenum, 1978.

Izard, C. E. *The maximally discriminative facial movement coding system (MAX)*. Unpublished manuscript. Available from Instructional Resource Center, University of Delaware, Newark, Delaware, 1979.

Izard, C. E. Differential emotions theory and the facial feedback hypothesis of emotion activation: Comments on Tourangeau and Ellsworth's "The role of facial response in the expression of emotion." *Journal of Personality and Social Psychology*, 1981, 40(2), 350–354.

Izard, C. E., & Tomkins, S. S. Affect and behavior: Anxiety as a negative affect. In C. D. Spielberger (Ed.), *Anxiety and behavior*, pp. 81–125. New York: Academic Press, 1966.

Jacobson, S., & Kagan, J. *Released responses in early infancy: Evidence contradicting selective imitation*. Paper presented at the International Conference on Infant Studies, Providence, R.I., 1978.

Janzen, E. K. A balanced smile – A most important treatment objective. *American Journal of Orthodontics*, 1977, 72, 359–372.

Jarden, E., & Fernberger, S. W. The effect of suggestion on the judgment of facial expression of emotion. *American Journal of Psychology*, 1926, 37, 565–570.

Jay, P. The common langur of North India. In I. De Vore (Ed.), *Primate behavior: Field studies of monkeys and apes*, pp. 197–249. New York: Holt, Rinehart and Winston, 1965.

Jolly, A. *Lemur behavior*. Chicago: University of Chicago Press, 1966.

Jones, H. The study of patterns of emotional expression. In L. Regment (Ed.), *Feelings and emotion.* New York: McGraw-Hill, 1950.

Josse, D., Leonard, M., Lezine, I., Robinot, F., & Rouchouse, J. Evolution de la communication entre l'enfant de 4 à 9 mois et un adulte, *Enfance,* 1973, *3*(4), 175–206.

Jung, P. Beziehungen zwischen Tests der socialen Intelligenz zu verbaler Testintelligenz und soziometrischen Variablen. *Diplomarbeit,* Universität des Saarlandes, Saarbrücken, 1972.

Kagan, N., Warner, D., & Schneider, J. *The affective sensitivity scale.* Paper presented at the convention of the American Psychological Association, San Francisco, 1977.

Kanner, L. Judging emotions from facial expressions. *Psychological Monographs,* 1931, *41* (3, Whole No. 186).

Karch, G. R., & Grant, C. W. Asymmetry in the perception of the sides of the human face. *Perceptual and Motor Skills,* 1978, *47,* 727–734.

Kaufman, I. C., & Rosenblum, L. A. A behavioral taxonomy for *Macaca nemestrina* and *Macaca radiata:* Based on longitudinal observation of family groups in the laboratory. *Primates,* 1966, *7,* 205–258.

Kaufmann, J. H. Behavior of infant rhesus monkeys and their mothers in a free-ranging band. *Zoologica,* 1966, *51,* 17–27.

Kaufmann, J. H. Social relations of adult males in a free-ranging band of rhesus monkeys. In S. A. Altmann (Ed.), *Social communication among primates,* pp. 73–98. Chicago: University of Chicago Press, 1967.

Kauranne, U. Qualitative factors of facial expression. *Scandinavian Journal of Psychology,* 1964, *5,* 136–142.

Kaye, K., & Marcus, J. Imitation over a series of trials without feedback: Age six months. *Infant Behavioral Development,* 1978, *1,* 141–155.

Kimura, D. Manual activity during speaking – I. Right-handers. *Neuropsychologia,* 1973, *11,* 45–50.

Kinsbourne, M. Eye and head turning indicates cerebral lateralization. *Science,* 1972, *176,* 539–541.

Kiritz, S. A., & Ekman, P. *The deviant judge of affect in facial expression: Affect-specific errors.* Unpublished manuscript, Langley Porter Neuropsychiatric Institute, San Francisco, 1971.

Kleck, R. E., Vaughan, R. C., Cartwright-Smith, J., Vaughan, K. B., Colby, C. Z., & Lanzetta, J. T. Effects of being observed on expressive, subjective and physiological responses to painful stimuli. *Journal of Personality and Social Psychology,* 1976, *34,* 1211–1218.

Klineberg, O. Emotional expression in Chinese literature. *Journal of Abnormal and Social Psychology,* 1938, *33,* 517–520.

Klineberg, O. *Social psychology.* New York: Henry Holt, 1940.

Klopfer, P. H. Evolution, behavior, and language. In M. E. Hahn & E. C. Simmel (Eds.), *Communicative behavior and evolution,* pp. 7–21. New York: Academic Press, 1976.

Knox, K. A. M. *An investigation of nonverbal behavior in relation to hemispheric dominance.* Unpublished master's thesis, San Francisco State University, 1972.

Kohara, Y. *Racial difference of facial expression–unilateral movement.* Unpublished manuscript. Department of Anatomy, Shinshu University, Matsumoto, Japan, n.d.

Köhler, W. [*The mentality of apes*] (Translated from the 2nd rev. ed. of *Intelligenzprüfungen an Menschenaffen* (E. Winter, trans.). New York: Harcourt Brace, 1925.

Kohts, N. [Infant ape and human child: Instincts, emotions, play, habits.] *Scientific Memoirs of the Museum Darwinianum*. Moscow, 1935, Vol. 3, xvi + 596 pp. (Russian text and English summary.)

Kozel, N. J. Perception of emotion: Race of expressor, sex of perceiver, and mode of presentation. *Proceedings of the 77th Annual Convention of the American Psychological Association*, 1969, 4, 39–40.

Kozel, N. J., & Gitter, A. G. *Perception of emotion: Differences in mode of presentation, sex of perceiver, and role of expressor*. (Tech. Rep. 18.) Boston: Boston University, 1968.

Krause, R. *Sprache und Affekt das Stottern und seine Behandlung*. Stuttgart: Verlag W. Kohlhammer, 1981.

Kummer, H. Tripartite relations in hamadryas baboons. In S. A. Altmann (Ed.), *Social communication among primates*, pp. 63–71. Chicago: University of Chicago Press, 1967.

LaBarbera, J. D., Izard, C. E., Vietze, P., Parisi, S. A. Four- and six-month-old infants' visual responses to joy, anger, and neutral expressions. *Child Development*, 1976, 47, 535–538.

LaBarre, W. The cultural basis of emotions and gestures. *Journal of Personality*, 1947, 16, 49–68.

LaBarre, W. *Paralanguage, kinesics, and cultural anthropology*. Report for the Interdisciplinary Work Conference on Paralangauge and Kinesics. Bloomington: Indiana University, Research Center in Anthropology, Folklore, and Linguistics, May 1962.

Ladygin-Kohts, N. *See* "Kohts, N."

Laird, J. D. Self-attribution of emotion: The effects of expressive behavior on the quality of emotional experience. *Journal of Personality and Social Psychology*, 1974, 29(4), 475–486.

Lalljee, M. The role of gaze in the expression of emotions. *Australian Journal of Psychology*, 1978, in press.

Lamendella, J. T. The limbic system in human communication. In H. Whitaker & H. A. Whitaker (Eds.), *Studies in neurolinguists* (Vol. 3). New York: Academic Press, 1977.

Landis, C. Studies of emotional reactions: II. General behavior and facial expression. *Journal of Comparative Psychology*, 1924, 4, 447–509.

Landis, C. Studies of emotional reactions: V. Severe emotional upset. *Journal of Comparative Psychology*, 1926, 6, 221–242.

Landis, C. The interpretation of facial expression in emotion. *Journal of General Psychology*, 1929, 2, 59–72.

Landis, C., & Hunt, W. A. *The startle pattern*. New York: Farrar, Straus & Giroux, 1939.

Langfeld, H. S. The judgment of emotions from facial expressions. *Journal of Abnormal and Social Psychology*, 1918, 13, 172–184. (a)

Langfeld, H. S. Judgments of facial expression and suggestion. *Psychological Review*, 1918, 25, 488–494. (b)

Lanzetta, J. T., & Kleck, R. Encoding and decoding of facial affect in humans. *Journal of Personality and Social Psychology*, 1970, 16(1), 12–19.

Lanzetta, J. T., Cartwright-Smith, J., & Kleck, R. E. Effects of nonverbal dissimulation on emotional experience and autonomic arousal. *Journal of Personality and Social Psychology*, 1976, 33(3), 354–370.

Leibowitz, H. The effect of pupil size on visual acuity for photometrically equated test fields at various levels of luminance. *Journal of the Optical Society of America*, 1952, 42, 416–422.

Letzer, G. M., & Kronman, J. H. A posteroanterior cephalometric evaluation of craniofacial asymmetry. *Angle Orthodontist*, 1967, *37*, 205–211.

Leventhal, H., & Sharp, E. Facial expressions as indicators of distress. In S. S. Tomkins & C. E. Izard (Eds.), *Affect, cognition and personality, empirical studies*, pp. 296–318. New York: Springer, 1965.

Levitt, E. A. the relationships between abilities to express emotional meaning vocally and facially. In J. R. Davitz (Ed.), *The communication of emotional meaning*, pp. 43–55. New York: McGraw-Hill, 1964.

Levy, D. M. The infant's earliest memory of innoculation: A contribution to public health procedures. *Journal of General Psychology*, 1960, *96*, 3–46.

Levy, P. K. The ability to express and perceive vocal communication of feeling. In J. R. Davitz (Ed.), *The communication of emotional meaning*, pp. 43–55. New York: McGraw-Hill, 1964.

Lewis, M., & Brooks, J. Self-knowledge and emotional development. In M. Lewis and L. A. Rosenblum (Eds.), *The development of affect*, pp. 205–226. New York: Plenum, 1978.

Lewis, M., Brooks, J., & Haviland, J. Hearts and faces: A study in the measurement of emotion. In M. Lewis and L. A. Rosenblum (Eds.), *The development of affect*, pp. 77–124. New York: Plenum, 1978.

Lewis, M., & Rosenblum, L. A. (Eds.). *The effect of the infant on its caregiver*. New York: Wiley, 1974.

Ley, R. G., & Bryden, M. P. Hemispheric differences in processing emotions and faces. *Brain and Language*, 1979, *7*, 127–138.

Lindzey, G. Prince, B., & Wright, H. R. A study of facial asymmetry. *Journal of Personality*, 1952, *21*, 68–84.

Lomax, A. *Folk song style & culture*. Washington, D.C.: American Association for the Advancement of Science, 1968.

Lynn, J. G. An apparatus and method for stimulating, recording and measuring facial expressions. *Journal of Experimental Psychology*, 1940, *27*, 81–88.

Lynn, J. G., & Lynn, D. R. Face–hand laterality in relation to personality. *Journal of Abnormal and Social Psychology*, 1938, *33*, 291–322.

Lynn, J. G., & Lynn, D. R. Smile and hand dominance in relation to basic modes of adaptation. *Journal of Abnormal and Social Psychology*, 1943, *38*, 250–276.

MacKinnon, J. The orang-utan in Sabah today. *Oryx*, 1971, *11*, 141–191.

Maley, M. J. Electrical stimulation of agonistic behavior in the mallard. *Behaviour*, 1969, *34*, 138–160.

Malmstrom, E., Ekman, P., & Friesen, W. V. *Autonomic changes with facial displays of surprise and disgust*. Paper presented at the meeting of the Western Psychological Association, Portland, Oregon, 1972.

Mandler, G. Emotion. In *New directions in psychology* (Vol. 1), pp. 267–343. New York: Holt, Rinehart and Winston, 1962.

Mandler, G. *Mind and emotion*. New York: Wiley, 1975.

Marler, P. Communication in monkeys and apes. In I. De Vore (Ed.), *Primate behavior: Field studies of monkeys and apes*, pp. 544–584. New York: Holt, Rinehart and Winston, 1965.

Marler, P. Vocalizations of East African monkeys. I. Red colobus. *Folia Primatologica*, 1970, *13*, 81–91.

Marler, P., & Tenaza, R. Signaling behavior of apes with special reference to vocalization. In T. A. Sebeok (Ed.), *How animals communicate*, pp. 965–1033. Bloomington: Indiana University Press, 1977.

Mayr, E. *Principles of systematic zoology*. New York: McGraw-Hill, 1969.

McCurdy, H. G. Experimental notes on the asymmetry of the human face. *Journal of Abnormal and Social Psychology*, 1949, *44*, 553–555.

McGrew, W. C. *An ethological study of children's behavior.* New York: Academic Press, 1972.

Mead, M. Review of *Darwin and facial expression. Journal of Communication*, 1975, *25*(1), 209–213.

Mehrabian, A. Nonverbal betrayal of feeling. *Journal of Experimental Research in Personality*, 1971, *5*(1), 64–73.

Mehrabian, A., & Ferris, S. Inference of attitudes from nonverbal communication in two channels. *Journal of Consulting Psychology*, 1967, *31*(3), 248–252.

Meltzoff, A. N., & Moore, M. K. Imitation of facial and manual gestures by human neonates. *Science*, 1977, *198*, 75–78.

Menzel, E. W., Jr. Communication about the environment in a group of young chimpanzees. *Folia Primatologica*, 1971, *15*, 220–232.

Menzel, E. W., Jr. A group of young chimpanzees in a one-acre field. In A. M. Schrier and F. Stollnitz (Eds.), *Behavior of nonhuman primates* (Vol. 5), pp. 83–153. New York: Academic Press, 1974.

Menzel, E. W., & Halperin, S. Purposive behavior as a basis for objective communication between chimpanzees. *Science*, 1975, *189*, 652–654.

Messick,, S. & Damarin, F. *Cognitive styles and memory for faces.* Princeton, N.J.: Educational Testing Service, 1963.

Michael, R. P., & Zumpe, D. Rhythmic changes in the copulatory frequency of rhesus monkeys (*Macaca mulatta*) in relation to the menstrual cycle and a comparison with the human cycle. *Journal of Reproduction and Fertility*, 1970, *21*, 199–201.

Milgram, S. *Obedience to authority.* New York: Harper & Row, 1974.

Miller, R. E. Experimental approaches to the physiological and behavioral concomitants of affective communication in rhesus monkeys. In S. A. Altmann (Ed.), *Social communication among primates*, pp. 125–134. Chicago: University of Chicago Press, 1967.

Miller, R. E., Levine, J. M., & Mirsky, I. A. Effects of psychoactive drugs on nonverbal communication and group social behavior of monkeys. *Journal of Personality and Social Psychology*, 1973, *28*(3), 581-588.

Mita, T. H., Dermer, M., & Knight, J. Reversed facial images and the mere-exposure hypothesis. *Journal of Personality and Social Psychology*, 1977, *35*, 597–601.

Monnier, M., Polc, P., & Böhmer, A. Visual acuity perception of field, position, distance, pattern and movement. In M. Monnier (Ed.), *Functions of the nervous system*, Vol. 3: *Sensory functions and perception*, pp. 763–796. New York: Elsevier North-Holland, 1975.

Monrad-Krohn, G. H. On the dissociation of voluntary and emotional innervation in facial paralysis of central origin. *Brain*, 1924, *47*, 22–35.

Mooney, C. M. Closure with negative afterimages under flickering light. *Canadian Journal of Psychology*, 1956, *10*, 191–199.

Mori, U. Inter-unit relationships. In M. Kawai (Ed.), *Ecological and sociological studies of gelada baboons. Contributions to primatology* (Vol. 16), pp. 83–92. Basel: Karger, 1979.

Moscovitch, M., & Olds, J. *Asymmetries in spontaneous, facial expressions and their possible relation to hemispheric specialization.* Paper presented at the meeting of the International Neuropsychology Society, Holland, June 1979.

Moses, R. A. The iris and the pupil. In R. A. Moses (Ed.), *Adler's physiology of the eye: Clinical application* (6th ed.), pp. 320–352. St. Louis: Mosby, 1975.

Moss, F. A., Hunt, T., Omwake, K. T., & Bonning, M. M. *Social Intelligence Test.* Washington, D.C.: Center for Psychological Services, 1972.

Moynihan, M. Remarks on the original sources of displays. *Auk*, 1955, *72*, 240–246.

Moynihan, M. Some behavior patterns of platyrrhine monkeys. I. The night monkey (*Aotus trivirgatus*). *Smithsonian Miscellaneous Collections*, 1964, *146*(5), 1–84.

Moynihan, M. Comparative aspects of communication in New World primates. In D. Morris (Ed.), *Primate ethology*, pp. 306-342. Garden City, N.Y., Anchor, 1969.

Moynihan, M. Control, suppression, decay, disappearance, and replacement of displays. *Journal of Theoretical Biology*, 1970, *29*, 85–112.

Mueller, C. G. *Sensory psychology*. Englewood Cliffs, N.J.: Prentice Hall, 1965.

Mulik, J. F. An investigation of craniofacial asymmetry using the serial twin-study method. *American Journal of Orthodontics*, 1965, *51*, 112–129.

Munn, N. L. The effect of knowledge of the situation upon judgment of emotion from facial expressions. *Journal of Abnormal and Social Psychology*, 1940, *35*, 324–338.

Murphy, G., Murphy, L. B., & Newcomb, T. M. *Experimental social psychology* (Rev. ed.). New York: Harper & Row, 1937.

Napier, J. R., & Napier, P. H. *A handbook of living primates*. New York: Academic Press, 1967.

Newman, M. Visual acuity. In R. A. Moses (Ed.), *Adler's physiology of the eye: Clinical application* (6th ed.), pp. 500–528. St. Louis: Mosby, 1975.

Nummenmaa, T. The language of the face. *Jyvaskyla studies in education, psychology, and social research.* Jyvaskyla, Finland: Jyvaskylan Yllopistoyhdistys, 1964.

Nummenmaa, T., & Kauranne, U. *Dimensions of facial expression* (Rep. No. 20). Department of Psychology, Institute of Pedagogics, University of Jyvaskyla, 1958.

Nunnally, J. C. *Psychometric theory*. New York: McGraw-Hill, 1967.

Nystrom, M. Neonatal facial–postural patterning during sleep: I. Description and reliability of observation. *Psychological Research Bulletin*, 1974, *14*, 7.

Orians, G. H. On the evolution of mating systems in birds and mammals. *American Naturalist*, 1969, *103*, 589–603.

Osgood, C. E. Dimensionality of the semantic space for communication via facial expressions. *Scandinavian Journal of Psychology*, 1966, *7*, 1–30.

Osipow, S. H., & Walsh, W. B. Social intelligence and the selection of counselors. *Journal of Counseling Psychology*, 1973, *20*(4), 366–369.

Oster, H. Facial expression and affect development. In M. Lewis & L. A. Rosenblum (Eds.), *The development of affect*, pp. 43–76. New York: Plenum, 1978.

Oster, H., & Ekman, P. Facial behavior in child development. *Minnesota Symposium on Child Psychology*, 1978, *11*, 231–276.

O'Sullivan, M., Fields, B., & Carney, S. *Construct validity in measuring nonverbal communication accuracy.* Unpublished manuscript, University of San Francisco, 1979.

O'Sullivan, M., & Guilford, J. P. Six factors of behavioral cognition: Understanding other people. *Journal of Educational Measurement*, 1975, *12*(4), 255–271.

O'Sullivan, M., Guilford, J. P., & de Mille, R. *The measurement of social intelligence* (Rep. No. 34) Los Angeles: University of Southern California, Psychology Laboratory, 1965.

O'Sullivan, M., & Hager, J. C. *Measuring person perception: New techniques, old problems.* Unpublished manuscript, University of San Francisco, 1980.

416   *References*

O'Sullivan, M., Micklewright, J., Ekman, P., Jones, R., & Friesen, W. V. *The influence of alcohol and marijuana on the perception of facial expressions of emotion.* Paper presented at the Western Psychological Association convention, Sacramento, April 1975.

Otte, D. Effects and functions in the evolution of signaling systems. *Annual Review of Ecology and Systematics,* 1974, *5,* 385–417.

Papadatos, C., Alexiou, D., Nicolopoulos, D., Mikropoulos, H., & Hadzigeorgiou, E. Congenital hypoplasia of depression *anguli oris* muscle: A genetically determined condition? *Archives of Disease in Childhood,* 1974, *49,* 927–931.

Papousek, H., & Papousek, M. Mothering and the cognitive head-start: psychobiological considerations. In H. R. Schaffer (Ed.), *Studies in mother–infant interaction,* pp. 63–85. New York: Academic Press, 1977.

Passemard, E. Quelques observations sur des chimpanzés. *Journal de Psychologie Normal et Pathologique,* 1927, *24,* 243–253.

Peiper, A. [*Cerebral function in infancy and childhood.*] (B. Nagler and H. Nagler, trans.) New York: Consultants Bureau, 1963. (Originally published, 1961.)

Petrinovich, L. Probabilistic functionalism: A conception of research method. *American Psychologist,* 1979, *34,* 373–390.

Piderit, T. *La mimique et la physiognomonie* (A. Girot, trans.). Paris: Ancienne Librairie Germer Bailliere et Cie, 1888.

Plimpton, E., & Rosenblum, L. A. *Responses of bonnet macaques to social stimulation presented by means of video recordings.* Paper presented at the annual meeting of the American Society of Primatologists, Atlanta, September 1978.

Plutchik, R., *The emotions: facts, theories, and a new model.* New York: Random House, 1962.

Plutchik, R. *Emotion: a psychoevolutionary synthesis.* New York: Harper & Row, 1980.

Poirier, F. E., Dominance structure of the Nilgiri langur (*Presbytis johnii*) of South India. *Folia Primatologica,* 1970, *12,* 161–186.

Polak, P. R., Emde, R. N., & Spitz, R. A. The smiling response. II. Visual discrimination and the onset of depth perception. *Journal of Nervous and Mental Disease,* 1964, *139,* 407–415.

Pritchard, R. M. Stabilized images on the retina. *Scientific American,* 1961, *204*(6), 72–78.

Rahaman, H., & Parthasarathy, M. D. The expressive movements of the bonnet macaque. *Primates,* 1968, *9,* 259–272.

Redican, W. K. Facial expressions in nonhuman primates. In L. A. Rosenblum (Ed.), *Primate behavior: Developments in field and laboratory research* (Vol. 4), pp. 103–194. New York: Academic Press, 1975.

Redican, W. K. A longitudinal study of behavioral interactions between adult male and infant rhesus monkeys (*Macaca mulatta*) (Doctoral dissertation, University of California, Davis, 1975). *Dissertation Abstracts International,* 1976, *36* (No. 12, Pt. 1). 6437-B.

Redican, W. K., Kellicutt, M. H., & Mitchell, G. Preferences for facial expressions in juvenile rhesus monkeys (*Macaca mulatta*). *Developmental Psychology,* 1971, *5,* 539.

Remillard, G. M., Andermann, F., Rhi-sausi, A., & Robbins, N. M. Facial asymmetry in patients with temporal lobe epilepsy. *Neurology,* 1977, *27,* 109–114.

Reuter-Lorenz, P., & Davidson, R. J. *Differential contributions of the two cerebral hemispheres to the perception of happy and sad faces.* Paper presented at the meeting of the International Neuropsychology Society, San Francisco, 1980.

Rombouts, H. *Sociale intelligentie*. Unpublished doctoral dissertation, University of Amsterdam, 1978.

Rosenthal, R. *Expectancy effects in behavioral research*. New York: Appleton-Century-Crofts, 1966.

Rosenthal, R., Judgment studies of emotion. In K. Scherer & P. Ekman (Eds.), *Handbook of research methods in nonverbal behavior*. Cambridge University Press, 1982.

Rosenthal, R., Hall, J. A., DiMatteo, M. R., Rogers, P. L., & Archer, D. *Sensitivity to nonverbal communication*. Baltimore: Johns Hopkins University Press, 1979.

Rosvold, H. E., Mirsky, A. F., & Pribram, K. H. Influence of amygdalectomy on social behavior in monkeys. *Journal of Comparative and Physiological Psychology*, 1954, *47*, 173–178.

Rowell, T. E. Hierarchy in the organization of a captive baboon group. *Animal Behaviour*, 1966, *14*, 430–443.

Rowell, T. E., Din, N. A., and Omar, A. The social development of baboons in their first three months. *Journal of Zoology*, 1968, *155*, 461–483.

Royal, D. C., & Hays, W. L. Empirical dimensions of emotional behavior. *Proceedings of the 15th International Congress of Psychology, Brussels*, 1959, 419.

Rubenstein, L. Facial expressions: An objective method in the quantitative evaluation of emotional change. *Behavior Research Methods and Instruments*, 1969, *1*, 305–306.

Ruckmick, C. A. A preliminary study of the emotions. *Psychological Monographs*, 1921, *30* (Nos. 134–139), 30–35.

Rudolph, H. *Der Ausdruck der Gemütsbewegungen des Menschen*. Dresden: von Gerhard Kühtmann, 1903.

Rump, E. E. Facial expression and situational cues: Demonstration of a logical error in Frijda's report. *Acta Psychologica*, 1960, *17*, 31–38.

Ruse, M. E. Functional statements in biology. *Philosophy of Science*, 1971, *38*, 87–95.

Saarni, C. *Acquisition of display rules for expressive behavior*. Paper presented at the meeting of the Eastern Psychological Association, Washington, D.C., 1978. (a)

Saarni, C. Cognitive and communicative features of emotional experience, or do you show what you think you feel? In M. Lewis & L. A. Rosenblum (Eds.), *The development of affect*, pp. 361–376. New York: Plenum, 1978. (b)

Sabatelli, R. M., Buck, R., & Dreyer, A. Communication via facial cues in intimate dyads. *Personality and Social Psychology Bulletin*, 1980, *6*, 242–247.

Sackeim, H. A., & Gur, R. C. Lateral asymmetry in intensity of emotional expression. *Neuropsychologia*, 1978, *16*, 473–481.

Sackeim, H. A., Gur, R. C., & Saucy, M. C. Emotions are expressed more intensely on the left side of the face. *Science*, 1978, *202*, 434–436.

Sackett, G. P. Monkeys reared in isolation with pictures as visual input: Evidence for an innate releasing mechanism. *Science*, 1966, *154*, 1468, 1471–1473.

Saha, G. B. Judgment of facial expression of emotion – a cross-cultural study. *Journal of Psychological Research*, 1973, *17*(2), 59–63.

Savitsky, J. C., Izard, C. E., Kotsch, W. E., & Christy, L. Aggressor's response to the victim's facial expression of emotion. *Journal of Research in Personality*, 1974, *7*, 346–357.

Schaller, G. B. *The mountain gorilla: Ecology and behavior*. Chicago: University of Chicago Press, 1963.

Schaller, G. B. The behavior of the mountain gorilla. In I. De Vore (Ed.), *Primate behavior: Field studies of monkeys and apes*, pp. 324–367. New York: Holt, Rinehart and Winston, 1965.

Schenkel, R. Zur Deutung der Balzleistungen einiger Phasianiden und Tetraoniden. *Ornithologische Beobachter*, 1956, *53*, 182–201.

Scherer, K. R., Scherer, U., Hall, J. A., & Rosenthal, R. Differential attribution of personality based on multichannel presentation of verbal and nonverbal cues. *Psychological Research*, 1977, *39*, 221–247.

Schiffenbauer, A. Effect of observer's emotional state on judgments of the emotional state of others. *Journal of Personality and Social Psychology*, 1974, *30*(1), 31–35.

Schlosberg, H. A scale for the judgment of facial expression. *Journal of Experimental Psychology*, 1941, *29*, 497–510.

Schlosberg, H. The description of facial expressions in terms of two dimensions. *Journal of Experimental Psychology*, 1952, *44*, 229–237.

Schlosberg, H. Three dimensions of emotion. *Psychological Review*, 1954, *61*, 81–88.

Schulze, R. *Experimental psychology and pedagogy: For teachers, normal colleges and universities* (P. Pintner, trans.). New York: Macmillan, 1912.

Schwartz, G. E., Ahern, G. L., & Brown, S. Lateralized facial muscle response to positive and negative emotional stimuli. *Psychophysiology*, 1979, *16*, 561–571.

Schwartz, G. E., Fair, P. L., Salt, P., Mandel, M. K., & Klerman, G. L. Facial muscle patterning to affective imagery in depressed and non-depressed subjects. *Science*, 1976, *192* (4238), 489–491.

Seaford, H. W. *Maximizing replicability in describing facial behavior*. Paper presented at the meeting of the American Anthropological Association, Washington, D.C., 1976.

Sebeok, T. A., Hayes, A. S., & Bateson, M. C. *Approaches to semiotics*. Hague: Mouton, 1964.

Secord, P. F. Facial features and inference processes in interpersonal perception. In R. Taguiri & L. Petrullo (Eds.), *Person perception and interpersonal behavior*. Stanford, Ca.: Stanford University Press, 1958.

Secord, P. F., Dukes, W. F., & Bevan, W. Personalities in faces: I. An experiment in social perceiving. *Genetic Psychology Monographs*, 1954, *49*, 231–279.

Seiler, R. Die Gesichtsmuskeln. *Primatologia*, 1976, *4*(6), 1–252.

Seinen, M., & Werff, J. J. van der. De waarneming van asymmetrie in het gelaat. *Nederlands Tijdschrift voor de Psychologie en Haar Grensgebieden*, 1969, *24*, 551–558.

Shafton, A., *Conditions of awareness: Subjective factors in the social adaptations of man and other primates*. Portland, Ore.: Riverstone Press, 1976.

Shah, S. M., & Joshi, M. R. The assessment of asymmetry in the normal craniofacial complex. *Angle Orthodontist*, 1978, *48*, 141–148.

Shannon, A. M. *Differences between depressives and schizophrenics in the recognition of facial expression of emotion*. Unpublished doctoral dissertation, University of California, San Francisco, 1970.

Shapiro, J. G. Responsivity to facial and linguistic cues. *Journal of Communication*, 1968, *18*, 11–17.

Shapiro, J. G. Variability and usefulness of facial and body cues. *Comparative Group Studies*, 1972, *3*(4), 437–442.

Shepard, F. N. The analysis of proximities: Multidimensional scaling with an unknown distance function. *Psychometrica*, 1963, *27*, 125–140.

Sherman, M. The differentiation of emotion responses in infants: I. Judgments of emotional responses from motion pictures views and from actual observation. *Journal of Comparative Psychology,* 1927, *7,* 265–284. (a)

Sherman, M. The differentiation of emotional responses in infants: II. The ability of observers to judge the emotional characteristics of the crying of infants and of the voice of an adult. *Journal of Comparative Psychology,* 1927, *7,* 335–351. (b)

Shipe, D., Prato, D., Rosser, M., & Sidhu, S. *Interpersonal competence, social competence, and affiliation motivation in non-academic youth.* Unpublished manuscript, Ontario Institute for Studies in Education, 1976.

Shultz, T. R., & Zigler, E. Emotional concomitants of visual mastery in infants: The effects of stimulus movement on smiling and vocalizing. *Journal of Experimental Child Psychology,* 1970, *10,* 390–402.

Silverthorne, C. P., Gibson, R., Micklewright, J., & O'Connell, M. *The effects of color environment on person perception.* Paper presented at the Western Psychological Association Convention, Sacramento, April 1975.

Sirota, A. D., & Schwartz, G. E. *Facial muscle patterning and lateralization during elation and depression imagery.* Paper presented at the meeting of the Society for Psychophysical Research, Vancouver, B. C., 1980. (For abstract see *Psychophysiology,* 1981, *18,* 196.)

Smith, R. P. *Frontalis* muscle tension and personality. *Psychophysiology,* 1973, *10*(3), 311–312.

Sokolowsky, A. *Beobachtungen über die Psyche der Menschenaffen.* Frankfurt: Neuer Frankfurter, 1908.

Southwick, C. H., Beg, M. A., & Siddiqi, M. R. Rhesus monkeys in North India. In I. De Vore (Ed.), *Primate behavior: Field studies of monkeys and apes,* pp. 111–159. New York: Holt, Rinehart and Winston, 1965.

Spencer, H. *Principles of Physiology* (2nd ed.), 1872.

Sprague, J. M., Chambers, W. W., & Stellar, E. Attentive, affective, and adaptive behavior in the car. *Science,* 1961, *133,* 165–173.

Sroufe, L. A. Wariness of strangers and the study of infant development. *Child Development,* 1977, *48,* 731–746.

Sroufe, L. A. The ontogenesis of emotion. In J. Osofosky (Ed.), *Handbook of infancy.* New York: Wiley, 1978.

Sroufe, L. A., & Waters, E. The ontogenesis of smiling and laughter: A perspective on the organization of development in infancy. *Psychological Review,* 1976, *83,* 173–189.

Stechler, G., & Carpenter, G. A viewpoint on early affect development. In J. Hellmuth (Ed.), *The Normal Infant* (Vol. I, *Exceptional Infant*) New York: Brunner/Mazel, 1967.

Steiner, J. E. The gustofacial response: Observation on normal and anencephalic newborn infants. In J. F. Bosma (Ed.), *Fourth Symposium on Oral Sensation and Perception,* pp. 254–278. Bethesda, Maryland, (DHEW Pub. No. (NIH) 73–546, 1973.

Stern, D. N., Beebe, B., Jaffe, J., & Bennett, S. L. The infant's stimulus world during social interaction: A study of caregiver behaviours with particular reference to repetition and timing. In H. R. Schaffer (Ed.), *Studies of Mother-Infant Interaction,* pp. 177–202. New York: Academic Press, 1977.

Stratton, G. M. The control of another person by obscure signs. *Psychological Review,* 1921, *28,* 301–314.

Stringer, P. Cluster analysis of non-verbal judgments of facial expressions. *British Journal of Mathematical Statistics of Psychology,* 1967, *20,* 71–79.

Stringer, P. *Sequential proximity as the basis for similarity judgments of facial expressions*. Mimeo, University College, London, 1968.

Stringer, P. Some effects of facial asymmetry on person perception. Final Rep. (HR5413.) Social Sciences Research Council, London, 1979.

Stringer, P., & May, P. *Bilateral facial asymmetry and trait attribution*. Manuscript submitted for publication, 1979.

Struhsaker, T. T. Auditory communication among vervet monkeys (*Cercopithecus aethiops*). In S. A. Altmann (Ed.), *Social communication among primates*, pp. 281–324. Chicago: University of Chicago Press, 1967. (a)

Struhsaker, T. T. Behavior of vervet monkeys and other cercopithecines. *Science*, 1967, *156*, 1197–1203. (b)

Struhsaker, T. T. Behavior of vervet monkeys (*Cercopithecus aethiops*). *University of California Publications in Zoology*, 1967, *82*, 1–74. (c)

Suberi, M., & McKeever, W. F. Differential right hemispheric memory storage of emotional and non-emotional faces. *Neuropsychologia*, 1977, *15*, 757–768.

Szondi, L. *Szondi Test: Experimentelle Triebdiagnostik; Textband*. Bern: Hans Huber, 1947.

Tagiuri, R. Person perception. In G. Lindzey & E. Aronson (Eds.), *The handbook of social psychology* (Vol. 3). pp. 395–449. Reading, Mass.: Addison-Wesley, 1969.

Tenopyr, M. Social intelligence and academic success. *Educational and Psychological Measurement*, 1967, *27*, 961–965.

Terry, M. W. Use of common and scientific nomenclature to designate laboratory primates. In A. M. Schrier (Ed.), *Behavioral primatology: Advances in research and theory* (Vol. 1), pp. 1–32. Hillsdale, N. J.: Erlbaum, 1977.

Terry, R. L. Veridicality of interpersonal perceptions based on physiognomic cues. *Journal of Psychology*, 1972, *81*, 205–208.

Thompson, D. F., & Meltzer, L. Communication of emotion intent by facial expression. *Journal of Abnormal and Social Psychology*, 1964, *68*, 129–135.

Thompson, J. Development of facial expression of emotion in blind and seeing children. *Archives of Psychology*, 1941, *37*, No. 264.

Thompson, J. R. Asymmetry of the face. *Journal of the American Dental Association*, 1943, *30*, 1859–1871.

Thomsen, C. E. Eye contact by non-human primates toward a human observer. *Animal Behaviour*, 1974, *22*, 144–149.

Tinbergen, N. "Derived" activities; Their causation, biological significance, origin, and emancipation during evolution. *Quarterly Review of Biology*, 1952, *27*, 1–32.

Tinbergen, N. Comparative studies of the behaviour of gulls (Laridae): A progress report. *Behaviour*, 1959, *15*, 1–70.

Tinbergen, N. Einige Gedanken über Beschwichtigungs-Gebaerden. *Zeitschrift für Tierpsychologie*, 1959, *16*, 651–665. (Reprinted as [On appeasement signals]. In N. Tinbergen (Ed.), *The animal in its world* (Vol. 2), pp. 113–129. Cambridge, Mass.: Harvard University Press, 1972.

Tokuda, K., Simons, R. C., & Jensen, G. D. Sexual behavior in a captive group of pigtailed monkeys (*Macaca nemestrina*). *Primates*, 1968, *9*, 283–294.

Tomkins, S. S. Consciousness and the unconscious in a model of the human being. *Proceedings of the 14th International Congress of Psychology*, pp. 160–161. Montreal: I. C. P., 1955.

Tomkins, S. S. *Affect, imagery, consciousness* (Vol. 1, *The positive affects*), New York: Springer, 1962.

Tomkins, S. S. *Affect, imagery, consciousness* (Vol. 2, *The negative affects*). New York: Springer, 1963.

Tomkins, S. S. A theory of memory. In J. Antrobus (Ed.), *Cognition and affect.* Boston: Little, Brown, 1971.

Tomkins, S. S. The phantasy behind the face. *Journal of Personality Assessment.* 1975, *39*, 551–562.

Tomkins, S. S. Script theory: Differential magnification of affects. In H. E. Howe & R. A. Dienstbier (Eds.), *Nebraska Symposium on Motivation*, 1978. (Vol. 26). Lincoln: University of Nebraska Press, 1979.

Tomkins, S. S. The role of facial response in the experience of emotion: A reply to Tourangeau and Ellsworth. *Journal of Personality and Social Psychology.* 1981, *40*(2), 355–359.

Tomkins, S. S. *Affect, Imagery and Consciousness* (Vol. 3. *Cognition and Affect*). New York: Springer, 1982.

Tomkins, S. S., & Izard, C. E. (Eds.) *Affect, cognition and personality.* New York: Springer, 1965.

Tomkins, S. S., & McCarter, R. What and where are the primary affects? Some evidence for a theory. *Perceptual and Motor Skills*, 1964, *18*(1), 119–158.

Tourangeau, R., & Ellsworth, P. C. The role of facial response in the experience of emotions. *Journal of Personality and Social Psychology*, 1979, *37*, 1519–1531.

Trevarthen, C. Descriptive analyses of infant communicative behavior. In H. R. Schaffer, (Ed.), *Studies of Mother-Infant Interaction*, pp. 227–70. New York: Academic Press, 1977.

Triandis, H. C., & Lambert, W. W. A restatement and test of Schlosberg's theory of emotion with two kinds of subjects from Greece. *Journal of Abnormal and Social Psychology*, 1958, *56*(3), 321–328.

Trivers, R. L. The evolution of reciprocal altruism. *The Quarterly Review of Biology*, 1971, *46*, 35–57.

Trujillo, N. P., & Warthin, T. A. The frowning sign multiple forehead furrows in peptic ulcer. *Journal of the American Medical Association*. 1968, *205*(6), 218.

Tschiassny, K. Eight syndromes of facial paralysis and their significance in locating the lesion. *Annals of Otology, Rhinology, and Laryngology*, 1953, *62*, 677–691.

Tuttle, R. H. (Ed.) *Socioecology and psychology of primates.* Chicago: Aldine, 1975.

Van de Creek, L., & Watkins, J. T. Responses to incongruent verbal and nonverbal emotional cues. *Journal of Communication*, 1972, *22*, 311–316.

van Hooff, J. A. R. A. M. The facial displays of the Catarrhine monkeys and apes. In D. Morris (Ed.), *Primate ethology*, pp. 9–88. Garden City, N. Y.: Anchor, 1969.

van Hooff, J. A. R. A. M. A comparative approach to the phylogeny of laughter and smiling. In R. A. Hinde (Ed.), *Non-verbal communication*, pp. 209–241. Cambridge University Press, 1972.

van Hooff, J. A. R. A. M. A structural analysis of the social behaviour of a semi-captive group of chimpanzees. In M. von Cranach and I. Vine (Eds.), *Social communication and movement: Studies of interaction and expression in man and chimpanzee*, pp. 75–162. London: Academic Press, 1973.

van Hooff, J. A. R. A. M. The comparison of facial expression in man and higher primates. In M. von Cranach (Ed.), *Methods of inference from animal to human behaviour*, pp. 165–196. Chicago: Aldine, 1976.

van Lawick-Goodall, J. The behaviour of free-living chimpanzees in the Gombe Stream Reserve. *Animal Behaviour Monographs*, 1968, *1*, 161–311. (a)

van Lawick-Goodall, J. A preliminary report on expressive movements and communication in the Gombe Stream chimpanzees. In P. Jay (Ed.), *Primates: Studies in adaptation and variability*, pp. 313–374. New York: Holt, Rinehart and Winston, 1968. (b)

van Lawick-Goodall, J. *In the shadow of man.* Boston: Houghton Mifflin, 1971.

Vasquez, J. *The face and ideology.* Unpublished doctoral dissertation, Rutgers University, 1975.

Vaughn, B. E., & Sroufe, L. A. *The face of surprise in infants.* Paper presented at the meeting of the Animal Behavior Society of Boulder, Colorado, 1976.

Vig, P. S., & Hewitt, A. B. Asymmetry of the human facial skeleton. *Angle Orthodontist,* 1975, *45,* 125–129.

Vinacke, W. E. The judgment of facial expressions by three national–racial groups in Hawaii: I. Caucasian faces. *Journal of Personality,* 1949, *17,* 407–429.

Vinacke, W. E., & Fong, R. W. The judgment of facial expressions by three national-racial groups in Hawaii: II. Oriental faces. *Journal of Social Psychology,* 1955, *41,* 184–195.

Vine, I. Communication by facial–visual signals: A review and analysis of their role in face-to-face encounters. In J. H. Crook (Ed.), *Social behavior in animals and man.* New York: Academic Press, 1969.

von Cranach, M. (Ed.) *Methods of inference from animal to human behaviour.* Chicago: Aldine, 1976.

Walker-Smith, G. J., Gale, A. G., & Findlay, J. M. Eye movement strategies involvied in face perception. *Perception,* 1977, *6,* 313–326.

Waters, E. Matas, L., & Sroufe, L. Infants' reaction to an approaching stranger: Description, validation, and functional significance of wariness. *Child Development,* 1975, *46,* 348–356.

Watson, J. S. Perception of contingency as a determinent of social responsiveness. In E. P. Thoman (Ed.), *The origin of the infant's social responsiveness.* Hillsdale, N.J.: Erlbaum, 1978.

Wedeck, J. The relationship between personality and "psychological ability." *British Journal of Psychology,* 1947, *37,* 133–141.

Weidmann, U. Some reproductive activities of the Common gull, *Larus canus* L. *Ardea,* 1955, *43,* 85–132.

Westbrook, M. Judgment of emotion: Attention versus accuracy. *British Journal of Social and Clinical Psychology,* 1974, *13,* 383–389.

Wexler, D. Methods for utilizing protocols of descriptions of emotional states. *Journal of Supplemental Abstract Services,* 1972, *2,* 116.

Wickler, W. *Mimicry in plants and animals.* New York: McGraw-Hill, 1968.

Wilson, E. O. *Sociobiology: The new synthesis.* Cambridge, Mass.: Harvard University Press, 1975.

Wilson, S. A. K. Some problems in neurology. II. Pathological laughing and crying. *Journal of Neurology and Psychopathology,* 1924, *4,* 299–330.

Winkelmayer, R., Exline, R. V., Gottheil, E., & Paredes, A. The relative accuracy of U. S., British, and Mexican raters in judging the emotional displays of schizophrenic and normal U. S. women. *Journal of Clinical Psychology,* 1978, *34*(3), 600–608.

Wolff, P. H. Observations on the early development of smiling. In B. M. Foss (Ed.), *Determinants of infant behavior* (Vol. 2). New York: Wiley, 1963.

Wolff, P. H. The causes, controls, and organization of behavior in the neonate. *Psychological Issues,* 1966, *5,* (Monograph 17).

Wolff, P. H. The natural history of crying and other vocalizations in early infancy. In B. M. Foss (Ed.), *Determinants of infant behavior* (Vol. 4). London: Methuen, 1969.

Wolff, W. The experimental study of forms of expression. *Character and Personality,* 1933, *2,* 168–176.

Wolff, W. *The expression of personality: Experimental depth psychology.* New York: Harper Brothers, 1943.

Woo, T. L. On the asymmetry of the human skull. *Biometrica*, 1931, 22, 324–341.

Woodworth, R. S. *Experimental psychology*. New York: Henry Holt, 1938.

Yerkes, R. M. *Chimpanzees: A laboratory colony*. New Haven, Conn.: Yale University Press, 1943.

Yerkes, R. M., & Yerkes, A. W. *The great apes: A study of anthropoid life*. New Haven, Conn.: Yale University Press, 1929.

Young, G. & Décarie, T. G. An ethology-based catalogue of facial/vocal behaviour in infancy. *Animal Behaviour*, 1977, 25, 95–107.

Young-Browne, G., Rosenfeld, H. M., & Horowitz, F. D. Infant discrimination of facial expressions. *Child Development*, 1977, 48, 555–562.

Zaidel, S., & Mehrabian, A. The ability to communicate and infer positive and negative attitudes facially and vocally. *Journal of Experimental Research in Personality*, 1969, 3, 233–241.

Zajonc, R. B. Attraction, affiliation, and attachment. In J. F. Eisenberg and W. S. Dillon (Eds.), *Man and beast: Comparative social behavior*, pp. 141–179. Washington, D. C.: Smithsonian Institution Press, 1971.

Zlatchin, C., & Ekman, P. *Misperception of facial affect*. Unpublished manuscript, Langley Porter Neuropsychiatric Institute, San Francisco, 1971.

Zuckerman, M., Hall, J. A., DeFrank, R. S., & Rosenthal, R. Encoding and decoding of spontaneous and posed facial expressions. *Journal of Personality and Social Psychology*, 1976, 34(5), 966–977.

Zuckerman, M., Larrance, D. T., Hall, J. A. DeFrank, R. S., & Rosenthal, R. Posed and spontaneous communication of emotion via facial and vocal cues. *Journal of Personality*, 1979, 47, 712–733.

Zuckerman, M., DeFrank, R. S., Hall, J. A., Larrance, D. T., & Rosenthal, R. Facial and vocal cues of deception and honesty. *Journal of Experimental Social Psychology*, 1979, 15, 378–396.

Name index

430   *Name index*

Subject index